T3-BOE-494

Only connect: readings on children's literature

Only connect

readings on children's literature

Edited by

Sheila Egoff, G. T. Stubbs, and L. F. Ashley

TORONTO NEW YORK / OXFORD UNIVERSITY PRESS / 1969

4 5 6 7 – 6 5 4

Printed in Canada by
JOHN DEYELL LIMITED

Contents

* By staff writers of *Fortune Magazine.*

* First published in *The Times Literary Supplement*, whose contributors are normally anonymous.

* First published in *The Times Literary Supplement*, whose contributors are normally anonymous.

Illustrations

Acknowledgements

EDWARD ARDIZZONE: *Creation of a Picture Book.* Reprinted from *Top of the News* (December 1959) by permission of the American Library Association.

Arthur Ransome: Charting the Course. Reprinted from *The Times Literary Supplement* (28 November 1963) by permission.

JORDAN BROTMAN: *A Late Wanderer in Oz.* Reprinted from the *Chicago Review* (vol. 18, no. 2) by permission of the author.

ROGER DUVOISIN: *Children's Book Illustration: The Pleasure and Problems.* Reprinted from *Top of the News* (November 1965) by permission of the American Library Association.

T.S. ELIOT: *Huckleberry Finn: A Critical Essay.* Reprinted by permission of Mrs Valerie Eliot.

JASON EPSTEIN: *'Good Bunnies Always Obey'.* Reprinted from *Commentary* (February 1963) by permission; copyright © 1963 by the American Jewish Committee.

CLIFTON FADIMAN: *Professionals and Confessionals: Dr Seuss and Kenneth Grahame.* Reprinted from *Enter, Conversing* by Clifton Fadiman by permission of The World Publishing Company, New York, and Fadiman Associates Ltd, New York.

For It Was Indeed He. Reprinted from the April 1934 issue of *Fortune Magazine* by special permission: © 1934 Time Inc.

MARTIN GARDNER: *A Child's Garden of Bewilderment.* Reprinted from *Saturday Review* (17 July 1965) (copyright 1965, Saturday Review, Inc.) by permission of the author.

RUMER GODDEN: *An Imaginary Correspondence.* Copyright © 1963 by Rumer Godden. Reprinted from *The Horn Book Magazine* (August 1963) by permission of Curtis Brown Ltd, New York, and Curtis Brown Ltd, London.

DIANA GOLDSBOROUGH: *Goodbye Humphrey, Hello Dick and Jane.* Reprinted from *The Tamarack Review* (Summer 1966) by permission of the author.

ROGER LANCELYN GREEN: *Andrew Lang in Fairyland.* Reprinted from *The Junior Bookshelf* (October 1962) by permission.

ROGER LANCELYN GREEN: *The Golden Age of Children's Books.* Included here by permission of the author, Roger Lancelyn Green, from *Essays and Studies 1962*, published for the English Association by Messrs John Murray Ltd and reprinted by Messrs Wm Dawson and Sons Ltd.

GRAHAM GREENE: *Beatrix Potter.* From *Collected Essays* by Grahame Greene. Copyright © 1951 by Graham Greene. Reprinted by permission of the author, The Viking Press, Inc., The Bodley Head Limited, and Laurence Pollinger Limited, London.

Henry Treece: Lament for a Maker. Reprinted from *T.L.S. 5, Essays and Reviews from The Times Literary Supplement 1966* by permission of *The Times.*

NAT HENTOFF: *Among the Wild Things.* From *The New Yorker* (22 January 1966). Reprinted by permission: © 1966 The New Yorker Magazine, Inc.

NAT HENTOFF: *Fiction for Teenagers.* From *The Atlantic* (December 1967). Copyright © 1967, by The Atlantic Monthly Company, Boston, Mass. Reprinted with permission.

MICHAEL HORNYANSKY: *The Truth of Fables.* Reprinted from *The Tamarack Review* (Autumn 1965) by permission of the author.

ELIZABETH JANEWAY: *Meg, Jo, Beth, Amy, and Louisa.* Reprinted from *The New York Times Book Review* (29 September 1968). Copyright © 1968 by Elizabeth Janeway. Reprinted by permission of Paul R. Reynolds, Inc. © 1968 by The New York Times Company. Reprinted by permission.

FREDERICK LAWS: *Randolph Caldecott.* Reprinted from *The Saturday Book,* No. 16, by permission of the Hutchinson Publishing Group Ltd.

EDMUND LEACH: *Babar's Civilization Analysed.* Reprinted from *New Society* (20 December 1962). Copyright *New Society,* London.

C.S. LEWIS: *On Three Ways of Writing for Children.* Reprinted from the *Proceedings* of the Bournemouth Conference, 1952, by permission of The Library Association, London.

MARION LOCHHEAD: *Clio Junior: Historical Novels for Children.* Reprinted from *Quarterly Review* (January 1961) by permission of the author.

HELEN LOURIE: *Where is Fancy Bred?* Reprinted from *New Society* (6 December 1962). Copyright *New Society,* London.

DONNARAE MAC CANN: *Wells of Fancy, 1865-1965.* Reprinted by permission from the December 1965 issue of the *Wilson Library Bulletin.* Copyright © 1965 by The H.W. Wilson Company.

WILLIAM H. MAGEE: *The Animal Story: A Challenge in Technique.* Reprinted from *The Dalhousie Review* (Summer 1964) by permission of the author.

PENELOPE MORTIMER: *Thoughts Concerning Children's Books.* Reprinted from the *New Statesman* (11 November 1966) by permission.

EDWARD W. ROSENHEIM, JR: *Children's Reading and Adults' Values.* Reprinted from *The Library Quarterly* (January 1967) by permission of The University of Chicago Press and the author.

The Search for Selfhood: The Historical Novels of Rosemary Sutcliff. Reprinted from *The Times Literary Supplement* (17 June 1965) by permission.

LILLIAN H. SMITH: *News from Narnia.* Reprinted from the *CLA Bulletin* (July 1958) by permission of the *Canadian Library Journal* and the author.

ANTHONY STORR: *The Child and the Book.* Reprinted from the *New Statesman* (12 November 1960) by permission.

ROSEMARY SUTCLIFF: *Combined Ops.* Reprinted from *The Junior Bookshelf* (July 1960) by permission.

J.R.R. TOLKIEN: *Children and Fairy Stories.* Reprinted from *Tree and Leaf* by J.R.R. Tolkien by permission of George Allen & Unwin Ltd, London, and Houghton Mifflin Company, Boston.

JOHN ROWE TOWNSEND: *Didacticism in Modern Dress.* Reprinted from *The Horn Book Magazine* (April 1967) by permission of The Horn Book, Inc. and the author.

JOHN ROWE TOWNSEND: *The Present State of English Children's Literature.* Reprinted by permission from the October 1968 issue of the *Wilson Library Bulletin.* Copyright © 1968 by The H.W. Wilson Company.

P.L. TRAVERS: *Only Connect.* Reprinted from the *Quarterly Journal of Acquisitions of the Library of Congress* (October 1967) by permission of the author's agents, David Higham Associates, Ltd, London.

ALISON WHITE: *With Birds in His Beard.* Reprinted from *Saturday Review* (15 January 1966) (copyright 1966, Saturday Review, Inc.) by permission of the author.

ALAN MORAY WILLIAMS: *Hans Christian Andersen.* Reprinted from *Time and Tide* (7-13 February 1963) by permission.

ILLUSTRATIONS

The illustration by JEAN DE BRUNHOFF is from *Babar the King.* Copyright, 1935, 1963, by Random House, Inc. Reprinted by permission of Random House, Inc., New York, and Librairie Hachette, Paris. Photograph courtesy Toronto Public Library.

The illustration by EDWARD LEAR is from *A Book of Nonsense* (Routledge, Warne and Routledge; fifth edition 1862) in The Osborne Collection of Early Children's Books, Toronto Public Library.

The illustration by BEATRIX POTTER from *The Tale of Tom Kitten* (1907) in The Osborne Collection of Early Children's Books, Toronto Public Library, is reprinted by permission of Frederick Warne & Co., Ltd, London.

The illustration from *Higglety Pigglety Pop!* by the author-artist MAURICE SENDAK, copyright © 1967 by Maurice Sendak, is reprinted with permission of Harper & Row, Publishers, New York.

The drawing by EDWARD ARDIZZONE from *Tim All Alone* is reprinted by permission of the Oxford University Press, London.

The illustration by ROGER DUVOISIN from *Petunia* (copyright 1950 by Alfred A. Knopf) is reprinted by permission of Alfred A. Knopf, Inc., New York. Photograph courtesy Toronto Public Library.

The illustration by RANDOLPH CALDECOTT is from *Sing a Song for Sixpence* (George Routledge and Sons, 1880) in The Osborne Collection of Early Children's Books, Toronto Public Library.

Preface

Every author or editor likes to think he is offering the public something unique. The editors of this volume are aware that a number of collections of articles and essays on children's literature have already been published. Without making any unreasonable claims, we feel justified in stating that in no previous collection has the material come from so many diverse quarters; nor has there been so broad a representation of writers from both North America and Great Britain.

Our primary aim has been to find selections that deal with children's literature as an essential part of the whole realm of literary activity, to be discussed in the same terms and judged by the same standards that would apply to any other branch of writing. We do not subscribe to the view that the criticism of children's books calls for the adoption of a special scale of values. We looked for insight and informed contemporary thinking, and rejected any material that was too concerned with recapturing childhood or with presenting coy and sentimental attitudes. With these criteria in mind we also sought writers who had a distinctive message to offer: one that is fresh, original, and illuminating and not necessarily unorthodox or provocative (though a few can be so described).

In the quest for material, byways of periodical literature were explored as well as more familiar ground, and before the process of compilation was finished, several hundred articles in journals and newspapers from all parts of the English-speaking world were examined. Essays and critical reviews were also considered, though in the final selection periodical articles are in the majority.

The original plan was to include only publications of the 1960s. Maintaining an arbitrary restriction to a single decade, however, seemed to impose an artificial limitation; therefore it was relaxed in some cases to admit important earlier contributions to the criticism of children's literature, such as the essays by T. S. Eliot and C. S. Lewis and the profile of Edward Stratemeyer, 'For It Was Indeed He'. This collection, then, is devoted mainly to topics of current interest, but a few pieces were written earlier than 1960.

Within the limits already defined, we have attempted to cover as many aspects of children's literature as possible. However, no article has been included simply because it discusses a certain subject or a certain writer: questions of balance or comprehensiveness have not taken precedence over literary considerations. For example, a careful search was made for a critical treatment of children's poetry, but nothing we read seemed to be significant enough to merit a place in the collection. That is the reason—the only reason–why no space has been allotted to the subject of poetry. However, two subjects that had not been adequately dealt with in the periodical literature we examined, of special interest to one of the editors, were written about specially for this book. One of these new essays is on science fiction and the other presents a capsule history of writing for children, 'Precepts and Pleasures'; both are by Sheila Egoff. Where there was a choice of articles on particular authors or illustrators, our decisions for inclusion were based mainly on the interest of the content and the quality of the writing rather than on the popularity or fame of the subject.

For the title *Only Connect* we are indebted both to E. M. Forster who made the phrase memorable in *Howards End* and to Pamela Travers who borrowed it to form the title and motif of her address at the Library of Congress, reproduced here in the second section. Our interpretation of the Forster epigraph, like Miss Travers's, implies a need to gain understanding through the linking of one world with another. In *Howards End* it was the life of warm personal relationships and that of unfeeling commercialism.

In this collection the two worlds that are brought into focus are Youth and Age, traditionally beset by problems of rapport, today perhaps more than ever before separated by mutual distrust. Some of our contributors, for example Jason Epstein and Nat Hentoff, feel that only here and there in contemporary writing for children is there evidence of a true understanding of young people's needs and interests. The connection between author and audience is often tenuous.

In 1965 a *Times Literary Supplement* article on a new study of children's literature began, 'Alas! This must be a review of a book yet to be written: *the* book about children's books.' The article was entitled 'Themes in Search of an Author' and the reviewer was pessimistic about the emergence of any single author who might succeed in producing a truly definitive work. He commented, however, on the existence of many 'interesting fragments' by notable writers 'mostly appearing—and therefore disappearing—in periodicals'.

We still do not have '*the* book about children's books'. Perhaps what is needed is a symposium. In the meantime the present volume gathers together some 'interesting fragments', of which a few are already well known while many have been rescued from obscure corners of specialized periodicals. We have wanted to make them permanently accessible because individually they are of more than merely passing interest and collectively they comprise a body of writing that we hope will be of lasting value. The book is designed to appeal particularly to librarians, parents, teachers, and students; but for anyone at all concerned with children and their literature there is material here that will repay scrutiny. We have reason to believe that the comment and discussion in the following pages will contribute to a better understanding of an important and influential field of writing.

G.T.S.

L.F.A.

1 *Books and children*

The golden age of children's books

ROGER LANCELYN GREEN

Histories of Literature seldom mention books written primarily for children, except when in cases like *Tales from Shakespeare* and *The Rose and the Ring* they represent amiable eccentricities on the part of writers famous for other and adult works.

Of recent years one or two favoured volumes have been promoted; but even for such works as *Alice in Wonderland* and *The Wind in the Willows* it has seemed that an excuse must be found, and painstaking (and painful) efforts have been made to prove that they are really allegories, or deeply psychological parables, intended to convey disguised truths to initiated adults.

The consideration of children's literature as such found its most noteworthy exponent in F. J. Harvey Darton, whose *Children's Books in England* was published in 1932. Even so, however, he felt constrained to add the sub-title 'Five Centuries of Social Life', and he does not in fact touch on anything which could be described as Literature until his last two chapters. Percy Muir's *English Children's Books 1600-1900* (1954) is written largely from the book-collector's point of view, and the delight in rare editions tends to divert both author and reader from consideration of content to that of format.

The most compendious and painstaking work on the subject

was published in America in the previous year (1953), *A Critical History of Children's Literature*, a 'survey' in four parts under the editorship of Cornelia Meigs.

Now while these excellent works describe the growth and development of writing for children over several centuries, they reveal curious differences in approach from any similar works on the whole or any section of adult literature. Not only are they apt to consider children's books as a separate species rather than a branch of literature, but they tend more and more to accumulate a vast sea of books in which the reader becomes lost as he struggles desperately between the few definite islands which are just allowed to emerge above the flood.

Under these circumstances there seems to be some point in attempting to write at least the first draft of what might be developed by some expert into a chapter in a future history of English Literature: an attempt to chart some of the more or less definite islands off a portion of the mainland of our more generally recognized literary heritage.

There were few books written before the middle of the nineteenth century which can be said to have more than an antiquarian interest today. Several adult books like *Robinson Crusoe*, *Gulliver's Travels*, and *Baron Munchausen* which have become nursery property (usually now in abridged or simplified versions) are beside the point, as are ballads, popular rhymes, and folktales. Beyond a few translations of foreign fairy tales (Perrault and Grimm) and of *The Arabian Nights*, Lamb's *Tales from Shakespeare* (1807) is the only book from before the middle of the century which is still read, or which deserves any place among children's classics. Apart from this, and from a few representative poems in anthologies, Marryat's *The Children of the New Forest* (1847) and Ruskin's *The King of the Golden River* (1851—but written some years earlier) are the only islands still visible in those early waters.

The only book which hovers on the border between actual and academic interest is Catherine Sinclair's *Holiday House*

(1839). From the historical point of view it is one of the most important books in the history of children's literature, for it was written with the intention of changing the quality and kind of reading supplied for young people, and it was so successful that not only did it achieve its purpose but it remained in print and was read by children for precisely a hundred years.

At a time when 'informative' books (they are now called, significantly, 'non-fiction') are once again swamping the junior-book counters, it is worth looking at what Catherine Sinclair wrote (for parents) in her preface:

Books written for young persons are generally a mere dry record of facts, unenlivened by any appeal to the heart, or any excitement to the fancy . . . but nothing on the habits and ways of thinking natural and suitable to the taste of children. Therefore, while such works are delightful to the parents and teachers who select them, the younger community are fed with strong meat instead of milk, and the reading which might be a relaxation from study becomes a study in itself . . .

In these pages, the author has endeavoured to paint that species of noisy, frolicsome, mischievous children which is now almost extinct, wishing to preserve a sort of fabulous remembrance of days long past, when young people were like wild horses on the prairies, rather than like well-broken hacks on the road; and when, amid many faults and many eccentricities there was still some individuality of character and feeling allowed to remain.

Her battle was not won without a long struggle, and her children seem fairly tame now in the light of subsequent developments. The only part of the book which stands out as a notable achievement that is still fresh and entertaining is the 'Wonderful Story' about Giant Snap-'em-up (who was so tall that he 'was obliged to climb up a ladder to comb his own hair'), which is the earliest example of Nonsense literature and a direct precursor of Lewis Carroll and E. Nesbit.

It was some time before either the nonsense fairy tale or the story of true-to-life childhood achieved any worthy representations; but meanwhile a new development was started by Marryat and developed by Charlotte Yonge—the simple historical romance, usually with a child hero. In an age when the Waverley Novels were read avidly even by young children (Mrs Molesworth, born 1839, was reading them at the age of six when *Peveril of the Peak* proved too difficult, though she had found *Ivanhoe* and *The Talisman* 'so much nicer and easier'), and when Scott's followers such as Bulwer Lytton and Harrison Ainsworth were not forbidden like the majority of adult novels, it was natural that, sooner or later, such books would be written with the young reader specially in view. An obvious development came also by way of the 'desert island' story, since *Robinson Crusoe* and *The Swiss Family Robinson* had been followed by the intensely pious *Masterman Ready:* R. M. Ballantyne avoided the didactic brilliantly in *The Coral Island* (1858), and followed it with excellent adventure stories in other fields which, like the meticulously historical thrillers of G. A. Henty, grew together towards the close of the century into the semi-adult movement of the 'storytellers' headed by Stevenson, Haggard, and Conan Doyle.

The really distinctive children's book grew more slowly and in less expected forms. Traditional fairy tales and stories from myth and legend found a period of great popularity about the time of the first translation of Hans Andersen (1846) and of Kingsley's *The Heroes* (1856), the Kearys' *Heroes of Asgard* (1857) and Dasent's *Tales from the Norse* (1859). But the original tale of fantasy developed slowly. Probably the earliest of any was F. E. Paget's *The Hope of the Katzekopfs* (1844), which showed real imagination and invention, but gave way to an undue weight of direct moral teaching which cripples its last two chapters hopelessly. It has not been reprinted since a shortened version renamed *The Self-willed Prince* came out about 1908.

Ruskin's *The King of the Golden River* (1851), a brilliant imitation of Grimm, made the grade, though an interesting experiment in the Border Ballad tradition of fairy tale, by Mrs Craik, *Alice Learmont* (1852), failed to hold its audience. But at Christmas 1854 (though dated 1855), Thackeray produced the first classic of fairy-tale nonsense and set the stage for all future stories of the 'Fairy Court' with *The Rose and the Ring*.

Although there is a basic moral in Thackeray's fantasy, the story, the characters, and the spirit of fun are all more important. With the paradox of all true originality, Thackeray owed several debts for the materials with which he built: the general fairy-tale background of writers like Madame d'Aulnoy and the pantomime tradition which was growing in the able works of Planché and H. J. Byron; perhaps *The Hope of the Katzekopfs*, certainly Fielding's heroic burlesque *Tom Thumb the Great* whose language is echoed in the royal blank verse and in the brilliant use of bathos ('He raised his hand to an anointed King, Hedzoff, and floored me with a warming pan!' 'Rebellion's dead—and now we'll go to breakfast').

The Rose and the Ring had very few direct followers, or few that survive. Tom Hood 'the Younger' wrote probably the best imitation, *Petsetilla's Posy* (1870), though it is too like its original to escape destructive criticism, and there were others of even less importance. It was not, in fact, until thirty-five years later that a major work in the same tradition appeared, Andrew Lang's *Prince Prigio* (1889)– which owes only the same kind of debt to *The Rose and the Ring* and the traditional fairy tales as Thackeray owed to his sources. In each case a writer of real genius was using, as it were, the same company and setting to put on a play of his own devising, and such as only he could have written.

Thackeray's indirect influence may, however, be traced in another original if somewhat controversial genius, George MacDonald, whose first children's story, *The Golden Key* (1861), was pure allegory in a setting only superficially that of any known fairyland, but who showed a strong dash of the comic Fairy Court tradition by the time he reached his third, *The*

Light Princess, in 1864 (written two years earlier). After this he attempted longer stories, beginning with the full-length *At the Back of the North Wind* (1870, dated 1871) which combines dream, allegory, and fairy tale in a not completely successful whole, but reached his real heights with the *The Princess and the Goblin* (1871) and its even better sequel *The Princess and Curdie* (1882, but serialized 1877).

Critical judgement of MacDonald's work is rendered difficult, as in the case of several writers with superlative powers of imagination which far out-run their skill as literary craftsmen. The classic example of this uncomfortable dualism is Rider Haggard, whose amazing imagination and narrative powers would place him among the truly great did not his woefully inept use of language and creation of character press him back amongst the very minor novelists.

MacDonald's deficiencies are most notable in his adult novels and least apparent in his *Unspoken Sermons* and the best of his children's books and imaginative works.

The quality of the *Princess* books to a child is that of a haunted house—but a house haunted by entirely good and desirable ghosts. They leave behind a feeling of awe and wonder, the excitement of the invisible world (we may call it Fairyland at the time, but it is always something more) coming within touchable distance: the door into the fourth dimension is situated in the places that we know best—we may chance upon it at any moment, and with the thrill of delight and excitement quite divorced from any fear of the unfamiliar. Though the stories are not memorable, the experience and its enriching quality remain vivid, and MacDonald's greatness is shown by the fact that to reread him in later life is equally rewarding and brings no sense of disappointment.

Two excursions into utterly different realms of the imagination which appeared at much the same time as MacDonald's finest children's books have also this quality of an appeal that continues through life: *Alice's Adventures in Wonderland* (1865) and *Through the Looking-Glass* (1871).

Coming when they did, these two books revolutionized writing for the young. They captured the irresponsible fantasy in the minds of most children, and with it the unrealized urge towards rebellion against the imposed order and decorum of the world of the Olympians; but the capture was made by a writer of exceptional powers, a scholar in love with the richness of language and the devastating precision of mathematics. This seemingly inharmonious concatenation of elements produced two masterpieces, of which the second, being a little farther away from the spontaneous inspiration of oral storytelling, is the more perfectly integrated whole.

It is unsafe to attempt to get nearer to Dodgson's sources of inspiration. There seems to be no doubt that he made up the stories on the spur of the moment, telling them to children who were supplying much of the inspiration while he told by the interruptions, suggestions, and criticism which are inseparable from composition in this kind. It is also true that on account of his stammer, from which he was only free when talking to children, Dodgson was seeking an escape into childhood and thereby recapturing or preserving his own to some extent past the normally allotted limits. The result is what matters, and in this case it was two of the best-known, best-loved, and most often quoted books in the language.

Although 'Lewis Carroll' set free the imagination, he had no original followers, though his imitators were legion—'People are always imitating *Alice*,' complained Lang in 1895. In fact the only writers to draw anywhere near him in his peculiar realm of fantasy, nonsense, and felicitously haunting turns of phrase are Rudyard Kipling with the *Just So Stories* (1902) and A. A. Milne with his two *Pooh* books in 1926 and 1928. One has only to turn to Tom Hood again (*From Nowhere to the North Pole*, 1875) to see how completely impossible it is to write a memorable imitation of *Alice*.

Perhaps because of this impossibility, the last quarter of the nineteenth century tended to produce fewer and fewer examples of the child's quest for the 'perilous seas' of fairyland and concentrate with more and more skill on the presentation of childhood in the world of every day.

This was the main theme of Catherine Sinclair's protest, but its application was slow and tortuous. Superficially it was not new, since Maria Edgeworth and Mrs Sherwood professed to be writing about real children in their daily lives. A distinct step forward was taken by Charlotte Yonge with her novels for teenage girls, such as *The Daisy Chain* (1856), and in the following year by Thomas Hughes in his outstanding story of public school boys, *Tom Brown's Schooldays*.

Smaller children, however, were still being subjected to the lachrymose-pious, as in *Jessica's First Prayer* (1867) and *Misunderstood* (1869), though a new writer first made her mark in the second of these years, Juliana Horatia Ewing (1841-85), with *Mrs. Overtheway's Remembrances*. She progressed to *A Flat Iron for a Farthing* in 1872 (which year also saw Elizabeth Anna Hart's one outstanding child-novel, *The Runaway*), and reached her greatest heights with *Six to Sixteen* (1875) and *Jan of the Windmill* (1876).

The impact of these first outstanding child-novels is shown by Kipling's reference to *Six to Sixteen* in his autobiography: 'I owe more in circuitous ways to that tale than I can tell. I knew it (in 1875) as I know it still, almost by heart. Here was a history of real people and real things.'

Although Mrs Ewing may have had a better style, and on a small scale could produce better work, she was far surpassed as a child-novelist by Mrs Molesworth (Mary Louisa, née Stewart, 1839-1921). Although several of her longer books remain popular and stand up to rereading, Mrs Ewing is best remembered by her miniature novels, or long short stories, *Jackanapes* (1884) and *The Story of a Short Life* (1885); but their appeal is now more strong to the adult than the child, since they both turn on child-deaths[1] which needs a conscious return to the days of high infant mortality on the part of the reader for any appreciation, and seem awkward and sentimental to a modern child. Though often derided, stories of this kind should not be condemned out of hand: Mrs Ewing's two remain classics, and they have close runners-up in Mrs Molesworth's *A Christmas Child* (1880) and Frances E. Crompton's *Friday's Child* (1889).

This was, however, almost the only death-bed in Mrs Molesworth's voluminous works for the young (two short stories and an opening chapter complete her list of early deaths; no parents meet their end during the course of any book, though a few endure dangerous illnesses, and only one child becomes a cripple). Her greatness lies in the fact that she was at once the faithful mirror of her own age and yet wrote, at her best, about the universal aspects of childhood.

It is no exaggeration to describe Mrs Molesworth as the Jane Austen of the nursery. Although her works are to Jane's as the miniature is to the great painting, such books as *The Carved Lions* and *Two Little Waifs* and *Nurse Heatherdale's Story* are as nearly perfect in their small kind as the great novelist's are in hers. Like her novel they are 'period' without being dated; they appeal to the heart as well as to the intellect; they remain in the memory and enrich the experience; they not only played an important part in their own branch of our literature but deserve an abiding place on our shelves to be read and reread by young and old.

Not only is one told in Mrs Molesworth's stories what it was like to be a child seventy-five years ago; as one reads one can experience all the hopes and fears, all the miniature loves and hates, passions and despairs, plots and counterplots of that distinct, if rather restricted, little world. She truly understood children and could see life again with their eyes, and give vividness

---

[1] Jackanapes in fact jumps into manhood before dying, but the effect is that of a child-death.

and poignancy to their small troubles in such a way that even to the adult reader the suspense may be as strong and as compelling as if it were a matter of life and death among grown men and women. So many of the basic problems and conflicts of life make themselves felt at all ages that this novel view of them back through the telescope into the eye of childhood seems in her best work to clarify and accentuate their relevance.

Although after such early stories as *Carrots* (1876) and *Hoodie* (1881) Mrs Molesworth avoided any hint of direct preaching, there is always a certain underlying intention in her stories. Well though she and such writers as Mrs Ewing and Mrs Hodgson Burnett understood children, they had not quite escaped from the tradition of the child as a miniature adult, as always in training for grownup life. This tends to make the children seem a little on their best behaviour, and it gives perhaps an undue emphasis to the continual moulding of character, occasionally an exaggerated importance to a small sin or backsliding. The children are just a little better than ourselves; to some extent the same is still true in such recent masterpieces as Arthur Ransome's stories of holiday adventures, but most of the conscious recognition of and combat with temptation has now gone. Acute introspection plays a relatively small part, however, in Mrs Molesworth's stories, though one told in the first person like *The Carved Lions* (1895), which is probably her masterpiece, gains greatly by the insight into the heroine's mind which it allows.

For more pronounced introspection we must turn to Mrs Hodgson Burnett, who wrote many minor works but only three which are on the definitely higher level which still makes them vividly alive. The first, *Little Lord Fauntleroy* (1886), suffers both from its intractable material—the balance without sentiment or patronizing between the democratic child of America and the aristocratic child in England—and from its unenviable reputation derived mainly from its translation into a stage sweetmeat for sentimental adults. Given a sympathetic reader who is ready to accept the limitations imposed by its period, the book is still remarkably readable both by young and old. Less difficult, though less convincing to the adult, is her second major story, *A Little Princess* (1905—but a revised version of an earlier book published in 1887), which exploits the theme of the lonely child fallen from high fortune to poverty and persecution and then rescued at the eleventh hour by means which seem supernatural until satisfactorily explained at the end. The book is brilliant fare for children, but not one which weathers the test of adult rereading with complete success.

Her last book, *The Secret Garden* (1911), is one of great individuality and astonishing staying power. It is the study of the development of a selfish and solitary little girl later in contact with an hysterical and hypochondriac boy of ten: a brilliant piece of work, showing unusual understanding of introspective unlikeable children with a sincerity that captures many young readers and most older ones.

Children with a country upbringing have found a similarly satisfying quality in *The Carved Lions*, with its less introspective and more sympathetic heroine, and Mrs Molesworth's less convincing *Sheila's Mystery* (also 1895), which deals not quite so happily with the salvation of one of her few unpleasant children. The significant difference is that while Sheila's solution is found for her by intelligent adults, Mary in *The Secret Garden* works out her salvation for herself–with the aid of an imposing array of coincidences. Between the writing of these two books another change had come over the child-novel and one of considerable importance; it seems to owe its main impetus to Kenneth Grahame's *The Golden Age*, also published in 1895.

Now *The Golden Age*, undoubtedly one of the most important landmarks in the history of children's literature, is not a children's book at all. Misguided parents have frequently thought that it was: so far as I can remember *The Golden Age* was the only book which, as a child, I really and violently hated. The reason, curiously enough, seems to be that Kenneth Grahame knew too much. Here was an adult writing in an adult style about things which touched the very heart of our mystery; he was profaning the holy places—perhaps (for his manner was elusive) he was laughing in his detestable Olympian fashion at the things which really mattered.

The Golden Age, said Oswald Bastable in *The Wouldbegoods,* 'is A1, except where it gets mixed with grown-up nonsense.' Even E. Nesbit did not quite realize where the trouble lay, since she had never read it as a child. For to the older reader *The Golden Age* (with its sequel *Dream Days,* 1898) is, as Swinburne said of it, 'well-nigh too praiseworthy for praise': it is not merely one of the greatest books of its period, but a classic in its own right and an outstanding example of English prose.

Its importance in the present survey rests in its approach to childhood and its amazing understanding of the workings of the child's imagination and outlook. Hitherto the child had been pictured to a greater or less extent as an undeveloped adult, and all his books were intended in some degree to help force him into life's full flowering. Sheer instruction may have faded into the background, but an undercurrent of teaching in morality, in manners, in the sense of duty was always present. Even Mrs Molesworth never escaped from this background purpose, close though she came to the real thoughts and sensations of childhood—to the child looking forward to adulthood rather than the adult pushing the child into it. In the greater writers even the conscious push was not necessarily a blot: Mrs Ewing, Mrs Molesworth, and Mrs Hodgson Burnett could make of it a triumph as, in a completely different way, could George MacDonald.

But *The Golden Age* suddenly presented childhood as a thing in itself: a good thing, a joyous thing—a new world to be explored, a new species to be observed and described. Suddenly children were not being written down to any more—they were being written up: you were enjoying the spring for itself, not looking on it anxiously as a prelude to summer.

The immediate result was a loosening of bonds similar to that wrought by the outbreak into mere amusement of *Alice* thirty years earlier. It had a marked effect even on writers already well in their stride; even Mrs Molesworth, nearing the end of her literary career, found it impossible to resist the new elixir altogether, and at least two of her later books, *The House that Grew* (1900) and *Peterkin* (1902), have a gaiety and a youthfulness that sets them among her half-dozen best child-novels. As for minor writers, one has only to compare the sickly sentimentality of S. R. Crockett's *Sweetheart Travellers* (1895) with the adventurous boyishness of *Sir Toady Lion* (1897) to see the difference at its most extreme.

The oddest omission from the majority of earlier child-novels which Kenneth Grahame brought into the front of the picture was the imaginative life of children, and its importance to the children themselves. It had cropped up in several books written with more than half an eye on the adult reader, notably in Dickens's *Holiday Romance* (1868), Jefferies's *Bevis* (published as a three-volume novel in 1882), and in Mark Twain's *Tom Sawyer* and *Huckleberry Finn* (1875, 1884). But when it appears in the child-novel proper, as in the first chapter of Mrs Molesworth's *Two Little Waifs* (1883), it is merely incidental, or a means (as in *Hermy*, 1881) of starting a train of incidents. Not until *The Three Witches* (1900) and *Peterkin* could she make it the centre of her story.

Grahame had many direct imitators, but only one broke away from imitation and produced great and original work, and that was Edith Nesbit. She had been a hack journalist whose ambition was to be a poet for nearly twenty years when, in July 1897, a series of reminiscences of her schooldays in *The Girl's Own* ran away with her when she came to write of her childhood games of 'Pirates and Explorers'. From this grew the idea of producing sketches or short stories of the *Golden Age* variety, but purporting to be written by one of the children concerned. Most of Oswald Bastable's earlier adventures were contributed to the *Windsor* and *Pall Mall* magazines, both intended purely for adults, and only in the autumn of 1899 did she revise and link them, with a little rewritten earlier material from *The Illustrated London News* and several of *Nister's Holiday Annuals*, as *The Story of the Treasure-Seekers.*

A few reviewers took it as an adult book: 'Don't be content to read *The Treasure Seekers*, but give it also to children. They will all bless the name of Mrs Nesbit,' wrote Andrew Lang, who described the Bastables as 'perfect little trumps' and preferred them to the heroes of *Stalky & Co.* which appeared at the same time. He went on to describe it as 'a truly novel and original set of adventures, and of the finest tone in the world'.

Lang himself was of an older generation and could still not quite reconcile the apparent lack of a moral with a children's book about contemporary children. Albeit with a twinkle in his eye, he had looked for and found a moral in his own original fairy stories (just as Dodgson had done with *Alice*, many years after its publication) and could at least make excuses for the moral shortcomings of such traditional tales as *Puss in Boots.*

E. Nesbit, though she could lapse into sentimentality with the best, made the shift from conscious 'elevation' to unconscious improvement, substituting tone for teaching with the untidy impetuosity which characterizes even her best work. In the second Bastable compilation, *The Wouldbegoods* (1901), she even rounded on the moral tale, made a face at *The Daisy Chain*, and (apart from the one monumental lapse over the supposed dead Boer War hero) wrote her best non-magical children's book. Most of the Bastable stories were based on incidents or inspirations from her own childhood, and the thorough assumption of the child's outlook in the person of the narrator, Oswald, allowed her to use the joyous freedom and colloquial verve which carried the child-novel right out into the spring sunshine once and for all.

In the 'real-life' line she could not follow up her initial success: *The New Treasure-Seekers* (1905) already shows strain and self-imitation, and *The Railway Children* (1906) tends to lapse back into the sentimentality from which she was usually able to escape. Moreover, surprisingly few child-novels followed hers that win anywhere near the status of classics (apart from *The Secret Garden*, 1911) until Arthur Ransome produced *Swallows and Amazons* in 1930.

Apart from achieving complete freedom, E. Nesbit's real claim to greatness lies, however, in her series of Wonder Tales. Short stories in the Fairy Court tradition accompanied the earlier Bastable tales into the world (they were collected as *The Book of Dragons*, 1900, and *Nine Unlikely Tales*, 1901) and she continued writing them, producing as many again over the next dozen years. The best of these would have assured her of a place not so very much lower than Thackeray and Lang; but by combining her styles and expanding her scope she produced eight full-length stories in which magic is introduced into family circles and surroundings as convincingly and prosaically real as those of the Bastables.

Magic to most children is only just out of reach: it fills their imaginings and informs their games. With the sure, deft touch and the rather pedestrian matter-of-factness which she knew so well how to use to advantage, E. Nesbit turned the games and the imaginings into actual events. 'Actual' is the key word; here she has never been equalled. She may have learnt how convincing magic can be, if strictly rationed and set in the most ordinary surroundings possible, from 'F. Anstey' (Thomas Anstey Guthrie, 1856–1934) of *Vice Versa* and *The Brass Bottle* fame; she certainly knew and admired Mrs Molesworth's blendings of fact and fantasy such as *The Cuckoo Clock* and *The Tapestry Room*—the Cuckoo and Dudu the Raven are close relations of the Psammead, the Phoenix, and the Mouldiwarp: but the total effect is, at its best, original with the originality of sheer genius.

Her mounting skill is shown in her first series of three, *Five Children and It* (1902), *The Phoenix and the Carpet* (1904), and *The Amulet* (1906), each better than the last. Then came perhaps her supreme achievement, *The Enchanted Castle* (1907), with a delightful new family, unexpected and most credible magic, and a really cohesive plot instead of the string of adventures in her other books. *The House of Arden* (1908) and its overlapping sequel *Harding's Luck* (1909) keep to the same high level, though the construction begins to falter; and then the decline comes, through *The Magic City* (1910) to *Wet Magic* (1913), after which she had written herself out.

The period ends sharply with E. Nesbit. But to follow out her career three notable writers have been shouldered aside, each author of individual works of such recognized importance and popularity as to need no comment: Kipling with *The Jungle Books* (1894-5), *Stalky & Co.* (1899), *Just So Stories* (1902), and *Puck of Pook's Hill* (1906); Kenneth Grahame for that ambivalent masterpiece *The Wind in the Willows* (1908), an adult's book for children written by one of the few adults who could re-enter childhood at will; and Beatrix Potter, the only writer for very small children to produce works of real literature which adults can still enjoy—helped perhaps by her inseparable and equally outstanding illustrations.

Finally, spilt over from another medium, comes *Peter Pan*, the essence and epitome of all that the writers of the Golden Age were striving to capture. 'It has influenced the spirit of children's books,' wrote Harvey Darton, 'more powerfully than any other work except the *Alices* and Andersen's *Fairy Tales*.' From its shores (the play has been revived every year but one since it began in 1904, and the book, *Peter Pan and Wendy*, 1911, is only a little less immortal) we may sail adventuring in I know not how many new directions, but to the Never, Never Land we shall always return–led away for magic moments by the Boy who wouldn't grow up, before turning refreshed and reinvigorated to seek those joys in the world of real men and women from which he was for ever shut out. For such, to all of us of whatever age, is the true message of the great children's books.

[1962]

Children's reading and adults' values

EDWARD W. ROSENHEIM, JR

The word 'reading', like the word 'literature', is far too broad to be useful for more than a few cheery generalizations, whether we are discussing the reading of adults or of children. Certainly one may begin with one familiar, necessary distinction—which can be simply, if controversially, expressed as the difference between reading conducted for its own sake and reading conducted for the sake of something else, usually learning or training. In the first category would fall the reading of what is sometimes called 'imaginative literature', including poetry, drama, fiction, certain kinds of essays and speculations; in the second category would fall all other books, juvenile and adult, which seek to tell us how things actually are or have been or ought to be. And I would think the problem of judging the excellence, the 'worthwhileness' of books in the second category—whether books on history or social questions or science or geography or religion or conduct or art itself—would simply involve determining the intelligibility, attractiveness, persuasiveness, importance, and usefulness of whatever could be learned from them. It may be very difficult to write such books—and difficult, too, to motivate children in reading them—but to assess and justify their role in the total reading experience seems relatively simple.

It is with the other type of reading, the imaginative, the reading that is pursued for its own sake, that the problems of justification and judgement become very troublesome indeed. They are, in fact, so controversial that they are precisely the questions to which critics and teachers of literature have characteristically addressed themselves during these recent decades, which some people have characterized as an Age of Criticism. Yet these questions produce answers, though never definitive ones, and they produce certain beliefs about literature, again never universally accepted, and these answers and beliefs do have a bearing on children's reading as well as adults'.

It is, in the first place, characteristic—though not by any means inevitable–that today's critic recognize that the greatest power of imaginative literature, in its various kinds, is to yield particular satisfactions—that is, unabashedly to assert that such literature is primarily read for pleasure. This may seem an unexciting, if debatable, commonplace, but I can assure you that, if so, it has only recently become one. I have dismal evidence that in classrooms—and even in recent printed curricular materials—the child's reading of a lyric poem or fantasy or even a comic short story is immediately followed by some such initial question as, 'What does the work teach us?' or 'What do we learn about so-and-so?'

Yet the primacy of pleasure as an end in reading is now quite widely accepted, and we have indeed gone further and asked some searching questions about the nature and sources of that pleasure. And because those sources properly lie in only two places—the written work before the reader and the mind of the reader himself—we have been led to concentrate upon that unique, immediate encounter between book and reader, largely and quite deliberately, neglecting such peripheral matters as the biography of the author, the circumstances under which the book was composed, its reputation, or—as I've already suggested—its 'lesson'. And in consequence we find ourselves driven to think, not primarily about authors and subject matters and 'reading' generally, but about specific books and their readers—what goes on in books, what goes on in the people, young and old, who read them.

Our thinking has prompted many of us to feel that there are

pleasures, even 'literary' pleasures, of many kinds. We recognize that certain species of work yield certain species of satisfaction. Beyond this, we have begun to suspect that there are degrees of pleasure that are largely determined by the degree of affirmative intellectual energy a reader is willing to invest. There are, we feel, the satisfactions, legitimate enough but rather flabby, that come only from a sort of effortless recognition of what is reassuringly and comfortably familiar, whether that familiarity is bred by authentic experience or by previous reading as in the case of 'series' books. There are the satisfactions of what I like to think of as 'easy fantasy'—often represented by the kind of escape-cum-identification literature one found in so many boys' books in my youth, in which, against a background of sport or youthful society that offered no challenge to the imagination, youngsters like myself enjoyed a more glamorous and triumphant life than their own. There are, again, the transient titillations afforded by flamboyant and minimally credible writings which exploit the violent or exotic or prurient or sentimental. The appeal of such work is assuredly the province of the psychologist, whose findings tend to remove these experiences from the area of intellectual—or at least aesthetic—satisfaction.

All these are pleasures, each authentic enough, frequently entirely respectable, that somehow fall short of the pleasures that can be achieved by reading, the pleasures proper to true humanistic experience. And I use the word 'humanistic' because in this kind of pleasure we inevitably make active exercise of our uniquely human gifts—the gifts of apprehension, of imagination, of discrimination, of relationship, of judgement. The humanistic satisfactions are not those of temporary, uncritical surrender (much as we like to speak of 'enchantment') but of sustained, active encounter—the kind of encounter that makes a Holden Caulfield want to telephone Old Thomas Hardy or causes a Mary Poppins to exist so vitally in the imaginations of her young admirers that, as many did, they reject her unconvincing embodiment on the movie screen.

Reading to achieve these satisfactions involves, obviously, an energetic act of the intellect—and the capacity for such an act requires cultivation which is certainly not that of mere literacy. It means, to put it bluntly, that we cannot have it two ways: if reading is to yield its deepest, most permanent, most humane satisfactions for our children, then the mere gesture of 'reading', mere uncritical pleasure in reading, is not quite enough. If we are concerned with reading for maximum satisfaction, we parents and teachers must be prepared to devise strategies, provide help, and—above all—make judgement about our children's books.

And these judgements are, of course, difficult to make. But I would suggest that, if my concept of the most satisfying reading is a correct one, we do not bother inordinately with questions such as, 'Is this a great book?' Or a wholesome one. Or an up-to-date one. Or an informative one. Or even a 'broadening' one. The questions I would ask would tend to be: Will this book call into play my child's imagination? Will it invite the exercise of genuine compassion or humour or even irony? Will it exploit his capacity for being curious? Will its language challenge his awareness of rhythms and structures? Will its characters and events call for—and even strengthen—his understanding of human motives and circumstances, of causes and effects? And will it provide him with a joy that is in some part the joy of achievement, of understanding, of triumphant encounter with the new?

All this may appear to put a somewhat pretentious light on the problem. Yet, after all, most of the special human satisfactions do require planning and training in their cultivation. Even the deepest, most appropriate satisfactions from sport—either of the participating or spectator variety—are achieved through training and practice in execution or experienced, sophisticated appreciation. And if we grant only that the satisfactions of imaginative literature are equally rich and permanent, then it seems reasonable that we think about their cultivation with equal care and responsibility. And thus, to accept the 'pleasure principle' is anything but an evasion of the duty to think about reading. It is, on the contrary, to accept the obligation to think resourcefully and carefully and devotedly in the interests of that motive which for most parents assumes the highest priority: the nature and magnitude of our children's happiness.

A second preoccupation of many critics in recent years has been with the question of literary kinds or genres—a problem that, at first glance, may seem rather lifeless and remote from the questions that should be concerning us. Yet I think it has some consequences for our thinking about children's literature. For many years, booklists, anthologies, and even literature courses and curriculums tended to classify works according to gross form—poems, plays, and novels—and, within such groups, according to 'topic' or 'subject matter'. Thus a typical anthology of poems or stories for young people might bear such headings as 'Nature', 'Foreign Lands', 'Sport', 'Other Times', 'Here and Now', 'Adventure', 'The World of Science', or whatnot. In short, classification was preceded by certain judgements—frequently not entirely accurate—as to what a work was 'about'—that is, into which very general category of human experience its contents might be pigeonholed. But the tendency of most modern criticism, especially in its educational implications, is to suggest that there are far more significant categories than these—that the structure and tone and, in particular, the peculiar effect of a literary work offer far more revealing modes for its classification. We have, that is, addressed ourselves (with, I admit, sometimes highly conflicting answers) to such questions as what is a lyric poem, a tragedy, a comedy, a naturalistic novel, an absurd play, an adventure tale, a satire—and we have recognized that such reliable old guides as subject matter or historical period have not proved very useful. For we ask, not 'What will the reader learn about?' but 'What kind of experience is he invited to undergo?'

The consequence of this for the high school and college classroom is easy to see. It is plain that *Oedipus* and *Othello* bear strong relationships, despite the 1,900 years that separate their composition; it is plain that *Gulliver's Travels* and *Catch-22* have powerful affinities, despite the disparity of their 'topics'; it is plain that *Huckleberry Finn* can afford closer comparison with the *Odyssey* than it can with *Penrod,* despite the fact that it might be lumped with the latter under some such heading as 'Books about Boys'. In short, we have become increasingly sophisticated about distinctions and relationships between literary kinds—and this has had profound effects both on criticism and pedagogy.

I would suggest, therefore, that in thinking about children's reading we relax somewhat about 'topics'. The boy whose consuming passion is the Civil War need not confine himself to century-old reprints of *Harper's Magazine* or special publications of *American Heritage,* but is likely, on the contrary, to find his way to biographies of Lincoln and Lee and the stories of Ida Tarbell and *The Red Badge of Courage* and even perhaps to 'When Lilacs Last in the Dooryard Bloomed'. The youthful baseball aficionado will quite likely come, at his own rate, to the comedy of Ring Lardner, the unique achievement of Mark Harris's *Bang the Drum Slowly,* the high art of Malamud's *The Natural.* The James Bond addict can be led on to Eric Ambler's intricate plotting and thence to Graham Greene's reflective 'entertainments' and thence, I venture to say, to Stevenson and even to Melville.

Thus, beneath the apparent uniformity of 'subject-matter' labels, there lies diversity of a far more important sort. No topic is intrinsically more 'worthwhile' than another; no topic is either a guarantee of, or a bar to, the sort of satisfactions I have mentioned previously. They can serve us as singularly useful devices by which to engage interest and by which, too, to exploit the happy diversity of literary experiences which, on the surface, they tend to obscure. In effect, if a youngster is entirely concerned with reading about the Civil War, we should view it neither apprehensively as 'obsessive' nor smugly as 'educational'. Instead, I should think we can view it as a natural and immensely promising channel, leading to a permanently rewarding diversity of humanistic encounters.

A third question that has interested many critics in recent years might be put as follows. Are there basic themes or 'motifs' whose expression and recognition in written and spoken literature help to explain the timeless appeal of certain kinds of stories and poems? I am talking here about something a little more fundamental than even such formulas as boy-meets-girl or the tale of revenge or the 'whodunit'.

The inquiries of such anthropologists as Frazer, such psychologists as Jung, and such scholar-critics as Northrop Frye have pointed to the fact that some of man's basic questions and doubts and hypothetical answers tend to take form in recurrent literary patterns—or archetypes, as they are often called.

To take an example from a field that interests me: one persuasive scholar has been able to talk about the nature of satire, even in its most sophisticated forms, by tracing its origins to certain tribal rituals, directed against hostile forces, and has gone even further back to various informal, minimally artful attempts to achieve, through extemporaneous curses, the same magical effects.[1] The work of another scholar, Philip Young, has noted the recurrence of such literary themes as the suspension of time (in stories like that of Rip Van Winkle or the many 'time machines') or the stories of kings' daughters who rescue their lovers from wrathful fathers (such as the tale of Pocahontas).[2] Not content with noting the origins of some of these literary motifs in folk literature, he has applied psychoanalytic insights into the reasons for their persistence—the needs and worries and wishes that thus find embodiment in mythic form.

In their particulars, many of these approaches still call for

---

[1] Robert C. Elliott, *The Power of Satire: Magic, Ritual, Art* (Princeton, N.J., 1960).

[2] Philip C. Young, 'Fallen from Time: The Mythic Rip Van Winkle', *Kenyon Review*, 22 (Autumn 1960), 547-73, and 'The Mother of Us All: Pocohontas Reconsidered', *Kenyon Review*, 24 (Summer 1962), 391-415.

refinement. But I am of the opinion that they are bringing us substantially closer than ever before to answering questions we have previously evaded or answered peremptorily and unsatisfactorily. They are questions, that is, that concern the unchanging appeal of certain basic kinds of literary construction.

I am not certain how thoroughly the implications of these studies have been explored with respect to children's literature—although it is plain that many of these motifs find their most uncomplicated and manifest embodiment in myths and fairy stories and folktales. What, for the moment, concerns me is their possible significance for that nagging problem, the problem that is variously defined as engagement or motivation.

I have, to be honest, been somewhat concerned with the manner in which I have discovered this problem is being handled in various curricular study centres and similar agencies designed to deal with children's reading in the schools. I have found, for example, that the principle of familiarity—of comfortable recognition—has been rather overworked in many places. It is argued that the child cannot be expected to show interest in the unfamiliar and even that literature should make no demands upon him that transcend the literal limits of his own experience. This has an odd effect on what we judge to be 'suitable'. If a story involves a city, let it be a city he knows—or knows a great deal about. If a poem involves a bird, let it be a native bird (exit nightingale). If a play is to be read, by all means let it be a play of the here and now.

Such a principle seems to me to be a pretty frail one. I believe it is in practice. Most teachers of English composition know that because a child owns a dog or has visited a farm there is no guarantee that he will write readily or enthusiastically about 'My Dog' or 'The Farm'. And most teachers of English and concerned parents soon recognize that the familiar is at best a partial handle on children's literary enthusiasm—doubtless for the very simple reason that the commonplace is the commonplace and therefore the most unexciting object to the imagination.

And one need not be a very subtle aesthetic theorist to sense the difficulties of a lopsided emphasis upon the familiar. Whether we quote Aristotle's dictum concerning the mixture of the probable and the marvelous in successful literature or Marianne Moore's lines about 'imaginary gardens with real toads in them', the principle seems pretty clear. Effective imaginative literature is an amalgam of the new and strange—what taxes credulity and complacency—with what is somehow believable, authentic, and immediate. And I should argue that if the balance is to be tipped it must be tipped in the direction of novelty, of the alien and challenging. For all genuinely memorable literary experience is, in some measure, an initiation into the previously unknown, and the overworked reviewer's phrase to the effect that after reading such and such one is 'never quite the same' is, quite literally, a criterion that may be applied to the judgement of any literary work.

The word 'romantic' is today a very unfashionable one, but it is the thrust toward romance, or at least toward the imaginative, that outruns experienced actuality and that, today as much as ever, remains a major weapon against sameness and stagnation. This is heartbreakingly apparent, for example, even in the street gangs of our cities, whose ritual and nomenclature and professed structure and self-image, it has been proven, far exceed the sordid actualities of their operations. The same phenomenon is present in the almost universal manifestations of Walter Mittyism, among the old and young, wherever the imagination is invoked in the struggle against the too familiar. Mittyism may be professionally explained as escapism or the buttressing of the *amour propre* or as protest, but, whatever its ends, the means plainly involve the enlistment of the imagination in combat against familiar reality.

I am rejecting the temptation to say that new, unfamiliar kinds of reading should be encouraged in order to 'stretch' the imagination and to 'broaden horizons'. I happen to believe that there's a good deal of truth (and some danger) in this position, but the question that immediately concerns me is that of engagement and motivation. And in this context I am simply urging that we can overdo the matter of familiarity—if it leads us to neglect the appeal of whatever strains against the boundaries of the commonplace.

But it is obvious, as I have suggested, that novelty must be balanced against the reassuring sensation of knowing where one is, that the totally alien lacks both intelligibility and consequence for any reader. As critics have always recognized, we can become engaged in literature only when it is, in some sense, 'credible', when it lays claim, in some fashion, on our sense of reality. Many writers—including writers of children's literature—have responded to this requirement by attempting to invest the familiar with the romantic, to exploit, as it were, the potential magic that is latent in everyday reality; or they seek to introduce the strange and incredible into the midst of the commonplace. This last, of course, is what has been done triumphantly in such works as *Mary Poppins* or *Stuart Little* or *Doctor Dolittle.* And the former kinds of things are worthily attempted in the familiar efforts to exploit the 'romance of coal' or the 'miracle of oatmeal' or 'the wonderful story of sewage disposal', largely for didactic reasons.

Awareness of motifs or archetypes, however, suggests that the recognizable to which we respond is not necessarily a matter of times, places, and institutions but of the basic needs we feel, questions we ask, answers we find—of the instinctive, universal challenge of the journey, tension of the conflict, the covert wish that magic mingle with reality, the complex drives of affection, the complex fears of death.

I am aware that talk of this kind breeds discomfort of sorts among parents and those who are devoted to children, professionally or otherwise. Because we love and cherish the childlike, we naturally seek to preserve it and to translate even children's reading into terms that reject many of the adult 'facts of life' as somehow corrupting. Talk of conflict and love and birth and death, of tension and terror and doubt, and even of driving curiosity seems hostile to the image some people foster of 'children's literature' as a world unsullied by the adult vision of reality—as a monument to wholesome naiveté. I am, in fact, tempted to speculate that the fatuous admiration professed by some sophisticated adults for the idyllic surroundings, the allegedly benign humour, the unworldly wisdom of *The Wizard of Oz* or *Alice* or *Winnie-the-Pooh* is not so much what it pretends to be—a recognition of 'adult' excellences in 'children's' books—as a wistful gesture of longing to recover an irretrievable, happy innocence.

It is certainly possible to view children's books as instruments for the confirmation of childishness— to rejoice in whatever preserves the guileless and ingenuous. I suspect that to do so is, in itself, an evocation of impossible magic. The child is, indeed, in all his growing faculties, the father of the man; the faculty of imagination is not a childlike gift but a faculty capable of robust, complex development. As I have mentioned archetypes, let me say that no archetype is more compelling and dangerous than that of the fall of our first ancestors, for it points to the most uncomfortable yet inevitable fact about the human condition. This fact is that the acquisition of wisdom is the loss of innocence. The fact has received ingenious evasions. From Plato, through Wordsworth, through Hugh Walpole's neglected, lovely, subversive *Golden Scarecrow* to the pubert-directed reassurances of *The Catcher in the Rye*, we have been told that the innocence of childhood somehow preserves a greater wisdom and virtue than the sagacity of adults.

Such doctrines, however attractive they may be, are mystical rather than humanistic. For the humanist, above all else, takes into account the realities of the human condition. And those realities do not lead us into a beautiful, passionless realm but are compounded of hope and fear, of doubt and reassurance, of need and the fulfilment of need. It is in encounter with these human facts that we develop uniquely human values; and they are the values we seek to develop in and share with our children.

What I have been trying to say is, first, that the problem of 'engagement' or motivation can only be met by a judicious blending of what is novel and unfamiliar with what is real and significant. And, second, I have suggested that the latter component is to be achieved, not necessarily through those overtly familiar sights and sounds and people and places we identify as what the child 'knows', but through the more basic recognitions of experienced needs and satisfactions, doubts and curiosities and preoccupations.

There is a story by Saki that may help me clarify my point. It is called 'The Toys of Peace'. In it two well-meaning, pacifically inclined parents are induced to substitute for their children's toy soldiers a set of new playthings, in which military installations and personnel are replaced by a model city hall, municipal disposal plant, figures of various worthy civic servants, and the like. The children are given these toys; but the parents return, after some absence, to discover that through the children's ingenuity the city hall has been converted into a fort, the garbage plant into another fort, and the street-sweepers, health officials, and doctors and nurses have been assigned the role of soldiers on both sides of a fierce and bloody imagined conflict. Leaving aside whatever motive was in the strange mind of Saki, the story still serves my purpose. The 'realistic', familiar, but dreary figures of civic virtue are rejected in place of the more remote, less recognizable, more 'romantic' figures of war. Yet in that act is a gesture not only toward romance but toward reality as well, toward a state of contest and dissension and uncertainty which has, in a sense, a greater authenticity than does the image of a benevolent and orderly universe.

The tendency of what I have been saying is toward the recognition of certain principles that may transcend such notions as 'maturity' and 'reading readiness' and 'suitability' and the like. It is designed to suggest that, if we don't fatuously accept children's literature as primarily a safe, sane, antiseptic device for the preservation of childishness, its most fundamental appeals are the appeals of all effective literature—it exploits our urge toward novelty as it exploits, too, our insistence on a human actuality that is an amalgam of glory and squalor, certainty and anxiety, nobility and baseness, or, for that matter 'good guys' and indubitably bad ones. And this belief, it seems to me, moves to close the gap between adults' values and children's reading. It suggests that we do not seek substitutes, in children's books, for the most cherished elements in the best adult books. It suggests the folly of 'approving' books that are mere superficial mirrors of what we think children are or ought to be, mere superficial representations of a children's world or what it ought to be. For the highest pleasures of literature to which I have already referred—whether in adults' reading or children's—combine the urgency and authenticity of life as we know it with the excitement and wonder of life as it may yet be known.

This is why I believe that 'great' children's literature, if I may use that tired term, is simply great literature. It is no accident, nor is it mere clinical curiosity, that accounts for the critics' interest in Greek myths or in *Robinson Crusoe* or *Treasure Island* or *Just So Stories* or even, for that matter, in the perennial fairy or folktales. The sources of adult curiosity, adult humour, adult suspense, adult terror, adult pity are exploited by the writers of such books with an art comparable to that of any author for any audience. If I happen to have been talking about what are called 'classics', I do not wish to be construed as believing that the existence of classics is central to any belief I have about reading by children or adults; the appetite for reading, in old and young, far outruns the capacity of a few men to produce books of transparently permanent greatness. But it seems only sensible that, when the satisfactions literature can offer are superlatively afforded by a certain, limited number of books, we should seek to experience these works. It seems equally sensible that our experience with these books should reveal, in some measure, the satisfaction that many other books are capable of affording—the satisfactions that young and old alike should seek from reading.

As great books differ from good books in degree rather than kind, so too, I think, successful children's books differ from successful adult books in degree rather than in kind. Obviously this view follows from a belief that, with respect to the faculties of understanding and the gift of appreciation, young human beings differ from older ones in degree rather than kind. Granted that youthful powers of attention and concentration are limited and thus raise real and difficult questions for us, our concern with these questions must not deter us from the recognition that neither attention nor concentration are the faculties to which literature ultimately addresses itself in children or adults.

The point of all this seems rather clear. What I have been trying to say expresses my belief that the judgement of children's literature—and all the adult efforts that proceed from that judgement—must be conducted without condescension, without turning one's adult collar in an effort to define and enforce values that are somehow uniquely juvenile. On the contrary, it seems to me that the proper satisfactions of reading, even in the newly literate child—even, indeed, in the non-literate, story-listening child—provide a robust affirmation of our common humanity, our capacity, whether we are young or old, to understand and to be moved by and to gather to ourselves the products of the creative imagination.

As I say these things I am deeply conscious of circumstances at this moment in history which may qualify my views and chasten my high hopes. Talk about rich literary experience may seem appallingly ironic in the context of the massive phenomena of minimal literacy, minimal ability to understand and communicate. A teacher of English cannot today carry on glibly about literary values without agonizing awareness of the presence of culturally deprived youngsters for whom literature can be expected to have little meaning, since such words as 'father' and 'bedtime' and even 'breakfast' have themselves virtually no meaning.

To the crushing, compelling challenge posed by such youngsters (as well as, I might add, by those ostensibly more privileged youngsters in whom parental apathy, television, and aggressive vulgarity have likewise engendered a brand of cultural privation) we must respond with whatever is relevant of our experience, our love, and our concern. Even in these instances, however, though we respond with total flexibility and undogmatic resourcefulness to problems of minimal communication, the imagination is an indispensable ally, and the awaking of the imagination a relevant province of art. For there are windows to be opened, and when they are open, they must reveal a vista of more than squalor and sameness and spiritual poverty.

It is common today to insist on a distinction between mere communication, including written communication, and literary art, whether or not that art is actually practiced in writing. Because, in practical and perhaps theoretical terms, some mode of communication is always antecedent to art, communication may well demand priority in much of our educational thinking, just as minimal questions of material well-being demand priority over questions of total well-being.

But, though we distinguish communication from art and concentrate upon the former in all its urgency, all its changes, all its opportunities, the nature and stature of literary art and its satisfactions suffer no change. Though in our folly we neglect literary art, though in our haste we seek substitutes for it, though in our complacency or cruelty we discourage access to it for many of our fellow men, art and its power remain unchanged.

The realm of the humanist (and by this time I hope it is clear that the values I have been describing are, in my view, humanistic) is the realm of what has been created by human wisdom and imagination, work that has achieved final form, work that waits to be known and savoured and remembered for the unique satisfactions it provides. And so it is that a belief in the value of reading leads to a concern, not primarily for what is desirable or appropriate, what is suitable or profitable, what is hard or easy, what can be or ought to be, but for what is *here*—here to be encountered, here to be understood, here to be responded to, here to be rejoiced in.

[1967]

Didacticism in modern dress

JOHN ROWE TOWNSEND

During most of the nineteenth century it was taken for granted that children's books had a didactic aim. The emphasis could be mainly instructional, as in the Peter Parley series or Jacob Abbott's Rollo books. It could be moral, as in Mary Butt Sherwood's alarming *Fairchild Family* or the tearful saga of Elsie Dinsmore or the novels-for-young-ladies of the impeccable Charlotte M. Yonge. It could serve other ideals: that of Empire in the boys' stories of Englishman George Alfred Henty or of self-help in the rags-to-riches novelettes of Horatio Alger. But simply giving children pleasure would have seemed too frivolous an aim to most nineteenth-century writers.

Most; not all. Didacticism began to break down with the Alice books, with *Treasure Island,* which seemed to its author to be 'as original as sin', with *The Adventures of Tom Sawyer* and *The Adventures of Huckleberry Finn,* in which, as Mark Twain said, 'persons attempting to find a moral . . . will be banished.' And today nearly all the old didactic books are dead; the survivors are those that rejected didacticism, with the addition of a few such as *Little Women* that transcended it.

Is the didactic spirit extinct in children's literature today? We tend to talk and write as though it were. It is contrary to our view of the happy, relaxed, and more-or-less-equal relationship between the generations which we now regard as ideal. Yet the urge to instruct the young is deeply built into human nature.

And if one looks at the 'quality' children's books of today, and still more at what is written about them, it is hard to avoid the conclusion that didacticism is still very much alive and that, by an engaging intellectual frailty, we are able to reject the concept while accepting the reality. We can accommodate this contradiction because of another of our frailties: we cannot extend any historical sense we may possess in order to look objectively at our own time. Years ago we threw the old didacticism (dowdy morality) out of the window; it has come back in at the door wearing modern dress (smart values) and we do not even recognize it.

The standards of those concerned with the assessment and selection of children's books are more often implicit than explicit; but in situations where these standards are being passed on they can be found stated plainly in print. Here are a few instances; I do not quote them with disapproval but only to make my point. May Hill Arbuthnot's *Children and Books* is the basic text for a great many teachers' courses, and the following passages are among a number of similar ones.

> *. . . such books as* Little Women *and the Wilder stories, without referring to specific religious practices or creeds, leave children with the conviction that decent, kindly people can maintain an inner serenity even as they struggle with and master the evils that threaten them.*
>
> *. . . they [children] need books that, in the course of a good story, help to develop clear standards of right and wrong.*
>
> *Above all, to balance the speed and confusions of our modern world, we need to find books which build strength and steadfastness in the child, books which develop his faith in the essential decency and nobility of life, books which give him a feeling for the wonder and the goodness of the universe.*

These views are not confined to one commentator. Charlotte S. Huck and Doris Young state in *Children's Literature in the Elementary School:*

Through reading and guided discussion of their reading experiences children may gain understanding of self and others. They may come to realize that all behavior is caused and results from individual needs. Children may gain insight into their own behavior and the process of growth by identifying with individuals or families in good literature.

Dr Bernice Cooper wrote, in an article on Laura Ingalls Wilder in a recent number of *Elementary English:*

. . . the value of the 'Little House' books is enhanced for boys and girls because Laura Ingalls Wilder's philosophy of life, without didacticism, permeates the series. That philosophy is expressed in the letter from Mrs Wilder which the sixth grade received in response to their letters to her. She wrote, 'But remember it is not the things you have that make you happy. It is love and kindness, helping each other and just plain being good.'

The use of the phrase 'without didacticism' seems to me to be a mere genuflection toward the accepted view that didacticism is out of fashion.

And here are two extracts from the excellent children's-book-selection policy of The Free Library of Philadelphia:

In the field of purely recreational reading, stress is laid upon those books which develop the imaginative faculties, promote understanding, and cultivate worthwhile ideals and values.

Recreational books of all kinds, whether story or fact, are purchased with a view towards giving pleasure in reading and developing healthy attitudes towards the family, the community, the nation, and the world.

The views of the critics and selectors of children's books are of importance because these people are so largely the ones who decide whether a children's book will be published and whether, if published, it will succeed. It is a platitude to say that when we talk of quality children's books today we are not talking about something that children buy for themselves. There is a relationship between a child's pocket money and the price of an ice cream or a root beer or a candy bar or a comic; there is no relationship between a child's pocket money and the price of a book. The child himself hardly enters into the process by which quality children's books are assessed and distributed. They are written by adults, they are read by adults for adult publishers, they are reviewed by adults, they are bought by adults. This is inevitable. But the result is that a children's book can go far on the road to success before a single child has seen it.

The expensive, approved children's book costing $3.95 or $5.50 will do well if the libraries take it and not too well if they do not. A small number of parents with taste and money will buy it too; like the librarians they will almost certainly be serious, well-meaning, conscientious people. Quality publishing for children is governed by a complex social-institutional-economic equation which replaces the law of supply and demand; and as a result the adults are uniquely able to procure on the child's behalf not so much the thing he wants as the thing they feel he ought to have.

And what the child ought to have is apt to be something that fits in with the image of our society as serious, well-meaning, conscientious people feel it ought to be. We see our ideal society as one in which everybody is thoughtful, gentle, compassionate, withal humorous and fun loving; in which everyone is integrated but nevertheless individual. We expect, consciously or otherwise, that writers for children will provide us with instruments for bringing this society into being. And if our hands are on the levers, we cannot merely expect this; we can practically insist upon it. Now is the time to recognize just what we are doing and consider the dangers we run.

The first danger is an obvious one: the child opts out of the whole procedure and reads comics or nothing. He has, after all, the ultimate veto; however much adults approve of a book, no power on earth can make him read it if he does not want to. Indeed, teachers may also opt out of the whole procedure. I have met some—more in England than in the United States—who are utterly cynical. They say in effect: 'It's no good trying to wish all this highbrow stuff on us. You just spend a day with the underprivileged kids I have in my class, and you'll see it's a blessed miracle if you can get them to read *any* kind of rubbish.' Even the child who is a natural reader is no longer, as in the nineteenth century, virtually a captive audience. There is no dearth of other reading matter or of other things that an intelligent child can do with his time.

The existence of approved books that children will not read is a sizeable danger, though somewhat diminished by the fact that librarians cannot afford to give space to shelf-sitters. If the reviewers like a certain author but the children do not, the news soon gets around. The book that no child will read cannot survive—at least as a children's book—nor does it deserve to. Authors have to write books that the child can and will read, and the effect has been to concentrate their minds wonderfully. Even so, the danger of undercutting by the comics or formula stories is there. The writer or publisher with an eye on the main chance has a long start over the one who is practising or encouraging an art.

The second danger is the effect upon authorship. Writers are human and have to eat. With a few dogged exceptions, they will not write the kind of books that are going to be unacceptable. The people who pay the piper can call the tune. In an article in the spring 1966 *Author*, Philippa Pearce describes the demand for values as insidious. If a writer has moral standards, she says, 'they will appear explicitly or implicitly in his books; or at least their corrupting contrary will not appear. He should not need to bother about values; his job is imaginative writing.' Arthur Ransome, author of *Swallows and Amazons*, would not have it that the author is responsible to anybody but himself: 'You write not for children but for yourself,' he says, 'and if by good fortune children enjoy what you enjoy, why then, you are a writer of children's books . . . no special credit to you, but simply thumping good luck.' But if you write for yourself and the result is dismissed as flippant or unwholesome, you will not feel like congratulating yourself on your luck.

The danger that the author is silenced, or more probably redirected toward producing acceptable work, must of course be seen in perspective. Plenty of good writers exist to whom the desired values are as natural as air. Ransome himself is an example. While there is no preaching in his books, they form in a sense a course for children, a powerful influence on them to look at life in a certain way—and a way that serious, well-meaning adults are likely to approve of. His children are truthful, loyal, straightforward; the things they do are sensible, constructive, character-building. And Philippa Pearce's *Tom's Midnight Garden* and *A Dog So Small* are just as firmly rooted in civilized values. Excellent authors may be found whose moral sense comes out still more explicitly in their books. One of many possible examples is Madeleine L'Engle, whose prize-winning *A Wrinkle in Time* describes a cosmic war of good against evil—evil here is the reduction of people to a mindless mass, while good is individuality, art, and love. Miss L'Engle finds it quite natural to bring in the great, and greatest, names on 'our' side:

'Who have our fighters been?' Calvin asked. . . .

'Jesus!' Charles Wallace said. 'Why, of course, Jesus!'

'Of course!' Mrs Whatsit said. 'Go on, Charles, love. There were others. All your great artists. They've been lights for us to see by.'

'Leonardo da Vinci?' Calvin suggested tentatively. 'And Michelangelo?'

'And Shakespeare,' Charles Wallace called out, 'and Bach! And Pasteur and Madame Curie and Einstein!'

Now Calvin's voice rang with confidence. 'And Schweitzer and Gandhi and Buddha and Beethoven and Rembrandt and St Francis!'

Miss L'Engle's was openly and joyfully a moral theme. I take not the slightest exception to her approach. But neither morality nor magnificent invocations will make a work of art live if the breath of life is not in it. And a moral posture assumed by an author in deference to current requirements could result in nauseating and disastrous work. A British literary editor suggested to me last year that I ought to write a children's novel 'against racial prejudice'; he was as much puzzled as disappointed when I politely declined. But it seems to me that an author will do best to write only the books that come naturally to him. Anything else is done at the peril of his soul.

A third danger, which follows closely from the second, is the evaluation of books by the wrong standards. We are, I think, getting onto critically shaky ground when books like Louisa Shotwell's *Roosevelt Grady,* which deals with the life of a Negro family of migrant workers, and Dorothy Sterling's *Mary Jane,* telling of the ordeal of a Negro girl who goes to a newly integrated junior high school, and even Ezra Jack Keats' *The Snowy Day,* a bright, cheerful picture book about a little coloured boy's day in the snow, are discussed not on their literary merits but only as representations of racial problems. It is natural if you feel as strongly as most decent people do about racial discrimination to welcome books that give it short shrift; but to assess books on their racial attitude rather than their literary value, and still more to look on books as ammunition in the battle, is to take a further and still more dangerous step from literature-as-morality to literature-as-propaganda—a move toward conditions in which, hitherto, literary art has signally failed to thrive.

I should emphasize again that I am not in general opposed to the system or standards by which children's books are chosen; it is hard to see a practical alternative, other than a lapse into commercialism with the mass production of titles aimed at the lowest common denominator. And we in the United States and Great Britain can congratulate ourselves that at least there is no official children's literature, no crude plugging of a national or party line. Authors, publishers, critics, teachers, and librarians would unite

—thank heaven—in horror at the very idea. All I am suggesting is that we should see our standards as they really are and should recognize that our emphasis on quality and on values exposes us to certain risks—which may be worth running but which we should be aware of. Let me sum them up, briefly. One is that if we are not careful the ordinary, unliterary child loses interest in books; for this problem the United States, through first-class work for children in the schools and libraries, is doing much better than England. Another is that we expect from authors what it is not right or wise to expect from them, and thus possibly stultify their creative impulse. And a third is that we judge books by the wrong standards. It is not irrelevant that a book may contribute to moral perception or social adjustment or the advancement of a minority group or the Great Society in general; but in writing there is no substitute for the creative imagination, and in criticism there is no criterion except literary merit.

[1967]

'For it was indeed he'

Satan adopts . . . devices to capture our youth and secure the ruin of immortal souls . . . Of this class the love story and cheap work of fiction captivate fancy and pervert taste. They defraud the future man or woman by capturing and enslaving the young imagination. The wild fancies and exaggerations of the unreal in the story supplant aspirations for that which ennobles and exalts . . . They forget the sweet poet's admonition, 'Life is real, life is earnest.'

—ANTHONY COMSTOCK: *Traps for the Young*

If Messrs Grosset & Dunlap, book publishers, were so inclined (which they certainly are not), they might erect on the grave of Anthony Comstock in Brooklyn's Evergreen Cemetery a monument 700 miles high composed exclusively of the 45,000,000 fifty-cent juveniles that they have sold during the past quarter century despite opinions set forth in *Traps for the Young*. By definition, every one of those books is pure, wild fancy, exaggerations of the unreal; in short, what reformers, intent upon ennobling, dub 'cheap'. And that is no reflection on the price.

Unobtrusively, like so many Guy Fawkes heaping gunpowder in the cellars of parliament, three publishing firms annually unload well over 5,000,000 explosive fifty-centers on the American adolescents, the foundation stones of human society.

Or that would be the version of the American Library Association. For pious people is the bitter statistical pill that in profitable but godless years like 1927 fifty-centers outsell Bibles two to one. Collectors of best-seller figures will find that the 9,000,000-copy sales of Harold Bell Wright novels, although supposedly a record for quantity production of one man's work, are a mere drop in the bucket beside the 20,000,000 copies of fifty-cent juveniles turned out by the late Mr Edward Stratemeyer—for practical purposes the inventor of the business.

Obviously the fifty-cent juvenile is no hothouse sport but a perennial of the hardiest variety and still blossoming. Of this there is no better proof than the U.S. government biennial census of book manufacture (figures given in round numbers):

1925:	Adult fiction	30,600,000—15 per cent[1]
	Juvenile	25,200,000—12.5 per cent
1931:	Adult fiction	19,200,000—12.4 per cent
	Juvenile	22,400,000—14.5 per cent

That the largest portion of these juveniles are fifty-centers is the final blasphemy that adolescent readers have flung in the beard of Mr Comstock.

The fifty-cent juvenile is, precisely, a book for boys and girls between the ages of ten and sixteen. It has few literary pretensions; it is a flat-footed account of the superhuman exploits of adolescent *Übermenschen*—and if it is successful it may have sequels that ramble on for as many as thirty-six volumes. It is a fortuitous cross between compound interest and perpetual motion. *The Rover Boys* is its quintessence; a substantial profit for author and publisher is its only, and unblushing, purpose.

In literature the fifty-center takes its place between the dime novel and the 'juvenile of distinction'. The ten-cent thriller, with the exception of *Frank Merriwell* (of whom more later), is a stir-

---

[1] Of all books manufactured in that year.

ring account of Homeric deeds accomplished by straight-shooting, hard-hitting, clean-living he-men. Decorous 'juveniles of distinction' are pseudo-novels in terms a child theoretically finds interesting and comprehensible. The fifty-center has its outward appearance of decorum, even in format, but the characters speed unflinchingly through adventures that would make even the ten-cent Deadwood Dick blanch. Most important is the rule that every fifty-cent hero must remain an adolescent in whose shoes the reader may easily imagine himself. But his accomplishments must surpass those of the bravest and most sagacious men. In other words, the fifty-center has a glorified dime-novel plot involving boys and girls, but is decked out in cloth covers to resemble *Stalky & Co.*

The nucleus of the fifty-cent theme is the fact that a hero cannot fail. With the definitive finality of a chemical formula, *The Rover Boys at School* is the pattern of elements from which every succeeding fifty-center has been compounded. Holding each volume together are the threads of some hair-raising adventure. Poverty empties the pockets of dastards only. Lack of funds in anyone so middle class as a Rover Boy would be something of a sin. Virtue and success are synonyms, for virtue is resolved to the business of thwarting the villains in their frantic efforts to appear greater men than the heroes. Women's place in the male fifty-center is to invoke manly strength, not venery. In a long series they serve another purpose: they bear the young for a junior set if popularity warrants it.

In order to hold the reader breathless, the fifty-cent plot whirls lickety-split from the first to the last chapter like an express train. Even the characters rush about at a breakneck rate in airplanes, racing cars, rocket ships, anything capable of breaking the speed limit. When Rover Boys are reduced to such slow means of locomotion as the horse, the reader is assured of at least one runaway. That idea is carried into the very names of the books: *Tom Swift, Dave Dashaway, The Motor Boys, Jack Ranger.*

On the surface none of this is insidious enough to undermine the morals of the nation. Then why the great hue and cry against the fifty-center? It is the embodiment of success-story idealism. If not exactly literary, it makes up by action for what it lacks of art. Certainly it will not fill the adolescent mind with ideas that adults might think too mature for it.

The reformer's answer to all of this is that the fify-center is over-exciting. A child intoxicated with *Tom Swift* would be not only intolerable but permanently warped by an overstimulated imagination. At least that was the cry of one Franklin K. Mathiews, whose enmity for the fifty-center will be particularized later.

Of all the scalps Mr Mathiews would have liked to hang on his belt, that of Edward Stratemeyer would have pleased him most. Grosset & Dunlap would be well justified in placing atop its whimsical 700-mile-high spire a monumental bronze of this Mr Stratemeyer—for he alone produced 250 miles of it. He was father of this fifty-cent literature. He wrote the first of it *(The Motor Boys, or Chums Through Thick and Thin)*, the most of it (under literally hundreds of pseudonyms), its best seller *(Tom Swift)*, its worst failure *(The White Ribbon Boys)*, its latest success *(Nancy Drew)*. With rare justice, he made the most money. When he died in 1930 he had hung up a record of having written, or conceived for others to write, more than 800 fifty-cent juveniles. He also left an estate worth a million dollars. That was his reward for discovering in the late nineties that, like many another natural resource of the time, the reading capacity of the American adolescent was limitless. As oil had its Rockefeller, literature had its Stratemeyer.

Today, librarians and champions of 'better books for children' would like to think that the fifty-cent thriller was interred with Mr Stratemeyer. But that is a reformer's dream. They forget the Writing Garises—Howard, Lilian, young Roger (Princeton '24), and Cleo—who today thump out fifty-centers faster than ever. They forget the Stratemeyer Syndicate founded by the late great Edward and lustily carried on by his daughters, Miss Edna Stratemeyer and Mrs Harriet Stratemeyer Adams (Wellesley '14), as well as many tenaciously prolific oldsters and newcomers. Barring acts of God, Grosset & Dunlap will go right on publishing its three million copies annually. Its competitors, A. L. Burt Co. and Cupples & Leon, will sell their million or so apiece.

If the generation brought up on *Tom Swift* were to dip into such currently popular works as *The Outboard Motor Boat Series,* few readers would notice any change in diet. The machinery of the story might seem strange but the eternal verities of plot and character would have a nostalgic familiarity. Superficially, time has wrought only two differences in the fifty-center. First, modern writers attempt to tell their stories with something more than the formal adequacy of *The Rover Boys* school. Airplanes, radio, television are no longer discussed with the cavalier nonchalance of total ignorance. Today, books concerned with such contrivances are written or revised with the greater authority of such men as Noel Sainsbury, a practicing pilot, or Jack Binns, a radio expert who in 1909 had the distinction, as 'wireless operator' on the sinking S. S. *Republic,* of sending the first Marconi 'CQD' message ever to bring about a major rescue at sea. The second change has to do with the mould in which the story is cast. The same jellies are poured in but the final form is, for the moment, a detective story. This matter of shaping the plot is a result of the discovery that adolescent reading tastes run about two years behind those of their elders. Thus the fifty-cent heroes went to war, thus they took up science seriously, and thus today they set about solving murders, apprehending international thieves.

Keeping the fifty-center close, but not too close, to adult fiction is perhaps the greatest problem of its publishers. In an earlier day sixteen-year-olds were unsophisticated enough to consume *Tom Swifts* with real relish. Now, Edgar Rice

Burroughs, Sax Rohmer, and the spicier thrillers claim the adolescent at fourteen. The average child is still initiated to the fifty-centers at ten, and therefore his exposure to them is cut from six to four years. Because the publisher knows that the percentage of children who will buy these books is practically constant, he figures his anticipated sales in terms of the number of years boys and girls spend in the fifty-cent reading period. Consequently, when their appetites are sated two years earlier, he faces a loss of one-third of his custom. It was to sustain interest after the crucial fourteenth year that *Bomba the Jungle Boy* was made in the youthful image of Tarzan, and *Nancy Drew* in that of Philo Vance.

Nancy is the greatest phenomenon among all the fifty-centers. She is a best seller. How she crashed a Valhalla that had been rigidly restricted to the male of her species is a mystery even to her publishers—for 'tomboy' rings like praise in the adolescent female ear, but 'sissy' is the anathema of anathemas to a boy. Thus it is that girls read boys' books, but woe betide the boy caught with a copy of *The Motor Girls at Camp Surprise!* It was the simple arithmetic of a census taker that boys' books should outsell girls'. Yet today, Nancy Drew tops even Bomba, the most popular of modern male heroes. The speed with which the public consumes this fabulous series is shown by the sales figures of one of the larger retailers, R. H. Macy & Co. In the six weeks of the last Christmas season Macy's sold 6,000 of the ten titles of *Nancy Drew* compared with 3,750 for the runner-up, *Bomba,* which had fifteen volumes to choose from. And Macy's would be disappointed if, during the holiday period, it did not find buyers for 50,000 fifty-centers.

Yet orginally this half-dollar bonanza was something of an ugly duckling. In the flamboyant half of the nineteenth century successful publishers of juveniles issued the works of Harry Castlemon, Edward S. Ellis, Oliver Optic, and Horatio Alger Jr at prices near a dollar. When *The Rover Boys* and *The Old Glory Series* came their way the price remained unchanged, and sales followed the usual pedestrian course of all books. Among publishers it remained for one American, two Scotsmen, an Englishman, and a German to fashion the fifty-center and make it a national phenomenon. The American was A. L. Burt, a pedagogue with publishing ambitions. His first ventures were a cheap edition of the classics entitled *The World's Best Books,* the few Algers he could lay his fingers on, and several nondescript juveniles. Today his house is rich, potent, and respected. Even more successful were the Scotsmen. They began as thrifty young men intent upon making their fortunes with the U. S. Book Co. When that firm failed, bookkeeper Alexander Grosset and salesman George Dunlap hit upon the idea of peddling the paperbound novels left in the U.S. Book Co.'s warehouses. As a special attraction they rebound them in cloth and boards. Demand at once exceeded supply. New grist for their mill they secured by renting plates of *passé* novels from the original publishers and reissuing them in cheap editions. Thus the highly profitable reprint business was born. They next added cheap juveniles to their list, and profits began to soar.

Then came the Englishman and German, Cupples and Leon. They were book salesmen casting about for an opportunity to make real money too. They saw the firms of Altemus in Philadelphia, Donohue in Chicago, Grosset & Dunlap and A. L. Burt in New York selling juveniles at whatever prices struck their fancy, all the way from $1.25 to twenty-five cents. One day Cupples & Leon was visited by Edward Stratemeyer, and from that meeting came a juvenile costing fifty cents but looking as if it were worth much more. The adolescent public at once decided that here was the place to get your money's worth. It did not take the other publishers long to follow Cupples' lead. Burt and Grosset, who had popular writers on their lists, rose merrily with them to opulence. Doubters like Donohue and Altemus slipped slowly but surely from the juvenile field.

Today virtually all fifty-centers are published by the Big Three—Grosset, Burt, and Cupples. Grosset is the biggest reprint publisher, and fifty-centers account for one-third of its business. Cupples does no reprinting, but is second largest publisher of fifty-centers. Burt, third in fifty-cent ranking, concentrates today on reprint fiction. How much money these firms have made from fifty-centers is their secret, and they hold on to it tenaciously. But a breakdown of fifty-centers could be estimated thus: twenty cents to fifteen cents, margin of profit to the retailer; five cents to three cents, royalty to the writer or the producing syndicate; seven cents to twelve cents, allowance for overhead; five cents to three cents, profit for the publisher; thirteen cents to seventeen cents, cost of manufacture. All of which adds up to fifty cents willingly paid by approximately 75,000,000 customers in the course of twenty-five years.

Some publishers would jack up overhead and allow themselves but one cent profit. Writers say that a five-cent royalty is the happy exception. But the above is a fair and average estimate.

When beginning a series of fifty-centers it is the convention to issue the first three volumes at once. Such a set must be a breeder, that is, go on for at least seven more volumes if it is to make money. It is a peculiarity of these books that they usually do come through with the progeny expected of them, which indicates one of the outstanding differences between fifty-cent and other publishing where even a single sequel has slim chances of success. Another condition that the average half-dollar juvenile usually meets is that each edition sells about 7,500 copies, a minimum for a profit. Usual printings are from 10,000 to 20,000. Editions of 2,000, usual in adult light fiction, would mean a good-sized loss for fifty-centers.

Once he has a sure-fire series, the publisher's next imperative is adequate distribution. Grosset & Dunlap owes much of its success to thirty salesmen who dash about finding outlets for books in department, drug, cigar, notion, and book stores. They sell their wares to newsstands, station lunch counters, holes-in-the-wall, trading posts. They are over the country like a plague of locusts. Similarly ubiquitous are Cupples & Leon and A. L. Burt. It is no mere accident that the executives of the Big Three—Harry Burt, George Dunlap, Arthur Leon—have all been star salesmen.

But there is more to marketing fifty-centers than putting them under the customer's nose. When competition jammed the shelves with *The Rover Boys* and the ilk, demand had to be stimulated. Conventional book advertising was useless. The potential customers were too busy shooting marbles to look at book announcements. Actual distribution was brought about by relatives' giving fifty-centers as presents. In cases where parents objected to them they were handed around from boy to boy by a grapevine. And, typical of boyhood economics, fifty-centers acquired a set of values. Thus, *The Boy Allies at Liége* might be worth two of *The Rover Boys,* or *Tom Swift and His Motorcycle* might purchase a baseball bat with a white door knob thrown in for good measure. Sales promotion was restricted to verbal recommendation by one boy to another. And there was no way to have boys praise, for example, only Cupples books. So Cupples decided to compile a colossal list of children's names. Included on the jacket of each of its books was a coupon which, when filled out with the names and addresses of ten friends, entitled the whole group to Cupples' illustrated catalogue. The catalogue was an insidious narcotic with the habit-forming properties of opium. In it were printed fetching bits from the more popular series. Cupples estimates that all in all 500,000 names have been on that list.

When the age of adolescent reading discretion began dropping from sixteen to fourteen, the increasingly rapid turnover of these names made the list too expensive to keep up to date. Cupples & Leon now issues a dollar omnibus book in which is included the first volumes of four series. This *apéritif* is just as effective as the catalogue. Such a volume presents, among other things, the best means of reviving a series that has dropped out of the adolescent eye.

Unlike some successful publishing ventures, the fifty-center was not pulled from a hat. The trick was to exploit a venerable part of the book industry. As early as 1767 Mein & Fleming of Boston was advertising 'A great variety of Entertaining and Instructive Books for Children'. Later came the famous pirated John Newbery books, written for the most part by Oliver Goldsmith, illustrated by the Bewicks, and very much sought after today by collectors. Cheap books pandering to the imagination of the maturing child did not appear until 1860—15 June to be exact—when Beadle & Adams of New York issued the first dime novel, Ann S. W. Stephens's *Malaeska, or the Indian Wife of the White Hunter.* So quickly did the germ spread that in the same year Edward S. Ellis's *Seth Jones, or the Captives of the Frontier* was bought by 750,000 avid readers.

By the eighties the demand for dime novels was raging like a forest fire. Nick Carter and Buffalo Bill were national heroes, Street & Smith succeeded Beadle & Adams and through the American News Co. began to distribute well over a hundred thousand different titles, old and new, in weekly editions. One of their most successful writers was William Gilbert Patten, who was probably the first man to exploit the self-perpetuating series for boys, about boys. Previously there had been the goody-goody Rollo books in which the hero always did just as mother said or quickly came to grief. For redblooded adolescents there was only Deadwood Dick or Ouray Jack, bad hombres from the Sunday School point of view. Patten, at the suggestion of Street & Smith, wrote a dime novel about a boy every bit as exciting as Jack, but without the barrier of mature age that separated the adolescent from Jack as a person. The book was *Frank Merriwell, or First Days at Fardale,* written in 1896 under the name of Burt L. Standish. Before he had finished Patten wrote 775 more Merriwell books that had an average weekly sale of 125,000 copies.

It is the success of Patten that lighted the fifty-cent juvenile blaze. Today, from the Orange Mountains of northeastern New Jersey still comes 90 per cent of the fuel for that conflagration. A literary geological survey would reveal particularly vast deposits of fifty-cent authors around East Orange, with the few remaining scattered deposits no further away than southern Connecticut. Noel Sainsbury, the major creator of airplane boys and girls, works in the Connecticut field. Eustace L. Adams, a nephew of Temple Bailey, and another writer of air stories, although in Florida at present, is a product of the same area. But East Orange itself is the real centre of the lode. There live the Writing Garises. All but young daughter Cleo have worked for the Stratemeyer Syndicate, and since the decease of Edward Stratemeyer they are well on the way to becoming a syndicate in themselves. Certainly Howard Garis who has written 400 juveniles, including the famous Uncle Wiggily books, is as well qualified as anyone to head any such company.

But the overwhelming colossus, past, present, and in all probability future, the Roan Antelope of this field, is the Stratemeyer Syndicate. Actually it is not a syndicate; it is merely an office at which hack writers call for and return pieces written to the Stratemeyer order. It was founded by Edward Stratemeyer about 1906, and since his death his daughters, Harriet and Edna, have been its jealous and able custodians. Smoothly, without interruption, the Stratemeyer plant turns out book upon book on a conveyor-belt system. Upon leaving the Stratemeyer brain, a fifty-center is crammed into a three-page, typewritten outline in which the time elements, names of characters, and their destinies are logically arranged. Then comes the writer who is given the outline and anywhere from a week to a month to fill it out into a book. Upon completing his job he is promptly given from $50 to $250, releases all claims to ownership of the piece, and the manuscript is thrown once again into the Stratemeyer hopper where it receives a final polishing. At the end of the chute stands a representative of the publisher who, acting like a U. S. government meat inspector in a packing plant, certifies the manuscript as factually fit for consumption. The finished product is a set of electrotypes for a fifty-center, ready to be turned by the printer into thousands of books for waiting adolescents. Some books are shipped to England, Canada, Australia. A few, like *The Rover Boys,* are translated into German and Czechoslovakian. The whole process takes perhaps forty days, although on occasion books have sped from the Stratemeyer brain to the immortality of print in considerably less time.

The chief reason for the continued dominance of the Stratemeyer Syndicate is the fact that it owns all of its copyrights.[2] In the days of the great Edward the publisher never even *saw* a manuscript. Instead he was shown electrotype proofs. He was given the opportunity of either renting the plates or letting some other publisher make a neat profit from them. Today, however, publishers frequently like to make minor corrections. No longer will they accept the plates. They rent the rights to the manuscript for a royalty of around five cents, do their own electrotyping. But they are no nearer to owning a Stratemeyer opus than they were twenty-five years ago.

For the Stratemeyer daughters have inherited from their father not only genius peculiar to fifty-cent juveniles, but his business acumen. After his death they moved the office from New York City to the top of East Orange's Hale Building. There they sit today at their ponderous roll-top desks dispatching the affairs of fifty-cent juveniles with a sincerity and belief in their work equal to that of the most serious adult novelist. Obscured in a fern-filled corner is a secretary. The only other occupants of the office are immortal: *Tom Swift, The Motor Boys, The Rover*

---

[2] Of the Big Three, Burt alone does no business with Stratemeyers. It has never published a Stratemeyer book because it is Burt's policy to buy manuscripts outright.

Boys, *Dave Dashaway*, and dozens of others who exist in the 800 fifty-centers that line the wall.

One who did not know that it is this office that keeps some twenty hack writers busy filling out the lives of superhuman heroes and heroines might readily mistake the Stratemeyer Syndicate for a private detective's office. As a source of open-handed information about fifty-cent juveniles it might as well be just that. Miss Edna, who stays at home managing affairs, waggles her bobbed grey head emphatically and says that their business is their business. Mrs Adams, who takes care of personal contacts with New York publishers, smiles graciously and says the same. What, the sisters demand in amazement, would their clients think if they knew that the great gallery of juvenile authors, Roy Rockwood, Victor Appleton, Lester Chadwick, Laura Lee Hope, May Hollis Barton, and so on, was nothing but a waxworks invented by their father? So greatly do they feel the need of maintaining the illusion of these fictitious literati that, in spite of the great veneration in which they hold their father, they have refused to authorize any of the many attempts to write his life history. Once, when Stratemeyer's readers insisted upon knowing the details of the life of his May Hollis Barton, a publisher's assistant took it upon himself to write a fabulous biography to satisfy the demand. Little did the readers of this work know that 'she' was a nervous, kindly, nearsighted, stocky man who looked like a deacon and from whom books came forth like an interminable string of sausages; that his business genius and literary horse sense earned for him a steady $50,000 a year.

Beyond the fact that he was born in Elizabeth, New Jersey, of middle-class German stock on 4 October 1862 and died in Newark 10 May 1930, Stratemeyer's real life is guarded as a trade secret. Actually, it was the antithesis of the lives about which he wrote. He never went to preparatory school or college. His sporting activity was confined to an avid interest in big-league baseball and mediocre bowling at the Roseville Athletic Association around the corner from his house. When he was not inventing plots, his recreation was reading travel books or going, like Dave Dashaway, to distant places. Modern fiction and problem novels he abominated as trash. Mr Stratemeyer created his fraternity of heroes out of dime novels, thin air, and the prompting of his own desires. His heart was the heart of Richard Rover.

When he was a boy he read the works of Alger and Optic with something akin to passion. His youth was the heyday of the success story with a moral and of the dime novel. It was the heroic age of American literature when any dime novelist could grind out his 100,000 words a month (at perhaps one-half cent a word) without turning a hair. It remained for Stratemeyer to inaugurate the golden age. With the rib of Deadwood Dick and the soul of Tom the Bootblack, he fashioned middle-class Richard Rover who made money for himself, his creator, and his publisher. And in all three cases it was a sizeable sum.

Stratemeyer's first story was a piece of 18,000 words which, just as Alger would have had it, he wrote on a piece of brown wrapping paper in between waiting on customers at his brother's tobacco store. *Golden Days*, a boys' magazine in Philadelphia, paid him $75 for it. Such success, young Edward decided, warranted a nom de plume. After casting about for one with the proper *ton*, he hit upon Arthur M. Winfield, which was explained thus: 'Arthur' was chosen as the nearest approach to author, while 'Winfield' expressed his hope of winning in his chosen field, and 'M', representing 'Million', was adopted as a suggestion that some day he might see a million copies of his books in print.

In the beginning, *Golden Days*, Munsey's *Golden Argosy* and his *Argosy* consumed Stratemeyer's products as fast as he put them on paper. But pay was irregular. He drifted to Street & Smith where he edited *Good News*, another boys' weekly, which he built up to a circulation of over 200,000. There he learned the art of mass production, and there he wrote his first dime novel, *Crazy Bob, the Terror of Creede.* Hundreds of others followed: *Cool Dan, or the Sport's Wonderful Nerve, Ouray Jack, The Collis Express Robbers, Dead Shot Dave.* They were signed with such names as Jim Bowie, Nat Woods, Jim Daly, and anything that popped into his head. The bibliography fills a big black book in Street & Smith's offices. Between times he wrote women's serials for the *New York Weekly* as Julia Edwards, did weekly pieces for the famous *Old Cap Collier Library,* and even ran a boys' paper of his own called *Bright Days.*

With Stratemeyer at Street & Smith were all the great dime novelists of the day. Doyen of the lot was Frederick Dey, in whose veins flowed a goodly portion of Van Rensselaer blood. Characteristic of his trade rather than his forebears, Dey's pleasures were simple. Policemen were his boon companions. That he was the one and only Nick Carter was his proudest boast. Upton Sinclair was there too, writing under the nom de plume of Ensign Clark Fitch, USN, to turn out such gems as *Through the Enemy's Lines, or Clif Faraday's Dangerous Mission,* for the *True Blue Series.* And then the aristocrats of the business would drop in occasionally, particularly H. R. Gordon (Edward S. Ellis), William T. Adams (Oliver Optic), and most famous of all, Horatio Alger Jr, author of, among other things, the 1853 Harvard Class Ode. Stratemeyer was still with Street & Smith when Alger died, and it was he who finished the posthumous works of Alger, probably the most pleasant duty of his life. Thus was he baptized in the dime novel, and thus was he fortified to write *The Rover Boys.*

Stratemeyer's first attempt at a serial was a book about boys on a battleship. He sent it to Mr W. F. Gregory of Lothrop, Lee & Shepard in Boston. Mr Gregory promptly put dime-novelist Stratemeyer's manuscript in his safe and went on worrying about Lothrop's pressing financial problems. It was a great stroke of luck that Dewey chose that moment to defeat the Spanish fleet at Manila. It was equally fortunate that Mr Gregory, upon reading the news, should suddenly remember the manuscript so summarily dumped in his safe. He got in touch with Stratemeyer. Could he change his book to something about Dewey in a few days? Could he indeed! Almost before the smoke of battle had cleared away Stratemeyer had produced *Under Dewey at Manila.* And as the popularity of the Little Admiral swelled and soared, so the book sold edition upon edition. It established Stratemeyer as a writer of juveniles and it re-established Lothrop's financial standing.

Thus began the *Old Glory Series,* which grew lustily until 1907 and which Lothrop still publishes. But more important than this were three books Stratemeyer dashed off betimes in 1899: *The Rover Boys at School, The Rover Boys on the Ocean,* and *The Rover Boys in the Jungle.* The immediate sire of *The Rover Boys* was Gilbert Patten's *Frank Merriwell.* But between Patten's immortal Frank and Stratemeyer's immortal Rovers there is one essential distinction. Merriwell appeared in the *Tip-Top Library* and sold for a nickel (most dime novels did). He was the first great boy hero, but the format in which he appeared naturally associated him with such dime-novel hillbillies as Rattlesnake Dick. This, for a squeamish middle class who appraised literature in terms of what it cost them, made Frank an undesirable. Smart Mr Stratemeyer, who wrote the same thing, put his dime novels in board covers and sold them at prices varying from a dollar to twenty-five cents. At once he gained the reputation of doing 'refined books', while Street & Smith, although it goes on publishing many dime-novel magazines a year, is still *persona non grata* in houses on the right ride of the railroad tracks.

But in the early days *The Rover Boys* showed no signs of reaching the million mark Stratemeyer had set for himself. By 1906 he was ready to try another idea. Under the name of Clarence Young he wrote a series for Cupples & Leon. They talked it over and decided to sell these books for fifty cents. This series, like dime novels, was designed to be sold directly to the customer without the divine intervention of parents, but with parental approval. The crux of the plan was that Stratemeyer took a small royalty, the publishers a minimum profit, and both earnestly prayed that the volume of sales would atone for the picayune return per book. It was like Noah praying for rain. That series was the now famous *Motor Boys*. The twenty-two volumes of this first fifty-center have gone through thirty-five printings, with the smallest of no less than 5,000 copies a title.

But that was just the beginning. When Grosset & Dunlap purchased the rights to publish *The Rover Boys* in 1908, Stratemeyer's star shot up like a rocket. The firm added more titles, and followed Cupples's lead in reducing the price. Aided by its tremendous sales activity, *The Rover Boys* broke out upon the country like measles. By 1930, 5,000,000 copies of the thirty volumes of that series had been sold, *The Rover Boys* had bred a second generation, become a tradition, made Stratemeyer wealthy. Modestly he reiterated in his prefaces: 'I hoped that the young people would like the stories, but I was hardly prepared for the very warm welcome the volumes received'. Actually, he was more than prepared. By the time *The Rover Boys Series* was an assured success he had at least ten parallel stories under way, had formed his Syndicate to set other people to writing new books as fast as he could think of plots. Thus began the Stratemeyer deluge.

On working days from nine to five he sat in his little office around the corner from Grosset & Dunlap in New York dictating two chapters a day, outlining plots to his hirelings, driving bargains with publishers. Second in command was Howard Garis, who filled in (from Stratemeyer's outlines, of course) all but the first few *Motor Boys*, every *Tom Swift, Great Marvel,* and hundreds more that even he forgets. Mrs Garis was the Syndicate's first woman writer. St George Rathbone, a dime novelist who wrote pieces for Sunday School papers, Stratemeyer brought with him from Street & Smith. There were many others, about twenty in all, but no one was any more than a cog in the

Stratemeyer machine. So unrelenting was his dominance that his writers were never allowed to meet one another in his office. They saw the master by appointment, and the appointments never overlapped.

Just who were the authors of the Stratemeyers books may some day be a matter for historians to wrangle over. But one point is clear: every work signed Arthur M. Winfield, Captain Ralph Bonehill, Edward Stratemeyer, was the product of Edward Stratemeyer—lock, stock, and barrel. None of these were, properly speaking, the property of the Syndicate, for Syndicate books were outlined by Stratemeyer but filled in by writers like Garis. Yet Stratemeyer was the author even of Syndicate books, in the sense that he conceived them. The supplementary work of hired writers constitutes a claim to a sort of literary foster parenthood. And certainly the names under which the Syndicate employees wrote were as indisputably Stratemeyer's as his shoes. They were assigned to whoever suited his fancy. Half a dozen people might use the same one in the course of a series. His reason for such tactics was obvious. It was good business to be able to replace a writer without losing a potent name like Victor Appleton. It was bad business for the public to know it.

And just how good the business was, the Winnetka Survey of 1926 revealed. This investigation was made under the auspices of the American Library Association and directed by Carleton Washburne, superintendent of the Winnetka, Illinois, public schools, who asked 36,750 pupils in thirty-four representative cities what they read. Ninety-eight per cent replied with titles of fifty-centers, and most of them added that they liked *Tom Swift* best. By 1913 *Tom Swift* had passed *The Rover Boys* as best seller, and was not routed from this eminence until 1931, when *Nancy Drew* made its astounding spurt. Today the sale of *Tom Swift* is the record of all time: 6,500,000 copies of thirty-six volumes and still lusty.

Librarians frothed at the mouth, banned the books from the stacks, but Stratemeyer merely shrugged his shoulders and went on piling up profits. If a child could not get his books free from the library he would have to buy them, and that was just so much more money in his pocket. Yet the opposition had a champion who gave Stratemeyer a run for his money. He was Franklin K. Mathiews, chief librarian of the Boy Scouts of America. And more than Dan Baxter and all the great gallery of black hearts, he hated the guts of Richard Rover.

Mr Mathiews is a kindly gentleman and one not likely to go about looking for trouble. But the state of adolescent literature in the early nineteen hundreds demanded action. In the five years that the Boy Scouts had been founded, over 5,000,000 cheap books about Boy Scouts had been sold. Excellent publicity for the young B. S. of A. though this might have been, these fifty-cent hair-raisers would lead small boys to sniff at anything so mundane as building campfires or tracking woodchucks. To purge the world of this infection, Mr Mathiews shortly took effective steps.

After a few preliminary negotiations with Ralph Henry Barbour, Joseph A. Altsheler, William Heyliger, and other writers of approved and expensive juveniles, Mr Mathiews put a list of their works in his briefcase and marched into the very citadel of the fifty-center, Grosset & Dunlap. To Mr Louis Reed of that office he expounded an idea that would first, he insisted, make money, and second, improve adolescent reading habits. Briefly, he had compiled a list of acceptable juveniles that could be sold for fifty cents like the thrillers. Grosset & Dunlap was to reprint them, the Boy Scouts of America would inaugurate 'Safety First Book Week' to publicize the series. Smart Mr Reed liked the idea. The books were prepared and on 1 November 1913 appeared the first 'Safety First' pamphlet, sent to all booksellers. Grosset's new list was on the back with, among other titles, *Williams of West Point* by NRA Hugh S. Johnson, then budding young littérateur of great industry. Since that time this collection has had a checkered career, becoming finally 'Juveniles of Distinction' costing a dollar. Grosset has sold over two million copies of the books thus advertised, and other publishers adopting the idea have had similar success.

Mr Mathiews's second blow was an article for the *Outlook* entitled 'Blowing Out the Boy's Brains'. 'One of the most valuable assets a boy has,' he announced, 'is his imagination . . . Storybooks of the right sort stimulate and conserve this noble faculty, while those of the . . . cheaper sort, by overstimulation, debauch and vitiate, as brain and body are debauched and destroyed by strong drink.'

'Blowing Out the Boy's Brains' became a tract that swept the country. Women in Portland, Ore. stood beside the counters of bookstores discouraging would-be buyers of fifty-centers. Disgusted booksellers packed up their *Tom Swift*s and shipped them back to the publishers.

Naturally, Stratemeyer was furious. He threatened to sue but was told by Grosset & Dunlap, notoriously considerate of its authors, that such a maneuver would necessitate choosing sides, and the firm was not sure whose side it would be. In a calmer and more practical frame of mind he issued a pamphlet of his own in which he included only Syndicate books as worthy of adolescent attention. The result of this counterattack was Mathiew's decision to fight Stratemeyer on his own ground. He persuaded Percy Keese Fitzhugh, who was working on historical encyclopedias for Harper's, to write the *Tom Slade* scout series. It was the fifty-cent material but presumably put together more adroitly than a Syndicate yarn. Over three million copies of that work have been sold to give Fitzhugh claim to fame as the only man whose books have been more popular than all but the three Olympians of the Syndicate (*Tom Swift, Rover Boys, Motor Boys*).

Today, as is fitting for a reasonably successful St George, Mr Mathiews is no longer rabid about the dragon fifty-centers. He admits that perhaps they engender the reading habit. But Stratemeyer never conceded that his books were, as Mr Mathiews had suggested 'of the cheaper sort'.

The fact that they were financially successful made excuses superfluous to Stratemeyer's mind. But he did attempt to justify them by making his later stories suggestively instructive. The flower of this idea was the *Don Sturdy* books, in which the hero follows explorations of the moment to find phenomena even stranger than those described in Sunday supplements.

Until the moment he took to his bed with fatal pneumonia he was devising new series. And the 'great juvenile' he was always going to write was forever lost in the deluge of his 20,000,000 potboilers that bestow upon him the fame of a colossus he never wanted to be.

But the fitfy-cent juvenile is not dead. Not by a long shot. Publishers will tell you today that even such moss-backed old standbys as *The Rover Boys* are, Rip Van Winkle-like, coming back to life. For a while the movies, then the depression, damaged them, but the fifty-centers have never really lost their place in the literary sun. Tripe they were in the beginning, tripe they are now, and tripe they always will be. But a wise publisher knows to his profit that they are pap to the maturing mind, and from the customer's point of view, most delectable pap to boot.

[1934]

An imaginary correspondence

RUMER GODDEN

An imaginary correspondence between Mr V. Andal, editor of the De Base Publishing Company, Inc., and the ghost of Miss Beatrix Potter,[1] *using the word* ghost *in the old meaning of soul or spirit. She would be shocked to its depth if she knew some of the things that are going on nowadays in the world of children's books.*

Mr V. Andal to Miss B. Potter

January 18, 1963

Dear Miss Potter:

I am editing for the De Base Publishing Company, Inc., an unusual series of books aimed at beginning readers. The general title is 'Masterpieces for Mini-Minds', and the series will consist of reissues, in a modern production, of famous books that have become classics for children, so that the first reading of the very young will also be an introduction to their own great authors. We are approaching, among others, Hans Andersen, Edward Lear, Lewis Carroll, George MacDonald, Anna Sewell, and Andrew Lang.

The works will be produced whole and entire, though with certain modifications to the text to make them suitable for

---

1 Some of Beatrix Potter's remarks are taken from her letters.

children of 1963: with this in view we have decided on a limited vocabulary of 450 different words. I have had a list of words prepared by a trio of philologists and I would be glad to send it to you if you are interested. Other words may be added as long as they are within the grasp of a reader from 5 to 8.

Mr Al Loy, our president, has authorized me to pay an advance of $3,000 against royalty upon receipt of an acceptable manuscript along the lines indicated. In addition to the advance, there should be continuing payments, for the books will have, besides quality writing, the collaboration of the best illustrators and should enjoy a huge sale.

I hope you will be one of the contributors to this project. If you like to edit your own book, I will be delighted to send you the word list, from which departures can, of course, be made (as long as they come within this age range). If you would rather we edited, this will be undertaken with the utmost care and the De Base Company will be pleased to send you a check for $3,000 as soon as I forward your work.

Cordially,

V. ANDAL

I send you Hans Andersen's 'Ti-ny Thum-my' to see. (Originally issued as 'Thumbelina', and I think now much improved.)

Miss B. Potter to Mr V. Andal

26th January, 1963.

Dear Mr Andal,

Thank you for your letter. That a request for a fresh issue of my books should reach me after so many years is heartening. The cheque you offer is certainly generous; there are several acres round Sawrey that could with advantage be purchased and given to our National Trust. Publication with another firm would vex my old publishers very much, and I don't like breaking with old friends, but possibly we might arrange to have something published on the American market that would not interfere with my normal sales.

I presume you will want *Peter Rabbit.* I believe my attitude of mind towards my own successful publications has been comical. At one time I almost loathed Peter Rabbit, I was so sick of him. I still cannot understand his perennial success. I myself prefer *The Tailor of Gloucester,* and send you both books to see.

Yours sincerely,
BEATRIX POTTER

N.B. My books are illustrated by myself.
N.B. I do not understand your second paragraph. How can a work be 'whole and entire' if it is modified? How can a philologist, however gifted, know what words I need? Perhaps I have misunderstood you.

Mr V. Andal to Miss Potter

February 4, 1963

Dear Miss Potter:

I hasten to thank you for 'Peter Rabbit', a most charming tale, and am sure that, when made larger (it must be enlarged—people like to get their money's worth) and given good illustrations, it will make a magnificent book for our series; we shall have our reader's report in a day or two when I shall write to you again. 'The Tailor of Gloucester' I have, for the moment, put aside. It has an old-fashioned air about it that might puzzle a child, but perhaps it might be reissued as a 'period piece'. The words would need a great deal of simplification: 'worn to a ravelling'—what could a child make of that?

I am sorry my letter was not clear. The modifications about such words are only those needed to make language more assimilatory to the children of today. In this connection, we believe the advice of our philologists is of value; they are often able to help an author to put his, or her, delightful thoughts into plain words—simple enough for a child to understand.

Yours very sincerely,

V. ANDAL

Miss Potter to Mr V. Andal

10th February, 1963.

Dear Mr Andal,

Again I do not understand. What do you mean by 'reader's report'? When I sent the manuscript of *Peter Rabbit* to Mr Warne, my original publisher, he read it, made up his mind he liked it, accepted it, and that was settled. Do you really need other people to do this for you? It seems to me a fuss over a very small matter.

I have too much common sense to think that *Peter Rabbit* could ever be magnificent; he is an ordinary small brown rabbit. Nor do I like the idea of the book being enlarged. I have never heard that size was a guarantee of quality, and must point out that my books were made small to fit children's hands, not to impress the grownups.

As for the philologists: if an author needs help in putting thought into plain and simple words he, or she, should not try to be an author. It would seem to me you are in danger of using 'simple' in the sense of mentally deficient. Are children nowadays so much less intelligent than their parents?

I have been told I write good prose. I think I write carefully because I enjoy my writing and enjoy taking pains over it. I write to please myself; my usual way is to scribble and cut out and write it again and again. The shorter, the plainer—the better. And read the Bible (unrevised version and Old Testament) if I feel my style wants chastening.

Yours sincerely,

BEATRIX POTTER

N.B. My books, as I said, *are* illustrated.

Mr Andal to Miss Potter

February 19, 1963

My dear respected lady:

While disliking having to cross swords with someone as eminent as yourself, I really must enlighten you to the fact that the Old Testament, as reading, is almost totally out of date, not only for children but adults. It has been replaced by the epic screen pictures which, sequestered as you are in your native Cumberland, you may not have seen. These movies are money-spinners, which is heartening as it endorses our belief that there is life in old tales yet—if properly presented. (One of our 'master-pieces' is Genesis, retold in uno-or duo-syllable words.)

Mr Warne could perhaps make his own decision to publish an important manuscript (which is what we want to make 'Peter Rabbit' in this new illustrated edition), but that was years ago. Publishing nowadays is such a costly business that we need expert advice. Properly handled, in attractive wrappers, perhaps packaged with one or two others, and well advertised, books for juveniles can become really big business, which is why I hope you will consider carefully our reader's report and let us guide you.

Your well-wisher,

V. ANDAL

Miss Potter to Mr Andal

22nd February, 1963.

Dear Sir,

I am not 'eminent' as you call it but a plain person who believes in saying what she thinks.

Your publishing would not be so costly without all these 'experts' and elaborate notions; indeed, your last letter reads as if you were selling grocery, not books. In my day, philologists kept to what is their real work: to enrich a child's heritage of words—not diminish it.

Yours faithfully,

BEATRIX POTTER

N.B. The illustrations in my books are integral with the text. They may *not* be separated.

Mr Andal to Miss Potter

March 7, 1963

Dear Miss Potter:

It is with pleasurable anticipation that I send you our detailed reader's report. It has taken a little time to get it—some work was necessary—but, as you will see, apart from some words in the text, some details of plot, new illustrations, fresh names and a larger size for the book, very little has had to be changed.

I very much hope you will co-operate in helping us to bring this classic little book within reach of our children.

Awaiting your favorable reactions,

Again yours cordially,

V. ANDAL

REPORT AND RECOMMENDATIONS FOR MODERNIZATION OF TEXT AND ILLUSTRATIONS OF 'PETER RABBIT' BY BEATRIX POTTER

'Mother' must read 'Momma' throughout.

p. 45 '. . . some friendly sparrows . . . flew to him in great excitement, and implored him to exert himself.'	Not all children will be able to identify sparrows; suggest the more general 'bird-ies'; last five words especially difficult; suggest 'to try again' or 'try harder'.
p. 52 'Kertyschoo' for sneezing	Unfamiliar. 'Tishoo' is more usual.
p. 58 'Lippity lippity'	Not in the dictionary.
p. 69 'Scr-r-ritch'	Might confuse. Onomatopoeia, though allowable, should not distort a word.
Same page 'Scuttered'	Unfamiliar again. Suggest 'ran away and hid', which has the advantage that three out of four words have only three letters.

p. 80	'Camomile tea'	Not in use now. Suggest 'tranquilizer' or 'sedative'.

As well as word limitation, the De Base Publishing Company has decided to use a certain 'thought limitation' so that parents may entrust their children's reading to us with complete confidence. In this connection:

p. 10 We do not think father should have been made into rabbit pie.
Mr McGregor is altogether a too Jehovah-like figure. We want children to *like* people rather than have that out-of-date respect. They must not be left thinking that a little rabbit can be blamed for trespassing and stealing: it was, rather, that he was deprived of lettuce and radishes. Mr McGregor must be made a sympathetic figure.

ILLUSTRATIONS
We now have a report from our art panel, and though these illustrations have charm we believe fresh ones should be used. The rabbits' furniture and clothing are out of date; i.e., the red cloaks used by Flopsy, Mopsy and Cottontail; the length of Mrs Rabbit's skirts; the suspended pan and open cooking fire on p. 8. We therefore propose to commission a young Mexican who specializes in vivid outline drawing. (Less expensive to reproduce.)

NOMENCLATURE
Our bureau reports that while 'Peter' is familiar to most children, Flopsy, Mopsy and Cottontail must be retitled.

Cable from Miss Potter to Mr Andal, 12 March 1963

RETURN PETER RABBIT AT ONCE

Mr Andal to Miss Potter

March 13, 1963

Dear Miss Potter:

We are sorry you have taken this attitude, which I confess seems to us unrealistic and does not take into account public opinion (supported by our own careful poll statistics). We are having much the same reaction from Mr Edward Lear. We saw a charming first version[2] of his poem, 'The Owl and the Pussy-Cat', which then had the lines:

---

[2] The lines that follow are authentic and are in the first draft of 'The Owl and the Pussy-Cat'.

They sailed away
For a year and a day
To the land where the palm tree grows.

and:

They dined on mince
and slices of quince
which they ate with a silver spoon.

lines quite innocuous and satisfactory; but now he has come up with 'bong tree' for the first lines, and 'runcible spoon' for the second, words not only unusual but not even in the dictionary.

As he insists on keeping these we have had to return his manuscript as, at your own request, we are returning yours. We can only tell you that it is our opinion, formed by expert advice, that in its present form, parents, teachers, and children will not buy, nor understand, nor like 'Peter Rabbit'.

Yours respectfully,

V. ANDAL

Miss Potter to Mr V. Andal

24th March, 1963.

Seven million have. I rest in peace.

[1963]

'Good bunnies always obey': books for American children

JASON EPSTEIN

The boy should enclose and keep, as his life, the child at the heart of him, and never let it go . . . the child is not meant to die but to be forever fresh born. —GEORGE MAC DONALD

Ever since an eighteenth-century bookseller named John Newbery commissioned Oliver Goldsmith to compile the first Mother Goose and thus launched an industry, the publication of books for children has been, among other things, a way of making money. Lately it has become a way of making a lot of money, and as more of the nation's effort comes to be invested in educating the young, the publication of books for children promises to become a major aspect of American business. Even more, it promises to become a business of great social and political importance, for it is trafficking in nothing less than the next generation, which is to say our whole future and the future of all our technological, political, and social machinery.

In 1961 some 1,700 new children's books were published. Total sales of all children's books, not counting school texts, came to 277,420,000 copies, mainly through some 25,000 toy, department, and novelty stores, five-and-tens, and supermarkets, and to a lesser extent through the 9,000 libraries in America and the 1,804 bookstores. A growing number have also found their way into the schools—through classroom libraries, of which there are now some 25,000—to supplement the dreary and often unreadable textbooks. But schools continue to buy mainly textbooks, which are not a part of this discussion—though much of what is wrong with American textbooks is also wrong with children's books in general and for the same reasons. Children's books have increasingly become part of a bureaucratically administered sub-culture, largely cut off by a dense fog of conventional and irrelevant theory from the best literary and scientific culture of the community at large.

Such isolation is relatively recent. The great children's books of the past, though they often represented a distinct genre, were simply a department of literature, and they were commonly written by authors who, in contrast to the situation today, were not primarily writers for children. Such figures as Defoe, Swift, Blake, Coleridge, Melville, Hawthorne, Mark Twain, Kipling, Doyle, etc., wrote for children either inadvertently or out of a romantic preoccupation with childhood itself. Childhood for them was sacred and superior, in its vitality and powers of perception, to maturity, which was compromised through having accommodated itself too much to the world. In one way or another these writers believed that the recollected vitality of childhood sustained a man, if anything did, throughout his entire life and that, conversely, civilization—Wordsworth's 'prison house'—was deadly. This same belief, in political terms, led Thomas Jefferson to demand a revolution every twenty years as each new generation coming of age asserted itself against the accumulated inhibitions of the generation in being. And one finds it again, less reasonably, in today's adults who occupy themselves with cowboy heroes and perhaps among the President and his friends playing touch football.

Before the eighteenth century there were no children's books as such, except for the chap-books, though works like Aesop's fables and the story of King Arthur in its various forms interested children as well as adults. And, of course, except for the catechisms and grammars, there were no textbooks. There was only the hornbook from which children learned the alphabet and the numbers from one to ten. Lessons were usually read by the teacher and the children learned nearly everything orally and by rote or by observation and imitation (a process which corresponds somewhat to the theory of conditioned reflexes according to which modern teaching machines have been developed; the older method was, however, less passive and more social).

The use of books in the classroom is rather recent and their pedagogic value, in view of the widespread criticisms that have lately been made of them, cannot yet be taken for granted. And if one watches young children growing up, it appears that even the schools themselves tend to inflate the part that they play in educating the young. Like other young animals, children seem to learn more or less directly from their environment and by testing and observing their parents, their playmates, and perhaps their teachers. Bright children, as they grow older, traditionally have found their schools dull and confining, except for the other children they meet there, and the brighter, the more explosive and spontaneous the youngsters are, the more their classes are likely to bore them. It is at least plausible to suggest that the fault may be in the process of formal education itself. Certainly there is something wrong with the programs and books that the children are expected to put up with.

The great body of children's literature and the really vital branch of it, despite the hundreds of children's books published last year and the even greater number that will appear this year, remains within the oral tradition—carried on over the centuries by the children themselves. The rhymes and songs, the crucial bits of information, the forms of behaviour, the loyalties and friendships, the superstitions and games, the sexual discoveries that children communicate to one another as they grow older have always formed the basis of early education. It is from these that the children learn, far more than they ever do from books or in their classes, the language, its rhythm, and the fundamental principles of ethics: i.e., how to keep out of trouble, the fatal knowledge of which begins the long, painful, and inevitable movement away from childhood. As Iona and Peter Opie remarked in their brilliant study, *The Lore and Language of School Children*, 'The world-wide fraternity of children is the greatest of savage tribes and the only one which shows no signs of dying out.'

But the Opies were optimistic. The savage tribe has suddenly become a market—a big one—and the woods are full of salesmen, typically disguised as missionaries. Education is the new religion and books are among the trinkets with which to lure the children into the civilized world. As Josette Frank, Reading Consultant to the Child Study Association of America, has written, '[Today] we have an opportunity to develop better educated, better informed, increasingly cultured citizens and more of them than was ever possible in times past. There is a new public for books, and this public includes children.' And later she adds, 'Our role is to be alert to all that goes on in a child's world, ready to offer a book that further explains a motion picture; or to direct attention to a television program that amplifies a book just read, or to discover how comics may lead to new avenues for a child to explore.'

The trouble with Miss Frank's point of view is its assumption that the civilized world as she conceives it is necessarily fit for children to grow up in and that children will unquestionably take part in it on the terms she proposes. 'Today,' Miss Frank goes on, 'long before [children] are ready for higher education, the arts and sciences are there for the taking, in pictures and stories. Political campaigns are suddenly intelligible to ten-year-olds. With the turn of a dial or the riffling of a picture magazine, they may have glimpses of scientific researches and of the men and women who are grappling with them. Perhaps they would never have known what an East Indian looked like, but now the United Nations delegate from India appears on their television screen and speaks to them in perfect English. The baseball hero comes to talk to them. So does the President of the United States. The people in the news are real to our boys and girls.'

In other words, it has now become possible to alienate children from childhood in ways that would have made Wordsworth's head swim. Today's children, hardly out of their cribs, can be shoved by the children's book industry and its affiliated bureaucracy of educators, reviewers, specialists, and consultants, straight into the 'civilized' world of television, advertising, and the cold war through processes which, when we hear of them in other societies, we call brainwashing.

In America there are some four thousand experts who, like Miss Frank, concern themselves with children's reading. Their influence on the kinds of books that are published and bought for children by schools, libraries, and parents is enormous, and their power, until recently, has been enhanced by the scornful indifference with which they have been regarded by the intellectual community at large. Though the experts' inclinations tend to be widely permissive and pluralistic—having devolved from Dewey's idea that a child should be encouraged to develop along the lines in which he is strongest into the quite contrary idea that anything goes so long as the children seem interested and the community doesn't object—their effect is radically inhibiting. Most of these experts work with schools and school boards or in teachers' colleges. Many have taught school themselves, but have given it up for the more prestigious, less frustrated role of administrators. Some are book reviewers or work as curriculum directors. A number of them have been hired by publishers or are engaged as consultants to the various children's book clubs. Most of them, to judge by their own writings, have read very little and are indifferent to the rhythm of English prose.

Nevertheless, they have as a group managed to encircle the children's book business to the point where a publisher has to be very fast on his feet, or unusually indifferent to profits, to break through and confront the children with his goods directly.

In the meantime, though the business flourishes, the children themselves increasingly ignore what the experts recommend. Marie Rankin, an expert herself, has noted that the books chosen for the Newbery Medal—a sort of Pulitzer Prize for juveniles awarded annually by members of the American Library Association—are among those the children read least. And while a few of the earlier selections were of a rather high order, if one examines some of the more recent prize-winners, one's sympathies tend to be with the children. Of the four winners for 1961, which presumably are typical of what expert opinion finds admirable these days, three are contemptible by even the most relaxed critical standard, and it is almost impossible to imagine from what point of view they may be considered to have any merits at all. With respect to vitality, inventiveness, and style, they are far inferior to the *Nancy Drews and Tom Swifts* of an earlier period, which children today continue to read in great quantities though the experts dismiss them now as they did then.

One of the prize-winners, a book called *Belling the Tiger* by Mary Stolz, pointlessly enlarges on the traditional tale: the mice find that they have inadvertently belled not a cat, but a tiger, an elaboration which requires sixty-four pages to complete and which sells for $2.50. But for this price the reader also gets a moral. As the mice are about to report to their elders on their adventures, they become aware that they will not be believed by the grownups, who are clearly less intelligent than themselves. So rather than create a disturbance they suppress their interesting news, wrap their tails around each other, and fall asleep.

Another prize-winner, in this case the winner of the Gold

Medal itself, is equally without accomplishment, though it represents more explicitly than *Belling the Tiger* the preoccupation these writers have with the idea that the young had better subdue, for the sake of avoiding a disturbance within the community, whatever tendencies they may have toward rebelliousness and originality. This book, *The Bronze Bow* by Elizabeth George Speare, is a biblical novel written for a somewhat older group of children than *Belling the Tiger*. It is thickly pious and its factitious historical setting is presented in language so drab and abstract and even, occasionally, illiterate, that it is impossible to adjust one's ear to it ('Prodded on by weary drivers, the camels swayed slowly.' 'The morsels of food had not begun to whet his hunger.') But the trouble is less with the book's prose or even with its fake historical and religious paraphernalia than with the smugness of its doctrine. The hero is a young Palestinian Jew at the time of Christ. He is meant to represent a juvenile rebel of the sort who today, with a less specific enemy to confront, has become a problem for the authorities. This young man—his name is Daniel—has joined a band of marauders and with them is determined to drive the Romans from his homeland. It is clear from the start—even to those who may not be familiar with Jewish history—that his rebellion is going to fail. But miraculously, a carpenter with magical powers to heal and persuade arrives in town and prevails upon Daniel to come down out of the mountains, return to his blacksmith shop and acquiesce, like everybody else, in the Roman occupation. Eventually Daniel takes this advice and we are led to believe that he will make a profitable marriage to a pretty girl who comes from a nearby suburb.

May Hill Arbuthnot, still another expert, has tried to account for the failure of children to become interested in such stories as these by suggesting that superior literature even among adults is often less admired than trash. But if *The Bronze Bow* is what Miss Arbuthnot means by good literature, then surely there are other reasons to account for this phenomenon. One need only recall the tactics of literature that children have always found interesting to see how far off the mark this sort of product is.

In *Gulliver's Travels*, for example, the hero, bored with his wife, sets out on a series of journeys in the course of which the absurdity of human society is variously illustrated; he concludes that horses are preferable to men. Robinson Crusoe discovers that he can live successfully with an absolute minimum of human society and create a satisfactory world of his own. Alice, tired of her book, escapes the everyday world and encounters a parody of it in which the logical categories that adults claim to think in are, if carried a few steps further, seen to be absurd. The children in E. Nesbit's novels are invariably wiser and enjoy themselves more than their elders, from whom they are forever escaping. Huckleberry Finn's only friend is an outcast, a fugitive slave, and the world from which they jointly flee is filled with sanctimonious frauds, false friends, and parvenus. Holden Caulfield grows up in a world which proves to be so untrustworthy that clearly he will never take part in it, but in his case there is neither fantasy nor wilderness to which to escape; he will remain 'maladjusted'.

Nor has this theme been limited to children's literature. That organized society is hostile to growth and freedom and defeats the individual as, in the literature of an earlier epoch, nature used to do, is a dominant idea in the literary tradition, especially for those modern writers who, in the aftermath of Romanticism, have deliberately concerned themselves with questions of rebellion, privacy, and their own authenticity. It is of interest, however, that in those works which have become great children's literature, the heroes, unlike the protagonists of much modern fiction, manage to survive the environment and even, in such cases as Robinson Crusoe and Doyle's Professor Challenger, to succeed in transforming it. The affection that children have for stories of this kind seems to confirm the affinity that the Romantic writers felt between themselves and childhood and helps to explain why so much fiction of the nineteenth century appealed, and still appeals, to the young. For until recently the typical literary hero was himself, so to speak, a child growing up and testing his mettle against the world. And if one thinks of that long line of literary adolescents from Don Quixote and Hamlet to Stephen Daedalus, then the idea of childhood and the problem of growing up will appear to be representative, for many of our great writers at least since Shakespeare and Milton, of the human condition itself. All that happened to Adam when he left Paradise is that he was condemned to grow up and become civilized, to put on clothes, deny his nature, and go to work. Mankind, ever since, has been trying, in one way or another, to find its way out of this dilemma.

In proposing a closer affiliation between childhood and the 'civilized world' in which the President addresses ten-year-olds, then, the experts have undertaken not only to alienate children from their own nature but to turn one of literature's great and characteristic themes upside down. Given the refractory nature of childhood, it is not surprising that the children increasingly refuse to take part in the world that the experts are trying to sell them. One suspects that they sense the fraudulence and despair of it, and that like such writers as Joyce and Faulkner, with whom they share this view, they have retreated, some more than others, to worlds of their own, while the juvenile authorities and the Sunday book reviewers irritably wonder what can have gone wrong.

In the case of disturbed children, for whom the world makes no sense and is terrifying, it is important to do nothing that will disturb them further and gradually to convince them that the world is not so hostile after all. And even where healthy children are concerned, the problem for society and their parents is to present them with an environment that they can trust, that is credible in itself and satisfies a child's growing need for a solid reality out there. What is wrong with prize-winners like *The Bronze Bow* or with Miss Frank's picture magazines is that they are deficient in reality, so deficient indeed that it requires an entire educational bureaucracy to talk the children into accepting them. One is encouraged by the extent to which the children are able to resist such persuasion and reject such products; but it is sad that the experts have given so little advice concerning alternatives, especially since so many parents and teachers must themselves be at a loss.

In the absence of viable alternatives, the children—who, as the experts proudly tell us, avidly read—buy more than 300,000,000 comic books a year, and nightly watch men and women die on television. Comics and television have, for the children, the dubious advantage of representing, however badly, their natural aggressiveness toward those elders whom they want both to destroy and become, a function previously fulfilled for them by the Brothers Grimm and by such representatives of adult authority as Mr MacGregor who put Peter's father into a pie. But in the new version of *Peter Rabbit*, 'specially edited in vocabulary and style to meet the needs of the young child', the pie is not mentioned and over Peter's bed is the sign 'Good Bunnies Always Obey'. Beatrix Potter's little masterpiece, language and all, has fallen apart in the hands of its modern adapter. Compare, for example, the original:

> *First he ate some lettuces and some French beans; and then he ate some radishes;*
> *and then, feeling rather sick, he went to look for some parsley.*

with the new version:

> *In the garden he saw carrots and beans and radishes.*
> *'Mmm,' said Peter to himself, 'Carrots, beans and radishes are what I like best.'*
> *He began to eat.*

He ate some carrots.
He ate some radishes.
He ate and ate and ate.
Peter ate so much he got sick.
He went to look for some parsley.

The value of this inane performance is impossible to grasp. There is nothing old-fashioned or obscure about Miss Potter's version and there is nothing in the new version to make it clearer or more interesting than the original.[1] A little of it is likely to go a long way with even a slow child and none of it is likely to go anywhere at all with parents and teachers who agree with Professor Jerome Bruner of Harvard that, 'We might ask as a criterion for any subject taught in primary school whether, when fully developed, it is worth an adult's knowing and whether having known it as a child makes a person a better adult. If the answer to both questions is negative or ambiguous, then the material is cluttering the curriculum.'

Thanks to the theories of children's literature which this adaptation exemplifies, the comic book publishers can look forward to even bigger sales and the children will probably never go on to read the sequel in which Peter and his cousin, Benjamin Bunny, who in Miss Potter's original have no inhibiting signs over their beds, steal some onions and retrieve Peter's clothes from Mr MacGregor's scarecrow. And they are nearly certain to miss *The Roly Poly Pudding,* which, according to Graham Greene, who has written the only mature essay on Miss Potter's achievement, is her best work.

---

[1] The pedagogical theory that is reflected by the repetition of words in this version of *Peter Rabbit* is that a child, in learning to read, has to encounter the same few words over and over again until he has mastered them: a perfectly sensible theory except that the modern adapter in this case has misapplied it and her version is so dull that it is hard to imagine that a child would want to read it at all, whereas the original is so lively that one can easily imagine a child's reading it over and over again and encountering, as according to the theory he should, the same set of words repeatedly.

To the extent that the children's book business is not an adjunct to modern educational theory, it is a branch of the toy industry; and those few enterprising publishers who manage to break out of the encirclement of the experts have found themselves, for better or worse, in the frantic, often insane, world of infantile mass merchandising, along with the producers of breakfast food, plastic rockets, and bubble gum. In this world the product is known for what it is—merchandise—and nearly everything depends upon the package. The merchandise either sells in quantity throughout the country in chain stores and supermarkets, five-and-tens, and department stores, or it is dropped and something new is tried that is more likely to sell in the mass market.

This is not to suggest that all merchandise juveniles are bad, any more than all breakfast food or bird seed is bad. But these books do tend, necessarily, to be pretty uniform. They must strike an average quality which precludes their ever being excellent, eccentric, or bold. The risks in this business are enormous and so are the profits, and until recently there has been little time for the prissy rationalizations of the children's book experts—except where the right educational endorsement might adapt the product to a school market and thus bring in an extra profit, or where some respectability is required to take advantage of the current nervousness among parents who want their children to be on the right cultural beam. In the world of merchandise juveniles the big factors are the production men who know how to shave a penny here and there, and the salesmen who are chosen for their aggressiveness and their ability to take a $100,000 order from a chain store or a mail-order house before thc competitors do.

The books themselves often reflect the latest television success or the national current worry, whatever it may be; lately it has been science. Sometimes they are historical accounts, and these, since they freqently describe heroic actions in a more or less revolutionary spirit, are often pretty effective. Though they are of doubtful value as history, they do, at their best, represent the kind of courageous and spontaneous action that used to be found in more forthrightly imaginative literature. But in the stores one pile of merchandise looks pretty much like another and the clientele is presumed to be in a hurry and not very discriminating. Except for such rarities as the works of Dr Seuss, who in his strange way is authentically a genius—a sort of supercharged Edward Lear—and whose books sell in the millions, most juveniles that are sold as merchandise can hardly be considered books at all. This is especially true of those specimens meant for children who are not yet able to read and which represent the bulk of merchandise juveniles. These products are really nursery fixtures made of paper.

Whereas the editors and publishers of books that are meant primarily for schools and libraries tend to be female, their counterparts in the merchandise lines are vigorously male, indistinguishable along Madison Avenue from their colleagues in advertising and TV, where Huckleberry Hound and Cape Canaveral are big business and where everything depends upon the package. And while the line followed by the children's specialists derives mainly from the intellectual debris of a generation or two ago—the progressivism, the liberalism, the 'social consciousness' and uplift of the thirties survive surprisingly in a stale and mindless parody in the educational journals–the producers of merchandise follow the mass culture on a more day-to-day basis. This does not, however, mean that the books aimed at schools and libraries and those sold in the supermarkets are fundamentally different. Often they are interchangeable, depending only upon adjustments of format. And some of the more enterprising experts have begun to make room for some of the drearier merchandise products in their theories. It is better, they argue, for children to read nearly anything, even if 'we' don't quite approve of it, than for them to read nothing at all—a rationalization which indicates an unlooked for area of agreement between the merchandisers and some of the experts. Both groups want to move the goods.

As the experts come more and more to work for the publishers, this area of agreement grows wider. And as the mass market gradually drifts away from the more obvious vulgarities of a generation ago toward the greater respectability of the new suburbs, and the shopping centres and the elementary schools which they create, it is an improvident merchandiser indeed who will fail to add an expert or two to his staff or to hire one to prepare modern editions of such books as *Peter Rabbit.*

The most nearly official expert publication intended for general consumption is *A Parent's Guide to Children's Reading* by Nancy Larrick, PH.D., former president of the International Reading Association and 'well known', according to the jacket, 'as a writer and lecturer on children's reading'. A wistful attempt on the part of publishers to promote the reading (i.e., the sale) of books, *A Parent's Guide* was sponsored by the National Book Committee, Inc. and prepared with the help of advisers from eighteen national organizations, including the Adult Education Association, The American Association of University Women, the Campfire Girls, the Child Study Association of America, the Children's Book Council, The Children's Services Division of the American Library Association, The General Federation of Women's Clubs, the National Council of Teachers of English, and the United States Junior Chamber of Commerce.

Not surprisingly, the *Guide* was awarded honorable mention in the competition for the Carey-Thomas Award, annually given (by the same people who offer the Newbery Medal) for the best example of creative publishing in America. We are dealing here with a rather small world. But for all these accolades it is difficult to find words that will describe Dr Larrick's book, for it is not, in fact, a book at all but a sales-talk (Shall we read aloud to them? Yes, by all means! They love it!), and a far more aggressive one than Miss Frank's. The point of Dr Larrick's exhortation is, as she says, to surround the children with books, a depressing enough thought given most of the books she has in mind, and especially when one thinks of those children, still in possession of their animal spirits, who may not feel like being surrounded by books or anything else. But books, Dr Larrick insists—and so presumably do the eighteen national organizations who helped her—can be 'fun', as much 'fun', in fact, as TV or the comics. Yet if one thinks of one's own childhood experience, the idea that books have to be 'fun' seems a little off centre. Radio was fun and the comics were great fun and so, most of the time, was playing baseball or walking in the woods or watching the trains go by, but going to the library to read a book was not primarily or even secondarily for fun. It was for the sake of learning something, or more precisely, for the sake of becoming something—something more grownup than one had been before. The impulse to go to the library was of a completely different sort from the one that led to reading the comics or going to the movies, which were, after all, more fun. Going to the library was something one did, as it were, 'for real', and the fantasies one managed to generate there among the books by Howard Pyle and George MacDonald, as one read them over and over, turned out in time to transform the idea of fun entirely. Through such books one acquired, without in the least knowing it at the time, a taste for reality and the holiness of the imagination operating at the far edges of human experience which, in later life, makes it so difficult to confront such performances as Dr Larrick's with patience.

The last forty-five pages of *A Parent's Guide* consist of lists of recommended titles, but from these lists 'Some Old Favorites, such as *Tom Sawyer* and *Little Women*, have been omitted because hardly any parent needs a reminder. The list is largely made up of books published since 1940.' But while Dr Larrick feels that most parents know all about Mark Twain and such other writers whom she fails to mention as E. Nesbit, John Buchan, and George MacDonald, she apparently doesn't feel that they know about bookcases, and she therefore devotes two pages to describing what they are and how to build one. (This seems to be a gesture on behalf of an unhappy attempt made some years ago by the publishers when they asked a famous public relations man to suggest ways of improving their business. After some thought the public relations man suggested that householders should be encouraged to build bookshelves which they would then have to fill up.)

One will not find on Dr Larrick's forty-five page list books by H. G. Wells or Howard Pyle, Jonathan Swift or Herman Melville, Frances Hodgson Burnett or Jane Austen, and one wonders if perhaps what is implied in her principle of choice may not, after all, have come to pass. Perhaps by now the great tradition is lost to most children. Perhaps only a marginal few can usefully be introduced to such authors and perhaps it is merely old fashioned to care. One wonders if the professor of education who a year or two ago advised the high school in Princeton, N.J. to get rid of 'fossilized classics' like *Ivanhoe* is not really marching forward with history, while the rest of us have, like the classics themselves, become fossilized in our affection for a dead past.

But where then do we draw the line? Do we slide all the way down to the new version of *Peter Rabbit* and those recent abridgements of the *Iliad* and *Odyssey* that have sacrificed everything to easy reading and are a waste of time to read, or to those colourful volumes which promise, in a hundred or so pages, to introduce the children to all the sciences known to man? Or do we stop halfway down and replace *Ivanhoe*, as the high school in Princeton has proposed to do, with *The Pearl* by John Steinbeck and Hemingway's *The Old Man and the Sea*, inferior works of their authors, but sexless and bloodless and therefore suitable? And if we set our standards at this level, how, when the children are older and go to college, will they deal with Shakespeare and Proust, and what will they do with a writer like

Joyce? Shall we find a way to drag these writers down so that they too can be read on the level of *The Old Man and the Sea* or perhaps even of the new version of *Peter Rabbit?* The problem is sad to contemplate and hard, and it includes the danger that the children may not grow up at all but simply grow older. For the appreciation of literature resembles the process of growing up in that they both involve the discovery of distinctions between the self and the world: the aim of both is differentiation, concreteness, and the development of a character of one's own. This is why literature is exciting and why it is, finally, inseparable from life. Where Nancy Larrick goes wrong is in her assumption that there is no particular need to distinguish oneself from the surrounding environment, that to take part uncritically in the common culture is the proper goal of growing up.

Still, it would be wrong to suggest that the level on which Josette Frank and Nancy Larrick operate necessarily represents the style in which all children's libraries and school teachers or even most experts themselves function when they are face to face with children; and it would also be wrong to suggest that *The Bronze Bow* necessarily reflects the real literary preferences of these people. Life, even in the schools, is full of its usual perplexity, and it is fair to assume that the stronger teachers consult their own experience and ideals, just as the weaker ones panic and submit, typically, to their own confusion. Though the experts on children's reading are, like experts everywhere, mistrustful of what they do not understand, a certain tough fibre occasionally appears in their otherwise undistinguished fabric. One of the recent Newbery winners is a book called *Frontier Living* by Edwin Tunis, which is a valuable and substantial account of daily life on the edge of the American wilderness as it gradually receded toward California. This book is not only full of uncommon information; it is surprisingly candid. Unlike most books in its category, it neither patronizes nor sentimentalizes the Indians, whose side it takes against the whites where it is necessary to do so. The Kentucky settlers are described as drunken and brutal, while it is revealed that the towns farther west were often bothered by gamblers and prostitutes. The directors of the Union Pacific and Central Pacific are described as thieves and exploiters who co-operated with the California legislature to rob the public, while the United States senate is shown to have been frequently faithless in its treaties with the Indians. In its attention to detail and the cleanliness of its style, *Frontier Living* is a considerable achievement—one of those books that is likely to inspire strong feelings of social justice and patriotism in certain young readers by providing them not only with a sense of their uniqueness but with a link to the common welfare.

One is surprised to discover that such a book was chosen by the same group who also chose *The Bronze Bow* and who are usually so careful not to offend against the standard impostures of American history. But this curious thread appears to run throughout the entire fabric of the children's book industry: while the formation of natural taste and the spontaneity and explosiveness associated with childhood are largely dampened by irrelevant theory, a certain stubbornness on behalf of real literature somehow prevails. Despite their omission from Nancy Larrick's list, the standard authors are likely to be available in most public libraries, even if, in some cases, only pro forma and even if the librarians, under pressure from the schools and knowing that their budgets in some cases depend on how many books they can circulate, feature the newer books that are easier to read. Most libraries too will include the handful of modern books like Hugh Lofting's *Dr Dolittle,* Kenneth Grahame's *The Wind in the Willows,* Mary Norton's *The Borrowers,* Laura Ingalls Wilder's *The Little House in the Big Woods,* and the works of Dr Seuss—books which even Dr Larrick finds room for and which, though they represent a sort of mannerist phase of the great tradition, are generally on a very high level. The libraries themselves are frequently stimulating and their collections and personnel are impressive. To visit the Donnell Library on Fifty-third Street in New York or the Children's Room of the New York Public Library is reassuring. The mindless eclecticism, the idea that children should know less and less about more and more, that characterize the writing of such experts as we have quoted here, are absent. Absent too is the notion that the books should be adjusted to the tempers and interests of the children, which is what is implied by the idea that books 'should meet the reading needs of the young child'—an idea that would, if fully carried into practice, reduce the children to idiocy and turn the libraries into madhouses.

But if the official experts are in practice largely ignored by superior librarians, how are teachers and librarians who may not be as good as those in the Donnell to know what books to make available? It is, after all, no easier to distinguish quality among children's books than among books in general: the same critical acumen is required in either case and such acumen has never been especially abundant in any society. The criterion generally applied by the experts is: 'Is this a book for children?" But the only relevant question—and the one which, to judge by their typical preferences, the experts are incompetent to decide—is: 'Is this a book at all?' The question 'Is this a book for children?' can properly be decided only by the children themselves as they fumble and experiment among what is available. And if a child decides, as one sixth-grader whom I know of has, to read the Greek tragedies, then Greek tragedy is, for him, a suitable book. It it bores and confuses him, he will soon enough turn to something that suits him better.

We have been considering not the more or less technical problem of teaching the children to read—which is properly a branch of cognitive psychology and is within the province of qualified experts—but of helping them to find and distinguish, once they have learned how to read, those books through which they can discover themselves as individuals and discern, gradually, the nature of the world in which they must function. 'Children read, through inexperience, whatever comes their way,' Lillian Smith, who was a Canadian librarian, has written in her admirable book *The Unreluctant Years,* published by the American Library Association. 'In a time when children's books are almost a matter of mass production,' Miss Smith goes on, 'it is possible that a child may pass from infancy to maturity without encounterng one book that will satisfy him in his search for experience and pleasure; that will offer him reality in the place of a shadow of reality.' But, she adds, 'children will defend themselves against encroaching mediocrity if books of genuine quality are put within their reach.'

Thus stated, the task of teachers and librarians and the experts who advise them is simple. It has nothing to do with 'being alert to all that goes on within a child's world', or with 'surrounding him with books', or with meeting 'the reading needs of the young child'. For it is absurd to suppose that the 'reading needs' of a child who is able to read by himself are, in principle, different from those of an adult, or that a child will or should submit to being surrounded by walls of books, or that alertness to the private world of childhood is a valuable or even possible desideratum. Proposals like these are useless in themselves and serve only to rationalize and certify the industry begun by John Newbery who, significantly, sold in his shop not only books for children but quack medicines for their parents.

As the market grows larger and the rate at which new books published for children expands, and as the standards proposed by the bureaucracy of experts increasingly conform to the surrounding mass culture and the commercial requirements of the publishers, the opportunity for children to find 'books of genuine quality' will necessarily diminish. In America there are hardly more than a hundred—certainly no more than two hundred—bookstores which are able to select and carry more than a bare minimum of the standard children's classics or which can by themselves distinguish among the new books published each year those that are of any value. And the number of such stores is decreasing as more and more of them come to depend for their profits on merchandise and as the schools and libraries, in their attempt 'to meet the reading needs' of the young child, increasingly make the children unfit for the 'fossilized classics'.

Though the children themselves wrote letters strongly rejecting the proposed modification in the curriculum of the Princeton High School when it appeared in the *New York Times*, the teachers grow weary. Dickens and Scott are, after all, harder to teach than low-grade Hemingway: for many teachers they may by now be impossible; and the community, except for an unimportant fraction, no longer cares very much. Perhaps, as Edgar Z. Friedenberg recently suggested,[2] the teachers have even come to resent the brightness of their students, for as Professor Friedenberg argues, the 'free-floating ill temper' so common throughout our society is particularly endemic among those people who, defeated like so many others by the conditions of American life, must nevertheless confront the abounding and as yet uncompromised energies of the young. And so the marvelous world of George MacDonald and Conan Doyle, John Buchan and Frances Hodgson Burnett may soon vanish, except for the happy few. Perhaps, since so much else has gone—and will go—it is pointless to care. Except, of course, that the children are always there to remind us. And one naturally wonders what they will become.

[1963]

---

[2] 'The Gifted Student and His Enemies', *Commentary*, May 1962.

The child and the book

ANTHONY STORR

All day long the boy stood at the window, looking over the sea by which the princess must travel; but there were no signs of her. And, as he stood, soldiers came and laid hands on him, and led him up to the cask, where a big fire was blazing, and the horrid black pitch boiling and bubbling over the sides. He looked and shuddered, but there was no escape; so he shut his eyes to avoid seeing.

Suddenly, some men were seen running with all their might, crying as they went that a large ship with its sails spread was making straight for the city. No one knew what the ship was or whence it came; but the king declared he would not have the boy burned before its arrival.

At this point in the story the five-year-old girl burst into tears. Her mother put down Andrew Lang's *Brown Fairy Book* and hastened to comfort her.

'Don't cry. The boy was quite all right. He didn't get thrown into the cask of pitch. He was saved.'

'But I *wanted* him to be thrown into the cask of pitch,' sobbed the little girl, unable to tolerate the disappointment of finding that this exciting threat was not after all, to be put into practice.

This true story may serve to demonstrate that the effects of a book upon a child are not always easy to predict; but, unfortunately, most of our knowledge remains at this anecdotal level, and there are, so far as I can discover, no large-scale studies of the effects of literature upon children comparable with the recent survey of the effects of television.

Parents, librarians, and educators often express alarm at what their children read. They are generally concerned, firstly, that the child shall not be made frightened or unhappy; secondly, that it shall not be prematurely sexually aroused; and thirdly, that it shall not be encouraged to behave in aggressive or delinquent ways. At the back of the adults' anxiety is usually the belief that children are innocent little creatures who must not have unpleasant ideas put into their heads; a belief which should have been, but is not yet, dispelled by psychoanalytic research. There is, of course, much to be said for not frightening children—although we all enjoy being frightened a little. And no one wants a child to be made miserable—although the shedding of a sentimental tear may be a pleasurable release. Sexual excitation can, in certain instances, be premature and create problems for the child whose ego is not yet strong enough to deal with it; and delinquent behaviour is certainly not to be encouraged. But it is extremely doubtful whether books in themselves ever cause any of the dreadful effects upon children which are attributed to them by anxious adults.

Many people will remember the publicity given to horror comics a few years ago; and some will have read Dr Wertham's book *Seduction of the Innocent*. This verbose and emotional work tells us more about Dr Wertham's reaction to horror comics than about that of the children who read them; and, although he blames horror comics for almost every psychological disturbance from fetishism to theft, his claims remain unsubstantiated.

I think they are likely to remain so. The fundamental objection to horror comics is not the themes with which they deal, but the crude and vulgar way in which these themes are presented. There is no convincing evidence that horror comics corrupt, and little to be found in them which cannot be met with in earlier publications. The adventures of Jack Harkaway, for instance, contain a description of the torture of a girl with red hot stones, and of the gradual eating of a man alive: and for the last thirty years of the Victorian era Jack Harkaway was a best-selling hero. Are we to suppose that our grandfathers often indulged themselves in such activities as a result of this boyhood reading? The Victorians, though more prudish about other aspects of sexuality, seem to have been less disturbed by sadistic themes than we are today. *The Mikado* and *The Yeomen of the Guard* are generally considered suitable entertainments for children; but in both W. S. Gilbert outspokenly reveals his preoccupation with torture, and some of the short stories of Conan Doyle disclose a similar interest. It seems that adults who are alarmed by comics must feel that illustrations are more potent for harm than the spoken or written word.

Why is it that the stories which children enjoy are so often full of horrors? We know that from the very beginning of life the child possesses an inner world of fantasy and the fantasies of the child mind are by no means the pretty stories with which the prolific Miss Blyton regales us. They are both richer and more primitive, and the driving forces behind them are those of sexuality and the aggressive urge to power: the forces which ultimately determine the emergence of the individual as a separate entity. For, in the long process of development, the child has two main tasks to perform if he is to reach maturity. He has to prove his strength, and he has to win a mate; and in order to do this he has to overcome the obstacles of his infantile dependency upon, and his infantile erotic attachment to, his parents. That the erotic strand in fairy tales is less obvious than the aggressive is partly due to bowdlerization and partly to the fact that the sexual component is in childish, pregenital form. The typical fairy story ends with the winning of the princess just as the typical Victorian novel ends with the marriage. It is only at this point that adult sexuality begins; and it is for this reason that books like *Lady Chatterley's Lover,* which describe the sexual behaviour of adults, are of little interest to children. It is not surprising that fairy stories should be both erotic and violent, or that they should appeal so powerfully to children. For the archetypal themes with which they deal mirror the contents of the childish psyche; and the same unconscious source gives origin to both the fairy tale and the fantasy life of the child.

Reading which produces an emotional effect rather than conveying information does not put things into the mind, but rather objectifies contents which are already present. If this were not so, we should be unable to react emotionally to a book at all. There has to be a lock within us which the key of the book can fit, and if it does not fit, the book is meaningless to us. The high value which we give to the artist or writer who pleases us is a tribute not so much to his power of invention as to his skill in objectifying the contents of our own minds; especially those contents which are only partially conscious, and thus unformulated. The thrill is one of recognition; and if there is no recognition there is no thrill, but only the cold admiration which we accord to some figure who achieves greatness in a field which is incomprehensible to us.

If children have heads full of fantasies of a violent and erotic kind, and if their delight in fairy tales and the like is due to the thrill of recognition, why is it that they do not act upon their fantasies, and is there not a risk that books might encourage them to do so?

A disturbed child who behaves in a delinquent way will sometimes say that he got the idea from a book, which is one way of disowning responsibility. But it is only the child who is already emotionally disturbed who will act out his fantasies. If this were not so we should all have strangled our brothers and sisters, slept with our mothers, castrated our fathers, and reduced to pulp all those who in any way opposed us. As a distinguished child-analyst has put it, the individual 'is engaged in the perpetual human task of keeping inner and outer reality separate yet interrelated.' The normal child can do this; but in the disturbed child, as in the psychotic adult, the two worlds may be confused, so that fantasies are acted upon and parents actually stolen from or pushed over cliffs. But I am sure that no book ever pulled the trigger of any gun but that upon which a finger was already quivering. Ultimately, what keeps us sane and makes us behave in a relatively civilized manner is our relationship with other people.

It is obviously quite hopeless to try and impose any kind of censorship upon children's reading, even if it were desirable to do so. If the normal child were as susceptible to the effects of literature as parents sometimes fear, we should have to proscribe reading altogether. A man told me that his masochistic interest in male slavery had been stimulated in childhood by pictures of the building of the Pyramids. Are we to ban history books on this account? Many people recall that, in early youth, they searched the pages of Leviticus for sexual information and puzzled over the mysterious sin of Onan. Should the Bible be withdrawn from all respectable households? Of course children may be sexually stimulated by their reading—just as adults are—but only when their development has reached a stage where they will look for something in a book which reflects the desires already half-formulated within them. And this they will certainly find somewhere, whatever censorship is attempted; or, if their search fails, they may write their own erotica.

It is probably reassuring for most children to read the violent tales in which they delight. We all like the comfort of finding that someone else feels as we do ourselves; nor need we be alarmed that the literature of childhood is likely to turn a child into a delinquent. For, as Gibbon remarks, 'the power of instruction is seldom of much efficacy except in those happy dispositions where it is largely superfluous.'

But although books cannot be blamed for causing either delinquency or neurosis, they do, of course, have their emotional effect; and it is probable that many adults can recall one book or one scene from a book which in childhood touched them particularly. Such scenes often stay in the mind for years, and may, like a Proustian *madeleine,* be more potent in evoking the memory of what it felt like to be child than the deliberate recollection of any actual external circumstance. My guess would be that such scenes in some way reflect a psychological situation within the child unrecognized by it at the time.

[1960]

Thoughts concerning children's books

PENELOPE MORTIMER

I strongly believe that a new look needs to be taken at the whole idea of children's books; that the necessity for having them at all needs at least to be questioned. I am not referring to books for the illiterate under-fives, and have no criticism to make of them beyond the fact that publishers and authors seem to think that the smaller the child, the larger the book must be—for what reason, since their arms are short and their eyesight usually at its best, it is hard to imagine. But once these tasteful if unwieldy volumes have lost their charm, the child begins to be given novels which are intended to mirror what psychiatrists and school teachers call 'the child's world'. These are frequently sold with time limits stamped on them, like cream cheese or Kodak film—to be read between the ages of 10 and 13, with no suggestion that this is roughly speaking. These books are, of course, written by adults, usually selected by adults, paid for by adults, published and printed and reviewed by adults. Will one child pore over this Supplement, library list in hand? Are there children who discuss, over the Ribena, the merits of the new Nesbit or Norton?[1] Or are children's books a form of literature which owes its continued existence to a minority of grownups who might as well be circulating

---

[1] E. Nesbit, *Long Ago When I Was Young*, illustrated by Edward Ardizzone (London, 1966). Mary Norton, *The Borrowers Omnibus*, illustrated by Diana Stanley (London, 1966).

Family Planning leaflets to guinea pigs for all that they understand of the requirements of the average child?

There is, of course, no such thing as the average child—however, for the purposes of argument, I mean those children who are as far from precocity as they are from stupidity. This includes all the children I know. Apart from messages on television—addresses for sending up for things, mostly—they read H. G. Wells, Daphne du Maurier, Conan Doyle, Ian Fleming, George Orwell, and the strip cartoons in the Sunday papers. Their interest in myth, magic, and anthropomorphism of all kinds is, on the whole, slightly less than mine. They are not as sentimental as I am. They like a good laugh, particularly at other people's misfortunes; they enjoy what seems to me an immoderate amount of fear and disgust and are often, through excessive affection, very beastly to animals; they have a very strong sense of justice in regard to themselves and none whatever in regard to anyone else. They are the perfect public for Shakespeare and the more disreputable parts of the Bible. Where did we get the idea that, apart from variations in taste and experience, they are any different from us?

The segregation between children and adults began to take place around the end of the seventeenth century—up until then, apart from the necessary period of infancy, children seem to have been regarded as normal people: hard working, capable of reading Ovid and slogging about battlefields, sexy, indistinguishable from men and women except in size. In 1693 John Locke publish his *Thoughts Concerning Education* and invented the Child. Character, he said, came before learning; the educator's aim must be to instil virtue, wisdom, and good breeding into the minds of the young; this must be done by means of 'sport and play' in a cosy family environment; children must not merely be, they must be brought up. The first missionary tracts appeared in the stately nurseries of England–'books of courtesy' designed to tame the little creatures and turn them, by gentle persuasion, into domestic pets. Eagerly exploiting a new market, aware that for the first time there was a captive audience which, if it couldn't read, was going to be read to, writers took up their quills and poured out their neuroses in fiercely moral bedtime stories beside which *The History of the Rod* reads like Eleanor Farjeon. Fathers who wouldn't be seen dead with the novels of the Duchess of Newcastle or Aphra Behn resonantly rendered tales of Batman heroism from the newly published adventures of King Arthur and Robin Hood. The prototype of the Victorian fairy—no resemblance to crafty sensualists like Titania and Oberon—fluttered over from the French court and settled, simpering, in the bottom of our garden. A few lady moralists tried to suppress her, believing that she would distract the tots from the doctrines of Rousseau, but she survived—largely, perhaps, because the mamas needed someone to identify with, a glamour image, asexual, radiant with virtue, ageless, and flimsy. By the time John Newbery began the profitable publishing of his 'pretty gilt toys for girls and boys', the children's book, as distinct from the book, had arrived, and Miss Enid Blyton was on her way.

The fact that seems to have been overlooked is simply that a good book cannot possibly be written for a particular age, sex, creed, or colour—if it is, the motive and the execution must be dishonest, and the result spurious. *Black Beauty* and *The Secret Garden* are more intelligent, even sophisticated, than the average women's magazine story; *Tom Sawyer* and *Huckleberry Finn* can be enjoyed by any fairly bright executive wanting a bit of escapism between ulcers. It is as foolish to confine these books to the nursery shelves as it is to assume that your ten-year-old is incapable of enjoying Colette or Kingsley Amis.

It is absurd to say that we do not think about such things because they are so obvious—obvious attitudes, particularly if they appear vaguely progressive or humane, are the last to be questioned. The subject of children's books has not, it seems to me, been thought about since Christopher Robin said his prayers. Children, over the last two decades, have changed radically: their expectation of child life has become shorter; they are rapidly returning to the pre-Spock, pre-Locke era and ceasing to be, in the traditional sense, children. They are no longer at the mercy of their parents' tastes and opinions, but are to a large extent 'brought up' by the Ideal Parents provided for them by television: scholarly, good-looking fathers, handy around the house, knowledgeable about space, rabbit hutches, the Gobi desert; pretty, calm, independent mothers who cook, swim about in coral reefs, make their own Christmas cards, nurse pregnant cats with patience. These splendid Super-Egos can be switched on or off at will; they have no moral axe to grind, you can sit there picking your nose or worse, they just keep smiling. They provide what the modern child really wants—information. In my local children's library, books on engineering *(Let's Take A Trip To A Cement Plant)*, pet-keeping, radio, magnetics, cookery, dress-making, outnumber the poetry and drama by twenty to one.

So, believing as I do that children have evolved and are now in many respects much brighter than we are, and that very few people in the literary or theatre worlds (will we, this Christmas, have Nicholas Stuart Grey *again?)* have recognized this fact—who will read these two books which I am, with infinite slowness, getting round to reviewing? For information—in the likely event of any child reading this—Miss Nesbit lived in the second great era of women novelists—the first was in the seventeenth century, the third, so the commercials say, is now—missing Charlotte Brontë by three years and dying just before the publication of *Mrs Dalloway*. Her writing had much of the wit, charm, and sense of privilege of her contemporaries. This little autobiography, so gentle and remote, adds no more than a whiff of camphor to *The Railway Children* and *The Wouldbegoods*.

'Supposing', the boy said, 'you saw a little man, about as tall as a pencil, with a blue patch in his trousers, half-way up a window

curtain, carrying a doll's tea-cup would you say it was a fairy?' 'No,' said Arrietty. 'I'd say it was my father.'

This kind of writing is good enough for anyone. The Borrowers are, it's true, Little People, living in terror of 'human beans', but they have appeared on radio and television, they are only small in relation to the gigantic hair-grips and safety-pins that they appropriate, their behaviour is in all respects entirely 'real'. This satisfactory bulk of a book contains the whole lot, *Afield, Afloat, and Aloft* as well as *The Borrowers* itself. I prefer the first, in which the family live snug under the floorboards and are very bourgeois and calm; when they become pioneers, making do in an old boot or kettle, they are less credible. There is also rather too much chat of the Archers variety, too many sympathetic human beans take over, and there are too many niggly little drawings. But I'd warmly recommend Miss Norton to any child—from, say, seven and a half to eleven and three-quarters—who has a few minutes to spare between finishing off the model railway and cooking a four-course meal.

One final thought, however: I saw a film recently in which a scientist's life was saved by 'miniaturizing' a submarine and its entire crew and injecting it into the bloodstream. Attacked by vast anti-bodies, storm-tossed inside a lung the size of Chartres Cathedral, threatened by a vast palpitating dragon of a heart, they escaped through the old boy's eye (Arrietty 'grew to know that ear quite well, with its curves and shadows and sunlit pinks and golds).' There was a spy and a blonde aboard, for good measure. The film was for adults only.

[1966]

Goodbye Humphrey, hello Dick and Jane

DIANA GOLDSBOROUGH

When my uncles and aunts were children, my grandmother used to take out a certain book every Sunday and read to them until they were all in tears and supplicating her to stop. The book was *Misunderstood,* by Florence Montgomery, and it has provided an irresistible jacket picture for Gillian Avery's *Nineteenth Century Children.* The scene is little Humphrey's deathbed, with father and uncle on each side, racked with remorseful sobs, and little brother Miles, dead centre, kneeling in his nightshirt, summoned from sleep for the event, the whole tableau under the portrait of sainted Mama. Miss Avery's subtitle is *Heroes and Heroines in English Children's Stories 1780–1900,* and her book makes an ideal companion volume to Leonard de Vries's *Flowers of Delight*—cullings from children's literature published between 1765 and 1830, from Toronto's Osborne Collection. Mr de Vries's bouquet is so colourful and engaging that you will be tempted to sniff heartily; but be warned—that nosegay is full of thorns. Interspersed among all those pretty pictures are some of the horridest tales you will ever encounter, worthy of *V* or *Last Exit to Brooklyn* and told with a perfect insouciance that might be envied by the authors of both those works. But these are just the nursery tales the late Georgians and Victorians considered suitable for the young.

Leafing through *Flowers,* you will find there is no end to the grue. There is the admirable father, for instance, who decides to put his foot down on fairy tales for his young. 'What benefit can you derive from them? [Speak up, Northrop Frye!] Absurdities like these serve only to vitiate your taste and weaken your mind, while some of them excite terror and disgust.' Instead, he tells them improving stories of his own, such as *Filial Affection* in which a boy sacrifices himself to a shark to save his father.

The monster . . . throwing himself above the waves, raised his horrid open mouth and swallowed half the body of the young Volney, separating it from the other half, which remained suspended by the cord. This direful spectacle petrified all the spectators . . . but the son cast his last look upon the author of his life and seemed, even while dying, to feel pleasure in having preserved his father.

And the one about the brave boy of Caracas (more filial piety —one suspects Papa's motives), son of a captured patriot, who appealed to the Spanish general for his father's life. The beast requires him to sacrifice one ear, then the other, for his father, then says: 'The father of such a boy is a danger to Spain!', and leads him off to witness his father' execution.

Well, back to Bluebeard.

Miss Avery is very good at showing the evolution from the piety and religiosity of the early Victorian children's book. In the early Victorian work, mother and father are right there, spouting morality and science like combination Wesleys and Darwins ('How is it, Papa,' asked little Franz, 'that with the aid of the instrument you can move objects which without it defy our united strength?') In the affluent late Victorian world, mama and papa vanish, to be replaced by nurse, and the nursery world is governed, not by Christian principles, but by the rules of what little ladies and gentlemen may and may not do. Religion is superseded by—or becomes—class-consciousness. In Mrs Molesworth's *The Cuckoo Clock*, still a classic, Griselda's aunts are distraught when they find she has been playing with a little boy they don't know, and not until they have made a thorough check into little Phil's background is she permitted to see him again. Luckily his origins prove to be awesomely gentlemanly, but his nurse earns a black mark for allowing him to appear misleadingly disheveled. No wonder few nurses took the risk, and preferred to raise their charges to be monstrous snobs.

Nevertheless, after the enthralling world of the Victorian children's book, the Dick-and-Jane world to today's juvenile seems awfully sterile. In reaction against the Victorians, religion and class-consciousness are now taboo, but so many other taboos have now been added. Almost any controversial opinion is banned. The gulf between adult's and child's literature is immense, as it never was for our forefathers. The Victorian author polemicized and proselytized for both young and old; he was ready to drop the plot at any moment and harangue the reader on his favourite cause, and he did this in stories for child and adult alike. Why discriminate? Life was real, life was earnest, and the earlier this was realized, the better. Children were spared few of the causes of the time. The slave trade, agricultural depression, conditions in the factories, alcoholism, the Irish problem (see *Castle Blair*), Tractarianism, child labour, slums, feminism, naval abuses, epidemic prevention, even homosexuality (see Dean Farrar's famous *Eric, or Little by Little)* were all treated in children's stories. Where is a problem of today to be seen in a children's book? Harsh realism and the macabre absurd may obtain in adult literature, but for children Protection and No License are the watchwords. Mrs Barbauld could espouse pacifism and attack soldiering as a profession, pointing out that a battle is nothing but organized murder: 'Let us correct our ideas of the matter, and no longer lavish admiration upon such a pest of the human race as a conqueror, how brilliant soever his qualities may be; nor ever think that a profession which binds a man to be the servile instrument of cruelty and injustice is an *honorable* calling.' Try ringing in an opinion like that in a juvenile of today and see how far your book gets with school boards and library committees.

Dick and Jane's world must be one of perfect harmony, without any of the threats from without, or splits from within, that menaced the Victorian fictional child. Home is in an antiseptic sunny suburbia, their dog never befouls the footpath, they never see a poverty pocket, or a car crash, or a rumble, and greatest irony of all, their mother is just as saintly as little Humphrey's —only she's alive. If Betty Friedan were living in 1860 she would write children's books, because that's the age to get them, that's where your ideas will really count. As it is, she can only look in envy at the mother in an 1888 short story, paying, apparently, her first visit to the nursery:

The nurse's heart welled anew with emotion and pleasure when her mistress said kindly, 'Ann, why did you never invite me before? You train these children to behave so nicely that I really must come sometimes, now that I have once found my way up.'

[1966]

2 *Fairy tales, fantasy, animals*

Where is fancy bred?

HELEN LOURIE

As Christmas inexorably approaches and the shop windows put forth their annual display of man's ingenuity to man; as red-coated Santa Clauses lurk in the recesses of the big stores, theatres are taken over by flying children, dragons, gnomes, and loquacious animals, and publishers let loose over 1,000 volumes of reading matter aimed at the population under sixteen it seems appropriate to examine the world of fantasy which the season invariably calls forth. For whose benefit is this wealth of the imagination? Why do we suppose that it is especially suitable to children? Who reads the literature of fantasy? Who writes it?

Since the age of reason set in, the wilder flights of man's fancy have had to find some framework in which to work. It was well for Sir John Mandeville to report from distant countries of men whose ears grew large enough to shield them from the sun, or who, being headless, had eyes in their shoulders. For nearly 300 years after he wrote, the extent of the earth and the laws of nature were so imperfectly understood that extraordinary events could be daily expected. Witches cast spells, alchemists searched for the philosopher's stone, scholars made pacts with the devil: at any moment one might find one's shape changed, one's status immeasurably raised, or access to infinite power within one's grasp.

The scientific discoveries of the last 200 years have altered this scene. The current image of Western man is now that of a rational creature slow to believe in anything that cannot be demonstrably proved; the password by which he gains credence, 'working hypothesis'. Travellers' tales today must be corroborated by maps and photographs, we have irrefutable means of testing gold, and if Faustus assured us that he had made a pact with Beelzebub, we could bring a battery of X-rays and expertise to disprove the authenticity of the fiend's signature. But wherever areas of ignorance remain, writers can still allow their imagination to work. It was possible in the last century for Rider Haggard to describe miraculous events, reincarnations, an immortal enchantress in the unexplored regions of darkest Africa. Conan Doyle postulated a Lost World on the high unknown plateaux of Brazil. Jules Verne, with a fecundity of invention which many better stylists might envy, populated the depths of the sea, the moon, the centre of the earth with the offspring of his fancy. Sheridan Le Fanu and Edgar Allan Poe appropriated the mysterious domains of the spirit after death. At the beginning of the twentieth century H. G. Wells explored the possibilities of unknown time; recently outer space has provided the field for the development of this particular vein of fantasy. Nature, we know, abhors a vacuum. In this she differs from man, who sees in the absence of positive knowledge a heaven-sent opportunity for invention.

This is the adult world of fantasy: a world of romance, adventure, ghosts and vampires, animals, men and machines. It is a world in which extraordinary phenomena appear, are recognized as being extraordinary, and are related to the world of scientific facts by some sort of explanation. The immortal

She learnt her magic arts from the Ancient Egyptians; the pterodactyls of the Lost World have escaped extinction by their geographical situation; one is able to fly through the air when one is beyond the pull of gravity. Given a primary assumption, itself often springing from a supposition difficult to disprove, these fantasies follow a logical course. It is possible to read them without forgetting one's place in society, one's moral responsibilities, one's age. They are written for the sane, the responsible, the grownup.

These books deal with a world of improbabilities. But there exists also a literature belonging to a world of impossibilities, and here one unlikely premise does not condition the rest of the story: here anything can happen at any time. In this world trunks fly, swineherds marry princesses, Jumblies go to sea in a sieve; a child is adopted by the North Wind, white rabbits carry watches in their waistcoat pockets, little boys can remain fluttering for ever between infancy and maturity, between the nursery ceiling and the wooded island in the middle of the Serpentine lake. In this world, immortality, Pobbles with or without toes, levitation, need no explanations—nor do ambition, ruthlessness, love, hate, or death. It is a world without rules, physical or moral, seen with the egoist's single eye. It is the amoral, polymorphous world of the infant. The writer who wants to express himself in terms of this world has learned to direct his appeal to the youngest readers; in some cases, but not all, he has needed the presence of a real child to enable him to reach this realm. Children pass easily from the incomprehensible adult world to the equally mysterious world of fantasy, partly because they are not steeped in the habit of convention, partly because they are still ignorant of so many of the laws by which our lives are governed that the discovery of new freedoms cannot surprise them. In their comparatively short sojourn in the world of scientific facts they have acquired less disbelief to be suspended before they can enter into the Kingdom of Never-Never.

The wilder the fantasy, the younger the reader. But who are the writers? Surprisingly it is not the very young themselves. Nor is it the sex conventionally supposed to be the more fanciful. If we exclude, as we must, the whimsy, the conscious allegory, the didactic fairies and unnatural animals who inculcate convenient moral principles into their not-so-innocent readers' minds, if we consider the unprincipled, violent, timeless, weightless, limitless literature of true magic, we find that it comes from an unexpected source. It is not the irresponsible, eccentric, or mad, not the explorers or the anthropologists, not necessarily the impractical or the dreamers. An unsuccessful dramatist of working-class origin; Queen Victoria's drawing master; an Oxford don of mathematics; a Congregationalist minister; and a flourishing writer of English stage comedy—it sounds a sober company. Yet Hans Christian Andersen, Edward Lear, Lewis Carroll, George MacDonald, and James Barrie produced, within an era of enormous respectability and veneration for order of every kind, an entry into as mad a world as could be found in any Bedlam, and achieved something that their often more accomplished contemporaries could not. While the great novelists were drawing unforgettable characters, were surveying the human scene with irony, pathos, humour, sympathy; while the Romantics were embroidering on the archetypal situations which cannot be too often restated; while innumerable gifted storytellers were entertaining the young and the old—these writers were fabricating that structure, like a spider's web at once delicate and resilient, that synthesis of the general and the particular which is the essence of the myth. For what distinguishes the story, the fable, the allegory from the myth is this: that whereas the former take an already existing shape, and embellish and enrich it with the writer's individuality and skill, the myth is the original pattern. Andersen's Ugly Duckling is as unforgettable an example of the difficulties of being undervalued as Oedipus is of another human predicament. Carroll's Red Queen, running furiously in order to stay in the same place, George Macdonald's child in the grip of the wind of inspiration too large for him to hold, Barrie's Peter Pan, an Oedipus in reverse, refusing to face the consequences of growing up: all these have taken their place in our mythology. Lear has no such striking figures to offer, but I would include him among the others for the sake of his emancipated attitude to language. He and Carroll share an art which tosses words about with as little regard for their common uses as a juggler shows for his poles and tumblers. Carroll was the more ingenious, Lear the less inhibited. In the countries they create, no event is predictable by any law of precedence. Birds mate with cats, chairs and tables promenade together, anything from a pair of tongs to a caterpillar or a playing card had its own individual voice; one can remember what is going to happen tomorrow and believe six impossible things before breakfast. These countries are not only mythological, they are themselves the myth of the freedom of the intellect.

Is it accident that all these writers and those in the same group who are writing today are men? No more, I would say, than it is by chance that the greatest works of art have been products of the male sex; and this can by no stretch of reasoning be attributed to women's want of education or of status. Women can be excellent storytellers: their powers of invention and fancy are not inferior to that of men. But what they lack is the whole-hearted abandonment to their inspiration: the power to enter the other world, whether it is through the Looking Glass or the Back of the North Wind, without keeping some conscious hold on normality. Is this why, of the incurably insane, women form over 60 per cent? Is it because those who can't voluntarily relinquish their foothold in reality run the greater risk of being involuntarily overtaken by the Eumenides? To be lunatic enough to experience the myth and to be at the same time sufficiently sane to present it to the public in the form of art, is genius; and this the great exponents of fantasy, at their best, share with the artist, the musician, and the poet.

[1962]

Children and fairy stories

J.R.R. TOLKIEN

What, if any, are the values and functions of fairy stories *now?* It is usually assumed that children are the natural or the specially appropriate audience for fairy stories. In describing a fairy story which they think adults might possibly read for their own entertainment, reviewers frequently indulge in such waggeries as: 'this book is for children from the ages of six to sixty.' But I have never yet seen the puff of a new motor-model that began thus: 'this toy will amuse infants from seventeen to seventy'; though that to my mind would be much more appropriate. Is there any *essential* connection between children and fairy stories? Is there any call for comment, if an adult reads them for himself? *Reads* them as tales, that is, not *studies* them as curios. Adults are allowed to collect and study anything, even old theatre programs or paper bags.

Among those who still have enough wisdom not to think fairy stories pernicious, the common opinion seems to be that there is a natural connection between the minds of children and fairy stories, of the same order as the connection between children's bodies and milk. I think this is an error; at best an error of false sentiment, and one that is therefore most often made by those who, for whatever private reason (such as childlessness), tend to think of children as a special kind of creature, almost a different race, rather than as normal, if immature, members of a particular family, and of the human family at large.

Actually, the association of children and fairy stories is an accident of our domestic history. Fairy stories have in the modern lettered world been relegated to the 'nursery', as shabby or old-fashioned furniture is relegated to the playroom, primarily because the adults do not want it, and do not mind if it is misused.[1] It is not the choice of the children which decides this. Children as a class—except in a common lack of experience they are not one—neither like fairy stories more, nor understand them better than adults do; and no more than they like many other things. They are young and growing, and normally have keen appetites, so the fairy stories as a rule go down well enough. But in fact only some children, and some adults, have any special taste for them; and when they have it, it is not exclusive, nor even necessarily dominant. It is a taste, too, that would not appear, I think, very early in childhood without artificial stimulus; it is certainly one that does not decrease but increases with age, if it is innate.

It is true that in recent times fairy stories have usually been written or 'adapted' for children. But so may music be, or verse, or novels, or history, or scientific manuals. It is a dangerous process, even when it is necessary. It is indeed only saved from disaster by the fact that the arts and sciences are not as a whole relegated to the nursery; the nursery and schoolroom are merely given such tastes and glimpses of the adult thing as seem fit for them in adult opinion (often much mistaken). Any one of these things would, if left altogether in the nursery, become gravely impaired. So would a beautiful table, a good picture, or a useful machine (such as a microscope), be defaced or broken,

---

[1] In the case of stories and other nursery lore, there is also another factor. Wealthier families employed women to look after their children, and the stories were provided by these nurses, who were sometimes in touch with rustic and traditional lore forgotten by their 'betters'. It is long since this source dried up, at any rate in England; but it once had some importance. But again there is no proof of the special fitness of children as the recipients of this vanishing 'folklore'. The nurses might just as well (or better) have been left to choose the pictures and furniture.

if it were left long unregarded in a schoolroom. Fairy stories banished in this way, cut off from a full adult art, would in the end be ruined; indeed in so far as they have been so banished, they have been ruined.

The value of fairy stories is thus not, in my opinion, to be found by considering children in particular. Collections of fairy stories are, in fact, by nature attics and lumber-rooms, only by temporary and local custom playrooms. Their contents are disordered, and often battered, a jumble of different dates, purposes, and tastes; but among them may occasionally be found a thing of permanent virtue: an old work of art, not too much damaged, that only stupidity would ever have stuffed away.

Andrew Lang's *Fairy Books* are not, perhaps, lumber-rooms. They are more like stalls in a rummage-sale. Someone with a duster and a fair eye for things that retain some value has been round the attics and boxrooms. His collections are largely a by-product of his adult study of mythology and folklore; but they were made into and presented as books for children.[2] Some of the reasons that Lang gave are worth considering.

The introduction to the first of the series speaks of 'children to whom and for whom they are told'. 'They represent,' he says, 'the young age of man true to his early loves, and have his unblunted edge of belief, a fresh appetite for marvels.' ' "Is it true?" ' he says, 'is the great question children ask'.

I suspect that *belief* and *appetite for marvels* are here regarded as identical or as closely related. They are radically different, though the appetite for marvels is not at once or at first differentiated by a growing human mind from its general appetite. It seems fairly clear that Lang was using *belief* in its ordinary sense: belief that a thing exists or can happen in the real (primary) world. If so, then I fear that Lang's words, stripped of sentiment, can only imply that the teller of marvellous tales to children must, or may, or at any rate does trade on their

---

2 By Lang and his helpers. It is not true of the majority of the contents in their original (or oldest surviving) forms.

credulity, on the lack of experience which makes it less easy for children to distinguish fact from fiction in particular cases, though the distinction in itself is fundamental to the sane human mind, and to fairy stories.

Children are capable, of course, of *literary belief,* when the story-maker's art is good enough to produce it. That state of mind has been called 'willing suspension of disbelief'. But this does not seem to me a good description of what happens. What really happens is that the story-maker proves a successful 'sub-creator'. He makes a Secondary World which your mind can enter. Inside it, what he relates is 'true': it accords with the laws of that world. You therefore believe it, while you are, as it were, inside. The moment disbelief arises, the spell is broken; the magic, or rather art, has failed. You are then out in the Primary World again, looking at the little abortive Secondary World from outside. If you are obliged, by kindliness or circumstance, to stay, then disbelief must be suspended (or stifled), otherwise listening and looking would become intolerable. But this suspension of disbelief is a substitute for the genuine thing, a subterfuge we use when condescending to games or make-believe, or when trying (more or less willingly) to find what virtue we can in the work of an art that has for us failed.

A real enthusiast for cricket is in the enchanted state: Secondary Belief. I, when I watch a match, am on the lower level. I can achieve (more or less) willing suspension of disbelief, when I am held there and supported by some other motive that will keep away boredom: for instance, a wild, heraldic, preference for dark blue rather than light. This suspension of disbelief may thus be a somewhat tired, shabby, or sentimental state of mind, and so lean to the 'adult'. I fancy it is often the state of adults in the presence of fairy story. They are held there and supported by sentiment (memories of childhood, or notions of what childhood ought to be like); they think they ought to like the tale. But if they really liked it, for itself, they would not have to suspend disbelief: they would believe—in this sense.

Now if Lang had meant anything like this there might have been some truth in his words. It may be argued that it is easier to work the spell with children. Perhaps it is, though I am not sure of this. The appearance that it is so is often, I think, an adult illusion produced by children's humility, their lack of critical experience and vocabulary, and their voracity (proper to their rapid growth). They like or try to like what is given to them: if they do not like it, they cannot well express their dislike or give reasons for it (and so may conceal it); and they like a great mass of different things indiscriminately, without troubling to analyse the planes of their belief. In any case I doubt if this portion—the enchantment of the effective fairy story—is really one of the kind that becomes 'blunted' by use, less potent after repeated draughts.

'"Is it true?' is the great question children ask,' Lang said. They do ask that question, I know; and it is not one to be rashly or idly answered.[3] But that question is hardly evidence of 'unblunted belief', or even of the desire for it. Most often it proceeds from the child's desire to know which kind of literature he is faced with. Children's knowledge of the world is often so small that they cannot judge, off-hand and without help, between the fantastic, the strange (that is rare or remote facts), the nonsensical, and the merely 'grownup' (that is ordinary things of their parents' world, much of which still remains unexplored). But they recognize the different classes, and may like all of them at times. Of course the borders between them are often fluctuating or confused; but that is not only true for children. We all know the differences in kind, but we are not always sure how to place anything that we hear. A child may well believe a report that there are ogres in the next county; many grown-up persons find it easy to believe of another country; and as

---

[3] Far more often they have asked me: 'Was he good? Was he wicked?' That is, they were more concerned to get the Right side and the Wrong side clear. For that is a question equally important in History and in Faerie.

for another planet, very few adults seem able to imagine it as peopled, if at all, by anything but monsters of iniquity.

Now I was one of the children whom Andrew Lang was addressing (I was born at about the same time as the *Green Fairy Book)*, the children for whom he seemed to think that fairy stories were the equivalent of the adult novel, and to whom he said: 'Their taste remains like the taste of their naked ancestors thousands of years ago; and they seem to like fairy-tales better than history, poetry, geography, or arithmetic.'[4] But do we really know much about these 'naked ancestors', except that they were certainly not naked? Our fairy stories, however old certain elements in them may be, are certainly not the same as theirs. Yet if it is assumed that we have fairy stories because they did, then probably we have history, geography, poetry, and arithmetic because they liked these things too, as far as they could get them, and in so far as they had yet separated the many branches of their general interest in everything.

And as for children of the present day, Lang's description does not fit my own memories, or my experience of children. Lang may have been mistaken about the children he knew, but if he was not, then at any rate children differ considerably, even within the narrow borders of Britain, and such generalizations which treat them as a class (disregarding their individual talents, and the influences of the countryside they live in, and their upbringing) are delusory. I had no special 'wish to believe'. I wanted to know. Belief depended on the way in which stories were presented to me, by older people, or by the authors, or on the inherent tone and quality of the tale. But at no time can I remember that the enjoyment of a story was dependent on belief that such things could happen, or had happened, in 'real life'. Fairy stories were plainly not primarily concerned with possibility, but with desirability. If they awakened *desire* satisfying it while often whetting it unbearably, they succeeded. It

---

[4] Preface to the *Violet Fairy Book.*

is not necessary to be more explicit here, for I hope to say something later about this desire, a complex of many ingredients, some universal, some particular to modern men (including modern children), or even to certain kinds of men. I had no desire to have either dreams or adventures like Alice, and the account of them merely amused me. I had very little desire to look for buried treasure or fight pirates, and *Treasure Island* left me cool. Red Indians were better: there were bows and arrows (I had and have a wholly unsatisfied desire to shoot well with a bow), and strange languages, and glimpses of an archaic mode of life, and, above all, forests in such stories. But the land of Merlin and Arthur was better than these, and best of all the nameless North of Sigurd of the Völsungs, and the prince of all dragons. Such lands were pre-eminently desirable. I never imagined that the dragon was of the same order as the horse. And that was not solely because I saw horses daily, but never even the footprint of a worm. The dragon had the trademark *Of Faërie* written plain upon him. In whatever world he had his being it was an Other-world. Fantasy, the making or glimpsing of Other-worlds, was the heart of the desire of Faërie. I desired dragons with a profound desire. Of course, I in my timid body did not wish to have them in the neighbourhood, intruding into my relatively safe world, in which it was, for instance, possible to read stories in peace of mind, free from fear.[5] But the world that contained even the imagination of Fáfnir was richer and more beautiful, at whatever cost of peril. The dweller in the quiet and fertile plains may hear of the tormented hills and the unharvested sea and long for them in his heart. For the heart is hard though the body be soft.

All the same, important as I now perceive the fairy story element in early reading to have been, speaking for myself as

---

[5] This is, naturally, often enough what children mean when they ask: 'Is is true?' They mean: 'I like this, but is it contemporary? Am I safe in my bed?' The answer: 'There is certainly no dragon in England today,' is all that they want to hear.

a child, I can only say that a liking for fairy stories was not a dominant characteristic of early taste. A real taste for them awoke after 'nursery' days, and after the years, few but long-seeming, between learning to read and going to school. In that (I nearly wrote 'happy' or 'golden', it was really a sad and troublous) time I liked many other things as well, or better: such as history, astronomy, botany, grammar, and etymology. I agreed with Lang's generalized 'children' not at all in principle, and only in some points by accident: I was, for instance, insensitive to poetry, and skipped it if it came in tales. Poetry I discovered much later in Latin and Greek, and especially through being made to try and translate English verse into classical verse. A real taste for fairy stories was wakened by philology on the threshold of manhood, and quickened to full life by war.

I have said, perhaps, more than enough on this point. At least it will be plain that in my opinion fairy stories should not be *specially* associated with children. They are associated with them: naturally, because children are human and fairy stories are a natural human taste (though not necessarily a universal one); accidentally, because fairy stories are a large part of the literary lumber that in latter-day Europe has been stuffed away in attics; unnaturally, because of erroneous sentiment about children, a sentiment that seems to increase with the decline in children.

It is true that the age of childhood-sentiment has produced some delightful books (especially charming, however, to adults) of the fairy kind or near to it; but it has also produced a dreadful undergrowth of stories written or adapted to what was or is conceived to be the measure of children's minds and needs. The old stories are mollified or bowdlerized, instead of being reserved; the imitations are often merely silly, Pigwiggenry without even the intrigue; or patronizing; or (deadliest of all) covertly sniggering, with an eye on the other grownups present. I will not accuse Andrew Lang of sniggering, but certainly he smiled to himself, and certainly too often he had an eye on the faces of other clever people over the heads of his child-audience —to the very grave detriment of the *Chronicles of Pantouflia.*

Dasent replied with vigour and justice to the prudish critics of his translations from Norse popular tales. Yet he committed the astonishing folly of particularly *forbidding* children to read the last two in his collection. That a man could study fairy stories and not learn better than that seems almost incredible. But neither criticism, rejoinder, nor prohibition would have been necessary if children had not unnecessarily been regarded as the inevitable readers of the book.

I do not deny that there is a truth in Andrew Lang's words (sentimental though they may sound): 'He who would enter into the Kingdom of Faërie should have the heart of a little child.' For that possession is necessary to all high adventure, into kingdoms both less and far greater than Faërie. But humility and innocence—these things 'the heart of a child' must mean in such a context—do not necessarily imply an uncritical wonder, nor indeed an uncritical tenderness. Chesterton once remarked that the children in whose company he saw Maeterlinck's *Blue Bird* were dissatisfied 'because it did not end with a Day of Judgement, and it was not revealed to the hero and the heroine that the Dog had been faithful and the Cat faithless.' 'For children,' he says, 'are innocent and love justice; while most of us are wicked and naturally prefer mercy.'

Andrew Lang was confused on this point. He was at pains to defend the slaying of the Yellow Dwarf by Prince Ricardo in one of his own fairy stories. 'I hate cruelty,' he said, '. . . but that was in fair fight, sword in hand, and the dwarf, peace to his ashes! died in harness.' Yet it is not clear that 'fair fight' is less cruel than 'fair judgement'; or that piercing a dwarf with a sword is more just than the execution of wicked kings and evil stepmothers—which Lang abjures: he sends the criminals (as he boasts) to retirement on ample pensions. That is mercy untempered by justice. It is true that this plea was not addressed to children but to parents and guardians, to whom Lang was recommending his own *Prince Prigio* and *Prince Ricardo* as suitable for their charges.[6] It is parents and guardians who have classified fairy stories as *Juvenilia*. And this is a small sample of the falsification of values that results.

If we use *child* in a good sense (it has also legitimately a bad one) we must not allow that to push us into the sentimentality of only using *adult* or *grownup* in a bad sense (it has also legitimately a good one). The process of growing older is not necessarily allied to growing wickeder, though the two do often happen together. Children are meant to grow up, and not to become Peter Pans. Not to lose innocence and wonder, but to proceed on the appointed journey: that journey upon which it is certainly not better to travel hopefully than to arrive, though we must travel hopefully if we are to arrive. But it is one of the lessons of fairy stories (if we can speak of the lessons of things that do not lecture) that on callow, lumpish, and selfish youth peril, sorrow, and the shadow of death can bestow dignity, and even sometimes wisdom.

Let us not divide the human race into Eloi and Morlocks: pretty children—'elves' as the eighteenth century often idiotically called them—with their fairy tales (carefully pruned), and dark Morlocks tending their machines. If fairy story as a kind is worth reading at all it is worthy to be written for and read by adults. They will, of course, put more in and get more out than children can. Then, as a branch of a genuine art, children may hope to get fairy stories fit for them to read and yet within their measure; as they may hope to get suitable introductions to poetry, history, and the sciences. Though it may be better for them to read some things, especially fairy stories, that are beyond their measure rather than short of it. Their books like their clothes should allow for growth, and their books at any rate should encourage it.

[1964]

---

[6] Preface to the *Lilac Fairy Book*.

The truth of fables

MICHAEL HORNYANSKY

Our own children are normal young citizens of the 1960s: addicted to television, well informed about Yogi Bear, Hercules, Robin Hood, Fireball XL-5, and so on. And yet, a cause for some surprise, they are also addicted to (even haunted by) the classic fairy stories. Why is this? Why should the old stories have such a grip, in this very different age? And why should their grip be so much stronger than the appeal of much else that has been written for children since, with our times clearly in mind—like *Tubby the Tuba, James the Red Train, Madeline,* even *Peter Pan?*

Don't imagine that our children's interest in the classics is narrow or exclusive. They read, or rather listen to, stories about machines, zoos, Saturday walks, dolls, magicians, children, and pets, without much apparent discrimination; and as I've suggested, they are avid consumers of the Hanna-Barbera products, even including such bilge as the Flintstones and the Jetsons. But the stories they want to hear last thing at night, and especially the stories they remember well enough to tell *us* (on the occasions when they decide to switch roles), are *Sleeping Beauty, Red Riding Hood, Cinderella, Snow White, Jack and the Beanstalk,* and that crowd: stories full of princes, princesses, giants, wicked witches, wolves, dwarfs, and other persons not normally encountered in modern life.

Why? The short answer, and the obvious one, is not that

such stories are 'imaginative, far from reality', and offer the child an escape into dreamland; but quite the contrary, that they do accurately reflect the child's picture of himself and his family. The father *is* king, mother *is* queen in this tiny world; and they ought to be wise, kind, and strong. The son, with light upon him from his parents' eyes, *is* a little prince; and our five-year-old daughter, for one, finds it quite natural to see herself as a princess–in fact she is prepared to look for her Prince Charming in England, because, as everyone knows, princes are scarce on this side of the water.

It is not only the royal scene that appeals to children for this reason, but also the basic situations or plots of the old-style folktale—for instance the pattern of the three princes or three princesses (it could be four, or two: but three is easier to remember, it is a magic number, with the feeling of a reliable sample), in which the two elder children miss the boat and the innocent simple-minded overlooked youngest child triumphs: what I call the Cinderella syndrome. What delight, what balm for the tiny downtrodden egotist! (And don't think I'm being scornful about egotism: it's the natural and normal place to start from.) Or take a more subtle example: *Beauty and the Beast* (or variations like 'The Frog Prince') which confirms a lesson that ought to have high priority among children: namely, you can't tell a book by its cover. *Beauty and the Beast* should be read early by every pretty girl, every girl who thinks she's pretty, and every unfortunate boy frog who knows he's a prince deep down. (Later, when you're mature enough, you can reverse the sexes in the story and watch Prince Charming learn that a hag may conceal a princess: Chaucer has already written this version in *The Wife of Bath's Tale,* which is recommended as adult entertainment.)

Stories like these are good moral propaganda. As people say, they 'teach children about life' through fables, in a way that *Tubby the Tuba* and *James the Red Train* do not, or do less successfully: because (oddly enough) these modern stories are more fantastic, farther from the child's view of life. After all, who is going to identify passionately with a tuba when he has the option of living as a prince?

But let's explore a bit further. Is this tight little kingdom (in which father is strong and just, mother kind and beautiful; the littlest prince or princess wins the day; and monsters or frogs turn into congenial mates)—is this a true picture of the world, even a child's world? We know it is not, even if we had to wait for Freud and company to tell us so. But some people have always known it—especially the tellers of stories, to men or children (as Freud was the first to admit: he recognized that most of the insights of the psychologist had been anticipated by the storyteller, the fabulist, the mythmaker). The child likewise soon learns that sometimes Daddy is not a good wise king but a fearsome giant whom the little prince or princess loves and hates at once (loves to the point of marriage, hates to the point of murder); that mother often seems cruel, tyrannical, a rival instead of a guide; and that the royal child is sometimes a forlorn waif lost in the dark wood, menaced by witches and monsters who go on being witches and monsters. We who have defeated or come to terms with these problems, at least in our waking lives, may need an effort to re-enter the child's real world, golden and pitch-dark by turns. We should recall the challenge of Al Capp, who puts it this way to the grownups: how would *you* like to be a pygmy in a world run by giants, without a dime to your name? It's a question worth pondering. Consider also that a genuine pygmy might be resolute and wholehearted even when terrified, but a child often believes, rightly or wrongly, that *he* is a monster, and deserves the dungeon.

The most haunting stories are the ones that recognize these facts and weave them into a reassuring pattern for the lost babe in the woods; the ones that accept the child's world directly, without bringing in grownup perspectives that the child doesn't know, and project it honestly, without any sentimental tidying up of the landscape. They do not distort the truth by filling the forest with cute, lovable little singing animals and motherly trees, in the manner of so many Disney cartoons; nor, at the other extreme, by filling the screen with fangs, glaring eyes, and other nightmares (as Disney used to do).

My way of putting the case is this: the fairy tales or folktales with real grip and staying power are genuine *myths* (and I trust you are grownup enough to know that myth is not an illusion or a lie: even children know better than that—it's a mistake made by foolish adults). A myth is a true story presented symbolically or indirectly instead of literally. At the moment I would distinguish two main forms of myth: one represents something that is true, but cannot or dare not be expressed directly (most of us dream this kind of myth, some time or other); the other represents something that is not always true in fact, but *ought* to be. Using these ideas as guides, I have been able to explain to myself the power of the old-time folktales, above all those of the brothers Grimm; and in a moment I'll show you what I've found.

But let me first put in a word for *some* modern myths (for it is not true, thank heaven, that we are past myth-making). Take the worlds of Hanna-Barbera, to which my children are so attached. Yakky Doodle's continuous story is a perfectly satisfactory myth: the little duck a perfect symbol (including his voice) for the lost orphan child, threatened at every turn by huge dangers (symbolized by one fox—with Jack Benny's voice; but that doesn't fool the kids, they know he's dangerous); and the bulldog Chopper a splendid *deus ex machina,* every child's dream of the all-powerful, kindly protector/good angel/fairy godmother, here in the comforting form of man's best friend. Or take Yogi Bear. Once you get past the adult jokes (like his name) aimed at the fourteen-year-old mind, you find another valid symbol for the child—this time a more robust child, with a timid younger brother to look after. To translate child into bear is of course comforting, because of the teddy-bear overtones;

but it is also psychologically right because it expresses the child's consciousness that he does not belong to the same species as grownups. However, the real secret of Yogi's appeal is first, his lust for food—which he must steal despite parental disapproval—and second his defiance, usually successful, of Daddy's authority—Daddy having dwindled to a rather silly park Ranger.

Now, back to the classics: the fairy tales which have lasted, and which will probably outlast Yogi Bear because they are good solid myths based in the child's own world and told directly, without archness or sentimentality or other adult nonsense. Let's start with *Snow White:* beautiful princess becomes rival of beautiful queen and is therefore ejected from family circle. This is one of those myths expressing a truth that dare not be faced directly—here, a clear case of mother-daughter rivalry (and presumably sexual rivalry, though it's presented as a straight beauty contest). The fact that the queen is called Snow White's stepmother shouldn't fool us for a moment. A child hesitates to accuse Mummy of being jealous enough to murder her, so Mummy turns into step-Mummy—which partly explains her behaviour, partly makes it okay for the child to hate *her*. The same device is useful to cover up one's normal hatred of brothers or sisters: Cinderella's sisters are so unkind that they can't be natural siblings.

What about Daddy, who ought to be the other corner of Snow White's triangle? Well, he's there, and kindly enough (we shall see this is the usual pattern: when mother is beastly father is sweet, and vice versa); but he's too much under Mummy's spell, or too busy at the office, to be very effective. Instead, the child is rescued by a father-substitute: first the woodsman or hunter who is too good-natured to obey the Queen and put Snow White to death; and afterwards the dwarfs. You may have read the other day of the latest anthropological theory about dwarfs. It's been discovered that dwarf legends all seem to originate from Roman settlements, because in the ruins of Roman towns the barbarians would find curious networks of underground passages and rooms far too small for normal folk to inhabit. Knowing nothing of Roman plumbing and heating systems, the barbarians invented the dwarf.

But that is an adult myth. To the child, the dwarf means something quite different. The seven little men who shelter Snow White are adults, but no bigger than children. She can look straight at them and see their faces instead of their knees. So Daddy has been cut down to manageable size, and split seven ways, which make him easier to love: in fact, on this basis you can set up housekeeping with him quite cosily and never have the neighbours gossip. Unfortunately, however, Daddy still cannot cope in the long run (he has to go off to work, hi ho). Mummy breaks through his defences with poisoned fruit, Snow White falls into a deathlike sleep, and the best that little daddy can do is to build her a pretty glass coffin. It remains for a passing prince to awaken her and take her away from all that. So she finally wins the beauty contest after all (you can't fool these magic mirrors). But notice that the ending is every bit as sound, psychologically speaking, as the beginning: the only real escape from the long sleep of childhood, hemmed in by a despotic mother, is to wake up into love and ride away with a prince who prefers *you* for his queen.

Hansel and Gretel has the same kind of theme, though more strongly stated—so strongly indeed that our own children would rather not hear this one, which nevertheless has a real grip on their memories. Or perhaps they shy away from it because they perceive that *their* mother, even at her worst, isn't as bad as this?

At any rate, this time we have two children in the same boat. Their nasty mother, again disguised as a stepmother, wants to get rid of them so she can have Daddy all to herself (though the line she hands out is that there isn't enough food to go round). Poor besotted Dad actually does the ejecting by losing his children in the forest. But Hansel is a bright lad, as every elder brother ought to be; thanks to his ingenuity with pebbles, they find their way back the first time. It's really not his fault that the breadcrumb system breaks down—children can't cope with everything.

So what we have here is not mother-daughter rivalry as in *Snow White,* but a straight battle between the pygmies and the giants: or rather, between the pygmies and the female giant—for mother hasn't finished with them yet. Deep in the forest they come upon a gingerbread house, presided over by an old woman who pops them into cages for fattening and proposes later to treat them as pot roast. She is a witch, so the story goes: but don't be deceived. She is really mother again, one stage further removed so that we can make some really serious charges against her. I ask you—can you imagine a better mother-symbol than a witch who offers you gingerbread with one hand and pens you in a cage with the other? And being devoured by her is a direct symbol straight from the dreaming mind—so direct that civilized people may miss it entirely. But children are not yet civilized, and express things as truthfully as their fears will let them. The witch who eats children is their version of smother-love, the overpowering meddling that prevents them from having lives of their own. And that oven really drives the point home. As every housewife knows in this day of cake-mix commercials, the oven is a natural symbol for the womb: which every normal child wants to get out of. So *Hansel and Gretel* turns out to be the children's version of *The Silver Cord*—and it adds a neat ending. The only way to deal with such a mother is to shove her into her own oven (rough justice, I grant you; but that's life). And sure enough, when the children have eliminated the witch and found their way home, they learn that by a curious coincidence the stepmother has 'gone away'—and they have dear old Dad all to themselves, happily ever after.

Daddy gets his lumps in that marvellous myth, *Jack and the Beanstalk.* Here the focus is on a solitary boy who lives alone with his mother. Daddy is not in evidence; dead, they say—but don't you believe it, he won't be dead until Jack makes sure of him. So far, it's mere wish-fulfilment.

We need not linger over Jack's misadventures at the marke except to note that they run parallel to the Cinderella patte the underrated child who turns out to know better or be be than his parents: for the wretched beans that Jack brings hom to his mother's chagrin, are of course magic beans, worth far more than the cow he began with. Their value is that they pr vide Jack with a magic entry to the adult world. By climbin up the overnight beanstalk, Jack reaches a level where he can challenge his giant-father face to face. Of course the father must still be represented as a giant, for this is a terribly naughty thing to dream of. No wonder father roars 'Fee fie fo fun, I smell the blood of my no-good son': for the true refrain, that dare not be expressed, is 'Fee fie fo fun, Here's Jack who wants to marry Mum.'

But there is never any real doubt that Jack will win, despit the difference in size. And you'll recall that Jack's mother turns up in disguise as the giant's wife; who is significantly friendly towards the boy but terrified of her husband (a dead giveaway: now Jack can save *her* from that monster too). Technically speaking she ought to be a giant as well, but it's never mentioned, and doesn't seem to matter. Jack not only wins, he makes a grand slam. First he plunders the giant of his treasures in a series of daring raids. This is a clear example of sympathetic magic: steal your enemy's valuables and you steal his power. (I dare say one could even spell out what the various treasures stand for—but let's take the high road.) Then he chops the beanstalk so that the great lumbering idiot comes a cropper, right there in the good old marketplace. (That'll show you, Dad. Who says I'm not a businessman?) And finally Jack winds up with his dreams of glory come true: manhood, money, and mother, all to himself.

I must add a footnote. Not long ago my daughter, who was listening to one of those kindly TV uncles tell the story of Jack and his beanstalk, came pelting into the kitchen with the news that the treasures belonged to Jack's father. I was astonished. Had he gone straight to the heart of the story without any help? I ied to the television to see who was spilling the beans. But at had happened was odder still: the TV storyteller had a eaned-up moral version of the story, in which the giant had orginally stolen the harp and treasure from Jack's 'real' father, ng before—so that in taking them back again Jack was no thief at all, but a hero of justice and property. Not very plausible, of course: why did that talking harp complain at being stolen if the giant wasn't its real owner? But it's a pretty piece of irony. As you see, in trying to tidy up the morality of the story, the bowdlerizers had unexpectedly confirmed its real moral.

Another footnote: our son Mark, who is not yet four (and who has already changed from frog to prince before our very eyes), chose to tell me this story one evening when I came to say goodnight. He got it a bit muddled, of course, but the main lines were unmistakable—until the very end, when the giant, having crashed to the ground, sat up, rubbed his hurt place, and said 'Ouch.' Then he gave Jack a chocolate bar and they lived happily ever after—because he was a friendly giant. No, I am not bragging about what a fine relationship I have with my son, or what clever things he says, or what a kindly dad I am (I do not hand out chocolate bars). I offer this simply as evidence that my son knew perfectly well what the story was about, and preferred not to hurt my feelings.

Exhibit four is *Rumpelstiltzkin:* a very different proposition indeed, and perhaps in its own way the most haunting of all (for good reasons). Who can forget the funny little man with the funny long name who spins gold for the miller's daughter and would have carried off her first-born had she not guessed his funny name? Yet he is a good deal less comfortable than the dwarfs we met in *Snow White;* and the rest of the characters are likewise a far cry from the hero-children, stepmothers, witches, and giants we've been dealing with. This time we are in an adult world—mythically treated, to be sure, but still significantly different in tone. In this world Daddy is a social-climbing miller who uses his daughter to curry favour with the local king. The king is moved purely by avarice; he will marry the girl simply to get legal title to her spun gold. No one so far has shown the least concern for her feelings—and the absence of concern is much more disturbing than hatred, for hatred is close kin to love, while callous indifference can never change. Even the funny little man who shows up to help her deliver the gold has his own axe to grind: his end of the bargain is her first child. And when he later returns to claim his rights, he is cheated—even though he has shown the only gleam of human decency in the tale, by modifying the bargain with his special name-guessing clause. Our natural sympathies lie with the young mother, but this should not disguise the fact that the dwarf has had a raw deal.

The prevailing moral climate in the story, then, is shabby—or at best ambiguous. Why is this so? One reason, already suggested, is that we have here a candid picture of the adult world, with all its shades of grey and double-dealing. But this doesn't go far enough: it doesn't account for Rumpelstiltzkin himself, who is an intruder in this everyday world, nor for the fact that we feel relieved and glad when he is defeated, despite the injustice of it. Who is this 'passionate deformed little creature' with the secret name? Consider the evidence: he pops up in a locked chamber and performs super-human tricks; in exchange he requires the dearest thing the young woman will ever own; he is accidentally overheard on a remote mountain-side, crowing over his victory and chanting his name around a campfire; and when he is beaten, he stamps his foot in rage so hard that he goes through the floor and straight on down. Where to? Why, home: where he came from. There are only two beings in the universe who have secret names, unknown to all but the adept: one of them is God, whose holy Name must not be spoken; the other, over whom mortal man may gain power by pronouncing his mysterious proper name, is the Devil. This explains why the funny little man isn't really funny, and why he is given a comic name that remains rather ominous: in German, *Rumpelstiltzchen* would appear to mean something like 'little roaring creature with strange legs'—and that is only amusing as long as you don't meet him. We can also see why we felt relieved at his defeat, however unjust: when you do business with the Devil, you have no time to worry about fair play. The story of Rumpelstiltzkin, then, is *Doctor Faustus* with a happy ending—or at least a satisfactory one.

Shall we draw general lessons in conclusion? Shall we say, for instance, that these classic fairy tales for children are in fact not children's stories at all but folktales from the half-conscious wisdom of the race, expressing in mythic form certain enduring human truths? We might say that. But we should add that this does not by any means make them unsuitable for children: far from it. And we should see once and for all the foolishness of any attempt to tamper with such tales, to pretty them up so as not to shock tender minds. I myself should prefer to take them, unaltered, as a guide to bringing up children sensibly: as examples of What Every Child Should Know, and as lessons presented in so cunning a fashion that a child can accept them before he fully understands.

If some of you should think that I've gone off the deep end, or trampled over precious flowers with my clumsy Freudian boots, I am not much worried: the evidence speaks for itself and will soon bring you round. If it doesn't, read Dr Spock. What does worry me a little is the thought that others among you will wonder why it took me so long to catch on. All I can reply is that the same uneasy thought kept occurring to me as I wrote all this down. It was all my own work, but hadn't somebody done it all before? I began to suspect that those cunning scholars, the brothers Grimm, were not at all the simpletons represented in the film, but knew exactly what they were collecting (how else could they hit the bull's-eye so often?), and that if I knew where to look, I should find that they h not only anticipated my every step, but soared far beyond m most daring guesses. Well, I have a friendly librarian working on this suspicion; and I can hardly wait to find out.

[1965]

Wells of fancy, 1865-1965

DONNARAE MacCANN

And ever, as the story drained
The wells of fancy dry,
And faintly strove that weary one
To put the subject by,
'The rest next time—' 'It is next time!'
The happy voices cry.

Thus grew the tale of Wonderland,' Lewis Carroll continues, the tale for which happy voices still cry. During this centennial year of its publication, it is especially timely to note children's enduring enthusiasm for *Alice's Adventures in Wonderland.* Besides being a source of play and refreshment for children and a pastime for scholars, *Alice* set a precedent in children's books. The influence of such imaginative and irreverent storytelling opened the way for the development of the fantastic genre in children's literature. Before 1865, children were hardpressed in their search for imaginative stories. They might borrow Swift's *Gulliver's Travels* or Bunyan's *The Pilgrim's Progress* from their parent's library, and some were blessed with a nurse who was familiar with folktales and could tell stories. But even so skilled a writer as Charles Kingsley to produce a superior fantasy. *The Water-Babies,* published in 1863, contains many essential elements, but as Herbert Read points out, 'it has a subjective, or moralizing, intent, and this not only destroys its rhetorical purity but in so doing destroys its rhetorical effect.'[1] This failing was typical of children's books throughout their early history.

Fantasies improved notably after the publication of *Alice*, as seen in the works of George MacDonald, Rudyard Kipling, and Edith Nesbit. By 1920 one of the outstanding contributions to this literature had appeared: Hugh Lofting's *The Story of Doctor Dolittle*. In Hugh Walpole's opinion, this was the first children's classic after *Alice;* but he has overlooked the Italian classic, *Pinocchio*, which became available in English in 1892.

Despite the increasing distinction of fantasies, they have met with a cool reception from certain segments of the public. The genre makes a special demand upon the reader, an adjustment which is easy for children but difficult for some adults. E. M. Forster discusses this special requirement imposed by the fantasist.

> *. . . other novelists say 'Here is something that might occur in your lives,' the fantasist says 'Here's something that could not occur. I must ask you to accept my book as a whole, and secondly to accept certain things in my book.' Many readers can grant the first request, but refuse the second. 'One knows a book isn't real,' they say, still one does expect it to be natural, and this angel or midget or ghost . . .—no, it is too much.'*[2]

For such a reader, there can be no communication and no appreciation of what a fantasist has achieved. Children, on the other hand, are at the height of their imaginative powers during the mid-elementary school years and often utilize supernatural characters in their play. It is not difficult for them to accept highly imaginative and unusual elements in a story. Furthermore, the fantasy's improvisations on reality are not a source of

---

[1] Herbert Read, *English Prose Style* (London: G. Bell and Sons, Ltd, 1937), p. 144.

[2] E. M. Forster, *Aspects of the Novel* (New York: Harcourt, 1954), p. 159.

confusion. By the time a child has reached the age of seven or eight, he has gained sufficient mastery of the real world, and sufficient mastery of his native tongue in particular, to enjoy the playful manipulations that literary fantasies provide.

Some adults distrust fantasies as being somehow 'unhealthy'. They raise the question, 'Won't these dwarfs and talking beasts encourage unwholesome fantasizing on the part of children or make them withdraw from the real world?' These fears result from a confusion of terms: confusion of the word fantasy when it refers to a *literary form* with fantasy as a *psychological illness.*

Fantasy, when used in the literary sense, has to do with the conception and construction of a story, its subject matter and treatment. The supernatural subject matter in the fantasy makes it an unlikely prompter of unhealthy daydreams. As C. S. Lewis has remarked:

The dangerous fantasy is always superficially realistic. The real victim of wishful reverie does not batten on The Odyssey, The Tempest, *or* The Worm Ouroboros: *he (or she) prefers stories about millionaires, irresistible beauties, posh hotels . . . things that really might happen. . . . For, as I say, there are two kinds of longing. The one is an* askesis, *a spiritual exercise, and the other is a disease.*[3]

One of the most characteristic features of fantasies for children is their sense of play. Although a feeling of mystery and foreboding can be the predominant mood (as in *The Jungle Book* or *The Children of Green Knowe),* more often the tone is one of playfulness. Even when the symbolic level of the story deals with social ills or philosophic questions, the writer's humour will pervade the book. His sharpest quips will be balanced by his benign attitude when addressing the young.

---

[3] C. S. Lewis, 'On Three Ways of Writing for Children', *The Horn Book Magazine,* October 1963, p. 466.

In *Alice's Adventures in Wonderland,* the sense of play emerges primarily as word play. Alice is forever talking to herself as well as to flowers, insects, mythical beasts, and the like; and this perpetual dialogue is the means for frequent puns and verbal jokes.

'And how many hours a day did you do lessons?' said Alice, in a hurry to change the subject.

'Ten hours the first day,' said the Mock Turtle: 'nine the next, and so on.'

'What a curious plan!' exclaimed Alice.

'That's the reason they're called lessons,' the Gryphon remarked: 'because they lessen from day to day.'

By the time the reader finishes *Through the Looking-Glass,* the sequel to *Alice's Adventures in Wonderland,* he has gained considerable mastery of this game. When Alice asks, ' "Where's the servant whose business it is to answer the door?" ' many children can predict the reply, ' "To answer the door? . . . What did it ask you?" '

The Phantom Tollbooth, published nearly a century later, is the most outstanding example of word play since the two *Alice* books. Its countless verbal jokes do not imitate the word play of those volumes, but there is the same remarkable ingenuity and wit. The plot itself is greatly involved with language and communication. There is a kingdom of Dictionopolis, ruled over by King Azaz the Unabridged; and at a royal banquet, the young hero, Milo, discovers that everyone must eat his own words and that's all one will get. Thus the guests, in their speeches, are careful to say 'hamburgers, corn on the cob, chocolate pudding' or 'frankfurters, sour pickles, strawberry jam' or, in the case of the king, 'soupe á l'oignon, faisan sous cloche, salade endive, fromages et fruits et demi-tasse'. Discussing the evening's entertainment, King Azaz tells Milo of all the clever tricks his cabinet members can perform:

'The duke here can make mountains out of molehills. The

minister splits hairs. The count makes hay while the sun shines. The earl leaves no stone unturned. And the under-secretary,' he finished ominously, 'hangs by a thread.'

In Roald Dahl's *Charlie and the Chocolate Factory*, there are surprising moments of word play, in addition to the nonsensical catalogues of factory supplies:

They passed a yellow door on which it said: STOREROOM NUMBER 77—ALL THE BEANS, CACAO BEANS, COFFEE BEANS, JELLY BEANS, AND HAS BEANS.

'Has beans?' cried Violet Beauregarde.

'You're one yourself!' said Mr Wonka.

Fanciful inventions have a playful aspect too, and invention is the major function of the chocolate factory, which manufactures such new gastronomic delights as 'eatable marshmallow pillows', 'lickable wallpaper for nurseries', 'strawberry-juice water pistols', 'exploding candy for your enemies', 'luminous lollies for eating in bed at night', and so on.

Mechanical inventions are the principal charm of William Pène Du Bois's fantasies. In *The Twenty-One Balloons*, a family changes the bed sheets by winding a crank which moves the sheets across the bed, across rollers, through a sideboard, and down through the floor to the cellar.

There, they pass through a boiler where they are washed, then through a drying machine. They next pass through steam-heated rollers where they are pressed; then come up through the floor, through the other sideboard of the bed on rollers, and back to the top of the bed.

When the writer himself makes a game of his storytelling, the child is apt to return to the fantasy again and again. And this is one of the most observable of the child's reactions to fantasies: he rereads them, apparently repeating his enjoyment of the game.

We readily associate play with children, but it is by no means their sole preoccupation. Inquisitiveness is perhaps an even more dominant trait in the elementary school child. On the one hand he is fascinated by the outward circumstances of experience, by action in and of itself. But it would be an oversimplification to assume that overt action in a story constitutes the limits of a child's literary enjoyment. His sympathy and curiosity are roused by all kinds of dramatic conflicts, not merely by physical feats.

Fantasies provide an ideal opportunity for observing the child's interest in inward aspects of life, in particular his fascination with the human personality. Because of its metaphorical possibilities, a fantasy is an opportune means for comment upon human nature; and for this reason, it is often more enlightening than the so-called 'realistic' forms of fiction offered to children. In many family stories, for example, characters are so idealized and incidents so contrived as to tax the gullibility of any intelligent reader. The fantasist's characters represent every conceivable human type, not just the loving family circle.

Child characters in a fantasy are often defined in quick strokes, yet with enough naturalness and distinctiveness to sustain credibility. In Edward Eager's fantasies, like *Half Magic* for example, children are endowed with the kind of contrasting personalities which invite kinship.

Jane was the oldest and Mark was the only boy, and between them they ran everything.

Katharine was the middle girl, of docile disposition and a comfort to her mother. She knew she was a comfort, and docile, because she'd heard her mother say so. And the others knew she was, too, by now, because ever since that day Katharine would *keep boasting about what a comfort she was, and how docile, until Jane declared she would utter a piercing shriek and fall over dead if she heard another word about it. . . .*

Martha was the youngest, and very difficult.

But the writer is usually most interested in the fantastic characters, and he uses them to create that wide diversity which one actually encounters in human experience. The gluttonous, self-seeking, self-pitying rat, Templeton, in *Charlotte's Web*, provides the story with a lifelike contrast in its cast of characters. Templeton is completely disreputable. After a characteristic night of self-indulgence:

Slowly Templeton dragged himself across the pen and threw himself down in a corner. . . .

'What a night!' he repeated, hoarsely. 'What feasting and carousing! A real gorge! Never have I seen such leavings, and everything well-ripened and seasoned with the passage of time and the heat of the day. Oh, it was rich, my friends, rich!'

The total effect of Templeton's charactization is comic relief, and his role in the plot is to help produce circumstances for a satisfying ending. Yet his nature never deviates from that of a scoundrel.

In *The Dolls' House*, the celluloid doll, Birdie, brings a tragic dimension to the tale. She is gay and kind-hearted, but her mind is forever distracted by pretty sounds or objects.

Now, as she stood at the sitting-room door, the tinkling of the musical box delighted her so much that it tinkled in her head and she could no longer remember what anyone had said.

When a fire threatens the doll family baby, Birdie's maternal instinct overrides 'the tinkling in her head' and she saves the child; but she is too simple-minded to know how to preserve her own life as well. Gradually, and sympathetically, Birdie's limited mentality is revealed and she becomes the most memorable character in the book. Tottie, 'with eyes . . . painted with bright firm paint, blue and very determined', is perhaps the most attractive. Marchpane is the beautiful but malevolent doll who causes Birdie's accident, and her villainy is never glossed over. Critics sometimes have a problem with such a character;

they fear that the child may imitate the wrongdoer. Such critics ignore or distrust the power of the writer, for an author who has produced strong characters is certainly capable of directing the sympathy of the reader toward one or another. Moreover, Forster's thesis applies to children's as well as adult books:

. . . novels, even when they are about wicked people, can solace us; they suggest a more comprehensible and thus a more manageable human race, they give us the illusion of perspicacity and of power.

In a novel, Forster continues, 'we can know people perfectly, and . . . find . . . a compensation for their dimness in life.'[4]

The most delightful of all pessimists, Eeyore the donkey in *Winnie-the-Pooh,* is well-known.

Sometimes he thought sadly to himself, 'Why?' and sometimes he thought, 'Wherefore?' and sometimes he thought, 'Inasmuch as which?'—and sometimes he didn't quite know what he was *thinking about.*

Ratty, in *The Wind in the Willows,* is the very embodiment of friendship. He never misses even the slightest opportunity to bolster the ego of his friend, the embarrassed, self-effacing Mole. When Ratty and Mole suddenly come upon Mole's long-neglected dwelling place, Mole is horrified that Ratty should see its shabbiness. Ratty, however, pays no attention.

'What a capital little house this is!' . . . So compact! So well planned! Everything here and everything in its place! We'll make a jolly night of it. . . . '

'No bread!' groaned the Mole dolorously; 'no butter, no—'

'No pâté de foie gras, *no champagne!' continued the Rat, grinning . . . 'what's that little door at the end of the passage? Your cellar, of course! Every luxury in this house!'*

---

[4] Forster, *op. cit.,* pp. 98-99.

Characterization and the interplay of personality are hallmarks of almost any well-written fantasy. Social comment is characteristic of some. Authors can make observations about society without indulging in direct preaching, and many writers have undoubtedly chosen the fantasy form for just this reason. Whatever his interest in philosophy, society, or the human condition, the writer finds a poetic device in fantasy for its expression. Antoine de Saint-Exupéry (author of *The Little Prince)* and Maurice Druon (author of *Tistou of the Green Thumbs)* are prominent examples; they are French fantasists with many similarities in their work, but each has a unique vision and voice.

Encounters by both the Little Prince and Tistou point to man's habit of rationalization and circular reasoning. The Little Prince meets a drunkard on one of his visits to a neighboring asteroid:

'What are you doing there?' he said to the tippler, whom he found settled down in silence before a collection of empty bottles and also a collection of full bottles.

'I am drinking,' replied the tippler, with a lugubrious air.

'Why are you drinking?' demanded the little prince.

'So that I may forget,' replied the tippler.

'Forget what?' inquired the little prince, who already was sorry for him.

'Forget that I am ashamed,' the tippler confessed, hanging his head.

'Ashamed of what?' insisted the little prince, who wanted to help him.

'Ashamed of drinking!'

The businessman on another asteriod seems just as foolish when he explains that he owns the stars in order to be rich, and the good of being rich is to be able to buy more stars, if any are discovered.

In *Tistou,* the hero questions his geography tutor about the nations of the Go-its and the Get-outs. A war is about to break out over an adjoining border country where there is oil:

> *'What do they want oil for?'*
>
> *'They want it so that the other can't have it. They want oil, because oil's an essential material for making war.'*
>
> *Tistou had known that Mr Turnbull's explanations would become very difficult to understand.*
>
> *He shut his eyes in order to think better.*
>
> *'If I've understood properly, the Go-its and the Get-outs are going to fight a war for oil because oil is essential material for fighting wars.' He opened his eyes.*
>
> *'Well, its stupid,' he said.*

Tistou is even more dismayed when he finds out that his father's munitions factory will supply guns to both sides: to the Go-its because they are friends, and to the Get-outs because 'that's business.'

Tistou of the Green Thumbs, although pointed in its criticism, deals primarily with the way the hero alleviates human suffering through the use of his magical thumbs. With a mere touch, Tistou can cause flowers and other plants to spring up overnight; he takes this strange power into the prison, the hospital, the homes of the poor, and finally, on to the battlefield.

> *That a modest wild flower should be able to create a panic among soldiers is perfectly comprehensible if you know that balsam has pods which explode at the slightest touch.*
>
> *The engines were all full of it. Balsam swarmed in the carburetors of the armored cars, in the tanks of the motorcycles. At first contact of the selfstarter. . . . there was a growing, spreading sound of dull explosions which, if they did no harm, nevertheless had a shattering effect on the morale of the troops. . . .*
>
> *A rain of foxgloves, bluebells and cornflowers had fallen on*

the Go-its' positions and they had replied, flooding the Get-outs with buttercups, daisies and roses.

Various professions are treated humorously or satirically in fantasies, and in such general terms as to be easily comprehended. James Thurber makes good-natural fun of the medical profession in *The White Deer.*

The Royal Physician was taking his temperature, but he shook the mercury down without looking at it.

'As a physician, I must take my temperature every three hours,' he said, 'but as a patient, I must not be told what it is' . . .

'I do not believe I can cure myself,' said the sick man. 'Now, now,' he retorted to himself, 'we mustn't lose faith in the skill of our physician, must we?'

The Phantom Tollbooth's commentary is devastatingly pertinent to twentieth-century urban living. It treats in symbolic terms the problems of excessive specialization, lack of communication, conformity, mercenary values, and other maladies highly characteristic of our time. The story revolves around the rescue of Rhyme and Reason (two banished princesses) and the many villains trying to prevent it, e.g., the Terrible Trivium, a demon of petty tasks and wasted effort, and the Senses Taker whose business it is to 'steal your sense of purpose, take your sense of duty, destroy your sense of proportion.'

'Now if you'll just tell me when you were born, where you were born, why you were born, how old you are now, how old you were then, how old you'll be in a little while . . . where you live, how long you've lived there, the schools you've attended, the schools you haven't attended. . . .'

The Senses Taker's queries fill nearly a page, but the hero can render him helpless as long as he keeps his sense of humour.

Whatever the specific area of commentary, it is the author's qualifications as craftsman, as well as philosopher, which give his work that sense of mastery which pleases and convinces children. The only notable difference in an author's stylistic treatment when he writes for the child audience is the overall tone of gaiety or sympathetic understanding pervading the story. The same writer, perhaps, may allow some bitterness to colour his communications with his peers.

If the illumination shed on social conditions is one pleasurable facet of reading, the uniqueness and totality of a fantastic conception is another. Seeing a newly created 'secondary world' is, in itself, an awesome experience. But the boundaries must be clear. In his essay, 'On Fairy Stories', J. R. R. Tolkien writes that the imaginary storyteller

> *. . . makes a Secondary World which your mind can enter. Inside it, what he relates is 'true' : it accords with the laws of that world. You therefore believe it, while you are, as it were, inside. The moment disbelief arises, the spell is broken; the magic, or rather art, has failed. You are then out in the Primary World again . . .*[5]

Without laws or boundaries the tale is both confusing and inconsequential, for 'the mind can do nothing with infinity, that most unmanageable commodity.'[6] The reader loses his sense of control. Some 'secondary worlds' which are compelling in the fullness and completeness of their conception include: the Land of Narnia in C. S. Lewis's *The Lion, the Witch and Wardrobe;* the Land Between the Mountains in *The Gammage Cup* ('It was quite untrue that the Minnipins . . . were a lost people, for *they* knew exactly where they were'); the elegant, but strangely twisted world of the Countess and the General in

---

[5] J. R. R. Tolkien, 'On Fairy Stories' in *Tree and Leaf* (Boston: Houghton Mifflin), 1965, p. 37.

[6] Elizabeth Sewell, *The Field of Nonsense* (London: Chatto and Windus, 1952), p. 5.

Loretta Mason Potts; the miniature, nautical world of the toy soldiers in *The Return of the Twelves;* and the island refuge of the few remaining Lilliputians in T. H. White's *Mistress Masham's Repose.*

Within the boundaries of the newly created world, a mass of corroborating detail is needed if the author hopes to inspire undeviating belief. Whether the story is about a 'hobbit' or a 'Borrower', the reader finds all sorts of data about the habits and history of their race, their domestic economy, their personality traits, etc.

The 'Borrowers' (in the book of this title) are a 'little people' race, and preventing them from becoming extinct becomes not only an adventure, but something of a game. The question is: how many real-world objects can the author utilize in a Borrowers' economy? These little people can 'borrow' and put to use only what they can carry away in their diminutive hands. In the first of four books, they have managed to tastefully decorate a tiny apartment.

> *. . . the walls had been papered with scraps of old letters out of waste-paper baskets, and Homily had arranged the handwriting sideways in vertical stripes which ran from floor to ceiling. On the walls, repeated in various colours, hung several portraits of Queen Victoria as a girl; these were postage stamps, borrowed by Pod some years ago from the stamp box on the desk in the morning room. . . . There was a round table with a red velvet cloth, which Pod had made from the wooden bottom of a pill box supported on the carved pedestal of a knight from the chess set. . . . The knight itself—its bust, so to speak—stood on a column in the corner, where it looked very fine, and lent that air to the room which only statuary can give.*

The discipline of working out a fantastic conception in all its vastness and detail has a bearing upon the author's style. When he conceives a story with such minute particularity as that required in a fantasy, he usually expresses it not only with clarity and euphony, but with a quality of voice which is as uniquely his own as the conception itself. His story is then a novel experience, irreplaceable by any other experience, any more than one individual is replaceable by another. This is the essence of style, and a distinguishing mark of many fantasies.

The child audience is the ideal audience to respond to this most subtle of literary gifts. Although the child doesn't know what has captured him, every line he reads or hears reveals the author's power and imaginative and expressive talent. The loyalties children exhibit toward certain authors indicate their sensitivity to the power and consistency of an individual style. There is clearly a pleasure in *how* things are written as well as *what*—a response to the writer's mode of thinking. Children refer to certain authors by name and know them as distinctive voices as well as creators of unique things. They request the C. S. Lewis books, the Edward Eager books, the Nesbit books. If the story is remembered for one dominant and striking character, the child asks for Mary Poppins, Doctor Dolittle, Pippi Longstocking, Freddy, etc. These are characters so thoroughly realized they appear to have voices of their own. Moreover, they are such entertaining company children want the relationship to continue, and they persistently inquire about sequels.

But the best indicator of responsiveness to style is when the child remains unmoved by what he hears about a book's characters or incidents until the librarian says, 'Here, sit down and read two pages.' He does, and all doubt dissolves. He becomes so absorbed that he is still trying to read as he checks the book out and feels his way toward the door. From the first few lines of the story such a reader knows immediately that this tale will keep him vitally attentive and will continuously make demands upon his curiosity, intelligence, sympathy, or sense of humour. Many fantasies could be cited which fulfill this promise.

There was once a boy named Milo who didn't know what to do with himself—not just sometimes, but always.

When he was in school he longed to be out, and when he was out he longed to be in. On the way he thought about coming home, and coming home he thought about going. Wherever he was he wished he were somewhere else, and when he got there he wondered why he'd bothered. Nothing really interested him—least of all things that should have. . . .

'And worst of all,' he continued sadly, 'there's nothing for me to do, nowhere I'd care to go, and hardly anything worth seeing.' He punctuated this last thought with such a deep sigh that a house sparrow singing nearby stopped and rushed home to be with his family. (The Phantom Tollbooth)

Maria was ten years old. She had dark hair in two pigtails, and brown eyes the colour of marmite, but more shiny. She wore spectacles for the time being, though she would not have to wear them always, and her nature was a loving one. She was one of those tough and friendly people who do things first and think about them afterward. When she met cows, however, she did not like to be alone with them, and there were other dangers, such as her governess, from which she would have liked to have had a protector. (Mistress Masham's Repose)

In a hole in the ground there lived a hobbit. Not a nasty, dirty, wet hole, filled with the ends of worms and an oozy smell, nor yet a dry, bare, sandy hole with nothing in it to sit down on or to eat: it was a hobbit-hole, and that means comfort. (The Hobbit)

If you should walk and wind and wander far enough on one of those afternoons in April when smoke goes down instead of up, and nearby things sound far away and far things near, you are more than likely to come at last to the enchanted forest that lies between the Moonstone Mines and Centaurs Mountain. You'll know the woods when you are still a long way off by virtue of a fragrance you can never quite forget and never quite remember. And there'll be a distant bell that causes boys to run and laugh and girls to stand and tremble. If you pluck one of the ten thousand toadstools that grow in the emerald grass at the edge of the wonderful woods, it will feel as heavy as a hammer in your hand, but if you let it go it will sail away over the trees like a tiny parachute, trailing . . . purple stars. (The White Deer)

Are these 'special' books to be limited to 'special' children? Fantasies, because they are of necessity unique, have too often been viewed as books for a 'special' reader only, for a child considered gifted in some vague way. *Tistou of the Green Thumbs* and *The Phantom Tollbooth* received this treatment, as have many others.

But what special demands does a fantasy make upon readers? Only that they be willing to encounter the supernatural and to receive the book as a whole. Certainly the playfulness of many fantasies, the conception of something new and completely self-contained, the distinctive voice, these are pleasures to offer to all children, not just to the few. As for the social commentary, this too is usually comprehended by a wide range of readers.

In the so-called 'disadvantaged' areas especially, educators underestimate what a child can read. They claim that the children lack background, that they scarcely know the difference between a camel and a cow. Fantasies, however, do not deal with the difference between a camel and a cow! They comment upon the most universal aspects of human nature, drawing attention to things with which everyone is familiar. What child has not seen, as Tistou did in one of his lessons, how newspapers sometimes exaggerate an incident by using an oversized headline? What child has not encountered a drunkard, a self-seeking businessman, or a character like good-hearted, light-headed Birdie? Perhaps he hasn't thought about these things consciously, but there is nothing here so very foreign. He reads and he has the satisfying, lightning-quick impression: 'Yes, I've seen this happen, I've seen people like that.'

Well-written fantasies have special advantages, but little in the way of special obstacles. Besides their wit and perspicacity, they are usually marked by a felicity of style which puts them within reach of many readers, not just a gifted minority.

In an age of dreary sameness in the mass media, it is indeed cause for celebration that the 'wells of fancy' have sprung up so plentifully during the last century.

[1965]

A child's garden of bewilderment

MARTIN GARDNER

It was just a century ago this month that Macmillan in London published its first edition—two thousand copies—of *Alice's Adventures in Wonderland.* Lewis Carroll himself had arranged this date. It had been on 4 July, three years earlier, that he and a friend had taken Alice Liddell and her two sisters on a boating trip up the Isis. 'On which occasion,' Carroll later noted in his diary, 'I told them the fairy tale of Alice's adventures underground.' *Through the Looking-Glass* appeared six years later, and the two dreams soon coalesced to become England's greatest fantasy tale.

If anyone had suggested to a Victorian critic that Alice was great literature, he would have been met with an incredulous snort. Clever and amusing, perhaps, but great literature? Reviews of the first Alice book were mixed. *The Athenaeum* called it a 'stiff, overwrought story' with 'square, and grim, and uncouth' illustrations. 'Too extravagantly absurd to produce more diversion than disappointment and irritation,' said the *Illustrated Times.*

But children and adults loved it, both in England and here, and before twenty years had passed a hundred thousand copies had been printed. Warren Weaver, in his recent book *Alice in Many Tongues,* lists more than forty languages into which *Alice's Adventures* are now translated. There are several Russian versions, including one written by Vladimir Nabokov when he was a young man living in Germany. ('Not the first Russian translation,' he once told a reporter, 'but the best.') How can one explain the persistent—indeed, the still growing—popularity of this strange, outlandish dream and its even stranger sequel?

My own view is—though it arouses some Carrollians to a pitch of frenzy—that *Alice* is no longer a children's book. I do not deny that here and there a few unusual children, more in England than here, are still capable of enjoying it, but I believe their number is steadily diminishing. Like *Gulliver's Travels, Robinson Crusoe,* and *Huckleberry Finn, Alice* has joined that curious list of books that librarians call 'children's classics' but which are read and relished mostly by grownups. I myself have never met a child who said that *Alice* was one of his or her favourite books, and I have met only two U.S. adults who said they had enjoyed it as a small child. (Please don't write me an angry letter saying you have just read *Alice* to your five-year-old and she *loved* it. Try reading to her *A Midsummer Night's Dream* or Norman Mailer's *American Dream;* you'll find she loves them, too.)

The truth is that, from a modern child's point of view, the Alice books are plotless, pointless, unfunny, and more frightening than a monster movie. Let me summon a few distinguished witnesses. Katherine Anne Porter, in a radio panel discussion of *Alice* in 1942, confessed that the book had badly frightened her as a little girl. All those household things going mad and reminding her of the uncertainty and insecurity she felt in an adult world she couldn't understand! Bertrand Russell agreed. *Alice,* he declared flatly, is unsuitable for any child younger than fifteen. 'There are many objections to it as a children's book. In fact, I should like to label it "For Adults Only".'

'I wonder,' said Mark Van Doren, 'if the young these days actually do like it as much as children used to like it.'

'My experience,' replied Lord Russell, 'is that they don't, and I think this because there are so many more children's books now and because, when I was young, it was the only children's book that hadn't got a moral. We all got very tired of the morals in books.'

Another great mathematician, Norbert Wiener, tells in his autobiography how Alice's metamorphoses terrified him as a boy, and how it was not until many years later that he learned to value the book. H. L. Mencken, in his autobiography, writes: 'I was a grown man, and far gone in sin, before I ever brought myself to tackle *Alice in Wonderland,* and even then I made some big skips.'

For intelligent children over fifteen and adults who, unlike Mencken, are not bored by fantasy, the Alice books are rich in subtle humour, social satire, and philosophical depth. Both books, especially the second, are crammed with paradoxical nonsense of exactly the sort that mathematicians and logicians revel in. It is no accident that you are likely to find more references to *Alice* in a book by a modern philosopher of science than in a book by a literary critic. The central symbol in Edward Albee's Broadway enigma, *Tiny Alice*—the infinite regress of the castle in the castle in the castle—is straight out of the looking-glass. Alice dreams about the Red King but the Red King, too, is dreaming, and Alice is only a 'thing' in *his* dream. This double regress of Alices and kings, into infinitely more dreamlike levels nested in the skulls of each, is a delicious thought to philosophers concerned with separating reality from illusion. But if a small child understands it at all, he is more likely to be upset than amused.

Moreover, *Alice* swarms with jokes that no American child will catch (e.g., the Ugly Duchess's clever double pun on the proverb 'Take care of the pence and the pounds will take care of themselves'). And there are jokes not even an English child today can understand (e.g., the parodies on poems, now forgotten, that Victorian children memorized). There are even jokes that a child in Carroll's time would not understand unless he was part of the Oxford community (e.g., the three Liddell-little puns in the first verse of the prefatory poem. The last name of Henry Liddell, dean of Christ Church and the father of Alice, rhymed with 'middle'.) It is all this, from the obscure word plays to the philosophical and mathematical paradoxes, that keeps the *Alice* books alive among adults long after they have ceased to delight the average child.

It is instructive to compare Carroll with our own greatest writer of fairy tales, L. Frank Baum. On the surface, the two men seem remarkably unalike: Carroll the shy, withdrawn, stammering, prim, devout, celibate teacher of mathematics; Baum the friendly, outgoing father of four boys, a man who acted and sang in his own Broadway shows, published a newspaper in North Dakota before that area became a state, started his own movie company in Hollywood. But underneath their differences they shared a deep love for children (though on Carroll's side, only for little girls), and a genius for entertaining them with brilliantly imagined stories of outrageous comic fantasy.

Baum's first juvenile book, *Mother Goose in Prose* (it was the first book, by the way, ever illustrated by Maxfield Parrish), weaves stories around nursery rhymes in a manner comparable to Carroll's episodes about the Tweedle brothers, Humpty Dumpty, the Knave of Hearts, and the Lion and the Unicorn. The title of Baum's book, *A New Wonderland*, published in 1900, is an obvious reference to *Alice*. *The Wonderful Wizard of Oz*, issued the same year, parallels *Alice* in many ways. Like Alice, Dorothy Gale is a healthy, bright, attractive, outspoken, unaffected, supremely self-confident and courageous little girl who suddenly finds herself in a mad world where animals talk and nature behaves in a thousand unexpected ways. Alice drops into wonderland through a rabbit hole. Dorothy is blown to Oz by a cyclone. Mother and Father are conveniently absent from both stories. (Dorothy is an orphan, Alice never thinks about her parents.)

Of course there are also profound differences between the two classics, both in style and content. Baum is less interested in mathematical and word play, more in telling a straightforward adventure story. No one would expect to meet that eminent Oxford linguistic philosopher, Humpty Dumpty, in Baum's Oz; though we do meet a Humpty in *Mother Goose in Prose,* and I suppose Baum's Wogglebug and Carroll's egg have much pride and pedantry in common. (The White Knight, wearing yellow armour, turns up as Sir Hocus of Pokes in Ruth Plumly Thompson's *Royal Book of Oz*). No one would expect to find the Scarecrow or Tin Woodman behind the looking-glass. You can no more imagine the Cheshire Cat in Oz than you can imagine Bungles, the glass cat, or Dorothy's cat Eureka in Carroll's wonderland, although the White Rabbit might have strayed from Bunnybury, in the Quadling Country of Oz. This is not the place to detail differences, but surely one outstanding difference is that Baum's characters are, for the most part, as lovable as they are outlandish. They are 'Ozzy', but seldom cruel or mad. Oz is a happy utopia. Indeed, it is so attractive to Dorothy that she finally settled there permanently with Uncle Henry and Aunt Em. Both of Alice's dreams turned into nightmares.

It is a funny little irony of our culture that there are still librarians around who keep *Alice* on the children's shelves and *The Wizard* off. As recently as 1957 Ralph Ulveling, director of the Detroit Public Library, explained in a letter to the *American Library Association Bulletin* (October issue) why his library kept *The Wizard* in its adult stacks only and did not permit it in the children's room. 'More than thirty years ago', he wrote, 'the decision was made that with so many far better books available for children than was the case when *The Wizard* was first published, the library would simply let the old copies wear out and not replace them. . . . This is not banning, it is selection.'

Well, as Humpty said, words can mean whatever we want them to mean. Personally, I find it easier to believe in the Scarecrow than in Mr Ulveling. My advice is: Give *The Wizard* (in its handsome Dover paperback edition, with its bibliography of Baum's other books) to that ten-year-old; send *Alice (The An-*

notated Alice, of course) to anyone over fifteen who is bored with reading novels about psychotics in a real world.

Fantasy, said G. K. Chesterton (in his marvelous essay 'The Dragon's Grandmother'), reminds us that the soul is sane 'but that the universe is wild and full of marvels. Realism means that the world is dull and full of routine, but that the soul is sick and screaming. . . . In the fairy tales the cosmos goes mad; but the hero does not go mad. In the modern novels the hero is mad before the book begins, and suffers from the harsh steadiness and cruel sanity of the cosmos.' It is a good bet that both *Alice* and *The Wizard* will be around for many centuries after *Tiny Alice* and *The American Dream*—even that monstrous, million-punned labyrinthine dream of H. C. Earwicker's—have been forgotten by everybody except the collectors and students of twentieth-century curiosa.

[1965]

A late wanderer in Oz

JORDAN BROTMAN

I never read an Oz book when I was a child! Not for me were the earthly paradise of the Emerald City and the surrounding four Oz countries with their swarming little utopias and nightmares and the enclosing Deadly Desert, nor the fairylands beyond and the far, far country of the American middlewest, nor little Dorothy from Kansas and Betsy Bobbin from Oklahoma and the Shaggy Man from Colorado and the humbug Wizard from Omaha, nor the crowd of Oz names and Oz faces, Ozma and Glinda the Good and Ozga the Rose Queen and Polychrome the Rainbow's Daughter, the Scarecrow, the Tin Woodman, Ojo the Unlucky and the Patchwork Girl, Tik Tok and the Gump and the Private Citizen and the Incubator Baby; these and all the children and simpletons, animals and freaks and fairies that make up Oz eluded me. I must have felt the lack, because when my little boy was four I started reading him Oz books.

My little boy now has a large collection of Oz books which he reads, rereads, and ignores on his own. I found most of them in second-hand bookstores. The Oz books are still in print, but the new printings omit the lavish and fantastic colour plates that graced the early editions. There must be attics all over the country—thousands of attics in the middlewest alone—where set upon set of the resplendent original Oz books, painstakingly gathered by children of two or three generations ago, lie neglected and preserved like so many child's gardens.

Those who read the Oz books when they were children say that you can never recapture the magic of Oz on rereading them. A stranger to Oz, I was spared such disappointment. Instead I found myself fascinated by an unfolding picture of childhood which was not my own but which belonged, somehow, to the childhood of the whole country. For one thing the Oz books had a kind of California extravagance about them, and I could remember the time when California with its sunshine and its golden oranges and movies was an earthy paradise hankered after by people all over the country, certainly in the middlewest. The further I got into the Oz books, the more obvious it was that these children's stories contained a lot of the dreams, the asperities, and the hard underlay of character of Americans of sixty and seventy years ago, when most of the country—certainly the middlewest—was still in its unrealized youth.

The Oz stories are fairy tales. In the background of all good fairy tales is the hardness of real existence: the fairy tale starts from life as it is and never really escapes from it. The Oz stories begin on a poor dirt farm in Kansas and take us to a green land abundant with fruits, flowers, birds, and streams. The contrast is always there: the empty plains and severe virtues of Kansas and the pastoral, humanized landscape of Oz. 'I cannot understand why you should wish to leave this for Kansas,' says the Scarecrow to little Dorothy as she wanders through Oz in search of a way home. 'That,' replies Dorothy 'is because you have no brains. No matter how dreary and gray our homes are, we people of flesh and blood would rather live there than in any other country.' 'Of course I cannot understand it,' says the Scarecrow. 'If your heads were stuffed with straw, like mine, you would probably all live in the beautiful places, and then Kansas would have no people at all. It is fortunate for Kansas that you have brains.'

Kansas life is a harsh one in the Oz books. Dorothy's Aunt Em and Uncle Henry are gaunt people worn by sun, wind, and hard labour, fighting a losing struggle with the land and the mortgage on it. The cyclone that whisks Dorothy off to Oz is also the ruin of the family, and in a later story Dorothy is obliged to take her foster-parents to Oz to save them from an impoverished end in the city, and herself from being put out to service as a nursemaid. The old people have a hard time adjusting to the little girl's fairyland. Drudgery has been their life and lot, and the permissive climate of Oz leaves them foundering—until at the last moment Aunt Em, with a cry of 'Why, Henry, we've been slaves all our lives!' decides to make a go of it.

The lot of the Kansas child is also hard, but the child's ingenuity always dominates circumstance. In the second Oz book *(The Land of Oz)* the story is about a boy named Tip, who is parentless like Dorothy and who lives in a remote corner of Oz that resembles Kansas. Tip's guardian is a foul witch named Mombi (there are no witches in Kansas), and the 'small and rather delicate' child does farm chores all day long. Tip has no playmates, but his boy's life is eked out in fantasy and private play. He makes a pumpkinhead man for a playmate, who comes to life and escapes with Tip when Mombi decides to turn the troublesome child into an ornament for her garden.

Tip understands without illusion or self-pity that Mombi has an evil heart. Children in Oz accept the world as it is, good and bad, and the fairyland they inhabit is full of shrewdly drawn human types. The basic outlook is rural and middlewestern, because the children come from the middlewest. 'Life was a serious thing to Dorothy,' we are told, and this is true because Dorothy is both a child and from Kansas. But Dorothy also has a yearning for the pleasures of life, and this too the middlewest has echoed and acted upon, without any apparent sense of moral contradiction. One result has been the great migration to southern California—that middlewestern paradise, where Oz suddenly grew up in life.

Among the primary middlewestern attitudes ingrained in the Oz books is mistrust of and fascination for the big city. In the heart of Oz is the Emerald City, ruled by a powerful Wizard who remains invisible to his subjects. 'I am Oz, the great and terrible,' booms the Wizard from behind his screen—to whch Dorothy replies, with proper Kansas forthrightness, 'I am Dorthy, the small and meek.' The Wizard is of course humbug; Dorothy returns from her battle with the Wicked Witch of the West, and the screen falls and reveals a little old man who shamefacedly confesses that he has no magic to send her home on. 'I think you are a very bad man,' Dorothy burst out, and the humbug answers, 'Oh, no, my dear; I'm really a very good man; but I'm a very bad Wizard, I must admit.'

There is always humbug in the heart of the great city; you can fool the big city people who wear green glasses, but not the plain people from back home. It turns out that the Wizard comes from Nebraska, where he was a balloonist with a circus. This opens the way to a keener prejudice: if you are a man from the country who has made good in the city, you have to be a humbug to have done it.

Culture and higher learning, associated with city life, are also targets of the mild and simple satire of Oz. The most learned figure in Oz is H. M. Wogglebug, T. E. (Thoroughly Educated), an insect who conducts a progressive college where students take learning in pill form. H. M. Wogglebug is verbose and harmless, a featherweight. There is a place in Oz called Foxville, a fox society where animals dress gorgeously, attend concerts, and exhibit all the vanities of high fashion and culture. But the children of Oz are not immune to such pleasures, be it noted. Ozma's palace is more lavish still.

Such rural and regional sentiments in the Oz stories sometimes run together in a current of populist feeling. In *The Emerald City of Oz,* for example, the city and the surrounding farm community take on a utopian socialist character. We learn that there are no poor people in Oz, because there is no money; each person produces for his neighbour's use, and each is given what he needs. The people work half the time and play half the time, and they enjoy their labour because there are no cruel overseers.

There is a prison where wrongdoers are treated as 'sick' and cured with kindness. There are other utopian features, but the point, although it leaves its mark, is not developed in any detail —no more than is needed, perhaps, to satisfy the child's understanding of a barter economy and his keen sense of fairness. There are also contradictions and extravagances that exist side by side with the pieties of utopia, because Oz is a much more human than hypothetical paradise.

In fact there are a multitude of utopias in Oz, each one putting into effect with more or less point some logical definition about nature. They carry out in children's-story terms the middle-western appetite for creating utopias, which of course have not always been for children—Technocracy and Dianetics and Moral Rearmament came from the middlewest, and they weren't. Most of the Oz utopias are absurd, some are funny, and some are merely the private worlds of animals, monsters, or lonely eccentrics like Miss Cuttenclip, who has a menagerie of live paper dolls. There is a place called the Valley of Voe, where the people are invisible because they believe that beauty is only skin deep, and that 'good actions and pleasant ways are what make us lovely to our companions'. The only drawback to the Valley of Voe is that there are also invisible bears, who occasionally bump into the invisible people and eat them up.

The guiding philosophy of Oz is homely, practical, and inventive—adapted to the situation. On one occasion, for instance, the Scarecrow will moralize that in this world it is best to submit to fate, and on another that you must strive to overcome all obstacles. Everything depends on circumstances.

This practicality is familiar and Kansan, but Oz isn't Kansas. Oz is a kindlier place where love is reciprocated and dreams, if you work hard for them, yield a fair return. But you must work hard to achieve your heart's desire. One difference between Oz and Kansas is that in Kansas people work so hard—for nothing. Oz has a California climate, the grim uncertainties of life are lessened, and people have more time to learn about one another. In Oz, just as in idyllic California, people stop and congratulate each other about the place and the climate. In a fairyland that possesses more merely mechanical magic than any place on earth it is natural, then, that the main point should be an entirely social one: 'In this world in which we live, simplicity and kindness are the only magic that works wonders'.

If you look at L. Frank Baum's introductions to his Oz books you will find them progressively dated: the first two (1900, 1904) are dated at Chicago; the next (1907) is dated Coronado. From 1910 to Baum's death in 1919 the rest of the Oz books are sent off from a place called Ozcot, in Hollywood.

Baum, then, moved from the middlewest to southern California. In so doing he wove his own life into the design of Oz, for as an early arrival in twentieth-century California, Baum was living out an Oz dream. He was also sharing it with thousands of others to come, and anticipating by several decades the time when America at large, taking southern California as its model, would come to look more and more like Oz.

Baum got to Hollywood just before the movies did; the movies grew up around him. He lived an efflorescent California life. He bred chrysanthemums at Ozcot; he was Dahlia King of California. He wrote every day in his flower garden, seated near an enormous birdcage filled with songbirds. He read philosophy at Ozcot, played the piano, composed music, painted. He was a member of a society called The Uplifters and dedicated one of his stories to them. He turned out an Oz book a year and other books besides. In 1914 he formed his own Oz movie company. The fairyland factory at Ozcot was a private world and quite different from Disneyland, a public exploitation, but it is worth noting that Ozcot and Disneyland are pretty much in the same place.

The career that wound up in Ozcot, Cal. was as indeterminate, diffuse, and hardy as any Oz adventure. Baum was born in

Chittenango, in New York, in 1856, the son of a pioneer Pennsylvania oilman. He was educated mainly at home (it was a place called Rose Lawn, and when he was twelve Baum was putting out a paper, the *Rose Lawn Journal*). At eighteen Baum was doing reporting for the *New York Globe;* a year later he went to Bradford, Penn. and established a weekly paper called *The New Era.* In the eighties Baum took his growing family deep into the middlewest. He bought and edited a weekly in the populist stronghold of Aberdeen county, in South Dakota. (A collection of Baum's shrewd observations of middlewestern life was later gathered from his newspaper, the *Saturday Pioneer,* and published by the South Dakota Writers' Project). Baum was also a wanderer through the middlewest at various times, and worked as a 'drummer', a travelling man, peddling chinawear from farm to farm in the country. This experience is reflected in the Oz books themselves, which in part are a kind of odyssey through the middlewest; they portray the eccentricities, the hardships, the timidity, the communal longings of the country life of the time.

Baum began sending off fiction and humorous verse to the magazines before he was twenty, and his literary output remained prolific for forty-years. In 1881, after a brief, disastrous experience as manager of an opera house in Olean, Penn., he brought out a hit play. It was an Irish melodrama called *The Maid of Arran,* and Baum quickly followed it with two other melodramas and a comedy. In the nineties—he now had four children to support—Baum wrote for the *Chicago Evening World* and edited a technical monthly for window trimmers called *The Show Window.* He founded the National Association of Window Trimmers of America, and in 1901 he wrote a book on decorating. Meanwhile he wrote fiction: when *The Wizard of Oz* appeared in 1900 Baum had already produced some twenty books for children, and some stories for adults. He became a purveyor to the fiction factories of the time, and wrote under a number of names. As Floyd Akers and Capt. Hugh Fitzgerald,

Baum wrote boys' books; as Edyth Van Dyne he wrote twenty-four girls' books. He was also Susanne Metcalf, Laura Bancroft, and John Estes Cook, and as Schuyler Stanton he wrote more-or-less grownup Gothic novels—among these, *The Fate of the Clown* and *Daughter of Destiny*.

Baum wrote most of his stories for younger children under his own name, and whatever significance we may attach to this, it was in the children's story that Baum became the great public entertainer of the era, the great moralist and prophet. In 1899 his *Father Goose, His Book* (illustrated by W. W. Denslow, who also did the pictures for the first Oz book) sold 90,000 copies in 90 days. The book was published in Chicago, and with the proceeds Baum built a summer home at Macatawa on Lake Michigan. This retreat—'The Sign of the Goose'—was a mock-up of the Californiana to come. Baum made all the furniture himself, and the heads of his upholstery tacks were in the form of brass geese. A vast stained-glass window portrayed a giant polychrome goose; the border decorations of the rooms were also geese.

By the time he wrote *Father Goose* Baum was already interested in the idea of providing a specifically 'American' fairy lore for children. *The Wizard of Oz* was the result. It was a quick success (it was made into a New York musical in 1902); it did so well, in fact, that Baum at first misunderstood its impact. He soon followed *The Wizard* with a new book, programmatically titled *Baum's American Fairy Tales: Stories of Astonishing Adventures of American Boys and Girls with the Fairies of Their Native Land*. It was not until 1904, after three other so-so children's stories, that Baum yielded to the peculiar demand for Oz.

Baum tells us what he had in mind for an 'American' fairy tale in his introduction to *The Wizard*. Here, with a brief tribute to the 'historical' European tales of Grimm and Andersen, he described the present need for a series of newer wonder tales, in which the stereotyped genie, dwarf, and fairy would be eliminated, 'together with all the horrible and blood-curdling incident devised by their authors to point a fearsome moral to each tale'. 'Modern education,' Baum observed, 'includes morality; therefore the modern child seeks only entertainment in its wonder-tales and gladly dispenses with all disagreeable incident.' *The Wizard of Oz* was in short to be 'a modernized-fairy tale, in which the wonderment and joy are retained and the heartaches and nightmares are left out'.

This sounds like a brochure for Forest Lawn, but Forest Lawn is fake Oz. Some people I have talked to remember the nightmares they had as children over this and that episode of the real Oz stories. Even for grownups, Baum's fancy can sometimes suggest a medieval hell (in fact in one of the Oz books there is a descent to the cavernous centre of the earth, complete with monsters, satanic powers, and even a limbo). The truth is that Baum had a better instinct for his story than he knew how to say in a preface, and this goes not only for 'horrible and blood-curdling incident'—Baum knew how to pinpoint a child's nightmare—but of course for morality too. Baum knew that children are natural moralists, and the pages of Oz are full of moral instruction, drawn from experience at every turn, that has satisfied children for generations.

Nevertheless Baum did feel strongly—and rightly—that the Oz stories were a departure from the older literature. He once told his publishers that he wanted to write children's stories that had no love and marriage in them, and that got away from the 'European background'. What Baum seems really to have been objecting to was the maturity of the older stories, particularly their fatalism—the fatalism of a historical people tied to their land, their lot, their picture of heaven and earth. In Oz you can literally transform your environment, and the Oz stories though fairy stories speak to a people who are indeed about to transform their own.

Like all fairylands Oz is a land where people are immortal,

but it is also a land where mechanical ingenuity and achievement are quite as marvelous as immortality. If people are more liberated from the spell of magic in Oz than anywhere else in the world, it is simply because there is so much magic—magic has liberated them from magic. Flying machines are in the sky; a creature named Johnny Doit appears by magic and invents a machine to take you out of your difficulties; incubators, food pills, walking phonographs, a hundred contrivances are met with. Apparently the old Calvinist doctrine of work has been transformed into assurance in the power of mechanical ingenuity and faith in a paradise of leisure here and now. The deities of Oz are not the stern gods of the Kansas fathers but permissive goddesses wearing a Gibsonesque American look. And the paradise they preside over—whether in Oz or in southern California—is an emphatically democratic one: mechanical skill is not the exclusive possession of aristocracy, which for that matter has always tended to despise it.

Los Angeles itself will tell us how far away L. Frank Baum actually got from Grimm and Andersen, for Los Angeles represents Oz by as much as it represents the middlewest transformed. The later Oz books, as if authenticating the step from middlewestern myth to reality, have a pronounced southern California flavour about them. Certainly Los Angeles has been as well documented for its children, freaks, and fantasies of immortality as Oz ever was. But the resemblance does not end there. Baum today would have little difficulty in recognizing the new southern California, where the skill of the technicians has put up the aircraft plants and mass-produced Ozma's magic mirror, and where mile after mile of real-estate subdivisions, of new houses and cars and television aerials and prefabricated pools, show us that the paradisiac socialism of the Emerald City has come true, if not for people-and-people, then certainly for people-and-things. Whatever lingering traditional doubts they may carry around with them about the lot of man, Americans have discovered that through technology they can transform a society. Baum did it in the Oz books. He was the children's historian of that discovery.

The Oz books were so popular that Baum in his later career became the entertainer trapped in his creation. Others have met this fate. Charlie Chaplin never quite succeeded in shaking the tramp off his back, despite *Limelight* and the other strenuous efforts he made, under pressure from intellectuals, to upgrade his public image. Al Capp, of *Li'l Abner,* actually had to violate a public interest in order to declare his independence from his own creation. He had Li'l Abner marry Daisy Mae, and when it happened the country woke up to the shocking realization that what belonged to it was being reclaimed by one man's violence. Baum in his turn had pressing need to escape from fairyland, and not only because the children were making public property of his creation. America was catching up with Oz. It was becoming harder and harder to secure fairyland from the rest of the world.

In introduction after introduction Baum vows that each new Oz book will be his last. His readers cry for more; children and grownups by the thousands send him story suggestions—'Why don't you bring Trot and Cap'n Bill to Oz, Mr Baum?'—and Baum gives in. Not without a struggle. From 1904 to 1907 he managed not to write an Oz book. In 1910, at the end of *The Emerald City,* he took a harsh measure and sealed off Oz forever by making it invisible—too many new airplanes, he explained, were getting across the Deadly Desert and invading Oz. The barrier held only until 1913. The children kept writing and telling Baum to get in touch with little Dorothy through the new gadget, wireless. From 1913 on Baum produced an Oz book every year. When he died he had done fourteen of them; the series was afterwards continued by others (notably John R. Neill, the great illustrator of Oz, and Ruth Plumly Thompson), but the decline of Oz in other hands was swift and sure.

Baum's appeal went further than to the children of his time

—a clergyman in England wrote to Baum in California praising him for the spiritual comfort of the Oz stories, thus reversing the moment when, only forty years earlier, a man in the wilds of California had written to George Eliot praising her for the same thing—but his appeal was also very much to the children. The sentiments of children, as Baum echoed them, naturally expressed the yearning for leisure and freedom of a country still held in a stern ethical mould; and Baum understood the sentiments of children. He gave the children a world to make and put them on their own. The children of Oz are separated from their parents; they have foster-parents or guardians, and these anyway cannot manage the world in the long run and have to be brought to Oz. In the Oz books it is the children (or the childlike adults, like the Wizard and the Shaggy Man) who are capable and effective people. They are serious too, reflecting Baum's own intimacy with seriousness of his child audience: Dorothy faces death time after time in Oz with philosophic calm, and her everyday speech, measured off in Baum's sedate literary style, is gave and sober. Oz itself, again, is not a passive fairyland but a very active one, full of arduous journeyings and doing without. A handful of blackberries is enough to satisfy Dorothy for a hard day's wandering.

The child's eye and the child's mind rule in Oz. There is continual name-making; Baum's name-fancy could range at will from erotic dreaminess (Glinda, Nimmie Amee) to the dreadful (the Long-Eared Hearer). There is constant punning and incantation, and the kind of word play that grows out of the child's sense of words as things. In one of the Oz stories Dorothy's kitten is put on trial for hiding or eating a piglet which the Wizard has given to Ozma for a gift. 'In either case,' says the prosecutor, 'a grave crime has been committed which deserves a grave punishment.' 'Do you mean,' exclaims Dorothy, 'that my kitten must be put in a grave?'

There is continual play upon the child's notions of his own identity in the world. When Tip's pumpkinhead man comes to life and learns that Tip has made him, he cries, 'Why, then, you must be my creator—my parent—my father!' 'Or your inventor,' laughs Tip, 'yes, my son; I really believe I am!' 'Then I owe you obedience,' says the man, 'and you owe me—support.' The reversal of roles between father and son provides much play through the book, at the end of which, to complicate things further, Tip becomes a girl. (He has really been Ozma all the time, but Mombi bewitched him into a boy when he was a baby.) The play on sexual character is unsentimental and childlike; Baum delighted as much as his child audience in upsetting the identity of things as given by the adult world.

Romantic love in the Oz world is, again, childlike (there are some curious and amusing romances in Oz, despite what Baum told his publishers). In *The Tin Woodman of Oz* the tin man decides, now that he has a heart, to find and woo the girl he lost long ago. On the journey he and Dorothy talk about Nimmie Amee and the married state; the exchange is ceremonial and learned. When at last the pair find Nimmie Amee, she is married to a tin soldier and has turned into a shrewish Kansas country wife. Of course pure love—love for children—is everywhere in Oz, and romantic playfulness takes place with all other adventures in an atmosphere of security. The Scarecrow, the Shaggy Man, and the other gentle Oz 'grownups' provide this atmosphere. Beyond them and beyond Ozma herself, the girl ruler of Oz, is the all-seeing sorceress Glinda the Good. Glinda has no mere temporal rule; she is the great mother, the authoress of love in Oz.

The Oz stories, clearly, have charm and variety and body enough to be real fairy tales. And for someone reading Oz books to a child—how else are you going to come across them?—there is also a familiar discovery to be made about the aspirations that have gone into the making of the American earthly paradise. The most interesting thing about Baum is that this popular writer of children's stories should have had so much to say about the most recent of the great migrations of the country's history. The move from the middlewest to southern California must now be written about as history; as an unfolding dream, Baum was writing about it in every Oz book he wrote, and his influence on the children was probably incalculable. It seems, anyway, that the new leisure that Baum was picturing belonged better in the children's story than anywhere else; in his time, and in part of the country, it was the children who were beginning to take the lead in determining what the whole country wanted.

[1965]

News from Narnia

LILLIAN H. SMITH

'Listen', said the Doctor. 'All you have heard about Old Narnia is true. It is not the land of men. It is the country of Aslan, the country of the Waking Trees and Visible Naiads, of Fauns and Satyrs, of Dwarfs and Giants, of the gods and Centaurs, of Talking Beasts.'

The world called Narnia is the world that C. S. Lewis has created in seven stories for children, each story having a beginning, a middle, and an end, and each may be read independently of the others. Yet in these seven books, taken as a whole, we see a complete story with a beginning, a middle, and an end, in much the same way that we see, first, single stars in the sky, and then see them as a constellation which takes on a pattern our eyes can follow and recognize.

Narnia is not in our world nor in our universe. Narnia has its own sun and moon and stars, its own time. Yet the landscape is a familiar one, a green and pleasant land of woods and glades, valleys and mountains, rivers and sea. The trees, shrubs, and flowers, many birds and animals, are those we know in our own world. Even the unfamiliar, the strange and fabulous ones, are in old stories we have heard and read.

Narnia's history is brief, as we reckon time in our world, though in Narnian time it covers many thousands of years. It began when 'Sherlock Holmes was still living in Baker Street and the Bastables were looking for treasure in the Lewisham

Road'. In London, too, lived Polly and Digory who were looking for adventure. It was Digory's Uncle Andrew, a dabbler in magic, who sent Polly and Digory out of our world and into a world of darkness, which was Narnia waiting to be born.

Digory was 'the sort of person who wants to know everything' and his curiosity brought great trouble to Narnia later on. For the children had visited a dying world before coming to Narnia, and because Digory could not resist the desire to know what would happen, he broke the spell that bound an evil witch to the dying world of Charn. When the children are drawn into a new world, the witch, though against their will, comes too. And so evil enters Narnia before it is five hours old.

As the children stand in the nothingness of this new, dark, and empty world, they hear a voice singing, and with the song suddenly there were stars overhead. Soon, the sky on the eastern horizon turned from dark to grey, then from pink to gold, and just as the voice swelled to the mightiest and most glorious sound, the sun arose and the Singer, himself stood facing the rising sun. 'It was a Lion.'

The Lion's song of creation changes as he paces the waste land, and, as Polly said, 'when you listened to his song you heard the things he was making up: when you looked round you, you saw them.' 'All things bright and beautiful, all creatures great and small'—Narnia is born.

But, since evil has already entered Narnia through the curiosity of two human children, the Lion, who is called 'Aslan', decrees that 'As Adam's race has done the harm, Adam's race shall help to heal it.'

Digory and Polly are sent, over the Western Wilds and mountains of ice, to a walled garden with gates of gold. Here, Aslan tells them, must be gathered the apple whose seeds will be Narnia's safeguard against the witch in the years ahead. And this was the first of 'the comings and goings' between

Narnia and our own world as it is told in *The Magician's Nephew*.

All our news of Narnia comes from the various human children who find themselves there whenever evil times fall on the land. Centuries of peace and plenty pass unrecorded until four other children, in the story of *The Lion, the Witch and the Wardrobe*, find all of Narnia wrapped in a blanket of snow and ice. Under the witch's spell, it is 'always winter and never Christmas'. The children and the Narnians are pitted against the witch, who calls to her aid all the 'abominations': Ghouls, Boggles, Ogres, Minotaurs, Cruels, Hags, and Spectres. But Aslan, the Lion, has been seen in Narnia, and with his coming the spell of evil over the land weakens, and signs of spring are followed by budding trees and rushing brooks as the children, with the talking beaver as their guide, journey to meet Aslan at the Great Stone Table where the battle against the witch will be decided.

Although not the first story in Narnian chronology, *The Lion, the Witch and the Wardrobe* was the first to be published, and is, I think, the first for children, themselves, to read. For, from the moment Lucy opens the wardrobe, steps inside to explore, and is suddenly standing in the middle of a winter forest with snow crunching underfoot, the adventure is a magnet that draws the reader deeper and deeper into the life of Narnia and into concern for all that happens there. At the same time, the reader is aware that there is more to the story than meets the eye, phrases that set young minds and hearts pondering, overtones that set up rhythms heard not only in this book, but in all the stories as they appeared year after year until the last two, *The Magician's Nephew* and *The Last Battle*. In these the children's questions are answered and the full harmony is heard and intuitively grasped at last.

Each story has its own landscape—or seascape. For C. S. Lewis, the face of nature, its changing moods and seasons whether seen in windswept wastes or in a small mossy glade where hawthorn is in bloom, has its part in his developing theme, in shaping the sequence of events and in giving reality to the reader's imaginings as he accompanies the characters of the story on their adventures in the magical land of Narnia.

The characters, themselves, apart from the human children who come there as visitors, reflect the author's mature and scholarly interest in mythology and mediaeval romances. They reflect and communicate his abiding love for the Old Things which belonged, perhaps, to a golden age, backwards in time, when men and birds and beasts spoke to each other in a common language, a fabulous age which, it may be, lived on in myth and fairy tale as a kind of race memory of another, more innocent, world.

It is Trufflehunter, the badger, whose sense of race hints at the prehistoric antiquity of animal traits, the unchanging persistent tenacity with which they pursue their own ends. 'You dwarfs,' says Trufflehunter, 'are as forgetful and changeable as the Humans themselves. I'm a beast, I am, and a Badger what's more. We don't change, we hold on.'

Among the other characters who live on in memory after we have closed the books, is that valiant Chief Mouse, Reepicheep, whose code of chivalry would seem to have been learned at King Arthur's Round Table, for 'his mind was full of forlorn hopes, death or glory charges and last stands.' He is one of the company who sails in *The Dawn Treader* 'towards Aslan's land and the morning and the eastern end of the world', and, after the last battle of all the battles, he is found at the open gates of Aslan's country to bid his friends welcome.

And there is Puddleglum, the Marsh-wiggle, who takes so dim a view of every prospect, but who is the faithful, hardy guide in the children's quest for the lost Prince Rilian. Says Puddleglum: 'How a job like this—a journey up north just as winter's beginning, looking for a prince that probably isn't there, by way of a ruined city that no one has ever seen—will be just the thing. If that doesn't steady a chap, I don't know what will.' When the Prince is found, in the underworld of the witch, and when she uses her black arts to persuade the children that only the underworld exists, and that Narnia is only a myth, it is Puddleglum who stamps out the flame whose evil fumes bewilder and confuse their minds and hearts. It is Puddleglum who throws the challenge to the witch: 'Suppose we *have* only dreamed, or made up, all those things—trees and grass and sun and moon and stars and Aslan himself. Suppose we have. Then all I can say is that, in that case, the made-up things seem a good deal more important than the real ones . . . I'm on Aslan's side even if there isn't any Aslan to lead it. I'm going to live as like a Narnian as I can even if there isn't any Narnia.'

And so we come to Aslan, the Lion, who is the heart and the periphery of these stories and their reason for being: Aslan, whose pervasive influence is felt at all times, in all places, whether visible or invisible, in the world of Narnia. He says to the children, 'Remember, remember, remember the signs . . . Here on the mountain I have spoken to you clearly; I will not often do so down in Narnia. Here on the mountain the air is clear and your mind is clear; as you drop down into Narnia, the air will thicken. Take great care that it does not confuse your mind.'

We may call these books fairy tales or allegories or parables, but there is no mistake about the significance of what C. S. Lewis has to say to the trusting, believing, seeking heart of childhood. But C. S. Lewis knows well that if children are to hear what it is he has to say to them, they must first find delight in the story he tells. And so the fresh and vigorous winds of his imagination carry his readers exuberantly through strange and wild adventures, adventures that, half consciously, they come to recognize are those of a spiritual journey toward the heart of reality. This is the final quality, I think, of C. S. Lewis's writing about the country of Narnia—that above and beneath and beyond the events of the story itself there is something to which the children can lay hold: belief in the essential truth of their own imaginings.

[1958]

Babar's civilization analysed

EDMUND LEACH

It is adult rather than childish preference which from time to time awards a classic accolade to particular characters in nursery literature. Two generations back it was Alice and Peter Rabbit, then, save our souls, Winnie-the-Pooh, and today Babar. What is it that the adults find so remarkable? Why does Babar reign among the immortals?

Perhaps it is simply the author's prophetic insight into French politics: Babar, born *c.* 1933, is a long-nosed gentleman who returns to his devastated country in the midst of a disastrous war against the rhinoceroses; under his paternal rule as *Général-Président* the elephants achieve unheard-of prosperity; Babar, like his human counterpart, now travels in a Citröen DS19 and leads a genteel bourgeois existence in a country château remote from the turmoil of Celesteville politics.

Or should we look for Freudian symbolism? Any overdressed European male must surely derive considerable exhibitionist delight from seeing himself displayed as an elephant, whichever end you approach the matter. And no doubt there are all sorts of other possibilities as far-fetched or as obvious as you will.

But let us consider some matters of fact. The Old Lady (La Vieille Dame) recurs in all the stories. She is a direct link with mundane reality and she is the only human character of any consequence. The others such as Fernando, a circus owner, a nameless sea captain, sundry Arabs and Africans etc. make only brief appearances, usually in crowd scenes. The Old Lady has no personal name. In the earlier (Jean de Brunhoff) books the geography is a nice blend of North Africa and Southern or even Central France. Real places are never mentioned by name, but the pictures imply that it is just a short scamper from darkest Africa to the banks of the Seine. A later (Laurent de Brunhoff) volume jumbles up Arabs and kangaroos. This seems to me a mistake; it is the wrong kind of inconsistency.

Babar himself is a thoroughly civilized elephant who sleeps in a bed, reads the newspaper, drives a car, and so on. To wear no clothes is a mark of savagery. This is a characteristic both of pre-Babar elephants and of post-Babar black men ('savages'). The increasing opulence of the elephant ruling class,—the consequences no doubt of an oil strike in the South Sahara—has regularly been marked by the ever-increasing complexity of their human attire.

Elephant society is strictly on a par with that of men, and intermingles with it directly without evoking astonishment on the part of either the elephants or the humans. This land of the elephants is merely a different country, as England is to France. Other animals occupy further countries in a similar way, but it is not the case that *all* animal species are elevated to an identical para-human status. There is a definite hierarchy. Rhinos, though unpleasant fellows, are as civilized as elephants; they fight on equal terms, and an elephant airline employs a rhino as pilot. Likewise Zephir, the monkey playmate of the younger elephants, has a monkey land of his own complete with a monkey fiancée, Princess Isabel. But the other animals, which are humanized in the sense that they attend parties and generally participate in Celesteville high jinks, all seem to be on a slightly lower plane—Asiatics as against Europeans perhaps? A Michelin guide to Babar's zoology would run something like this:

FROM *Babar the King* BY JEAN DE BRUNHOFF

★★★★ CIVILIZED RULERS
White Men, Elephants, Rhinoceroses, Monkeys

★★★ SERVILE COLONIAL POPULATIONS:
Black Men, Dromedaries, Hippopotamuses, Kangaroos

★★ HUMANIZED ANIMALS (appearing only occasionally and then as individuals):
Lion, Tiger, Giraffe, Deer, Tortoise, Mouse, Porcupine, Lizard. Various exotic birds (e.g. Flamingo, Ibis, Pelican, Marabout)

★ WILD BEASTS (hostile to elephants as they would be to man):
Crocodile, Snake

DOMESTIC ANIMALS

Domestic animals, e.g. horses, cows, sheep, goats, pigs, frequently appear in the pictures but never as 'characters' in the story; they remain domestic animals quite devoid of human qualities. Animals which rate as pets for humans (i.e. cats and dogs) are eliminated altogether with one exception: when Babar goes in search of Father Christmas—a sort of fantasy within a fantasy—he is accompanied by a talking dog (which is rather surprisingly called Duck).

The allocation of names in Babar's world has a definite pattern. The Old Lady, the only 'real' human, has no name. Babar's closest associates, that is those who are closest to being human, have names appropriate to real humans or to pets: Babar, Celeste, Pom, Flora, Alexander, Arthur, Zephir, Isabel, Eleanor (a mermaid), Cornelius.

Beyond this there is a list of Celesteville elephants who have 'real' occupations but fanciful names. Tapitor, the shoemaker, Pilophage, the officer, Capoulosse, the doctor, Barbacol, the tailor, Podula, the sculptor, Hatchibombator, the road sweeper, Doulamour, the musician, Olur, the mechanic, Poutifour, the farmer, Fandango, the scholar, Justinien, the painter, Coco, the clown, and Ottilie, a girl friend of Arthur. The names of the rhinos are rather similar: Rataxes, Pamir, Baribarbottom. Likewise the minor characters associated with Zephir: Huc and Aristobel are monkeys; Aunt Crustadel and Polomoche are 'monsters' which look like nursery toys, and it is never stated whose aunt they are. None of the three-, two-, or one-star animals have personal names except the tortoise, who on one occasion is called Martha.

It will be seen that Babar's world is very urban. The humanized animals and birds are those one might meet in a zoo, behind bars. The list of professions suggests the atmosphere of a small-town street.

The naming pattern has the effect of setting up class discriminations even within the category of four-star animals. The reader is coerced into making a self-identification with one or the other of the members of Babar's own household; the rest of the universe of humanized animals is then ranged round about in categories of inferior status.

The ethnographers provide us with other evidence concerning Babar's ideas of social class. Though Babar is elected as 'King', he is not an hereditary aristocrat. There is no suggestion that he is a relative of the previous monarch who died from eating a poisonous mushroom. Nor do any of Babar's associates carry hereditary titles such as Count; they are all Mr and Mrs plain and simple. True, Babar has covered the walls of his new château with portraits of sixteenth-century 'ancestors', but this is obviously a completely fake piece of snobbery. Further evidence of class sensitivity may be seen in the fact that Babar marries his cousin Celeste, and that the only other elephant outsider with whom the family have intimate relations is another cousin, Arthur. When Babar and Celeste amuse themselves in the Celesteville Garden of Pleasure they play tennis with Mr and Mrs Pilophage, Pilophage being a military officer. In the same context, General Cornelius plays bowls with a sort of intellectual élite: Fandango the scholar, Podula the sculptor,

Capoulosse the doctor. But Babar does not associate with tradesmen.

All this is as it should be. It is important that the comfortable bourgeois adult readers should not have their basic assumptions about social relationships in any way disturbed. Babar has the prejudices of a middle class *colon* of the 1930s.

I have a theory about all this. I think that Babar appeals to adults because the fantasy is so carefully contrived, so fully under control. In the ordinary way we tend to categorize living creatures in terms of social distance, depending upon the degree of remoteness from 'myself', thus:

	1	2	3	4
ME	VERY NEAR	NEAR	FAR	VERY FAR
	very tame	tame	wild	very wild
		domestic	familiar	unfamiliar
	pets	animals	wild animals	wild animals
	inedible	edible	some edible	inedible
	family members	neighbours	strangers	total strangers savages
	incest	marriageable	some marriageable	not marriageable

The categories of animals and humans falling into columns 1 and 4 are both abnormal and sacred, and the sacredness is in both cases marked by the taboo on edibility and sex relations.

This I admit is a complicated matter. The English have tended to accept biblical injunctions so that all meat-eating creatures and creeping things are inedible, also horses. But the French eat snails and frogs and horse. In Canton the restaurants serve up dog and snake as delicacies, also unborn mice and a soup made of bird saliva. Cannibal connoisseurs consider human rumpsteak delicious. But the point is that eating and sex are both matters of social convention and in all cases there is a 'very near' and a 'very far' category, *both* of which are alike inedible and sexually illegitimate.

I find it significant that almost all the humanized beasts in the Babar books belong to column 4, whereas surely the child's natural interests must lie in columns 1 and 2? Children's books in which the leading characters are humanized pets and humanized domestic animals are published with great regularity but seem to have no staying power—this can only be because the adults disapprove. But why? Might not the explanation be something like this:

For the child, fantasy is obvious. The category distinction real/unreal (true/false) is vague and unimportant; for the adult it is crucial. And in the adult's painfully constructed image of the real world the categories which are very close—those relating to the parts and excretions of the body—to family relations, to pets and familiar creatures—are the basic discriminations which serve as a rather shaky foundation for a vast superstructure of precisely defined linguistic concepts. As we get older the uncertainty of these early discriminations becomes a source of great anxiety, sex and excretion become 'obscene', they are loaded with a taboo which infects even Chanticleer and the harmless pussycat. Small wonder then that the adult finds this kind of country uncomfortable. We may blandly assure ourselves that we thoroughly approve of childish fantasy, but at the same time we want to be quite sure that the real and the unreal never get muddled up in our own imagination. Alice can do what she likes on the other side of the looking-glass or down the rabbit hole, but not too close please, not too close. If you want to see a real elephant go to the zoo: I don't want any of Mr Ionesco's rhinoceroses around here if you please.

[1962]

Only connect

P. L. TRAVERS

It was suggested to me when the Library of Congress did me the honour of asking me to address you that I should talk about how *Mary Poppins* came to be written. Now, I know that there are many people who can talk, and at great length, on subjects of which they are totally ignorant. But I'm not one of them. I can't speak of what I don't know and this is not from an excess of modesty but from lack of relevant data. Any work of fiction, any work of imagination, has inevitably something of the quality of poetry, or of those strange flashes of realization that happen for no apparent reason or rhyme—it can't be described. Words are like the notes on a piano, instruments of communication, not the poem—or the music—itself. Once a piece of work is finished, it has said all there is to be said. My instinct is always to whittle down, not to enlarge upon, and hasn't your own poet Randall Jarrell said—I forget the exact phrase for the moment—that a writer must remain silent about the way in which he writes? Even what he writes. Nothing, however, prevents a writer from speaking about the earth—the compost, as it were—from which his work arises. He can't help knowing something about that because it is, of course, his very self.

And this brings me to my title. I don't have to tell you where it comes from. When I was at Radcliffe last year students from that college and Harvard used to crowd into my small apartment once a week and the talk was so good, they were all so alive, so open to ideas, and so ready to fight me for them. I liked that. And I remember that on one occasion I said—and it still seems to me true—that thinking was linking. At that, one marvellous girl blazed out at me, 'Yes! Only connect!' and began searching for pencil and paper. But I begged her not, for the life of her, to write it down in a notebook. E. M. Forster had made the connection already, and now it was really her own. Once you write things down you've lost them. They are simply dead words on dead paper.

But 'Only connect' was the exact phrase I had been leading up to and it has been precious to me ever since I read *Howards End*, of which it is the epigraph. Perhaps, indeed, it's the theme of all Forster's writing, the attempt to link a passionate scepticism with the desire for meaning, to find the human key to the inhuman world about us; to connect the individual with the community, the known with the unknown; to relate the past to the present and both to the future. Oh, it's a marvellous phrase and I seized upon it for this lecture because—well, what else *is* there to seize upon? This question of linking is, anyway, very close to me, and since that is what I am talking about tonight inevitably I have to go back to the past.

You remember Blake's 'Little Black Boy'? 'My mother bore me in the Southern wild.' In that sense I was a little black boy, too, for I was born in the subtropics of Australia. Not that I spent all my life there, only my young years, and most of it far from cities. I lived a life that was at once new and old. The country was new and the land itself very old—the oldest in the world, geologists say, and in spite of all the brash pioneering atmosphere that still existed, even a child could sense the antiquity of it. We had also strong family traditions; we couldn't escape them, caught as we were between the horns of an Irish father and a mother of Scottish and Irish descent. It was simple, not rich, not centred at all on possessions or the search for status symbols. It seems to me that there were few *things* of any kind—furniture, of course, clothes and food, all the modest necessities. But of toys, and personal treasures, very few. If we wanted them we had to invent them, not by parental edict but from necessity. And there were few books: Dickens and Scott, of course, Shakespeare, Tennyson, and some of the Irish poets. I ate my way through these like a bookworm not because of any highbrow leanings but simply because they were books. But for the children, who as far as I can remember were seldom specially catered for, it was the grownup world that was important. There was a modest hodge-podge of good and bad: Beatrix Potter, simple—even babyish—comics, an odd book that nobody else seems ever to have heard of called *The Wallypug of Why*, Ethel Turner's stories, *Alice*, Kingsley's *Heroes*. Hawthorne I never met till I was grown up and it seems to me, as I read him now, though perhaps I wouldn't have thought so then, that he rather talks down to children, 'tinifying', if I may coin the word, and inventing dear little curly haired daughters to make people like Midas more acceptable. Kingsley doesn't do those things. He gives you the myths straight.

Then, too, we had something that no child could find today, not anywhere in the world. We had penny books. You could buy a fairy tale for a penny—that's how their lore went into me. And just as good, perhaps even better at the age, you could buy a *Buffalo Bill*. I don't know whether anybody in this audience remembers such books? Indeed, not long ago—for it seemed so unlikely—I began to wonder whether I hadn't made them up. It was a great relief to me when Rosamond Lehmann, the novelist, assured me that I hadn't. 'Of *course* we had penny books,' she said, and we dreamed over them together. Oh, why didn't I keep them? What grownup, with no eye for the future, tossed the raggedy little morsels—as I myself have done since with many a child's tattered paper treasure—into a nearby dust-bin? Last year, when I was in Toronto visiting the Osborne collection of children's books that goes back to the seventeenth century, I eagerly searched the glass cases. 'If only,' I said, quite by chance, 'I could see a penny book.' A conspiratorial, Guy Fawkes sort of look passed between the librarians, and one hurried away and quickly came back with something held secretively behind her. She put it on the case before me and there was a *Buffalo Bill*—almost, it seemed, the very one, in the faded blacks and blues and reds that I had so long remembered. On the back of the cover was the advertisement for the two-and-sixpenny alarm clock that I had saved up for long ago but never quite achieved. And there, also—much more important—was the air rifle for nineteen-and-elevenpence that would kill an elephant at five yards. Alas, I never got that, either. What would I have done with it if I had, you may ask. I never had a moment's doubt about what I was saving for. It was to slay the enemies of Ireland! The sorrows of the 'most distressful country' got into me very early—how could it help doing so with my father's nostalagia for it continually feeding the imagination? My body ran about in the southern sunlight but my inner world had subtler colours, the greys and snows of England where Little Joe swept all the crossings and the numberless greens of Ireland which seemed to me to be inhabited solely by poets plucking harps, heroes lordily cutting off each other's heads, and veiled ladies sitting on the ground keening.

I think, perhaps, if there was any special virtue in my upbringing, it lay in the fact that my parents, both of them, were very allusive talkers. Neither of them ever read anything that didn't very quickly come out in conversation and from there pass into the family idiom. If my father discovered a poem he liked, even a piece of doggerel, it would presently be, as it were, on the breakfast table. Many a phrase, as ordinary to me then as the daily porridge, began its life, as I later learned, as a quotation from a poem or snatch from a ballad. As an instance, my father, who was a great lover of horses—and tricky, dangerous horses at that—would call out, whenever he returned from riding or driving, 'Bonnie George Campbell is home!' And my mother from somewhere in the house would always answer 'Thank God!' But *who* has come home, I used to wonder, for my father was neither George nor Campbell. It was not until much later, when I began to read the Scottish ballads, that I understood. You remember it?

Booted and saddled
And bridled rade he,
To hame cam' his guid horse
But never cam' he.

For all Bonnie Georges that come safely home the Lord should, indeed, be praised.

'Oh, what can ail thee, knight-at-arms?' my mother would sometimes say to a weeping child. Who was this knight, I often wondered. And yet, when you come to think of it, all children are knights-at-arms at times, alone and palely loitering. It is then they need to be comforted. But sometimes my father would prevent that. 'No, no,' he would say, 'let her weep. You know we need the rain.' Thinking of this, with hindsight, I see how really antique that was, that we cannot really escape the myths, even if we wish to. You can call it, perhaps, sympathetic magic. And it is a fact that still, in countries suffering from drought, a cup of water is poured on the ground in the hope of bringing rain. In Sumeria, the oldest civilization the world knows, the rain god was invoked by the pouring of a cup of wine. I remembered this recently when a journalist, who had been talking to people in Ireland about the assassination of President Kennedy, told me that one old man said gravely, 'We cried the rain down for him that night.' What an epitaph! The rain cried down!

Then, too, there were maxims galore and proverbs and aphorisms. I was so often told—being a passionately lazy child—to 'Make an effort, Mrs Dombey', that I began to think that Dombey was one of my own names. How could I know it was out of Dickens?

Then there were other, closer, connections with myth. In those lucky days there was always help to be had in the house. Such people are wonderful meat for children. The life they live, from the child's point of view—because to him it is strange and unknown—seems to be filled with glamour that his own dailiness lacks. One of them—Bella, or was it Bertha?—had a parrot-headed umbrella. This fascinated me. On days out, it swung besides Bella's furbelows—she was far more elegant, I then thought, than my mother—and was carefully put away in tissue paper on her return, while she told us the always fantastic story of what she had done and seen. Well, she never *quite* told—she did more, she hinted. 'Ah,' she would say, looking like Cassandra, 'if you could know what's happened to me cousin's brother-in-law!' But all too often, when prayed to continue, she would assure us, looking doomed and splendid, that the story was really beyond all telling and not for the ears of children. Oh, those inadequate ears of children! We were left to wonder, always mythologically—had he perhaps been chained to the mast because of someone's siren voice? Was his liver being slowly eaten by a baldheaded local eagle? Whatever they were, the things she didn't tell, they were always larger than life. Once, however, she spoke plain. 'I saw Paddy Liston in the gutter,' she said, 'and him as drunk as an English duke!' Well, what a sight for the inward eye! It filled out imagination to such an extent that now I can never think of our poor, probably sober, dukes without seeing then en masse under tables, robed and crowned and in the last stages of alcoholic dissolution. We didn't, as you see, need television! In a world where there are few possessions, where nobody answers questions, where nobody explains—I say this with joy not sorrow!—children must build life for themselves. One child is forced this way, one another. I went into imagination and poetry—perhaps I should more modestly say versifying—and never with grownup approbation. Come to that, I never sought it.

'Hardly W. B. Yeats,' said my father once, when my mother showed him a scrap of mine. And remembering it now I feel bound to agree with him, though at the age of seven it would have been hard even for *Yeats* to be W. B. Yeats. My father, as you see, perhaps because he was so far away from her, was in love with Cathleen ni Houlihan. Nothing that Ireland did was wrong, nothing that other countries did was completely right. Even his maxims came from Ireland. 'Never put a baby in a drawer', was one of them. But who would ever do such a thing? Even if he saw a doll in a drawer, he would pluck it out, saying 'Remember Parnell!' We had never even *heard* of Parnell, and I had to wait to make the connection till I read a life of him a few years ago. Soon after he was born his mother, called away on some pretext, put him down quickly and came back to discover that her baby had disappeared. She looked everywhere, servants searched the house, gardeners rummaged in the shrubberies—no sign of Charles Stewart Parnell. I hope I'm not inventing it, but I think the police, too, were sent for. And while they were once more searching the nursery a mewling little sound came from the bureau. And there was Charles Stewart, six weeks old and at his last gasp because his mother, absent-mindedly dumping him into a open drawer had, also absent-mindedly, shut it! I am sure my father knew this story. Where else could the maxim have come from?

So you see, I was drenched in the Celtic twilight before I ever came to it. Indeed I only came to it when it was over and had practically turned into night. I had dreamed of it all my life, and although my father was long dead, I had to test what my childhood had taught me. So the first thing I did on arriving in England was to send a piece of writing to Æ (George Russell), who was then editor of *The Irish Statesman.* With all the hauteur of youth I deliberately sent no covering letter, just a stamped addressed envelope for return. And sure enough the stamped envelope came back, as I had fully expected it to do, but inside—instead of my manuscript—was a cheque for three guineas and a letter from Æ. It said 'If you have any more, please let me see them and if you are ever in Ireland let us meet.' So, you see, even if I hadn't been already going to Ireland I would have been off on the next train.

That was how I came under the wing of Æ and got to know Yeats and the gifted people in their circle, all of whom cheerfully licked me into shape like a set of mother cats with a kitten. As you can imagine, this was blessing and far beyond my deserving. But I was not the only kitten; no young person was ever sent empty away, the riches were poured out upon all. It was strong meat, this first introduction to my father's country, among the poets and the makers of history. Perhaps it was just as well that my first contact with my Irish relatives should take me down several pegs. I needed it. They, I discovered, were not all in love with Cathleen ni Houlihan. Living cheek by jowl with her, they saw her without any trappings. Irish to the marrow, full of local lore and story, lovers of horses and the countryside, they weren't at all sure that life depended on poetry and they took the Celtic Renaissance with more than a grain of salt. 'I don't like you gallivanting around with men who see fairies,' said one. 'And the thought of you, a young girl, in Fleet Street, that terrible place—it's beyond thinking about!' From his description of it, I saw myself suffering nameless indignities at the hands of newspaper tycoons or being dragged up dark alleys by drunken reporters, and looked forward to it all with the greatest enthusiasm—though of course I didn't say so. 'And you'll meet such frightful people,' he said. 'There's one who lived down the road a way—old now, of course, but a terrible great boastful fellow. If you meet him, be courteous, but do not pursue the acquaintance. His name is Shaw, George Bernard Shaw.'

Gradually I learned to dissemble my enthusiasm for all that the elderly relatives of my father's generation found so reprehensible. One of them even remarked approvingly, 'You're not nearly so mad as you used to be.' Yet he was the one who, on his death-bed, hearing his wife asking the doctor if he was likely to last till next morning, remarked sardonically, 'I don't need to. I've seen plenty of mornings. All I want to know is, will I live to hear the result of the boat race?' Among last words this spartan, if eccentric, phrase deserves, I think, a place.

Not so mad as I used to be? Little did he know! It was coming back from visiting him that one of what he would have called my maddest moments occurred. I knew that on the way back to Dublin the train would pass Lough Gill. And I remembered that in Lough Gill lay Yeats's Lake Isle of Innisfree. So I leapt from the carriage and charged a boatman on the lapping shore to take me there.

'Ach, ther's no such place,' he said.

'Oh, but there is, I assure you. W. B. Yeats wrote about it.'

'And who would he be?'

I told him.

'Ah, I know them, those poets, always stravaiging through their minds, inventing outlandish things. *We* call it Rat Island!' Rat Island! Well!

So we set out, under grey hovering clouds, with me in the bows and a young priest, who suddenly arose out of the earth, it seemed, joining us in the stern. At last, after a rough passage, there was Innisfree. No hive for the honeybee and no log cabin, but of course I hadn't expected them. They were only in the bee-loud glade of Yeats's stravaiging mind. But the whole island was covered with rowan trees, wearing their red berries like jewels, and the thought suddenly came to me—a most disastrous one, as it turned out—'I'll take back some branches to the poet.' In no time, for the island is diminutive, I had broken off pretty nearly every branch from the rowans and was staggering with them towards the boat. By now a strong wind had sprung up and the rain was falling and the lake was wild. Those Irish loughs beat up into a great sea very quickly. As we embarked, the waves seemed as high as the Statue of Liberty and I wished I'd had more swimming practice. Then I noticed, between one trough and the next, that the priest, pale as paper, was telling his beads with one hand and with the other plucking off my rowan berries and dropping them into the water. 'Ah, Father,' said the boatman, pulling stertorously on the oars, 'it's not the weight of a berry of two that will save us now.' He gave me a reflective glance and I got the idea, remembering that in times of shipwreck women are notoriously unlucky, that he was planning to throw me overboard, if the worse came to worst. I wished *I* had a string of beads! However, perhaps because of the priest's prayers, we came at last safely to shore. I hurried through the rain with my burden and took the next train for Dublin. The other passengers edged away from my streaming garments as though I were some sort of ancient mariner. I should never have started this, I knew, but there is an unfortunate streak of obstinacy in me that would not let me stop. From Dublin station, through curtains of cloud—taxis did not exist for me in those days—I carried the great branches to Yeats's house in Merrion Square and stood there, with my hair like rats' tails, my tattered branches equally ratlike, looking like Birnam come to Dunsinane and wishing I was dead. I prayed, as I rang the bell, that Yeats would not open the door himself, but my prayer went unheard.

For an articulate man to be struck dumb is, you can imagine, rare. But struck dumb he was at the sight of me. In shame, I heard him cry a name into the dark beyond of the house and saw him hurriedly escape upstairs. Then the name came forward in human shape and took me gently, as though I were ill or lost or witless, down to the basement kitchen. There I was warmed and dried and given cocoa; the dreadful branches were taken away. I felt like someone who had died and was now contentedly on the other side, certain that nothing more could happen. In this dreamlike state, I was gathering myself to go—out the back way if possible—never to be seen again. But a maid came bustling kindly in and said—as though to someone still alive!—'The master will see you now.' I was horrified. This was the last straw. 'What for?' I wanted to know. 'Ah, then, you'll see. He has his ways.'

And so, up the stairs—or the seven-storey mountain—I went, and there he was in his room with the blue curtains.

'My canary has laid an egg!' he said and joyously led me to

the cages by the window. From there we went round the room together, I getting better every minute and he telling me which of his books he liked and how, when he got an idea for a poem—there was a long momentous pause here: he was always the bard, always filling the role of poet, not play-acting but knowing well the role's requirements and giving them their due. He never came into a room, he *entered* it; walking around his study was a ceremonial peregrination, wonderful to witness. 'When I get an idea for a poem,' he went on, oracularly, 'I take down one of my own books and read it and then I go on from there.' Moses explaining his tablets couldn't have moved me more. And so, serenely, we came to the end of the pilgrimage and I was just about to bid him good-bye, when I noticed on his desk a vase of water and in it one sprig of fruiting rowan. I glanced at him distrustfully. 'Was he teaching me a lesson?' I wondered, for at that age one cannot accept to be taught. But he wasn't; I knew it by the look on his face. He would do nothing so banal. He was not trying to enlighten me, and so I was enlightened and found a connection in the process. It needed only a sprig, said the lesson. And I learned, also, something about writing. The secret is to say less than you need. You don't want a forest, a leaf will do.

Next day, when I was lunching with Æ, he said to me, 'Yeats was very touched that you brought him a sprig of rowan from Innisfree.' So I had to tell him the whole story. You couldn't be untruthful with Æ. 'I hope,' he said slyly, 'when you go to Dunfanaghay'—his own favourite part of Ireland—'you won't cut down all the willows for me. What about the tree spirits? Remember the dryads!' Dryads! I'd grown up on a diet of mythology and on Innisfree I'd forgotten it all. It was Æ who had to remind me, Æ whose thought was crystal—clear and hard—and still had room for dryads. These men—he, Yeats, James Stephens, and the rest—had aristocratic minds. For them, the world was not fragmented. An idea did not suddenly grow, like Topsy, all alone and separate. For them, all things had antecedents, and long family trees. They saw nothing shameful or silly in myths and fairy stories, nor did they shovel them out of sight in some cupboard marked 'Only for Children'. They were always willing to concede that there were more things in heaven and earth than philosophy dreamed of. They allowed for the unknown. And, as you can imagine, I took great heart from this.

It was Æ who showed me how to look at and learn from one's own writing. 'Popkins,' he said once—he always called her just plain Popkins, whether deliberately mistaking the name or not, I never knew, his humour was always subtle—'Popkins, had she lived in another age, in the old times to which she certainly belongs, would undoubtedly have had long golden tresses, a wreath of flowers in one hand, and perhaps a spear in the other. Her eyes would have been like the sea, her nose comely, and on her feet winged sandals. But, this being Kali Yuga, as the Hindus call it—in our terms, the Iron Age—she comes in the habiliments most suited to it.'

Well, golden tresses and all that pretty paraphernalia didn't interest me; she could only be as she *was*. But that Æ could really know so much about it astonished me, that he should guess at her antecedents and genealogy when I hadn't thought of them myself—it put me on my mettle. I began to *read* the book. But it was only after many years that I realized what he meant, that she had come out of the same world as the fairy tales.

My childish love for the tales had continued in increase in me —Tolkien says somewhere that if you are natively attached to the fairy tales (lots of people are not and there's no blame in that), that habit grows on you as you grow older. And it has certainly grown on me. 'Only connect' comes strongly into this. Not long ago I read in the *New York Times* about how the eels from America and Europe make their way to the Sargasso Sea to mate and lay their eggs, the journey for American eels taking one year, for Europeans two. Afterwards, they make their long way back to their respective homes and apparently feel, it was worth it. Well, for me the tales are a sort of Sargasso Sea and I am a kind of eel. And all these years of pondering on the fairy tale, first of all for love of it—because to learn about anything, it seems to me, you have to love it first—and later because I became enthralled by it, all this pondering has led me to believe that the true fairy tales (I'm not talking now about invented ones) come straight out of myth; they are, as it were, miniscule reaffirmations of myth, or perhaps the myth made accessible to the local folkly mind. In the nineteenth century, as you know, Andrew Lang and all his fellow pundits treated them as the meanderings of the primitive intelligence—and therefore, apparently, suitable for children! Then the anthropologists had a go at them and later they descended, if I may so put it, to the psychoanalysts. But none of these seem to have been able to exhaust their meaning; there is still plenty left. They're like the magic pitcher in the Greek myth of Baucis and Philemon—you remember it retold in Hawthorne?—no matter how much milk you poured out, it was still full to the brim. This, of course, is where Jack's magic purse comes from; whenever you take out the last coin there is always another there.

Of course, you may ask—indeed, people are always asking—who invented the myths? And do you think they are true? Well, true? What is true? As far as I am concerned it doesn't matter tuppence if the incidents in the myths never happened. That does not make them any less true, for, indeed, in one way or another, they're happening all the time. You only have to open a newspaper to find them crowding into it. Life itself continually re-enacts them. Not long ago, staying with friends in Virginia, I watched from the terrace as two little girls of six and four performed the rite of burial over a dead bird. I guessed that they did not want to touch it, but they gathered all their grandfather's flowers and covered the body with them. Over these they laid branches and set a fence of sticks around them. Then they stood up and began to dance, not wildly, not gaily, not childishly, but formally, with measured steps. After that they knelt down, one on either side of the grave—were they praying? I couldn't see—and then they leaned across the sticks and gravely embraced each other. They had never been to church or a funeral, never before seen anything dead, knew nothing about the rite they were enacting out of ancestral memory, and the whole performance was true. I don't insist that you make anything out of it, but it meant something to me—the assurance that the myths and rites run around in our blood; that when old drums beat we stamp our feet, if only metaphorically. Time and the past are getting at us. The Australian aborigines have a word for this. To any happening further back than a grandmother their memories cannot go, any event further forward than a grandson, they cannot pretend to envisage. Beyond these times, when knowing is relatively possible, they can only reach by speaking of what lies there as the Dreaming. 'It is gone into Dreaming,' they say of the past. 'It will come in the Dreaming,' they say of the future.

There is a wonderful Japanese phrase, used as a Zen koan, which says, 'Not created but summoned'. It seems to me that this is all that can be said of the myths, 'They are in the Dreaming. They are not created but summoned.' But it is the fairy tale, not the myth that is really my province. One might say that fairy tales are the myths fallen into time and locality. For instance, if this glass of water is myth and I drink it, the last drop—or the lees of the wine—is the fairy tale. The drop is the same stuff, all the essentials are there; it is small, but perfect. Not minimized, not to be made digestible for children. I think it is more and more realized that the fairy tales are not entertainments for children at all. In their primal state, that is. They've been bowdlerized and had the essentials removed in order not to frighten—but to my mind it is better not to tell them at all than to take out all the vital organs and leave only the skin. And what *isn't* frightening, after all? What *doesn't* carry a stern lesson? Even the nursery rhymes present us with very difficult truths. And they, too, like the fairy tales, have long family trees, though it would not be easy, I admit, to prove it legally. Take Humpty Dumpty. All the King's horses and all the king's men couldn't put him together again. That some things are broken irrevocably, never to be whole again, is a hard truth and this is a good way of teaching it. Away back in Egypt, the myth was telling the same thing. You remember how, when the body of Osiris was cut up and scattered, his sister-wife Isis searched the world for the fourteen pieces, trying to re-member him and always unable to recover the fourteenth. I'm not trying here to suggest that whoever wrote 'Humpty Dumpty' had Isis and Osiris in mind. Of course not. I merely make the connection between them. And what about the cow that jumped over the moon? In Egypt the sky was always thought of as a cow, her body arching over the earth and her four legs standing firmly upon it. Again, it is I who make the link, not the writer of the rhyme. 'How many miles to Babylon?' What is that telling us, I wonder, with its three score and ten, the life of man? There is a gloss upon this rhyme that makes it perhaps a little clearer.

How many miles to Babylon?
If it's three score and ten
Bury me under the cold gravestone
For my time is come, but make no moan,
I shall be back by candle-light—
Many times again!

You may think this is hocus-pocus and mumbo-jumbo—and well it may be, except to me—but if you look in the Oxford dictionary, you will find that hocus-pocus itself derives from *hoc est corpus* —and we are, after all, talking here about the body, if I may so put it, of an idea. Mumbo-jumbo has, alas, no known derivation. It is a figure supposed to have been invented by African chiefs in order to keep their wives properly disciplined and to give them a sense of awe. As for fee fi fo fum, you must go back to ancient Greece for that. It was the great incantation of the Erinyes, the triple furies born from the drops of blood of Cronus; and the old world rang with it as they pursued their prey. What a long and circuitous way it took before it found a home in our western nurseries!

You may, of course, feel that this is drawing a long bow. But, as I see it, what is a long bow for but to be drawn? And our phrase 'the long bow' itself comes from the great bow of Philoctetes, one of the Argonauts, who inherited it from Hercules. A man came to be a hero inwardly and outwardly to be able to draw that bow.

Or it may be that you will categorize all this as 'old wives' tales'. But I am one who believes in old wives' tales and that it is the proper function of old wives to tell tales. Old wives have the best stories in the world, and long memories. Why should we treat them with contempt? The tales have to be told in order that we may understand that in the long run, whatever it may be, every man must become the hero of his own story; his own fairy tale, if you like, a real fairy tale. Hans Andersen for me, in spite of the fact that he often used old material, is an inventor of fairy tales; so is Oscar Wilde. Their tales have an element of nostalgia in them, a devitalizing element that the true tale never has. Perhaps those that most clearly derive from myth, those that clearly show their antecedents, are the Greek stories, the Norse tales, and Grimms'. These are old trees, rooted in the folk, full of meaning and ritual; they retell the myths in terms that can be understood by unlettered people. For originally they were for the listener rather than the reader; they came long before books. Every one of these tales, it seems to me, is asking something of us, telling us something about life. Of course I am now on my hobby-horse and anyone who wishes may get up and shoot at me or at any rate ask a question. I am not here to stand and assert but to share my questioning with you.

Doesn't it seem to you, too, that there is more in the tales than meets the eye? Think of all those stories of the three brothers who go off in search of various treasures. As a child, naturally, I thought of them as separate entities—the eldest so handsome, always delayed at the crossroads, or prevented from going farther because of some temptation. He's handsome and brave, and relying on this, he assures himself that when the time comes, he'll find the treasure. Then the second, sure of his cleverness, a cleverness that proves to be groundless, also fails in the quest. Lastly, the third brother sets out, realizing his ignorance, knowing himself a simpleton. And so he is. Simple and humble, willing to accept help from anyone who will give it. You'll remember the story of 'Puddocky', a prime example of this. I always loved that youngest son. Nowadays, however, I think of the brothers, not as single adventurers, but as three stages of one man. In the beginning he sets out bravely, young and handsome, and quickly gets to the end of that; but 'I'm still clever,' he thinks to himself; yet soon he finds even that's not true. He ends by knowing he knows nothing. And once he knows nothing he begins to know something, and from there it is really only a step to happy ever after.

The fairy tales also tell us a great deal about women—or perhaps about woman and her role in life, the triple role of maiden, mother, and crone. Each one of us, of course, begins as a maiden, and whether she becomes a physical mother or not makes no difference, the role of mother is the next step, the flowering of the bud. Last of all comes the grandmother—again, not the physical grandmother, but the stage where the flower withers into seed pod. To become a crone, it seems to me, is the last great hope of woman, supremely worth achieving. An old woman who remembers, who has gathered up all the threads of life and sits by the fire with her hands in her lap—not doing anything any more—what a marvellous thing! This is what it is to become wise. There you sit in your rocking-chair as in the fairy tales—I hope I shall, anyway—aware of all you have learned and garnered and having it available in case the young ones want it. You will not force it on them, but simply tell it.

That's what the crones—all those good and bad fairies—are doing in the tales.

Of course, it is not always easy to see the relation between the fairy tale and the myth. They do not *all* insist on telling you of their great-grandparents. But many of them have lineaments that loudly proclaim their breeding. Cinderella, for instance, whose story is so ancient that she is found in one guise or another in practically every mythology known to man. She has been grossly ill-treated, however, by writers of pantomime and by illustrators who retell the tales in terms of their own illustrations. Chop off a nose or leg, what does it matter? All tellers of the Cinderella story, ever since Perrault himself retold it, make the mistake of assuming that it is because she wishes that she goes to the ball. If that were so, wouldn't we all be married to princes? No, the wishing has much more behind it; it must be so if the happy ending is to be achieved. Grimms' comes near to the true theme. There, it is not because she wishes but because she has performed the necessary rites at her mother's grave, and because, above all, she has accepted her fate, that she meets the little benevolent bird who gives her the golden gown and all the magnificent rest. And then, the story has so many sisters. There is a book—the author's name is Cox—which has over 300 versions of the Cinderella story. But I like to make my own connections. Would you not say she was the girl in 'King Cophetua and the Beggar Maid'? Isn't she, as near as makes no matter, Patient Griselda? And who but Cinderella is Lear's Cordelia, with those two monstrous sisters? Going back to myth, you will find her in the garb of Sita, the prototype of all feminine virtue in the epic of the Ramayana, in India, which is as old as history.

And what about that recurrent theme where a character in the story agrees—for a price—to give the villain the first thing that runs to greet him on his return home? It's a wonderful story. You find it in 'The King of the Golden Mountain' and 'The Singing, Soaring Lark', and it goes back to Methuselah—

or at any rate the Old Testament, in the story of Jephthah's daughter. None of the true stories was born yesterday; they all come from far and have a long way yet to go. One that was dear to me as a child—I still think it most beautiful, even though others protest that it is brutal and bloody—was 'The Juniper Tree'. There is a wicked stepmother, of course, who, when the little stepson bends down to get an apple from a chest, drops the lid and cuts his head off. Even now I never bend over a chest without making quite sure that the top won't fall on me. And so the story goes from bad to worse. Sitting the body at the table, with the head balanced on top of it, she orders the little sister to call her brother to supper. Naturally, he does not answer, so the little sister gives him a shake and down falls the severed head. And now worse hurries on to worst. The stepmother cooks the child in a stew and gives this meal to the father when he comes home from work. 'Ah,' he exclaims, 'how truly delicious. I feel as though it were all mine.' As, indeed, of course, it is. Eventually the little watching bird puts all to rights, the little sister is freed of her supposed guilt, the little boy comes alive again, the stepmother—and serve her right!—is finished off with a millstone. It sounds, I admit, like a mess of horrors. But it never bothered me at all. Knowing the power of the little bird I never doubted that the boy would be safe. If, indeed, the father ate him, it was inevitable, even natural, that the boy would somehow, and in good time, return to his proper shape. After all, hadn't Cronus, the father of the gods, eaten up his children? Son after son was born to Rhea and each time Cronus said 'He'll supplant me!' and promptly swallowed him down. But with her last child Rhea grew cunning, swaddled a stone and gave it to her husband who, feeling—though erroneously—that it was all his, let it go the way of the others. Thus Zeus was saved to become king of the gods. And, once on his throne, he himself performed the same act—or an aspect of it—when he took his unborn son Dionysus into his own thigh—his mother having been burnt to death—and at the full period of nine months brought him forth, unharmed and perfect.

And then there are the countless stories that warn against trying to see too much; of the demon lover who persuades the maiden to marry him on the understanding that she must never, once the night falls, attempt to look at him. And always the maiden—who could help it?—always the maiden fails. Either she is persuaded by her family as—again!—in the 'Singing Soaring Lark' and 'Melusine', or she is overcome by curiosity, as in 'Cupid and Psyche'. And as a result he disappears or has to go through grave vicissitudes before he comes to himself once more. This theme comes directly out of myth; it goes back to the farthest limits of time when Semele, not knowing that her bridegroom was divine, yet suspecting it, begs him to grant her one boon, that she may see him in all his splendour. Reluctantly Zeus unveils himself and she, unable to endure the lightning, is herself turned to ash. The story is a warning, repeated down the centuries, through myth, folk and fairy tale, that it is dangerous to look upon the face of the god. Seek him rather with the inward eye.

'Rumpelstiltskin' was another of my favourities, for its meaning lay very close to me. Everyone knows the story of how the miller's daughter, in order to become a queen, promises the little old man her first child if he will spin her straw into gold. Of course he does it. It is no problem. To him they are one and the same. But when the child is born she cannot bear to part with it and he agrees to let her off if she can discover his name. So for three days she tries this and she tries that, always unsuccessfully, and he warns her that when tomorrow comes he will take the child away. In despair, she sends riders far and wide, east of the sun and west of the moon. Only one comes back with a clue. 'In the land where the wolf and the hare say good night to each other, I came upon an old man jumping up and down and singing, "My name is Rumpelstiltskin."' And so, the next day, making a great pretence of it, she asks the old man 'Is it Tom, is it Dick, is it Harry?' 'No!' 'Then is it Rumpelstiltskin?' And with that he shrieks a great 'Yes!' and stamps his foot into the earth and tears himself in two. His name is known, therefore he is finished. This role has been played out.

This idea of the secrecy of the name, the taboo against making it known, goes back to man's very early days, to the time, perhaps, when he had no name. During the war I spent two summers with the Navaho Indians, and when they gave me an Indian name they warned me that it would be bad luck both for me and the tribe if I ever disclosed it to anyone. And I never have. For one thing, I do not want to receive or give bad luck, and for another I have a strong atavistic feeling—one, I think, that is strongly shared by unlettered people all over the world—that to disclose one's name, or take another's before the time for it is ripe—well, it's dangerous. I tremble inwardly and withdraw when my Christian name is seized before I have given it, and I have the same hesitancy about using that of another person. An Indian—or a gypsy—would understand this very well. It is very ancient taboo and I relate it—though I don't suggest that anyone else relate it—to the earliest times when men built altars 'To the Unknown God'. If I were ever to build an altar, I would put that inscription above it.

In making these connections, I do not want to assert or impose. But, in fact, all things are separate and fragmentary until man himself connects them, sometimes wrongly and sometimes rightly. As far as I am concerned, it is all a matter of hint and suggestion, something seen at the corner of the eye and linked with another thing, equally fleeting. You remember Walt Whitman's poem, 'On the Beach at Night'. 'I give you the first suggestion, the problem, the indirection.' Isn't that wonderful? Turn your back on it and you'll find it! It's like Shakespeare's 'By indirection find direction out.' And with these quotations I connect Swift's dictum, 'Vision is the art of seeing things invisible.' Doesn't this relate to the unknown name?

But now let me make one last link. I was rereading recently how Aeneas came to Campania—which is now Naples—seeking some means of getting into contact with the ghost of his father, Anchises. First, for piety, he prays at the temple of Apollo, begging the god to inspire the Cumean Sybil, whose cave is at hand, to help him on his way to the underworld. Nearby is the great forest where lies the terrible Lake of Avernus over which no bird flies, and at the edge of that is the rift between the great rocks that guard the way to the realm of Pluto. You know the story. She tells him to break from one tree in the forest a small golden branch. With that in his hand he will be able to descend into the depths. So, holding the branch before him as an amulet, he begins the dreadful journey. Of course, the whole of Frazer's *Golden Bough* is about this branch and many of the fairy stories repeat it; 'The Shoes That Were Danced to Pieces', for instance, where the twelve princesses are followed each night to the underworld by a soldier who breaks off a little golden branch to bring back as a sign that he has, indeed, been there. Not for nothing, I thought, as I read again of Aeneas, were those four sites so close together—the temple of Apollo, the cave of the Sybil, the Lake of Avernus, the Land of the Dead. It is inevitable that they should touch and interpenetrate each other, not only in myth, but in life. Life, in a sense, *is* myth, one might say; the one is a part of the other. In both of them, the good and the bad, the dangerous and the safe, live very close together. And I remembered, as I thought about this, how Aeneas had begged the Sybil to speak her oracle in words and not, as was her usual practice, to write it on leaves that would blow away. That struck a chord in me, for I knew a story where this had actually happened. In this story the wind blows leaves into the hands of two children. And on each leaf a message is written. One says 'Come' and the other 'Tonight'. Now the story I'm talking about is 'Halloween'. It is in *Mary Poppins in the Park*. And there is the Sybil obeying Aeneas by writing the oracle down on leaves!

And I thought I had invented it! There's a poem by Rupert Brooke, one verse of which says:

There's wisdom in women, of more than they have known,
And thoughts go blowing through them, are wiser than their own.

Truly, I had far wiser thoughts than my own when I wrote that story. You may remember—though why should you?—that it is about a party in the park where all the shadows are free. They go out to enjoy themselves and leave their owners at home. The only one whose shadow refuses to go without her is—guess!—Mary Poppins.

I find another connection here in the fact that tonight happens to be Halloween. In ancient times this used to be the festival of the dead. I think it was one of the Popes, Boniface IV, perhaps, in the seventh century, who decided to do away with all the pagan saturnalia and turn it from what it so significantly was, into a commemoration of the saints and martyrs. But in spite of him the myth never lost its mystery: men needed the festival rites for the dead; they needed to find a way out of grieving that would ease their fear that the spirits of the dead might come back to earth and haunt them. They put on masks and disguised their faces, wrapping themselves, to cheat the ghosts, in the garments of black that became for us, their late descendants, simply mourning clothes. The wake that the Irish hold for the dead is part of this ancient saturnalia. It gives an opportunity and a justification for the living to turn their faces again to life; it also provides a propitious moment, a ritual moment one could say, a kind of crack through which some element of the unknown can be brought into the known.

Is anyone thinking of saints and martyrs on this Halloween, I wonder? And who knows, when they leave this hall, that their shadows will be with them? For me the fairy tales are abroad tonight. Good fairies and demons, Beauty and the Beast—they are all knocking at the doors, rattling their money boxes and holding out grubby hands for candy. It's a pagan festival still, be sure, swinging between trick and treat, angel and devil, yes and no. It is a night of ghosts and shadows, a night that links the past and the present, a night perhaps when that crack between known and unknown could open, and we could believe the old Greek poet, Aratus, when he declared: 'Full of Zeus are the cities, full of Zeus are the harbours, full of Zeus are all the ways of men.'

If it was true then, it is true always; time cannot change the timeless. It could be—could it not?—*this* city, full of lighted, grinning pumpkin faces; *that* harbour out on Chesapeake Bay; *we* men—if we could only connect. What do you think?

[1967]

On three ways of writing for children

C. S. LEWIS

I think there are three ways in which those who write for children may approach their work: two good ways and one that is generally a bad way.

I came to know of the bad way quite recently and from two unconscious witnesses. One was a lady who sent me the MS. of a story she had written in which a fairy placed at a child's disposal a wonderful gadget. I say 'gadget' because it was not a magic ring or hat or cloak or any such traditional matter. It was a machine, a thing of taps and handles and buttons you could press. You could press one and get an ice cream, another and get a live puppy, and so forth. I had to tell the author honestly that I didn't much care for that sort of thing. She replied, 'No more do I, it bores me to distraction. But it is what the modern child wants'. My other bit of evidence was this. In my own first story I had described at length what I thought was a rather fine high tea given by a hospitable faun to the little girl who was my heroine. A man who has children of his own said, 'Ah, I see how you got to that. If you want to please grown-up readers you give them sex, so you thought to yourself, "that won't do for children, what shall I give them instead? I know! The little blighters like plenty of good eating!" ' In reality, however, I myself like eating and drinking. I put in what I would have liked to read when I was a child and what I still like reading now that I am in my fifties.

The lady in my first example, and the married man in my second, both conceived writing for children as a special department of 'giving the public what it wants'. Children are, of course, a special public, and you find out what they want and give them that, however little you like it yourself.

The next way may seem at first to be very much the same, but I think the resemblance is superficial. This is the way of Lewis Carroll, Kenneth Grahame, and Tolkien. The printed story grows out of a story told to a particular child with the living voice and perhaps *ex tempore*. It resembles the first way because you are certainly trying to give that child what it wants. But then you are dealing with a concrete person, this child who, of course, differs from all other children. There is no question of 'children' conceived as a strange species whose habits you have 'made up' like an anthropologist or a commercial traveller. Nor, I suspect, would it be possible, thus face to face, to regale the child with things calculated to please it but regarded by yourself with indifference or contempt. The child, I am certain, would see through that. In any personal relation the two participants modify each other. You would become slightly different because you were talking to a child and the child would become slightly different because it was being talked to by an adult. A community, a composite personality, is created and out of that the story grows.

The third way, which is the only one I could ever use myself, consists in writing a children's story because a children's story is the best art-form for something you have to say: just as a composer might write a Dead March not because there was a public funeral in view but because certain musical ideas that had occurred to him went best into that form. This method could apply to other kinds of children's literature besides stories. I have been told that Arthur Mee never met a child and never wished to: it was, from his point of view, a bit of luck that boys liked reading what he liked writing. This anecdote may be untrue in fact but it illustrates my meaning.

Within the species 'children's story' the sub-species which happened to suit me is the fantasy or (in a loose sense of that word) the fairy tale. There are, of course, other sub-species. E. Nesbit's trilogy about the Bastable family is a very good specimen of another kind. It is a 'children's story' in the sense that children can and do read it, but it is also the only form in which E. Nesbit could have given us so much of the humours of childhood. It is true that the Bastable children appear, successfully treated from the adult point of view, in one of her grownup novels, but they appear only for a moment. I do not think she would have kept it up. Sentimentality is so apt to creep in if we write at length about children as seen by their elders. And the reality of childhood, as we all experienced it, creeps out. For we all remember that our childhood, as lived, was immeasurably different from what our elders saw. Hence Sir Michael Sadler, when I asked his opinion about a certain new experimental school, replied, 'I never give an opinion on any of those experiments till the children have grown up and can tell *us what really happened*.' Thus the Bastable trilogy, however improbable many of its episodes may be, provides even adults, in one sense, with more realistic reading about children than they could find in most books addressed to adults. But also, conversely, it enables the children who read it to do something much more mature than they realize. For the whole book is a character study of Oswald, an unconsciously satiric self-portrait, which every intelligent child can fully appreciate: but no child would sit down to read a character study in any other form. There is another way in which children's stories mediate this psychological interest, but I will reserve that for later treatment.

In this short glance at the Bastable trilogy I think we have stumbled on a principle. Where the children's story is simply the right form for what the author has to say, then of course readers who want to hear that will read the story or reread it at any age. I never met *The Wind in the Willows* or the Bastable books till I was in my late twenties, and I do not think I have enjoyed them any the less on that account. I am almost inclined to set it up as a canon that a children's story which is enjoyed only by children is a bad children's story. The good ones last. A waltz which you can like only when you are waltzing is a bad waltz.

This canon seems to me most obviously true of that particular type of children's story which is dearest to my own taste, the fantasy or fairy tale. Now the modern critical world uses 'adult' as a term of approval. It is hostile to what it calls 'nostalgia' and contemptuous of what it calls 'Peter Pantheism'. Hence a man who admits that dwarfs and giants and talking beasts and witches are still dear to him in his fifty-third year is now less likely to be praised for his perennial youth than scorned and pitied for arrested development. If I spend some little time defending myself against these charges, this is not so much because it matters greatly whether I am scorned and pitied as because the defence is germane to my whole view of the fairy tale and even of literature in general. My defence consists of three propositions.

1. I reply with a *tu quoque*. Critics who treat *adult* as a term of approval, instead of as a merely descriptive term, cannot be adult themselves. To be concerned about being grownup, to admire the grownup because it is grownup, to blush at the suspicion of being childish—these things are the marks of childhood and adolescence. And in childhood and adolescence they are, in moderation, healthy symptoms. Young things ought to want to grow. But to carry on into middle life or even into early manhood this concern about being adult is a mark of really arrested development. When I was ten, I read fairy tales in secret and would have been ashamed if I had been found doing so. Now that I am fifty I read them openly. When I became a man I put away childish things, including the fear of childishness and the desire to be very grownup.

2. The modern view seems to me to involve a false conception of growth. They accuse us of arrested development because we

have not lost a taste we had in childhood. But surely arrested development consists not in refusing to lose old things but in failing to add new things? I now like hock, which I am sure I should not have liked as a child. But I still like lemon-squash. I call this growth or development because I have been enriched: where I formerly had only one pleasure, I now have two. But if I had to lose the taste for lemon-squash before I acquired the taste for hock, that would not be growth but simple change. I now enjoy Tolstoy and Jane Austen and Trollope as well as fairy tales and I call that growth; if I had had to lose the fairy tales in order to acquire the novelists, I would not say that I had grown but only that I had changed. A tree grows because it adds rings; a train doesn't grow by leaving one station behind and puffing on to the next. In reality, the case is stronger and more complicated than this. I think my growth is just as apparent when I now read the fairy tales as when I read the novelists, for I now enjoy the fairy tales better than I did in childhood: being now able to put more in, of course I get more out. But I do not here stress that point. Even if it were merely a taste for grownup literature added to an unchanged taste for children's literature, addition would still be entitled to the name 'growth', and the process of merely dropping one parcel when you pick up another would not. It is, of course, true that the process of growing does, incidently and unfortunately, involve some more losses. But that is not the essence of growth, certainly not what makes growth admirable or desirable. If it were, if to drop parcels and to leave stations behind were the essence and virture of growth, why should we stop at the adult? Why should not *senile* be equally a term of approval? Why are we not to be congratulated on losing our teeth and hair? Some critics seem to confuse growth with the cost of growth and also to wish to make that costs far higher than, in nature, it need be.

3. The whole association of fairy tale and fantasy with childhood is local and accidental. I hope everyone has read Tolkien's

essay on fairy tales,[1] which is perhaps the most important contribution to the subject that anyone has yet made. If so, you will know already that, in most places and times, the fairy tale has not been specially made for, nor exclusively enjoyed by, children. It has gravitated to the nursery when it became unfashionable in literary circles, just as unfashionable furniture gravitated to the nursery in Victorian houses. In fact, many children do not like this kind of book, just as many children do not like horsehair sofas: and many adults do like it, just as many adults like rocking-chairs. And those who do like it, whether young or old, probably like it for the same reason. And none of us can say with any certainty what that reason is. The two theories which are most often in my mind are those of Tolkien and of Jung.

According to Tolkien the appeal of the fairy story lies in the fact that man there most fully exercises his function as a 'sub-creator'; not, as they love to say now, making a 'comment upon life' but making, so far as possible, a subordinate world of his own. Since, in Tolkien's view, this is one of man's proper functions, delight naturally arises whenever it is successfully performed. For Jung, fairy tale liberates the Archetypes which dwell in the collective unconscious, and when we read a good fairy tale we are obeying the old precept 'Know thyself'. I would venture to add to this my own theory, not indeed of the Kind as a whole, but of one feature in it: I mean, the presence of beings other than human which yet behave, in varying degrees, humanly—the giants and dwarfs and talking beasts. I believe these to be at least (for they may have many other sources of power and beauty) an admirable hieroglyphic which conveys psychology, types of character, more briefly than novelistic presentation and to readers whom novelistic presentation could not yet reach. Consider Mr Badger in *The Wind in the Willows*—that extraordinary amalgam of high rank, coarse manners, gruffness, shyness, and goodness. The child who has once met Mr Badger has

---

[1] [See pages 111 to 120 for a long extract from this essay.]

ever afterwards in its bones a knowledge of humanity and of English social history which it could not get in any other way.

Of course as all children's literature is not fantastic, so all fantastic books need not be children's books. It is still possible, even in an age so ferociously anti-romantic as our own, to write fantastic stories for adults—though you will usually need to have made a name in some more fashionable kind of literature before anyone will publish them. But there may be an author who at a particular moment finds not only fantasy but fantasy-for-children the exactly right form for what he wants to say. The distinction is a fine one. His fantasies for children and his fantasies for adults will have very much more in common with one another than either has with the ordinary novel or with what is sometimes called 'the novel of child life'. Indeed the same readers will probably read both his fantastic 'juveniles' and his fantastic stories for adults. For I need not remind such an audience as this that the neat sorting-out of books into age-groups, so dear to publishers, has only a very sketchy relation with the habits of any real readers. Those of us who are blamed when old for reading childish books were blamed when children for reading books too old for us. No reader worth his salt trots along in obedience to a time-table. The distinction then is a fine one; and I am not quite sure what made me, in a particular year of my life, feel that not only a fairy tale, but a fairy tale addressed to children, was exactly what I must write—or burst. Partly, I think that this form permits, or compels, you to leave out things I wanted to leave out. It compels you to throw all the force of the book into what was done and said. It checks what a kind but discerning critic called 'the expository demon' in me. It also imposes certain very fruitful necessities about length.

If I have allowed the fantastic type of children's story to run away with this discussion, that is because it is the kind I know and love best, not because I wish to condemn any other. But the patrons of the other kinds very frequently want to condemn it. About once every hundred years some wiseacre gets up and tries to banish the fairy tale. Perhaps I had better say a few words in its defence, as reading for children.

It is accused of giving a false impression of the world they live in. But I think no literature that children could read gives them less of a false impression. I think what profess to be realistic stories for children are far more likely to deceive them. I never expected the real world to be like the fairy tales. I think that I did expect school to be like the school stories. The fantasies did not deceive me: the school stories did. All stories in which children have adventures and successes which are possible, in the sense that they do not break the laws of nature, but almost infinitely improbable, are in more danger than the fairy tales of raising false expectations.

Almost the same answer serves for the popular charge of escapism, though here the question is not so simple. Do fairy tales teach children to retreat into a world of wish-fulfilment—'fantasy' in the technical psychological sense of the word—instead of facing the problems of the real world? Now it is here that the problem becomes subtle. Let us again lay the fairy tale side by side with the school story or any other story which is labelled a 'Boy's Book' or a Girl's Book', as distinct from a 'Children's Book.' There is no doubt that both arouse, and imaginatively satisfy, wishes. We long to go through the looking-glass, to reach fairyland. We also long to be the immensely popular and successful schoolboy or schoolgirl, or the lucky boy or girl who discovers the spy's plot or rides the horse that none of the cowboys can manage. But the two longings are very different. The second, especially when directed on something so close as school life, is ravenous and deadly serious. Its fulfilment on the level of imagination is in very truth compensatory: we run to it from the disappointments and humiliations of the real world; it sends us back to the real world undivinely discontented. For it is all flattery to the ego. The pleasure consists in picturing oneself the object of admiration. The other longing, that for fairyland, is very different. In a sense a child does not long for fairyland as a boy longs to be the hero of the first eleven. Does anyone suppose that he really and prosaically longs for all the dangers and discomforts of a fairy tale?—really wants dragons in contemporary England? It is not so. It would be much truer to say that fairyland arouses a longing for he knows not what. It stirs and troubles him (to his lifelong enrichment) with the dim sense of something beyond his reach and, far from dulling or emptying the actual world, gives it a new dimension of depth. He does not despise real woods because he has read of enchanted woods: the reading makes all real woods a little enchanted. This is a special kind of longing. The boy reading the school story of the type I have in mind desires success and is unhappy (once the book is over) because he can't get it: the boy reading the fairy tale desires and is happy in the very fact of desiring. For his mind has not been concentrated on himself, as it often is in the more realistic story.

I do not mean that school stories for boys and girls ought not be written. I am only saying that they are far more liable to become 'fantasies' in the clinical sense than fantastic stories are. And this distinction holds for adult reading too. The dangerous fantasy is always superficially realistic. The real victim of wishful reverie does not batten on *The Odyssey*, *The Tempest*, or *The Worm Ouroboros*: he (or she) prefers stories about millionaires, irresistible beauties, posh hotels, palm beaches, and bedroom scenes—things that really might happen, that ought to happen, that would have happened if the reader had had a fair chance. For, as I say, there are two kinds of longing. The one is an *askesis*, a spiritual exercise, and the other is a disease.

A far more serious attack on the fairy tale as children's literature comes from those who do not wish children to be frightened. I suffered too much from night-fears myself in childhood to undervalue this objection. I would not wish to heat the fires of that private hell for any child. On the other hand, none of my fears came from fairy tales. Giant insects were my specialty, with ghosts a bad second. I suppose the ghosts came directly or indirectly from stories, though certainly not from fairy stories, but I don't think the insects did. I don't know anything my parents could have done or left undone which would have saved me from the pincers, mandibles, and eyes of those many-legged abominations. And that, as so many people have pointed out, is the difficulty. We do not know what will or will not frighten a child in this particular way. I say 'in this particular way' for we must here make a distinction. Those who say that children must not be frightened may mean two things. They may mean (1) that we must not do anything likely to give the child those haunting, disabling, pathological fears against which ordinary courage is helpless: in fact, *phobias*. His mind must, if possible, be kept clear of things he can't bear to think of. Or they may mean (2) that we must try to keep out of his mind the knowledge that he is born into a world of death, violence, wounds, adventure, heroism and cowardice, good and evil. If they mean the first I agree with them: but not if they mean the second. The second would indeed be to give children a false impression and feed them on escapism in the bad sense. There is something ludicrous in the idea of so educating a generation which is born to the Ogpu and the atomic bomb. Since it is so likely that they will meet cruel enemies, let them at least have heard of brave knights and heroic courage. Otherwise you are making their destiny not brighter but darker. Nor do most of us find that violence and bloodshed, in a story, produce any haunting dread in the minds of children. As far as that goes, I side impenitently with the human race against the modern reformer. Let there be wicked kings and beheadings, battles and dungeons, giants and dragons, and let villains be soundly killed at the end of the book. Nothing will persuade me that this causes an ordinary child any kind or degree of fear beyond what it wants, and needs, to feel. For, of course, it wants to be a little frightened.

The other fears—the phobias—are a different matter. I do not believe one can control them by literary means. We seem to bring them into the world with us ready made. No doubt the particular image on which the child's terror is fixed can sometimes be traced to a book. But is that the source, or only the occasion, of the fear? If he had been spared that image, would not some other, quite unpredictable by you, have had the same effect? Chesterton has told us of a boy who was more afraid of the Albert Memorial than anything else in the world. I know a man whose great childhood terror was the India paper edition of the *Encyclopaedia Britannica*—for a reason I defy you to guess. And I think it possible that by confining your child to blameless stories of child life in which nothing at all alarming ever happens, you would fail to banish the terrors, and would succeed in banishing all that can ennoble them or make them endurable. For in the fairy tales, side by side with the terrible figures, we find the immemorial comforters and protectors, the radiant ones: and the terrible figures are not merely terrible, but sublime. It would be nice if no little boy in bed, hearing, or thinking he hears, a sound, were ever at all frightened. But if he is going to be frightened, I think it better that he should think of giants and dragons than merely of burglars. And I think St George, or any bright champion in armour, is a better comfort than the idea of the police.

I will even go further. If I could have escaped all my own night-fears at the price of never having known 'faerie', would I now be the gainer by that bargain? I am not speaking carelessly. The fears were very bad. But I think the price would have been too high.

But I have strayed far from my theme. This has been inevitable for, of the three methods, I know by experience only the third. I hope my title did not lead anyone to think that I was conceited enough to give you advice on how to write a story for children. There were two very good reasons for not doing that. One is that many people have written very much better stories than I, and I would rather learn about the art than set up to teach it. The other is that, in a certain sense, I have never exactly 'made' a story. With me the process is much more like bird-watching than like either talking or building. I see pictures. Some of these pictures have a common flavour, almost a common smell, which groups them together. Keep quiet and watch and they will begin joining themselves up. If you were very lucky (I have never been as lucky as all that), a whole set might join themselves so consistently that there you had a complete story without doing anything yourself. But more often (in my experience always) there are gaps. Then at last you have to do some deliberate inventing, have to contrive reasons why these characters should be in these various places doing these various things. I have no idea whether this is the usual way of writing stories, still less whether it is the best. It is the only one I know: images always come first.

Before closing, I would like to return to what I said at the beginning. I rejected any approach which begins with the question 'What do modern children like?' I might be asked 'Do you equally reject the approach which begins with the question "What do modern children need?"—in other words, with the moral or didactic approach?' I think the answer is Yes. Not because I don't like stories to have a moral: certainly not because I think children dislike a moral. Rather because I feel sure that the question 'What do modern children need?' will not lead you to a good moral. If we ask that question we are assuming too superior an attitude. It would be better to ask 'What moral do I need?', for I think we can be sure that what does not concern us deeply will not deeply interest our readers, whatever their age. But it is better not to ask the question at all. Let the pictures tell you their own moral. For the moral inherent in them will rise from whatever spiritual roots you have succeeded in striking during the whole course of your life. But if they don't show you any moral, don't put one in. For the moral you put in is likely to be a platitude, or even a falsehood, skimmed from the surface of your consciousness. It is impertinent to offer the children that. For we have been told on high authority that in the moral sphere they are probably at least as wise as we. Anyone who *can* write a children's story without a moral, had better do so: that is, if he is going to write children's stories at all. The only moral that is of any value is that which arises inevitably from the whole cast of the author's mind.

Indeed everything in the story should arise from the whole cast of the author's mind. We must write for children out of those elements in our own imagination which we share with children: differing from our child readers not by any less, or less serious, interest in the things we handle, but by the fact that we have other interests which children would not share with us. The matter of our story should be a part of the habitual furniture of our minds. This, I fancy, has been so with all great writers for children, but it is not generally understood. A critic not long ago said in praise of a very serious fairy tale that the author's tongue 'never once got into his cheek'. But why on earth should it?—unless he had been eating a seed-cake. Nothing seems to me more fatal, for this art, than an idea that whatever we share with children is, in the privative sense, 'childish' and that whatever is childish is somehow comic. We must meet children as equals in that area of our nature where we are their equals. Our superiority consists partly in commanding other areas, and partly (which is more relevant) in the fact that we are better at telling stories than they are. The child as reader is neither to be patronized nor idolized: we talk to him as man to man. But the worst attitude of all would be the professional attitude which regards children in the lump as a sort of raw material which we have to handle. We must of course try to do them no harm: we may, under the Omnipotence, sometimes dare to hope that we may do them good. But only such good as involves treating them with respect. We must not imagine that we are Providence or Destiny. I will not say that a good story for children could never be written by someone in the Ministry of Education, for all things are possible. But I should lay very long odds against it.

Once in a hotel dining-room I said, rather too loudly, 'I loathe prunes.' 'So do I' came an unexpected six-year-old voice from another table. Sympathy was instantaneous. Neither of us thought it funny. We both knew that prunes are far too nasty to be funny. That is the proper meeting between man and child as independent personalities. Of the far higher and more difficult relations between child and parent or child and teacher, I say nothing. An author, as a mere author, is outside all that. He is not even an uncle. He is a freeman and an equal, like the postman, the butcher, and the dog next door.

[1952]

The animal story: a challenge in technique

WILLIAM H. MAGEE

In art realistic animals are as old as the caveman drawing on his stone wall, but in the novel and short story they are as new as the theory of evolution. A direct if minor effect on literature of the controversy over that theory appeared in the sudden creation of animal heroes in the closing quarters of the nineteenth century. Although a consciousness of such an inspiration would probably have shocked some of the first modern writers with four-legged heroes, particularly moralists who made a cause of the prevention of cruelty to animals, Sir Charles G. D. Roberts made the connection. He also described the first consistently realistic animals in literature, thus giving Canada a founding influence in this development in modern literature.

Ancient and medieval writers who had used animals in fiction usually had had purposes which discouraged or even prevented realistic characterization. Primitive storytellers used animals as antagonists of human heroes to depict man's struggle for survival against nature. Those animals might possibly have been created as true to life as had those in the cave drawings, but in fact the temptation of making them almost human antagonists, of having them think human thoughts and speak, beguiled the storytellers away from the simple truth of the cave artistry. In contrast, didactic stories called for animal figures that were strictly human except for some single superficial characteristic. For classical writers Aesop's *Fables* provided virtually the archetype for animal heroes. Likewise medieval writers used animals to point up human morals for human readers, in allegory as well as in fable. Bestiaries perhaps partook no more of the fantastic than did most medieval literature, but the animal characters were easier to pervert than the human ones. Medieval romance encouraged fantasy still more, with dreamland dragons and questing beasts. None of these classical or medieval literary purposes encouraged the depicting of animals as characters leading independent lives.

Renaissance and neo-classical writers showed much less interest in using animals as characters. For although their object in writing remained essentially didactic, the new spirit of representational art controlled their technique. In their man-oriented world, too, new literary uses for animals were not likely to develop, and even stories in earlier forms touched on the animal characters more lightly. Romances used considerably fewer animals, pastoral heroes and heroines ignored their sheep, and La Fontaine forced a satire of his human contemporaries on animals in the Aesop tradition. Indeed the customary bent towards satire made neo-classical animals still less realistic, for they were required to expose this or that human foible. Perhaps it was unconscious remorse for this falsification, together with increased knowledge of geography, that sent the fanciful beasts migrating to the then much smaller unknown world. Although the temper of the times encouraged such writers as Swift to make such creatures conform to common sense, with the houyhnhnms a didactic aim still thwarts realism in the characterization of animals. Before animals could again come into general use in literature, two changes had to occur. First, the nonhuman heroes had to live for their own ends, not just to echo the concerns of human readers. Second, some new techniques had to be found for drawing in words a truly representational character study of animals. Neither their primitive use as daily antagonists of man nor their medieval use for allegory or romance appealed to writers in the early nineteenth century, and no new one developed. Only single lesser writers who watched them with objective interest, such as Mrs Catharine Parr Traill, or who hunted, like Robert Surtees, thought of building simple stories around them.

The widespread use of animals in modern literature dates from the last quarter of the nineteenth century. In 1877 Anna Sewell began the vogue with *Black Beauty,* the best selling horse story which pleaded for more humane treatment of domestic animals. Through her philanthropy Miss Sewell had hit on a purpose for her story which distinguishes animal characters from man, instead of stressing similarities. The artistic appeal for human readers is genuinely indirect, a good will based perhaps on the misery and cruelty suffered by all living creatures and caused by bad men. For the first time in literary history it was no longer desirable or even artistically sensible to draw manlike animals. Any failure to make the domestic animals credible on the part of Anna Sewell or her followers is the result only of failures in technique.

Pets can beguile readers into tears even more readily than horses can, and so it is that the Canadian contribution to Anna Sewell's type of animal story is even more sentimental than *Black Beauty.* When Margaret Marshall Saunders wrote her famous dog story, *Beautiful Joe* (1894), she won a competition for a companion piece to *Black Beauty.* Again the animal is at the centre of the scene, and again the author stresses needs peculiar to it rather than common with man. Indeed *Beautiful Joe* seems for chapter at a time to be less a story than a manual in the care of animals. Chapter headings read 'Training a Puppy', Goldfish and Canaries', 'A Neglected Stable', 'A Talk about Sheep'; but these at least avoid the sentimentality and melodrama of the rest of the book. At first the dog hero is, as he puts it, merely a dumb animal, but he quickly finds a way to communicate the author's message to younger puppies, such as Billy the fox terrier: 'I used to tell him that he would kill himself if he could eat all he wanted to.' The characterization of Beautiful Joe takes on a clarity of outline through its new, nonhuman perspective, and some continuing credibility results from the marked simplicity of the dog's reflections and its lack of dialogue. Miss Saunder's failure came in the more advanced challenge of devising a credible plot for her dog hero. Confronted with the need to develop a conflict, she borrowed a melodramatic villain and weeping young woman from the traditions of nineteenth-century human fiction. The cruel master Jenkins not only demonstrates man's cruelty to animals by disfiguring the hero, he also destroys the initial authenticity of the story when he tries to rob and burn a house which the hero dog is defending. The constant Christian didacticism in the book suggests another literary tradition of the times. As a result, the story which begins from a distinctive and credible nonhuman point of view ends in a medley of long popular conventions of fiction. They sufficed to make *Beautiful Joe* the most popular Canadian best seller to date, as well as to launch Miss Saunders on a career which ran to nearly a dozen domestic animal novels, none of which shows any advances in technique.

Also in 1894, Rudyard Kipling introduced a different widespread use of animals in modern literature with his first *Jungle Book*. It is a pure romance of man living among the beasts of the jungle, with the boy Mowgli as the typical hero of an adventure which differs from the hackneyed only because of the rest of the cast. Sometimes Kipling reverted to the primitive use of animals as antagonists of man, sometimes his characters echo human virtues and vices. The animals would suit Kipling's purpose at least as well if they were characterized realistically. As with Miss Sewell and Miss Saunders, the old hybrid characters no longer were essential to the purpose, and the incredible humanness is merely a difficulty of technique. The chief literary advance in Kipling's animal stories results from the more unified atmosphere provided by his romantic approach. Kipling subdued the attendant artistic dangers of triviality, sentimentality, and melodrama, although his sprawling progeny of Tarzan and other yarns of men living among somewhat nonhuman beasts has carried the art of fiction close to its nadir. Sir Charles G. D. Roberts objected to the falsified animals of both traditions and started a third and accurate one in *Earth's Enigmas* (1896).

When Roberts turned to the animal world to populate his stories, he tried to look at life from the animals' point of view. To do so he would choose an animal or animal family going about its daily business of searching for food, the most common concern of such creatures, Roberts felt. Their chief obstacle is the threat of danger or death from the intended victim or from another hungry animal. Consequently the typical character has a serious outlook on life, with no time for fun, no concern for outsiders, and the stories seethe with this solemnity. When the simple wants of two such hungry animals clash, when the one eats the other, or more often the young of the other, the irreconcilable conflict creates an effect of stark tragedy. Roberts usually increased the poignancy of this effect by making the animals either pregnant or starving from trying to feed their young. In 'The Young Ravens That Call upon Him' *(Earth's Enigmas)*, a starving eagle seizes a newborn lamb to feed the starving eaglets, bringing momentary contentment to the nest but leaving the wandering ewe utterly forlorn. Such a juxtaposition can make the animal story a profound comment on the tragedy of life on earth.

Having focused his animal characters on the central concern of their lives, Roberts went on to draw them as convincingly nonhuman. Anna Sewell and Miss Saunders had chosen a special rather than a central problem of animals in the world, one in which man plays a unique and godlike rather than a similar role. Without any men at all in some of his stories, Roberts was driven back to consider the first principles of animal characterization. His animals do not talk, and their thoughts are single, immediate, and simple. Most of the time their behaviour is habitual or instinctive, as when the male eagle always hunts the

Squatook Lakes and his mate hunts the Tuladi in 'The Lord of the Air' (from *The Kindred of the Wild*). When the environment changes, as when an Indian trapper regularly leaves food for the male eagle, and later a net under the food, the eagle comes to accept the change as habitual too. After being captured, the bird can think of one quick move to escape, but only pride provides the continuing urge to escape, and an unexpected ferocity makes it succeed. As the story closes, the eagle has returned to its habitual perch over the Squatooks. The dominion of the eagle, and his determination, make the character heroic, but the simplicity of his outlook helps retain the conviction of reality.

At best Roberts developed a powerful new literary form out of the simple stories of such realistic animals. The climax of two stories of starving animals in the same incident lends depth to the view of the world, and the joining at the climax turns their innocent wants into pathetic tragedy. A rare irony deepens the effect still further at the end of 'When Twilight Falls on the Stump Lots' *(Kindred of the Wild)*, after a mother cow has fatally gored a bear looking for food for its cubs:

The merry little cubs within the den were beginning to expect her, and getting restless. As the night wore on, and no mother came, they ceased to be merry. By morning they were shivering with hunger and desolate fear. But the doom of the ancient wood was less harsh than its wont, and spared them some days of starving anguish; for about noon a pair of foxes discovered the dead mother, astutely estimated the situation, and then, with the boldness of good appetite, made their way into the unguarded den.

As for the red calf, its fortune was ordinary. Its mother, for all her wounds, was able to nurse and cherish it through the night; and with morning came a searcher from the farm and took it, with the bleeding mother, safely back to the settlement. There it was tended and fattened, and within a few weeks found its way to the cool marble slabs of a city market.

The curtailed lives of both groups in the conflict, dams and offspring alike, add a perspective of the futility of survival that makes this Robert's most moving story. Perhaps a less conscious irony underlies the treatment of man as just another animal with the same hunger to satisfy. In 'Savoury Meats' *(Kindred of the Wild)*, a man shoots a doe to give his invalid father the red food to live, but a wildcat eats the abandoned fawn. In 'Wild Motherhood' *(Kindred of the Wild)*, which tells three parallel stories, a man with a meat-hungry wife and son shoots not only a wolf who is trying to feed a pregnant mate who cannot hunt because of missing a paw, but also the moose that the wolf is hunting. In stories like these man is an animal competing with his fellows in satisfying the same wants, and succeeding because he is the most fit.

Other variations on the basic characters and plots proved less rewarding. Stories of men trapping tended to distract Roberts into sentimental studies of tender-hearted human beings. 'The Moonlight Trails' *(Kindred of the Wild)* ends with a boy, who has excitedly been snaring rabbits, repenting at the sight of dead rabbits hanging in the noose. Even more sentimental is the longing of a goose that has been raised on a farm from a wild egg to be off with the migration ('The Homesickness of Kehonka', *Kindred of the Wild*). The young goose, with his wings clipped, falls easy prey to a red fox, but by then his untamable spirit has no doubt done its intended work on the reader. Once in a while man even enters as a god looking after animals like a puppet master. In 'The Watchers of the Camp-Fire' *(Kindred of the Wild)*, the man shoots a hungry panther just to save a doe which has been attracted to the site by the light of his campfire. In casting around for the necessary variety in the development of his plots, Roberts fell back more and more on the repertoire of human fiction, particularly in his later volumes. Roberts also had an instinctive bent towards romantic justice which clashed with the air of objectivity so important to his best effects. In 'The Haunter of the Pine Gloom' *(Kindred of the Wild)*, the animal-loving young boy of 'The Moonlight Trails' turns out to hate lynx while loving all other creatures. With romance entered nostalgia, with nostalgia sentimentality. A heightened scene produces a heightened emotion, and so melodrama was pressed in service.

Ultimately Roberts was unable to develop a general repertoire of fresh characters and situations for his new genre. Deliberately giving up the dialogue, the extended descriptions, and the casual plotting of traditional fiction, he found it difficult to fill up his stories without repetition. The juxtaposition of two or even three parallel searchers for food, climaxing in tragedy for at least one, eked out the material for several well-rounded stories, but it did not provide a pattern which was repeatedly reusable and fresh. The restriction to simple wants also worked against variety. In effect Roberts seldom wrote well with any other want for his heroes than food. In 'The King of the Mamozekel' *(Kindred of the Wild)*, the long biography of a bull moose from birth to adult domination of a herd is tied together only by the dubious psychological dread of bears suggested as unique to this moose. The wintertime longing of a young ox for the dream pastures of the previous June makes 'Strayed' *(Earth's Enigmas)* an untypical romance of minimal interest. Roberts developed a new literary form, but then he found no reliable means to give it variety.

'Alike in matter and in method, the animal story, as we have it to-day, may be regarded as a culmination.' When Roberts began his essay on 'The Animal Story' (in *The Kindred of the Wild)* with these words, he was recording his technical frustration. He was also rejoicing in the sense of his own accomplishment and his new recognition of the significance of the history of animals in literature. He saw that the keys to his discovery were the recent advances in psychology and the biological sciences, declaring that 'the animal story at its highest point of development is a psychological romance constructed on a framework of natural science.' Consequently he sets his own stories and those of

Ernest Thompson Seton against those of Anna Sewell, Marshall Saunders, and Kipling, pointing out their errors in the representation of animals. Although he is rather distressed that Christianity with its 'Dispensation of Love' had not stimulated this advance long before, he rejoices ultimately that his stories appeal to the heart and the spirit of evolutionary man after 'the long upward march of being'. Perhaps the delight in this 'potent emancipation' provided the stimulus for Roberts to produce a score of animal story books despite his conviction that he had reached the culmination of the genre: 'There would seem to be no further evolution possible.'

The example provided by Roberts in *Earth's Enigmas* stimulated several kinds of animal stories, but neither the naturalists nor the romancers succeeded in discovering any other distinctive patterns in plots. Naturalists and wild-animal lovers like Ernest Thompson Seton and Grey Owl tried using the form to make natural history memorable, but they also made it bizarre. Explaining the choice in the prefatory 'Note to the Reader' in *Wild Animals I have Known* (1898), the first of more than a dozen volumes, Seton applies hero worship to the animal world as the most memorable device for informing the reader about a species. In the stories themselves, however, he stresses individual rather than representative aspects or heroism. Lobo the wolf organizes a pack in deliberate opposition to man, and Lobo proves his superiority to man in incident after incident ('Lobo, the King of Currumpaw'). Vixen the fox eludes a watch at both the hen house and the kennel, to bring freshly killed chickens to his captured cub night after night ('The Springfield Fox'). At best these stories create a dramatic tension comparable with Roberts's, and Seton can deepen them with a similarly tragic vision: 'No wild animal dies of old age. Its life has soon or late a tragic end. It is only a question of how long it can hold out against its foes' ('Raggylug, the Story of a Cottontail Rabbit'). Thus Vixen the fox counters every human attempt to thwart her feeding her cub, but when she concludes that she can never free the cub she kills it, in a particularly moving climax. Most of Seton's stories, however, are too episodic to build up such drama. Without a representative unifying drive like the constant search for food in Roberts's stories (in these stories the animals seldom eat), Seton's animals usually drift from crisis to unrelated crisis. Silverspot the crow learns many separate things in his recounted life ('Silverspot, the Story of a Crow'), and Redruff the partridge sees his young die one by one ('Redruff, the Story of the Don Valley Partridge'), and then each is by chance eaten by an owl. Even less promising are the stories in which Seton turned desperately to conventions of human fiction, which are not only trite but gratuitous in the animal world. Lobo the wonder wolf abandons its fight against man and lets itself be trapped when its mate is caught. Seton was unable to expand the genre of the animal story with any new patterns of plot or characterization.

The many romances of wild animals in our century share the general interest of Roberts and Seton in animal psychology, but for unity and emotion they rely on trite models of human fiction. Individual incidents can dramatize conflicts peculiar to the animal world, as in Jack London's *The Call of the Wild* (1903), when Buck wins the leadership of the dog team in a fierce fight for survival. For London as well as Seton, however, survival or simple leadership proved insufficient material for a worthy plot. The chosen animal must be a hero, and with heroism enters villainy, moral insight, and active affections. These animals typically move more and more from the simple, single thoughts reminiscent of Roberts's stories the further the author ekes out their lives.

As well as centring animals in fiction, modern writers have sometimes adopted the methods and even the attitudes of the tradition for animals in secondary roles. Then animals can draw off the point of view for observing human characters and situations to an unusual perspective, either serious or amusing. Stories of sports which climax in the killing of an animal, like bullfighting or fox hunting, have gained intense poignancy through a sensing of the beast's plight. John Masefield carries the emotional identity to its ultimate in *Reynard the Fox* (1919), when he forsakes the hunters and pants ahead of the chase with the fox. Among the humorists, authors who deal in the comedy of human manners can gain from the startling perspective of how loving ones look to pets. Tobermory, the infamous talking cat of Saki's story, says only what would sound trite or obvious from a human being. Yet what Tobermory says seems in keeping with the nastiness suggested by a cat's smug face. Other writers have found animals useful in fixing human characterization. The impudent, loud parrot of *Jalna* helped Mazo de la Roche to her most memorable character study, grandmother Adeline, reinforcing the image with repetitive traits. Galsworthy's atmosphere of beautiful old age in 'Indian Summer of a Forsyte' draws impressively from the dog Balthasar. The dog shows how admirable Old Jolyon's repose is, and reflects his security. Steinbeck exploited symbolic beauty and security still more in 'The Red Pony'. Here the elemental dramas of death and birth in the lives of horses catch a romantic vision of life lost by the farmer amid his daily chores and cares. Animals convincingly drawn can lend a tangible reality to everyday associations.

The successful representation of animals in modern fiction, developing rapidly since the beginnings in *Black Beauty, Beautiful Joe,* and *The Jungle Books,* has added to literature a huge range of possible character long ago exploited by sculptors and painters. In the careful inner studies as prompted by zoology and psychology, writers have found the means to a success denied to ancient, medieval, and Renaissance writers alike. Animals, who live in nature and even in the house for themselves and not for man, are credible in fiction only so long as they care about themselves first. The early modern stories, in which animals plead for human kindness or support romances of men raised by beasts, ventured on the new animal hero through special, nontypical applications of this care. From them Roberts developed the wider exploitation of animal heroes for general stories in which conflicts outside the repertoire of human fiction are centred on animals. No matter whether they were emphasizing science or adventure, Roberts and his followers depended for their artistic appeal on the universality of the earthly challenges facing man and animal alike. They ask their readers to feel at one with their heroes in contrast to the myriad enemies to both. They also expose the limits as well as the vastness of the expanded range of characters and topics for fiction. Art and life may be one, but stories of animals living only for themselves must still appeal to readers that are human.

[1964]

3 Historical fiction

Clio Junior: historical novels for children

MARION LOCHHEAD

'Such good news! Such good news! The Black Knight has got into the castle!' So two of his twelve children once greeted Dr Moberly, headmaster of Winchester. They spoke of *Ivanhoe,* and their jubilation was typical not only of their own book-loving family but of more than one generation of Victorian children to whom Sir Walter Scott made history a delight, an excitement, almost a passion. Indeed, one of the differences between them and the modern young is that the former regarded the Waverley novels as a treat not a task, and, far from being driven to read them, were allowed, as reward and privilege after lessons were done, to indulge in one of those enchanting volumes. Charlotte Yonge, friend of 'they Mulberries', as an old woman called them, could recall that way of reading them in her own schoolroom in the 1830s. Towards the end of the century Maurice Baring saw his sisters promoted to reading Scott at a suitable age. The Barings also read the historical novels of Miss Yonge herself, who besides being a devotee of Sir Walter, was by that time his spiritual daughter and heiress, and with him a great historical influence upon the children of the century.

History was her own favourite study, and her excellent education by her mother and father gave her that sure foundation of learning—a habit of solid reading. She was well equipped in mind and knowledge when she began her long career as author. Her first novel, *Abbeychurch,* appeared anonymously in 1844; then in 1850 began the double stream of domestic and historical fiction with, respectively, *Henrietta's Wish* and *Kenneth; or, The Rearguard of the Grand Army*—a tale of the Retreat from Moscow. In 1851 she began editing *The Monthly Packet,* which continued for more than forty years, every number with two serials by herself: a domestic chronicle and an historical. Besides these, she contributed her *Cameos from History:* scenes and episodes from our rough island story and that of the rest of Europe. Girls in the schoolroom, having learned a chapter of Mrs Markham or some other approved historian (the elder among them perhaps reading Miss Strickland's *Queens of England),* then relaxed over one of Miss Yonge's novels, could hardly help developing a sense of history. The list of her historical tales is impressive, and makes no mean contribution to English fiction, indeed no meagre lifework altogether: *The Little Duke, Pigeon Pie, The Lances of Lynwood, The Chaplet of Pearls, The Dove in the Eagle's Nest, The Prince and the Page, The Armourer's Apprentice. The Caged Lion, Two Penniless Princesses, Unknown to History*—these and others take us on a journey through many countries and many centuries. A few are still read by children: *The Little Duke, The Lances of Lynwood,* perhaps *The Chaplet of Pearls*; but from the 1850s till the end of the century their readers were legion, their influence was profound. For girls, they supplemented and enlivened history lessons in the schoolroom; for their brothers they were sometimes the only approach to the past, except that of Greece and Rome.

At school these boys were drilled in the classics. In imbibing Thucydides and Xenophon, Cæsar and Livy, they might absorb some ancient history, but that of their own country and Christian

Europe was rarely imparted to them in formal lessons. Thanks to Clio junior, daughter of the Muse of History and of a father who can only be guessed (though we might hint at an entirely chaste liaison with Sir Walter Scott), they were led into the past through the pleasant gate of fiction. Scott undoubtedly began it, and his influence endured. He told a story, he gave pictures; children in the last century may have had a quicker sense of selection, more agility in skipping than they have to-day. Those long first chapters did not appear to hamper enjoyment. Indeed one Edwardian child was captivated by *The Talisman*—admittedly not one of the great novels—because of the incident in the chapel, where Sir Kenneth keeping vigil sees the procession of veiled ladies, one of whom, his own lady-to-be, drops a rose at his feet. Great as was his influence, it was possibly surpassed by that of some of his successors, whether they wrote directly for youth, as Charlotte did and as he himself did in *Tales of a Grandfather*, or found themselves being adopted by children and given the unexpected accolade of their approval.

Among the latter is Harrison Ainsworth, whose *Tower of London* (1840) began for children the visible renaissance of the city, in her buildings and memorials. It also presented a heroine whose reign in the schoolroom would be so much longer than her pitiful ten-days' queenship of England—Lady Jane Grey: a model for girls in her devoutness, her learning, her virtue and courage. At the same time he could do justice to Mary Tudor, giving some sense of her personal tragedy as well as of the fearful complications of the time. Readers of every age were captivated by a story packed with incident and rich in colour, while girls in particular were pleased by the details of costume and appearance: so useful if one wanted to dress up and act the story. *Old St Paul's* continued this tradition—or renaissance—and the author's native Lancashire was given what is almost a county history in a series of novels, ranging from Tudor to Georgian times. The Civil War was treated in more than one tale; the Fifteen and the Forty-Five were not forgotten.

The Civil War might be regarded as the favourite period of Clio junior. Charlotte Yonge dealt with it in a short serial, *Pigeon Pie;* and before she had begun her *Monthly Packet*, Captain Marryat published, in 1847, his *Children of the New Forest,* which would win many young adherents to the Royal cause and strengthen others in their allegiance to the Martyr King. The adventures of Edward and Humphrey, Alice and Edith in old Jacob's cottage in the Forest made excellent reading. The story was warmly approved by parents and governesses, for it inculcated sound morals and piety, showing how brave and resourceful boys could be, how diligent and adaptable little girls. The example of Alice and Edith may well have made her task of sewing a long seam endurable to many a reluctant small needlewoman. In masculine eyes, it was all the better for being so meagre in love interest. Edward, certainly, complicated matters by falling in love with Patience, a Puritan maid; but her father, always moderate in opinion, saw the light and abjured Cromwell and his cause. A suitable wife was found for Humphrey—after an exciting adventure—two gallant and virtuous cavaliers paired off with Alice and Edith grownup. There was a fine wedding feast after King Charles II came into his own, but there was no silly love-making. It was indeed a capital story, and the spell of it endures. The Edwardian child aforementioned was so confirmed in Royalism by reading it that any novel that presented Cromwell with sympathy—such as Marjorie Bowen's *Governor of England*—seemed improper and heretical.

This leads to the question of how far historical convictions and prejudices are made for us by Clio junior before we begin to listen to the mature Muse. Charlotte Yonge, out of her own deep loyalty, strengthened her readers in allegiance to High Church and Royalist ideals. She was English and Anglican to the marrow, but she scrupulously avoided attacking Roman Catholicism, which was, indeed, a very good religion for foreigners and for people in the Middle Ages and earlier. One of the great lacks in Roman Catholic literature and culture in

England is that of the two kinds of novel Charlotte so delightfully wrote: the *roman jeune fille,* showing the life and ethos of contemporary families, and the historical novel for children; but young papists could read Charlotte's without hurt to their faith or feelings.

Charles Kingsley on the other hand, who came near her in popularity, was as much her opposite in style as in churchmanship: strident and voluble in his patriotism, his Protestantism, his views on education, social reform, and everything that came within his survey. He was at all times the preacher and lecturer, though one with a gift for storytelling. *The Water Babies* has too much magic to be spoiled by the moral remarks; these are pleasantly few in *The Heroes;* and no one who has discovered the enchantment of Greek legend through his rendering can ever lack gratitude to Kingsley. *Hereward the Wake* is introduced by a lecture on history and thereafter weighted by comments. There are hints of Protestant animosity, as in the description of Edward the Confessor, whose sanctity did not appeal to Kingsley. (So unlike the Prince Consort!)

The conduct which earned him the title of Confessor was the direct cause of the Norman Conquest and the ruin of his people.

Instruction's warning voice may be uplifted overmuch; but after all a child can skip, and *Hereward,* being so remote in time, is comparatively free from prejudice. The patriotism is objective, emotion is expressed in action; as everyone who was not a pagan was at that time a papist, there is no need to inveigh against Roman corruption. In *Westward Ho!* instruction's warning voice becomes louder and still louder, to the accompaniment of a trumpet-blast against popery. Any contemplation of our separated brethren of Rome drove Kingsley into a frenzy bordering on hysteria; his attitude was not so much fraternal as fratricidal. Nowhere in his work are the two strains in his mentality—the religious mania and the narrative gusto—more apparent than in this epic of seafaring and patriotism: the former in the prelude of praise for those Devon men who destroyed the Armada, but for which victory 'what had we been by now but a popish appanage of a world-tyranny as cruel as heathen Rome itself and far more devilish?', and in a chapter which resembles too closely our knowledge of Nazi and Communist ways to make good reading. Amyas Leigh, having captured a bishop and a Dominican, reviles them for their sins and refuses them time to make their confession before being hanged: " 'I will have no such mummery where I command," said Amyas sternly. "I will be no accomplice in cheating the devil of his due!' "

But if one skips the introduction to *Westward Ho!* one may begin with a promising description of young Amyas:

One bright summer's morning in the year of grace, 1575, a tall and fair boy came lingering along Bideford Quay in his scholar's gown, with satchel and slate in hand, watching wistfully the shipping and the sailors,

and presently coming upon John Oxenham as he holds forth upon his own exploits and those of Francis Drake. Children probably did skip the outburst, but Protestant parents may have read it with approval and then looked benignly upon juvenile absorption in the tale. Clio junior owed much of her popularity to the pervading desire for improvement. Food for the young mind, as for the growing body, should be both nourishing and delectable, and historical novels fulfilled this ideal. Children read them with pleasure, and in the process were edified. These books were not precisely powder in jam; they were more like porridge with lashings of cream, or a well-made rice pudding with plenty of sugar and raisins 'intil't' and an agreeable hint of lemon or cinnamon.

Scott, honest man, was not without his prejudices, but everything in his writing is mellowed and transfused by a double warmth: that of genius and that of his own generous temper. His influence did not lessen, but it was enhanced and complemented by that of Dumas—especially upon Robert Louis Stevenson. This adherent of Clio junior has left a delightful account, in one of his essays, of his enthralment by Dumas: reading him on a winter's night in Swanston Cottage, rising at intervals to draw back the curtains and look out on the snow, then returning to the warmth and lamplight and the magic of the tale. From that enchantment he emerged to write his own spell-binders: *The Black Arrow* being directly in the Dumas tradition, *Kidnapped* containing the historical mystery of the Appin Murder.

Stevenson was still playing the sedulous ape when, in the 1870s, G. A. Henty began his long series of books for boys—and usually for their sisters as well. 'He took all history for his province'—to quote his biographer in the *Dictionary of National Biography*—from the recent Franco-Prussian War in *The Young Franc Tireurs*, backwards to ancient Egypt, enlivening nearly every century and every war or expedition with his narratives: *With Clive in India; Under Drake's Flag; St George for England; In Freedom's Cause: a Story of Wallace and Bruce* (which might have been called *St Andrew for Scotland*). The Civil War, Ireland, Orange and Green, of 1688, Venice, Holland, Mexico, Russia—he swept through them all in a gusto of action that left little breath for preaching; and was followed by a crowd of enthralled young readers with a goodly group of elders in the rear. Journalism was by this time paying some attention to youth, and he edited three periodicals for boys: *The Union Jack, Boys' Own Magazine*, and *Camps and Quarters*. Dying in 1902 he lived long enough to write of Roberts in Pretoria and Kitchener in the Soudan. Kingston, his predecessor in editing *The Union Jack*, was copious in producing historical tales as well as those of adventure and travel. The popularity of both these authors has long outlived their century.

And Stevenson was still alive, fragile in body, the beloved Tusitala of Vailima, when Conan Doyle began his twofold career—in romance and in detective fiction. In the nineties, too, came that treasury of tales of every kind, *The Strand Magazine*, of beloved and lamented memory. The engaging Brigadier Gerard made his bow and proceeded to relate the adventures of himself and the Emperor, introducing a Napoleonic saga. In the nineties and the early nineteen-hundreds came *Sir Nigel* and *The White Company* making vivid and real the late Middle Ages, and *Micah Clark* with his memories of Monmouth's rising. These heroes and others made *The Strand* a vehicle of delight which must have disrupted the peace of many a household as the young defied paternal claims to first possession. These romances continued a tradition; they did not create a form and mould as did the Sherlock Holmes stories, nor have their heroes the sure immortality of the great detective, but their spell lingers, and not only in memory.

France, especially of the late Middle Ages and Renaissance, was the favourite field of Stanley Weyman. His *House of the Wolf* was published in 1890, seven years after it had appeared in serial in *The English Illustrated Magazine.* (The contribution of the Victorian periodical, especially in the latter decades of the reign, to juvenile happiness would demand an essay to itself.) Other admirable chronicles followed: *A Gentleman of France, Under the Red Robe, The Man in Black, The Red Cockade.* By this time there was plenty of fine, rich feeding, possibly confused through very abundance, and the disciple of Clio junior may have had a kaleidoscopic view of history. But it was vivid enough. History was now much more commonly taught at school, but not always inspiringly. The Victorian discipline of the memory was long maintained: children must learn lists of dates, of kings and queens, and great events; and too often they 'did' history up to a particular period and thereafter knew nothing. Nor were they shown any relation between English and European history. There were, no doubt, exceptions: inspired teachers who brought the past to life, and some who used historical novels wisely and well, along with lessons. But for most children history at school was something different from history as presented in those minor masterpieces in fiction.

If Charlotte Yonge remains first among the female devotees

of Clio junior, we must not overlook her companions and followers. Emma Marshal, though remembered now only by amateurs of Victoriana, was in her own day popular, and with reason; she wrote, with charm and knowledge, tales of many periods, in tone and principle akin to Charlotte's. Towards the end of the nineteenth and well into the twentieth century came Evelyn Everett Green's accomplished and pleasant stories—also wide in range: *After Worcester; Cloister and Court; The Church and the King; The Children's Crusade* being only a few of them.

The tendency is more and more towards entertainment, towards illustration and re-creation of a period, with less and less instruction and interpolation. History, whether in learned treatise or enticing novel, whether written for scholars or for children, must answer two questions: 'What happened then?' and 'What were they like?'—the kings and queens, the leaders and warriors, the great and the common folk, old and young in this century or that: the people who caused or who witnessed events. Historical fiction should perhaps answer the second question even more fully than the first, and the characters of romance beloved—or hated—by the schoolroom were, for the most part, convincingly alive.

We have been considering almost but not quite exclusively the work of the Victorians, because this was a form that began and flourished in their century; but we cannot end abruptly in 1899 or 1900. One of the most beloved writers for children of yesterday and today and probably tomorrow, E. Nesbit, created the last of the great Victorian families in her Bastables of *The Wouldbegoods*. They inevitably became Edwardian and were succeeded by other families. E. Nesbit had Charlotte Yonge's talent for making each child in a family alive, separate and different from the rest, at once typical and individual, and very like their readers. Presently she infused magic into domesticity in her *Five Children and It* and its sequels, always with the same realism of character and background. Finally she combined the domestic, the magic, and the historical in *House of Arden* and

Harding's Luck. In these two books the young Ardens, children of an ancient but impoverished house, return one, two, three, and four centuries back in their family history, the spell being worked by the Mouldiewarp or Mole, which is the animal on their badge and crest and coat of arms. The children remain themselves, whether in their own home or in the castle or mansion to which they are transported through the door of time. In their first adventure, incidentally, one of them—Elfrida—throws a sidelight on her own history lessons: 'I wish I could remember what was happening in 1807, but we never get past Edward IV. We always have to go back to the Saxons because of the new girls.'

Kipling took up this idea in his *Puck of Pook's Hill* and *Rewards and Fairies*, where Dan and Una are taken by Puck into that old, enduring England whose reality they had not guessed.

Charlotte Yonge, in all her creative energy and versatility, never dallied with magic. It may be improper to wish she had; certainly it is a whimsy to imagine a book in which her young Underwoods are translated into the past of their own family, preferably to the seventeenth century. It is easy to see Felix and Wilmet as Pillars of the House during the troubles of the Civil War: brave and resourceful, Felix in defending the house, Wilmet in managing its welfare; all of them sheltering fugitives, perhaps the king himself; worshipping in the chapel, their prayer-books and sacred vessels hidden from marauding Cromwellians; coming again to prosperity at the Restoration.

But even her contemporary domestic chronicles are now period pieces, and in another generation or so will rank as historical romances!

Meanwhile, the inspiration has not been lost. Clio junior has still her servants. The present generation has been given many delights: some by novelists of distinction in mature work, some by those who concentrate on 'juveniles'. There is still the romance of adventure, as for example Rosemary Sutcliff's novel of Roman Britain, *The Lantern Bearers;* and the vogue for biography-on-fiction has been followed in juvenile as in adult literature: Jane Oliver has told the life of Saint Columba in *The Eaglet and the Angry Dove* and of Robert the Bruce in *Young Man With a Sword;* Elisabeth Kyle that of *The Maid of Orleans* and the *Queen of Scots.* To make any approach to a catalogue would prolong this article beyond measure. It is enough to show that the tradition continues. The teaching of history has changed and developed; writing for children changes under our eyes. There is a new approach, a new technique. But human nature continues to be the most fascinating study for human readers of every age and in every period. The question of what heroes and heroines and the common people of history were like, especially when young, of what they wore and what they ate, how they talked, what games they played—all that must always interest modern children of any intelligence and curiosity.

It is fairly safe to predict that a hundred years or more hence someone will write an article on 'Historical Novels for Children in the Twentieth Century' and possibly another on 'The Period Interest of Children's Books in the Reign of Queen Elizabeth' (Windsor, whom God preserve!).

[1961]

Combined ops

ROSEMARY SUTCLIFF

Once, and only once to date, my Daemon has completely taken over the making of a book for me, telling me what to write and how to write it, and presenting me with a set of ready-made characters who only required putting down on paper, as though they were people I had known and loved rather than creations of my own imagination. The result was *The Eagle of the Ninth,* for which I have had a very special affection ever since. All my other books, save for the very early ones which came lightly and with ease, have been laboriously spun out of my own being, like spider's silk—but probably with considerably more effort and discomfort, stress and exasperation than any spider has to put up with. My Daemon, however, still decides what each book is to be about, which is to say that it is the subject which chooses me and not the other way round. No good for me, having finished one book, to look round anxiously for an idea for the next, even if I know the kind of idea I should like. (I have always wanted to write an eighteenth century story with smugglers in it, but my Daemon says No, and the thing turns to mere cloak-and-dagger in my hands.) I have to wait, keeping, as it were, my doors and windows open; and one day something comes along—a paragraph in a book of local history, a few lines of a poem, a stretch of country that catches my imagination, or simply an idea out of the blue for no apparent reason at all—and my Daemon says, small but unmistakable, 'All right, this is It. Now let's begin.'

The Lantern Bearers was one of these ideas out of the blue.

Not even an idea really, just a thought drifting around and looking for somewhere to settle. I was making the toast and tea for breakfast one morning and thinking of nothing in particular, when it occurred to me (that is the undisciplined way my mind works) how very wide of the mark the usual history book accounts of the withdrawal of the Roman Legions must be.

One leaves school with a vague idea that the Romans came, remained in Britain as a military occupation force—never becoming mingled with the native population—for approximately the same time as lies between the accession of the first Queen Elizabeth and the present day, and were then recalled to defend their native land against the Goths and Vandals. The truth is of course far otherwise. The Legionaries were forbidden to marry while still with the Eagles; but being far from home, with twenty years or so of military service in front of them, they overcame the difficulty by taking unofficial wives from the native population, and making honest women of them when they retired. They then settled in the land of their long service, and their sons joined the Legions after them. There was no marriage ban on the civilian officials, nor on officers above the rank of centurion, and they intermarried freely from the first. So by the time the empire fell to pieces and the order for withdrawal came in 410, the matter had become a far more complicated and tragic one than the mere withdrawing of an occupation force. Many of the men who now made up the three Legions in Britain were native born and bred, they had British mothers and grandmothers and anything up to four hundred years of British roots behind them. They were not being called home from occupied territory, they were being ordered to leave their own country to the Barbarians and go off to die in defence of a concept called Rome that no longer meant very much to them. For many of them there must have been a heartbreaking conflict of loyalties before the transports sailed; and suddenly, standing over the grill and waiting for the kettle to boil, I wondered how many of them went 'wilful missing' at the last moment.

With rising excitement I began to see the situation personified in one young soldier faced with that appalling choice. A boy bred (to make it as hard as possible for him) in the Service tradition of the type of family which in later years sent its sons for generation after generation into the Ghurka Rifles or an English County regiment. I began to wonder what he would feel like if he chose Britain, took the way of a deserter and let his comrades sail without him; and what would happen to him afterwards. While I was wondering, the kettle boiled over and the toast went up in flames.

I dealt with the crisis, and later consumed charred toast and marmalade with my mind in fifth-century Britain, my family wondering the while whether I was overcome with remorse for past sins, trying to remember the name of something, or had merely been taken worse with an idea.

I began by going through any books of my own that might provide a page or two on the end of the Roman era. Arthur Weigell's *Wanderings in Roman Britain* and *Wanderings in Anglo-Saxon Britain* gave me a little; so did *The Romans in Britain* by Bertram Windle, Collingwood's *Roman Britain*, and volume 1 of the *Pelican History of England*. Arthur Bryant's *The Makers of the Realm* yielded only a few words, but they were written in fire. One of the first things I discovered was that although the last regular Legions were withdrawn in 410, the last Auxiliary troops did not follow them until about forty years later. That pushed the start of my story on to 449 and made my hero an Auxiliary and not a Legionary officer; for if there were imperial troops of any kind still in Britain after he made his choice, the story lost most of its force. It also opened up the tremendously exciting possibility that he might have come in contact with the historical hero who stood behind the legends of King Arthur; for it is, I think, generally accepted now that the fighting years of that hero, chieftain or war lord or whatever he was, lay in the second half of the fifth century and the beginning of the sixth.

I turned to Gildas, Nennius, William of Malmesbury, and Geoffrey of Monmouth. They made enchanting reading, save for Gildas who was too busy telling everybody what he thought of them to be pleasant, but they either didn't mention Arthur at all or seemed too full of dragons to be really reliable.

After that I started on the county library. I wanted books about the Roman withdrawal, the coming of the Saxons, the Dark Ages in general, Arthur in particular. I didn't know the names of any of the books I wanted, but that was what they had to be *about*. The county library, as always, rose nobly to the occasion and after a frustrating delay while they searched the rest of the United Kingdom on my behalf, produced, among other books, the *Battle for Britain in the 5th Century* and *The Rise of Wessex*, both by T. Dayrell Reed. These proved to be treasure trove. They provided a possible and coherent reconstruction of the years between the fall of Roman Britain and the rise of Saxon England—desperate and heroic years when the British people, far from lying down passively to be slaughtered, as was at one time believed, were fighting to the last ditch. Also, in the first volume the author had a good deal to say about the historical Arthur, even a theory to offer as to who he might have been by birth. And the theory seemed to me a good one.

So gradually the background grew and took shape, and against this more or less fixed background my own particular young soldier, his character and his fortunes and his reactions to those fortunes, began to develop.

He was another decendant of Marcus's, and therefore he had to be called by one of Marcus's names or a name derived from one of them. I had already used Flavius for the hero of *The Silver Branch,* so he became Aquila and developed a character to suit his name. His home was the farm that Marcus had made below the South Downs three hundred years before, and Marcus's signet ring with its flawed emerald was still in the family.

But if the story was to deal with the Romano-British resistance to the Saxons as well as with the fortunes of Aquila, that aspect of it, as well as Aquila's private affairs, must be brought to a fit ending-off place; one of those places where history reaches a climax or pauses for breath. The only place for the ending of *The Lantern Bearers* (the name had come already) was the Battle of Wallop, where the Romano-British won the first of a series of resounding victories over the Saxon hordes. It was, for the time being, the turning of the tide. But it did not happen until 472. So if Aquila was nineteen, which seemed a likely age, at the start of the story, he was going to be forty-three by the end. Since it was supposed to be a children's book, that meant a son to carry on the interest, and presumably a wife to produce the son. I gave him Ness and an 'arranged' marriage ripening slowly into something else; and I gave him Flavian, called after his father but commonly known as The Minnow because of one of those family jokes so small that viewed from outside the family they are almost invisible. I gave him the tragedy of his greatly loved sister because it was the kind of thing that must have happened so often; as Flavia herself says, 'Isn't it always so? The men fight, and after the fighting, the women fall to the Conquerors.' And having done that, I knew (for I was beginning to understand him reasonably well by that time) what effect it would have on him: the hard defensive shell of bitterness and the fear of being hurt more than he could bear a second time that would maim his relationships with other people, especially anyone he loved, from that time forward; and that it would take the rest of the book, and the help of most of the other characters in it, for him to work out his salvation.

At which point my Daemon, ignoring the existence already of a large red exercise book dropsical with notes, and a vast number of hieroglyphics on the back of envelopes, said 'Enough! Now come down to earth and start writing.'

And so, on a clean new sheet of foolscap, *The Lantern Bearers* was begun.

[1960]

The search for selfhood: the historical novels of Rosemary Sutcliff

For those who submit willingly to magic, Rosemary Sutcliff's new novel, *The Mark of the Horse Lord,* will cast its spell no less powerfully than any of her books since *The Eagle of the Ninth.* This is her fifteenth book for children, the flowering since 1950 of a remarkable talent which enchants readers old and young, exercises critics, and makes irrelevant the notion that the historical novel is barely concealed didacticism or an escape from the difficulty of writing for adolescents about contemporary problems. Miss Sutcliff's books have an organic unity which sets them apart from the extrovert 'good yarn' or historical fiction, and they make no concessions to ideas of what is a suitable book for children. This said, it must be admitted that *The Mark of the Horse Lord* may well daunt a reader who, attracted by the '11 up' age-group on the book jacket, comes to this novelist for the first time, although he is encountering some of her best work.

Rosemary Sutcliff is developmentally involved in everything she writes, not only as an artist but as a person. A cramping disease contracted in her earliest years restricted her physical movement and deprived her of the normal experiences of childhood. The compensation was a rich store of myths and legends and the historical tales of Kipling which became the springboard of her books. These are the product of vicarious experience vividly realized, penetrative imagination, and much hard work. She is more closely identified with her readers than is usual in children's authors, and consequently, because her artistry in the later books is fully developed, she makes adult demands on them and sketches their reading skill to the utmost. This is particularly true of *The Mark of the Horse Lord.* Its merits can best be seen by setting it in its place in Miss Sutcliff's development.

Timid as they now seem, her early books are not without significance, especially as historical stories for the under-tens are thin on the ground. *The Chronicles of Robin Hood, The Queen Elizabeth Story, The Armourer's House,* and *Brother Dusty-Feet* enjoy a continuing popularity with the young who identify history with legend. The heroes and heroines are the idealized playmates of the only child. *Simon* is the first novel to show the power that the later books developed. Miss Sutcliff sketches a vigorous hero and shows unexpected skill in describing battles.

In discussing the novels after *Simon* one moves back and forth between the relevance of the thematic material to the growing points of adolescence and the varied response of the readers. Think of a twelve-year-old who, on being asked to tell of a book she had recently enjoyed, related to a spellbound class in one unbroken sweep the story of *The Eagle of the Ninth* and confidently summarized it by saying that 'the eagle was lost because the men had lost their loyalty to it.' These Roman books, notably the trilogy of *The Eagle of the Ninth, The Silver Branch,* and *The Lantern Bearers,* are the most generally appreciated. The grave virtues of the maimed heroes chime in with the serious idealism of adolescence. Miss Sutcliff's theme is the struggle of the Roman ideal, the light, against the dark ignorance of the barbarians. Aquila in *The Lantern Bearers* learns that an ideal persists even when empires totter, and the reader knows that history is the continuity of the past and present; the soil and the people remain. Owain in *Dawn Wind* discovers that a nation grows when warring tribes join in a common cause. These books provide the definition of authentic Sutcliff material: symbolic action, the heroic figure who surmounts his disability, the father figure, the links with the past in the timeless characters of seers and 'little dark people'. There are hosts of other good books for children on the Roman period; these are among the best because the universality of Miss Sutcliff's themes is balanced by detailed description.

The secret of their success is the close identification of the author, reader, and hero. The books seem to be written from the inside so that the author's imagination is fused with the reader's response. One discovers this in discussion with enthusiasts. Another point emerges. Adolescents recognize the adult complexity of Miss Sutcliff's themes and respond to it while continuing to read the stories with the total involvement which is the best feature of the reading done by children.

This becomes even clearer in *Warrior Scarlet*, which is central in Miss Sutcliff's development. In this book many strands come together—awareness of historical continuity, the significance of the countryside, tribal rituals—to explore the theme of initiation into manhood. Drem with his withered arm is so determined to conquer his disability that he ignores the fact that to be a Warrior is to be more than strong and skilful. It is to be magnanimous and humble, to accept a disability, to lose the self-regard of the child. *Warrior Scarlet*, with its flashing bronze and gold colouring, its archetypal issues and conflicts, is the strongest emotional experience Miss Sutcliff provides and is outstanding among children's books of any kind.

Where the historical record is scant the author's penetrative imagination has the greater scope. Miss Sutcliff illuminates the blank pages with an intensity which comes from her reading of heroic legends which *are* the history of these times in that they portray what greatness, fealty, and sacrifice meant to the followers and descendants of the warrior kings. She is fortunate in that she has no self-consciousness when writing about sublimity. Her style rises to a bardic strain and, while some passages are over-written, there is, on the whole, more restraint than excess. Charles Keeping has served Miss Sutcliff well with his stark illustrations. There is no lack of realism. The Britain of *Warrior Scarlet*, *Outcast*, and *The Shield Ring* is mist-shrouded, cold and dark, huddling in a forgotten corner of the world. The fire of passionate loyalty and conflict illuminates the landscape and the action so that the reader sees that the *rite de passage* to manhood is more than the accomplishment of a set task. It is the growth of responsibility, the free acceptance of obligation.

In her modern versions of *Beowulf* and the stories of Cuchulain in *The Hound of Ulster*, Miss Sutcliff returns to the sources of her inspiration. Her Arthurian novel, *Sword at Sunset*, which was written for adults, is a working-out at length of her preoccupation with the 'leader whose divine right is to die for his people'. *The Mark of the Horse Lord* has traces of all three. In action and tone it is the most truly epic of the novels and, so far as readers are concerned, the most adult. It shows how far Miss Sutcliff has come from the wounded Marcus in *The Eagle of the Ninth*. The problem is: will she take her usual readers with her?

They will recognize the setting from the first paragraph:

In the long cavern of the changing room, the light of the fat-oil lamps cast jumping shadows on the walls; skeleton shadows of the spear-stacked arms-racks, giant shadows of the men who crowded the benches or moved about still busy with their weapons and gear; here and there the stallion shadow of a plume-crested helmet. The stink of the wild beasts' den close by seeped in to mingle with the sharper smell of men waiting for the trumpets and sweating a little as they waited. Hard to believe that overhead where the crowd had been gathering since cock-crow, the June sun was shining and a fresh wind blowing in from the moors to set the brightly coloured pennants flying.

The Roman games at Corstopitum. The story soon moves from

the arena to the dark west coast of Argyll, the land of the Dalriads who are fighting for their identity as a people against the powerful matriarchal Caledones. These struggles are of no concern to Phaedrus the gladiator until he wins his wooden foil by killing his friend and finds that freedom is the long boredom of a lost identity. After a drunken brawl he is bought out of the town gaol by a horse trader who has noticed his extraordinary resemblance to Midir, the lost leader of the Dalriads. Midir was blinded as a youth by his father's half-sister, who with the help of the Caledones rules over the Dalriads and seeks to enforce the old ways, including the sacrifice of the king every seven years. Phaedrus has little choice but to accept the role of the Horse Lord, but as he assumes the title he gradually earns the dignity. Finally, by dying to save the tribe, he is confirmed in his kingship.

The theme is the next step in Miss Sutcliff's exploration of what constitutes one's real self. As a gladiator Phaedrus is a slave; his life is his only as he fights successfully to retain it. In the arena he has a sham heroic identity. In the world outside he has none at all. In the role-playing spirit of his trade he accepts the leadership thrust upon him and later grows to greatness. The real Midir is concerned with private vengeance; Phaedrus's final sacrifice is the heroic immolation which could never have come in the arena. This awareness that public excellence is the extension of private integrity links this novel with *The Lantern Bearers*, *Warrior Scarlet*, and *Knight's Fee*. The familiar elements recur: the dark patch of history, the tribal feud, the hunts, the battles. The plot is slight, apart from the central action, so that each scene is described in detail to carry the intensity of the feud. The reader needs more experience than can generally be assumed of eleven-year-olds. For the first time in her novels for the young Miss Sutcliff may have outstripped her readers.

Unlike the other Roman stories, this book has a Gaelic rather than a British background: the hero goes into the darkness of the land beyond the Wall and stays there. Phaedrus stands alone: the old man of the tribe and the faithful friend are left behind.

The Horse Lord becomes larger than life until he becomes Arthur, Cuchulain, and Beowulf in one. There is enough artistry and complexity to extend an adolescent's experience. Undoubtedly the book is another success for Miss Sutcliff. The battle scenes are as grand as ever, but even in the descriptive passages there is a sharper edge on the prose which makes the style more taut. The quality of the whole confirms Margery Fisher's assertion that 'the best historical stories for children have little or nothing of the juvenile in them.'

They were pouring in through the gaps, like the squadrons of some terrible ghost army, tattered and bloody; chariots with only one man in them, chariots with driver and warrior slumped against the wicker side or dragged askew by one wild-eyed and wounded horse with the harness dangling where a dead teammate had been cut free. The wild cavalry were swinging right and left towards either flank of the War Host. The weary horses in the chariot lines, roused by their comrades and the tumult and the smell of blood, had forgotten their weariness and were fighting for their heads. Cocory, next in line, was looking to him, but Phaedrus, sweating with more than the heat now, set his teeth and held the whole War Host in leash that one moment longer, until the very last of the retreating chariots were safely through: while the enemy behind them, maybe in fear of a trap, reined their horses in and swerved aside for a few moments from their charge, and the waiting bands in the rear were swinging forward to close the gaps; waited one racing heartbeat of time longer, then with the Caledones on the very lip of spilling forward again, raised the bronze ox-horn to his lips, and winded one sharp blast that flung to and fro among the hills until the high corries of Cruachan caught and flung it back, startling every shore bird in Earra-Ghyl.

The Mark of the Horse Lord shows the coming-of-age of Miss Sutcliff's hero and the total assurance of the writing indicates an author fully in command of her power. One question remains.

When young people have the reading skill and experience to make the most of a book like this, they have moved on from books written 'for the young' and cannot bear to return to them until they are assuredly adult. Yet many of the authors they read have little to offer them compared with this universality of experience. Who then will see to it that this challenge comes their way?

[1965]

Henry Treece: lament for a maker

Henry Treece was a prolific and regular writer, though until 1959 a full-time teacher. As well as his nine deeply imagined historical novels, much poetry, some plays and criticism, he produced more than thirty stories for the young. In one field in particular he was making himself a master, in his Viking stories. Perhaps his ability to get inside the Viking skin, to produce an utterly convincing extension of the saga tone of voice, is due to his own evident delight in fast, suspenseful, surprising action: and also, surely, to an imaginative sympathy with their way of meeting life.

The picaresque, take-what-comes kind of action arising from the Northmen's voyages of discovery, plunder, or revenge, is almost bound to make a rapid episodic story, and suited Treece. He first uses the voyaging pattern in *Viking's Dawn,* which begins the story of one Harald Sigurdson, who goes with a Northman, Thorkell Fairhair, and his sinister Danish blood-brother, Ragnar Raven, in a ship the *Nameless.* The modern writer for the young is hard put to it to make plunder and treachery part of his story without seeming to extol them. Treece manages this problem well, using the Dane Ragnar as scapegoat. Sworn brother though he is, Ragnar has left a longship of his own lying in wait to take Thorkell's. But it is wrecked by the storm-raising powers of a brilliantly drawn character, Horic the Laplander. The incident is told with the starkness of a ballad and shows how Treece's often over-colourful writing gains in pungency and strength when he willingly submits to the saga style—an objective, allusive economy. When they pass the wreck, Thorkell changes course to pick up a survivor, but Ragnar reaches for his seal-spike and silences this last witness to his treachery:

Horic whispered to himself, but every man near him heard, 'Look, there is blood upon the point of Ragnar's sealspike.'

So we know what Ragnar is, who later treacherously robs hospitable Picts and steals treasure from a boatload of unarmed Christian monks. Convincingly he gets his deserts when he loses his treasure and his life to some wreckers. Ragnar's tortuous character, as discussed by the others, is real enough. The book explores, too, the Viking character in general: their love of ridiculous, exaggerated tales and jokes (like Horic's about bears); their interest in philosophical talk; their courage, fatalism, and humour in disaster. There is a man called Smörke, convinced, though all laughed at him, that this voyage would be his last:

As he was swept overboard, Gnorre swore that he heard the man yell out, 'There, I told you so!'

More important still is the seafarers' love for and faith in their leader, movingly shown when Thorkell goes blind. Wolf comforts him:

'I will be your eyes, Thorkell Fairhair,' he said. 'You have lost nothing.'

'I will be your right arm, Thorkell Fairhair,' said Aun, 'you have gained something.'

'I will be your spell-master, Thorkell Fairhair,' said Horic, crying a little as he said it. 'You will gain everything.'

The Road to Miklagard, a second book about this Harald, is not a complete success. The richness of Constantinople tempts Treece into lush writing and melodramatic action. Also, a comical fairy-tale quality enters with the giant Grummoch, alien to the saga kind of supernatural—omen, dream, and vision—which

Treece later uses so well. Yet there is grim comedy in Radbard drowning their treasure (with some of themselves) rather than letting it fall to the enemy. Treasure is often elusive in these stories: Prince Nial reburies the lot when he rifles a barrow too clumsily in *Splintered Sword*, and the Vikings who raid the howe in *Horned Helmet* pay for the treasure with Gauk's death. Both these stories, written rather later, are different in having their emphasis upon a young hero rather than upon a whole crew, and are of vintage quality while slighter in scope. Set late in the Viking period they show, subtly, its drawbacks as a way of life.

The last tale of Harald, *Viking's Sunset*, is splendid. The taut, ironical tone and the shipmen's conversation are better than ever. Harald and Grummoch (now perfectly convincing and endearing as Harald's blood-brother) chase Haakon Redeye in the *Long Snake*, in revenge for his burning their village. From Greenland, where there is a humorous Eskimo interlude, they finally reach Vinland, and their story becomes intertwined with the red men with whom they settle. The fusion is as happy as this image of it:

The longship sailed among them . . . like a mother goose among her many goslings, for in truth the canoes of the Boethuk floated as thick as seeds upon the broad waters.

But the jealousy of the red chief's maimed son brings Harald and his own brother down with him, and *Long Snake* is sent burning over the lake with the three bodies upon her, an ending superb in its epic restraint and sadness. (A longship prow *was* found, Treece tells us, in one of the Lakes.) Grummoch and Thorgeif turn away from the ship-burial, comforting each other with a Jomsborg ditty, but are soon silent again:

For a while there would be nothing worth the saying. They knew that well enough.

Now although the Northmen's 'joy in doing' (including the frenzied action of the berserk or 'baresark' which Treece often describes) is the mainspring of these stories, there is no doubt of the importance of 'the saying'. Henry Treece has forged and used a pointed weapon of conversation between his Northmen which has a flash and twist and bite peculiar to itself. Inspired by the old sagas, yet individual and more expansive, the flavour of this talk is as recognizable as a favourite wine. Maturing with time, it has perhaps reached perfection in *Swords from the North*. Irony is its basic ingredient: 'the men of the North were not given to self-pity', as Treece remarks, and the ironical, stoical attitude is part of their very nature. But its shifts and variations are like the glitter of sword-play. It ranges from plain irony—'A man would not know unless he was told . . .' replies Summerbird of Harald Hardrada's protest that he is a Christian—to the euphemism that brings a shiver: 'And I speak for my brothers, who do not wish to talk . . .' says a warrior in his death-verse, his brothers being dead. It includes a constant grim or comic use of understatement—'Something must have kept them awake . . .' remarks a Varangian escaped from a Byzantine 'death-cell' and hearing his agonized shipmates loudly planning revenge—and a balancing use of gloriously exaggerated bombast. It explodes into that kind of banter heard among schoolboys or service men (the sound of it still, no doubt, in Treece's ears), as when Hardrada protests that

'we will be drinking out of our cupped hands like dogs before long.'

Wulf laughed and said, 'When you next see a dog drinking out of his cupped hands, call to me.'

and so on, for a page of uproarious absurdity. It includes much brusquer teasing—'No one wants your front teeth, friend . . .' remarks Gyric to Haldor, who has wagered these—and a gentler kind, as is Hardrada's solemn reply to young Helge, who says he dreamed of flying, tried it, and fell in the fjord:

'So you cannot fly eh? I should have thought that a brisk young fellow like you could fly, Helge.'

For Treece's great achievement in individual characterization in these tales is this re-creation of the Norway giant King Harald Hardrada into so awesome yet lovable a figure: audacious, joyous, poetical, warm-hearted, immensely brave, yet also hard, calculating, savage, and proud. In *The Last of the Vikings*, a haunting and shapely book (perhaps artistically the best of these), the author draws all Harald's young life into the compass of his thoughts on the battlefield of Stamford Bridge, where he is to die. *Swords from the North* tells of Harald as head of the Varangian guard in Byzantium and remains episodic—but what episodes and changes of mood! Scenes of violence, mystery, stark drama, controlled pathos, and wild comedy follow one another with unflagging gusto, related with crisp, ironic invention. When the not young Empress Zoe proposes marriage to Harald (a hint the author has taken from the *Heimskringla Saga*, which he uses skilfully and imaginatively), the Varangian sits on the mosaic floor and laughs like a maniac. When the two boatloads of Vikings rush the harbour-chain to escape from Byzantium and Harald's boat rides over while the other breaks her back, drowning two of his dear friends, grief gets Harald in its grip like ice. When he ruthlessly sends ashore the stolen Princess Maria, for whom he has a passion (beautifully indicated in more than one scene), because she keeps reminding him that he owes her his life, he retires to his cabin and does not watch her go. Saint Olaf, Harald's dead brother, is a familiar and convincing visitor throughout Harald's life, and it is he who has come to Maria the last night in Byzantium and said:

> *'Be about it and send a ladder to my brother.'*
>
> *'Northern Saints [remarks Harald] are brisk fellows and stand on no ceremony. But they get things done.'*

Treece always describes Harald's faith—genuine, calculating, and virile—with perfect insight, and uses Olaf's interventions with great dramatic effect.

Closely connected with these two books in conception and period is *Man with a Sword,* a life of Hereward the Wake. Little is known for fact of Hereward, and the author has imagined an episode when Hereward is Hardrada's man, so that we see the middle-aged king of hard counsel in Norway. Hereward has suffered a loss of memory after a cowardly attack by the English Godwines, and his moods, his foolish wisdom, and uncalculated wit (delighting Hardrada, the good conversationalist) are partly due to this. Coming with Hardrada to England in the fateful year 1066, Hereward leaves behind his wife and son, who are taken into his court by the wily Sweyn of Denmark. It is the promise of their return to him which Treece uses as Hereward's main motive in leading the fen men to help King Sweyn in the sack of Peterborough. The Isle of Ely episode is hauntingly done and includes an encounter between Hereward and a strange Norman —the Conqueror himself: a long and stormy friendship develops between them. Hereward emerges as individualist and outlaw, but also as a peace-loving family man, driven mad when William removes his wife and son to his court. Sometimes immensely pathetic, this picture of Hereward is a high achievement and remains unaffected by an overwrought last few chapters.

The Godwines, naturally enough, are ill-thought-of in this book. In a much earlier story, *Hounds of the King,* Treece dealt interestingly with the making of Harold's housecarls, conditioned into dog-like loyalty at Wallingford. But Harold Godwinson's magnetism is described rather than felt, and we remain looking at events as well-told history rather than rapt by the tragedy of Hastings at the end. The book deals also, for the first time, with the battle of Stamford Bridge.

Treece's three versions of this famous battle in this famous year are a fascinating study in imaginative and emotional concentration. He has not made us care much about Godwinson, and the housecarls Beornoth and Finn are slight figures, so their battle moves us least. We care considerably about Hereward, through whose eyes we have a fine sense of the shield ring and the fall of Hardrada. But in *The Last of the Vikings* Treece seemed to gain the freedom of that battlefield through the eyes of Hardrada himself: and the glow of reality spreads outwards, lighting up English Harold and all the figures around, with that kind of passionate sympathy which is creative love.

In what appears to be his last story of all, *The Dream-time,* Treece, touchingly enough, has written a lucid poetical fable, set back in the dawn of time, about a 'maker' among warriors. In it there are some statements of simple profundity about the artist among ordinary men. There is a time when Twilight, the boy who can draw and work in metal, tries to make the likeness of his girl who is lost:

At first he was afraid that he could not make the right shape . . . but his hand caught his dream and he drew her so rightly that he felt she might speak . . .

Treece's hand often 'caught his dream' among the men of the North, and when it did they speak most splendidly. His choice of material is skilful, his treatment of it increasingly 'adult'.

Treece's other earlier historical stories are ambitious in theme, sometimes uncritically bold in scope, giving an impression of impatience to reach the end. This may be because they have a recurring tendency to compress too much material into too short a book, with a consequent sacrifice of depth to breadth, both in plot and characterization. This is in turn partly due to his fascination with themes from cross-roads in history and the desire to hitch his young heroes on to those historical characters of huge stature who are so often centred there. In doing so he sets his sights very high, gives himself two major (but differing) imaginative tasks. Treece loved British history and myth, and in his use of the Arthurian material in *The Eagles have Flown* he discarded Malory and Tennyson (and did T.H. White's brilliant conception of the boy Arthur go too?) and presented Artos, Count of Britain, only half-willingly Romanized, leading the three kings of the west against Aella and Cissa, the Saxon invaders. Merlin is the spirit of paganism, the round table is the great round shield

Artos throws down to teach his men equality. But the young hero Festus and his slave-friend remain thin. The interested young reader had best go straight to *The Great Captains*, the novel for which this story seems a blueprint. Despite doubtful things, like equating Camelot with Camulodunum, the book is fully imagined and powerful.

Other unsettled periods Treece chose as themes were the Claudian invasion in *Legions of the Eagle* and the new waves of herdsmen-invaders in the bronze-age story *Men of the Hills*. Caught up in the vast movements of history, Treece failed to create flesh and blood people within small pockets of convincingly woven circumstances against these panoramic backgrounds, so that the books somehow do not move us. We feel little for Lala, but we weep with Drem of Rosemary Sutcliff's *Warrior Scarlet*.

A new story, *The Queen's Brooch*, tells of Boudicca's uprising through the eyes of a young tribune of the Ninth Legion at Lincoln. The liberal-minded young tribune's attempts to keep good relations with the tribesmen of the Coritani (whom he has grown up among and loves) and the edgy uneasiness of Cynwas, their chieftain, the insolence of a tactless decurion, the army-bound mind of the faithful old centurion Tigidius: these are described from inside with tremendous conviction. But once among the hordes of the Iceni, Treece loses the concentrated vision and the story becomes broad instead of deep, panoramic rather than moving. The Marcus of the beginning, loyal to the Legion yet brother to the Britons, would not so easily have thrown in his hand.

There is needed a fusion of the personal and the historical vision, and this is more easily achieved in private than public events. *The Bombard*, for instance, really comes alive when a youth and his friends, returned from Crecy, make their own bombard and fire it at the crack in their enemy's castle wall (a magnificent piece of description). The young man's love of the bombard they have so arduously made, the horror of the priest whose skill has helped them, and his death when the bombard is blown to pieces at his order, are entirely convincing and moving.

An author of immense creative verve, Treece wrote six suspense stories with contemporary settings which show that same pleasure in (almost *need* for) fast, dangerous opportunist action as his Viking tales, and are compulsively readable. The author makes skilful use of all the devices of the thriller, from double-chase to hidden identity. In *Ask for King Billy*, for instance (the first story to deal with Gordon Stewart, private detective, who later works for government intelligence), we do not know until the end which side the sinister large man in black is on. The pace in these stories never flags, the suspense mounts, there is a reckless uninterest in minor, inexplicable details and a certain repetition of situations. Only rarely is Treece's considerable ingenuity misplaced. There is a most enjoyable use of place—London, the Humber, the Welsh borders, Spain, Gibraltar, Sark—and a detailed knowledge of boxing and of firearms. The characters that lodge in the mind are the pointed miniatures (a West Indian boxer, an old Boer War shepherd) rather than the main characters, caught up in a game which moves too fast for us to see their features. A slighter story for younger children, *The Jet Beads*, has, on the other hand, a very live picture of an eleven-plus boy, and such humorous school scenes as to make one wish he had done more in this line.

In a letter in 1965 Henry Treece confirmed his belief in that wholeness of intention in writing for the young which must be the guide of all serious writers for them: the expression of something important to the writer himself, within 'that common territory shared by human beings of all ages'. He saw the gap between books for children and books plain and simple narrowing, and it is sad that he should not have had longer in helping to bridge it.

[1966]

4 Some writers and their books

Hans Christian Andersen

ALAN MORAY WILLIAMS

Since 1835, when the first of his *Eventyr Fortalte for Boern* were published in Copenhagen, Danish writer Hans Christian Andersen's fairy tales have been translated into eighty-two languages. In England alone more than five hundred different editions have appeared, by twenty-five different translators. For generations of children *The Tinderbox, The Ugly Duckling, The Little Mermaid, The Emperor's New Clothes, The Staunch Tin Soldier,* and the rest have held a magic which they have never quite forgotten.

Yet comparatively few know the story of Andersen's life, which, as he was fond himself of saying, was as colourful and romantic as any of his stories. Few realize, either, that the fairy tales—'those trifles', he first called them—were only a by-product of his inventive mind and that he was disappointed that his fame rested on them rather than on the novels, plays, travel books, poetry and prose sketches which compose the bulk of the thirty-three volumes of his posthumous collected works.

Born in Odense, a country town of 7,000 inhabitants, then

twenty hours' journey from Copenhagen, the capital, he was the only child of an unsuccessful cobbler who loved books and an illiterate washerwoman eight years older than her husband. His parents were so poor that they lived, worked, and slept in a single room (today charmingly preserved as a museum). There was a streak of lunacy in the family and the boy himself sometimes had fits. As a small child he was dreamy and reclusive, and, teased for his oddness by other children, spent much time playing on his own with a home-made puppet-theatre. Sent to a school for poor men's sons, he received almost no education; but his imagination was spiced by avid reading (*The Arabian Nights*, Holberg's and Shakespeare's plays, and Scott's novels), relished theatre-visits, and tales of ghosts and goblins told him by superstitious old women.

When he was eleven, his father died. Two years later his mother remarried. At fourteen he decided to be an actor and told his mother (who wanted him to be a tailor): 'I am going to Copenhagen and I'm going to be famous. First one must go through all kinds of hardships and *then* one becomes famous.' Local worthies, who had counselled him to 'learn a trade', tapped their heads ominously; but he was fortified in his 'craziness' by an old fortune-teller, who had told his parents that some day he'd be something great and fine and 'all Odense would be illuminated for him.'

In September 1819 he arrived by mail-coach in Copenhagen with nothing but a bundle of clothes, twelve silver pieces from his clay savings pig, and a vague letter of introduction to an actress. Disproportionately lanky and thin, rather ugly, and with comically ill-fitting clothes, he was ill-equipped to realize his dreams. In three years Copenhagen's Royal Theatre gave him, as a pupil, only one part—as an anonymous troll. A petition for aid which he sent to the king, 'equipped only with a fervent desire for the theatre and a trust in noble souls to help him', was turned down. A callow tragedy he submitted to the directors was returned after six weeks' hopes as showing 'absolute lack of elementary culture and necessary education.'

Three things sustained him in the hungry garret-existence he led: an unshakable determination, a deep though unorthodox religious faith which he maintained all his life, and an ingratiating naivety which made people of all walks of life want to help him, even if they secretly laughed at him a little.

Of the many writers, officials, and others who kept him going with gifts of money or clothes, meals at their homes, useful introductions, etc., the most important was Jonas Collin (pronounced *Colleen)*, a state councillor and one of the Royal Theatre's directors. One of the great patrons in the history of literature, he early sensed the boy's possibilities and not only got him free schooling, at state expense, at Slagelse Grammar School, but took him into his cultured middle-class home and made him one of the family.

His five years at school were, according to his autobiography, the blackest in his life. Though he had already written and published (at his own expense) a story in imitation of Walter Scott, he knew no Latin, Greek, history, geography, or arithmetic, and had to start from scratch. The headmaster, who lashed boys as viciously with his tongue as Wackford Squeers did with his cane, nicknamed him 'Shakespeare with the vampire eyes' and humiliated him in every way, telling him his writings were only fit for the wastepaper-basket and that he'd end up in an asylum.

But his five years' cramming proved a precious bane, for soon after matriculation in 1827 he managed to produce three books: a travel journal which achieved some success, a comedy which was performed at the theatre, and a book of poems. These established him as a professional author, but brought him little money. For five years he floundered in the muddy waters of freelance writing, painfully dependent on the life-belt of his friends' charity.

It was not until 1832, when Collin secured him a travel-scholarship to visit Italy for two years, that his genius expanded in the warm south and he wrote a novel, *The Improvisator,* which gained international fame and led to his being given a small state pension. From then on, honours and fame piled on him and his work till in 1869—fifty years after his arrival in Copenhagen—his native Odense was duly illuminated for him at a ceremony in his honour.

His first tales (Andersen always distinguished carefully between his 'fairy' tales—concerned with the supernatural—and the rest) were written as a kind of afterthought, mainly to make money. They were a logical outcome of his childhood puppet-plays. In a letter to the poet Ingemann in 1843 he described how he wrote them:

> *The first ones were, of course, some which I had heard in my childhood and re-told, but then I found that those which I created myself such as* The Little Mermaid *got the most applause, and that has started me off. Now I dip into my own bosom, find an idea for the older people and tell it to the children, but remembering that father and mother are listening! . . . I have masses of material, more than for any other kind of work; often it seems to me that every fence, every little flower said: 'Just look at me, then you'll know my story,' and if I so desire, the story is mine.*

If Danish was a world-language like German, a handful of Andersen's poems, lyrics, and patriotic songs would probably be as well known as Goethe's. An opera he wrote, *Little Kerstin,* is still performed in Denmark. But apart from the tales and his autobiography, *The Fairy-Tale of My Life,* little of his prose work is read today. Two of his novels, *The Improvisator* and *Only A Fiddler*—romantic projections of his own early struggles—can still be read with enjoyment, however.

The tales combine the freshness of vision and the innocence of childhood with the gentle irony and knowledge of human psychology that only hard experience can produce. They are racy with the homely speech of the Danish common people and warm with the simple beauty of the countryside. There are 158 of them, not all equally good. A few seem potboilers, and some are marred by what Mr W. H. Auden has called the 'Sensitive-Plantishness and Namby-Pamby Christianity of their heroes'. But most are little masterpieces, as perfect in their way as Tanagra statuettes. One wishes they were available singly in Britain, like the Beatrix Potter books, with the original illustrations by Vilhelm Pedersen.

Like Kierkegaard, Andersen was celibate. Like Oliver Goldsmith (with whose gawky, ungainly personality he had something in common) he was able to travel very widely between 1838 and his death in 1875 and feel himself a citizen, if not of the world, at least of Europe. He twice visited England, was given a great reception (you *need* no introductions, the Danish Ambassador, Count Reventlow, told him) and stayed with Dickens at Gad's Hill—but the Dickens family, it must be recorded, found him 'a bony bore' and Dickens, though he admired Andersen's work greatly, stuck a notice on the dressing-table in the room he'd occupied:' Hans Andersen stayed in this room for five weeks—which seemed to the family AGES!'

Andersen was a man with a chronic inferiority complex. All his career was a struggle to compensate for his lowly origins and early humilations and snubbings. Hence his faults: his vanity, morbid sensitiveness to criticism, inverted snobbery, and neurotic quirks. But unlike that all-too-familiar figure, the self-made man who, success's mountain once climbed, scorns or ignores those still toiling at its base, he never lost touch with the humble and the handicapped. Though in his years of fame counts and princes competed for the honour of his celebrated company, he never, one feels, belonged to their privileged world, but remained a part of ordinary suffering humanity. This is what makes him sympathetic and lovable.

[1963]

Andrew Lang in fairyland

ROGER LANCELYN GREEN

The name of Andrew Lang is more closely connected with fairy tales than that of any other writer who used the English language, and indeed it seems that he now holds as secure a place as historian of fairyland as do Perrault, Grimm, and Andersen. Although he did not collect folktales from the peasants like the brothers Grimm, Lang occupies an important niche among those folklorists and anthropologists whose researches are carried on with the aid of printed sources, and he is remembered among scholars as the author of the first full refutation of Max Muller's theory of mythology derived from 'a disease of language' stemming from the Aryans, as well as for the more controversial suggestion that the 'lower mythology' derived from the 'higher' and even perhaps from monotheism.

Lang's long and gruelling studies as a folklorist and desk-anthropologist, like his Classical studies which resulted in the finest prose translations of the *Iliad* and *Odyssey* and three important books on the Homeric Problem, supplied the solid foundations on which his more famous collections of fairy tales were built. His own personal background also contributed to the turn which his genius was to take, and his character and the chances of his career gave him a ready 'pass' into fairyland.

He was born at 'Viewfields', Selkirk, on 31 March 1844, the eldest son of John Lang, Sherriff Clerk of Selkirk, whose father

Andrew had held the same position under and become a trusted friend of Sir Walter Scott.

Andrew Lang had several brothers and one sister, and passed a happy boyhood in the Border Country, fishing in the burns, digging for hidden treasure among the ruined keeps and peel-towers, and playing cricket for the Selkirk team against those of the neighbouring townships.

He was always, however, a bookish and imaginative child, and took particular pleasure in the tales and legends of the Borders. He and other boys would seek out an ancient shepherd learned in fairy tales; Nancy Hall, the old nurse at 'Viewfields', had all the local legends of magic, ghosts, and hidden treasures at her finger-tips—and they lost nothing in the telling. Scott's poems opened a new world of enchantment to him, and the good laird of Abbotsford was a living memory wherever he went by Tweed and Yarrow and Ettrick.

Apparently Lang was always delicate, shy, and hypersensitive—always ready to escape from the rough and tumble of everyday life in some literary or legendary fairyland of the imagination. His early schooldays at Selkirk Grammar School gave him the right leavening of solitude and society, but when at the age of ten he proceeded to Edinburgh Academy he found his contemporaries less to his taste and read more and more voraciously. Inspired Classical instruction turned him from a loathing of Greek to his life-long devotion to Homer, and a scholarly career was already opening before him when he entered St Andrews University in 1861.

He spent almost two years at 'the college of the scarlet gown' and always looked back on them as the happiest of his life, though they closed with the death of the college friend, Henry Brown, on whose account he wrote of

St Andrews by the northern sea
That is a haunted town to me.

Lang's earliest surviving writings date from 1862 when he

edited *The St Leonard's Magazine* (a manuscript affair produced in his hall of residence, of which a selection was printed the following year), and contributed to the more formal *St Andrews University Magazine* articles on such subjects as 'Scottish Nursery Tales' and 'Spiritualism Medieval and Modern'.

He was already reading any volume on ancient medieval magic he could find in the university library, and the more accessible collections of folktales; but his Classical studies did not suffer, and he was moved to Glasgow University in 1863 to qualify for a Snell Exhibition to Balliol College, Oxford, which he obtained in 1864. At Balliol he took Firsts in Classical Moderations and Literae Humaniores, and won an Open Fellowship to Merton College in December 1868, which he held for seven years.

The academic career so auspiciously started did not prosper, however. The period at Merton proved that it was contrary to Lang's temperament and talents. Dons in those days were expected to stick rigorously to the normal fields of scholarship and not to flirt with each of the Muses in turn. After staying with Lang at Merton in 1874, Robert Louis Stevenson in his poem to 'Dear Andrew of the brindled hair' described Oxford as 'The abhorred pedantic sanhedrin', and Lang, though he wrote that there 'Youth an hour came back to me', also realized that 'at last, if men linger there too late, Oxford grows a prison.' Outside influences also came to upset him: his parents died within a few days of one another in September 1869, there was perhaps an unhappy love affair, and certainly in 1872 Lang's health broke down completely and he spent two winters in the south of France in danger of his life through lung trouble.

When he won back to something like health in 1874 he became engaged to Leonora Blanche Alleyne, whom he married the following year. He resigned his Fellowship and they settled at 1 Marloes Road, Kensington, their home for the rest of his life.

Already at the beginning of 1874 Lang was writing reviews for a newly founded weekly, *The Academy*; and on settling in London he plunged into journalism, writing regularly for many years for *The Daily News* and *The Saturday Review*, besides an astonishing number of contributions on all kinds of subjects to numerous other papers and magazines, popular or learned. He published over a hundred books, and it has been reckoned that his uncollected works would fill more than that number of volumes over again.

It would be possible to write of Lang in many other fields besides journalism. He began as a minor poet of some distinction and considerable promise, though disappointment over the poor reception of his narrative poem *Helen of Troy* (1882) turned him towards light verse and parody. He wrote two amusing and absolutely distinctive novels which were popular only with a minimum of more literary readers; and historical romance, which he also essayed, proved in his own words 'too bitterly historical' for readers glutted with more thrilling works of Stanley Weyman, Conan Doyle, S. R. Crockett, and A. E. W. Mason. As a literary critic he was for many years the most popular and influential of his time; but criticism is transitory, though he left several volumes of permanent interest. In more academic fields his book on folklore, totemism, Homeric scholarship, Scottish history, and 'historical mysteries' are still remembered by specialists in each; and all that he wrote in prose or verse is still readable on account of the charm and individuality of his style, through which shines the illusive, yet strangely attractive mind and character of their author.

Lang wrote no masterpiece in the accepted sense, and only those who fall captive to the magic of his personality as glimpsed through his writings will follow him now beyond an odd volume or two appealing to some special interest.

Yet by an odd irony of fate he is remembered and known throughout the world for a group of books which contain little of his actual writing—the Fairy Book series. For of the twelve volumes of fairy tales, named according to colour, though he was the collector and presiding genius, hardly any were actually retold by him.

His early interest in folklore took a strictly scientific bent while he was at Merton, and he wrote most learnedly on the origin and diffusion of popular tales. 'There was a time,' he recalled, 'when I considered all *contes*, except *contes populaires*, as frivolous and vexatious.' He was never enthusiastic about literary fairy stories, though he had a special affection for *The Rose and the Ring* and was an early admirer of George MacDonald's *Phantastes*.

This did not however prevent him from trying his hand at a little fairy story, which he called *The Princess Nobody*, in 1884 at the suggestion of his friend and publisher Charles Longman. This pleasant trifle (recently reprinted in Dent's *Modern Fairy Stories)* was written to fit a series of pictures of fairyland by Richard Doyle, and Lang showed great ingenuity in arranging them and fitting together a number of the stock incidents of folklore for them to illustrate in such a way that *The Princess Nobody* appears to be a completely spontaneous tale written simply in the traditional vein, rather as Mrs Ewing did in her *Old Fashioned Fairy Tales*.

The success of this effort broke down Lang's resistance to the literary use of the fairy *genre*, and he ventured still further with *The Gold of Fairnilee* in 1888, for which the inspiration was drawn from the Border Ballads and the old superstitions that still lingered by Tweedside when he was a boy, and the setting was the ruined house near Selkirk where he and his brother had dug for the fabled treasure in vain.

This is the most completely original of Lang's own fairy stories, and the most perfectly written. That it was not the most popular is due mainly to the unfamiliar background among the evil fairies of the north, so alien to the English nursery tradition derived from Perrault, Madame d'Aulnoy, and Grimm.

By far his most successful venture came the following year when Lang first introduced his readers to the Kingdom of Pantouflia, situated on the borders of fairyland in a region not far from Thackeray's Paflagonia, where the adventures of *Prince Prigio* take place. This book was at once recognized as a classic, the leading American critic, Brander Matthews, for example, writing that he 'unhesitatingly proclaimed it the most delightful of modern fairy-tales since *The Rose and the Ring*', and it has been constantly reprinted ever since, the last edition, in company with its sequel, *Prince Ricardo* (1893), being in Dent's *Children's Illustrated Classics* in 1961. Lang's attempt at a return to Pantouflia, *Tales of a Fairy Court* in 1907, could not recapture the spontaneity and irresistible charm of the earlier adventures, though it contains authentic echoes. But the original *Prince Prigio* can stand comparison with all but the greatest children's books, even of that golden age which began with *The Rose and the Ring* and *Alice* and ended with *The Wind in the Willows* and the Nesbit series.

It is not, however, so well known as another book with Lang's name on the title page which also appeared in 1889. *The Blue Fairy Book* was a daring venture at a time when even the traditional fairy tales were in eclipse and the child-novels of Mrs Ewing and Mrs Molesworth held the centre of the stage. Its only important predecessor, *The Fairy Book* prepared by Mrs Craik, had appeared as early as 1863, and was drawn almost entirely from the obvious French sources and from Grimm.

Lang's collection, 'made for the pleasure of children, and without scientific purpose, includes nursery tales which have a purely literary origin'—as he was careful to explain in the introduction to the limited large-paper edition. This accounts for the unexpected appearance in it of a shortened version of 'Gulliver in Lilliput', three tales from *The Arabian Nights* and five from Madame d'Aulnoy, besides three from the *Cabinet des Fées;* but of the truly traditional tales Lang included seven from Perrault, seven from Grimm, four Norse tales, two Scottish, one from Asia Minor, and his own brilliant version of the ancient Greek story of Perseus recast in its original fairy-tale form.

The book was published in an edition of 5000 at six shillings, with numerous illustrations by H. J. Ford and P. Jacomb Hood, and was very much of an experiment. It was certainly not intended as the first of a series. But its success was immediate and amazing: it changed the whole trend of children's literature and brought back the fairies in full force.

A sequel was called for, and *The Red Fairy Book* followed for Christmas 1890—now in an edition of 10,000 and containing only traditional fairy tales (except for Lang's retelling of the *Volsunga Saga*)—eleven French, eleven Norse, eight German, two Russian, two Romanian, and one English. By the time *The Yellow Fairy Book* arrived in 1894, the first edition was of 15,000 copies, and the contents included Norse, Estonian, German, French, Modern Greek, Hungarian, Russian, Polish, Red Indian, Chinese, and Icelandic folktales.

In the preface to *The Green Fairy Book* (1892) Lang wrote: 'This is the third, and probably the last, of the Fairy Books of many colours . . . If we have a book for you next year, it shall not be a fairy book.' But the demand for fairy tales showed no sign of slackening, and in the end the series ran to twenty-five annual volumes (1889-1913), of which twelve were Fairy Books, though several others such as *The Arabian Nights*, the two *Romance Books*, and the final *Strange Story Book* hail almost entirely from the realms of faerie.

'There is no story quite so worth reading as a fairy story,' wrote G. K. Chesterton when *The Violet Fairy Book* appeared in 1901. 'A fairy story is, perhaps, more artistic in the strict sense of the word than any other form of art.' That adults should admit to reading and enjoying the old fairy tales was a great triumph for Lang who, in 1889, was fighting against the critics and educationists of the day who considered their unreality, brutality, and escapism to be harmful for young readers, while holding that such stories were beneath the serious consideration of those of mature age. Already the accolade of a truly 'adult' taste was the appreciation of Henry James, Ibsen, and the Russians, to the exclusion of anything that might be termed romantic as a sign of escapism or arrested development.

Lang insisted, however, that fairy tales contain more fundamental truth than the most 'realistic' novel by Tolstoy or Thomas Hardy, and 'unobtrusively teach the true lessons of our wayfaring in a world of perplexities and obstructions'. He had already, in a more apologetic vein, preached from the same text in the introduction (for adults) to the large-paper edition of *The Blue Fairy Book*, pointing out, for example, that 'when the Princess wakens, after her betrothal to the Yellow Dwarf, and hopes it was a dream, and finds on her finger the fatal ring of one red hair, we have a brave touch of horror and of truth. All of us have wakened and struggled with a dim evil memory, and trusted it was a dream, and found, in one form or other, a proof, a shape of that ring of red hair.'

Nevertheless, as he grew old, Lang longed more and more to escape from the changing age which had outgrown him. Like his friend's Dr Jekyll, he found himself more and more inclined to slip out of his own personality without meaning to—though it was to the fairylands of legend and literature.

His later literary criticism suffers from this form of escapism —in his case a kind of melancholia which caused him to take events both private and public more and more to heart; when he died suddenly of angina pectoris on 20 July 1912, his wife wrote: 'It was the Strikes that killed him.' But it increased his understanding of fairy tales and the romances of the past. The later Fairy Books are better than the more famous earlier ones. Though Mrs Lang was responsible for most of the writing, Lang 'superintended' them to an extent which it is now impossible to discover—but he left his touch on nearly all of them.

One of the best things he ever wrote appeared in 1907: *Tales of Troy and Greece*, of which two-thirds consists of *The Adventures of Odysseus* (reprinted in Dent's *Children's Illustrated Classics* in 1962). The retelling is entirely by Lang, and into his re-creation of the Old Greek legends he put all the love and understanding of a life-long devotion to Homer, besides the underlying realization of the fairy world behind the adventures of Theseus, Perseus, and Jason—as well as of Odysseus when he wandered among one-eyed giants, beautiful witches, fairies on magic islands, and princesses in kingdoms beyond this world on his way from the cruel reality of fallen Troy to the final happiness of the simple, everyday world of his home in Ithaca.

Among all retellers of Greek myth and legend, Lang best understood 'how a child's mind worked' and alone succeeded in capturing the necessary simplicity of style without losing any of 'the old original magic', as an anonymous writer in *The Times Literary Supplement* put it recently in reviewing some modern retellings; and he went on 'How one longs for Lang's *Tales of Troy and Greece* to be reprinted; in their chosen field they were, and remain, unequalled.'

The Fairy Books are also, in their own way, still unequalled. Even in the new editions, lacking the inspired illustrations by Henry Justice Ford, which seemed an essential part of the original volumes, they capture and hold new generations of children. And those who, like Lang himself, enjoy the best of the old fairy tales at any age, turn back to them again and again—to pick out one story, perhaps, but then to fall under the spell and read tale after tale, forgetful of all but the eternal world of fairyland when led into its magic purlieus by that great enchanter, Andrew Lang.

[1962]

With birds in his beard

ALISON WHITE

In the late 1830s when the young Victoria came to the throne, English ladies and gentlemen passed the social evenings by improvising comic verse. An early example is:

There was an old man of Tobago
Who lived on rice gruel and sago.
But at last to his bliss the physician said this:
To a roast leg of mutton you may go.

After each absurdity the company would chorus: 'Will you come up to Limerick?' And so the limerick was born.

In the 1840s a young artist whose name was Edward Lear found that children liked his original limericks, patterned upon the popular Old Man of Tobago. To illustrate these Lear sketched inane and preposterous people. Edward Lear was funny-looking himself, with thick spectacles, a really inordinate nose (it is hard to avoid the Lear idiom), and a beard that according to him resembled a wig. We have his self-portrait in the lines beginning 'How pleasant to know Mr Lear', in which Lear says of Lear:

His mind is concrete and fastidious,
  His nose is remarkably big;
His visage is more or less hideous
  His beard it resembles a wig.

He has many friends, laymen and clerical,
Old Foss is the name of his cat;
His body is perfectly spherical,
He weareth a runcible hat.

Though comic, this poem does not ignore the sad aspects of Edward Lear's life. It observes:

He weeps by the side of the ocean,
He weeps on the top of the hill.

Why should the creator of the 'Jumblies' or the 'Dong with the Luminous Nose' weep? To start with, his life began in a melodrama of misery as outlandish as any in Dickens. As a child Edward Lear saw his palatial home, complete with footmen, vanish like some fairy dream as his bankrupt father was borne off to King's Bench Prison. Edward's mother, who seems to have been all wife, lightly abandoned her twenty-one (yes, twenty-one) children to carry daily, year after year, a six-course dinner to her husband in jail. Helpless in their attempts to make their own way, a number of her sons and daughters died soon, four of them within four months. Like figures in a limerick they expired, it seems, out of pure discouragement. Edward was mothered by his sister Ann, twenty-one years his senior. Apart from a deep attachment to Ann, he never attained to many of the usual personal happinesses. He lived the life of a lonely, self-exiled wanderer, prey to an astonishing number of ailments. As uncouth as Hans Andersen, he also suffered, like Andersen, the dimly comprehended pangs of unendurable friendships.

This agonized invalid, an epileptic and asthmatic, suffered almost everything that the pre-aspirin age could inflict. Forever seasick when at sea, on land, despite his ills, he roved the wilds of Corsica, Albania, Syria, painting landscapes that are still admired. His companion was his cat, Old Foss. The pair of them must have looked like one of Lear's own comic inventions.

In his limericks the grotesque, ailing, exiled, lonely poet and painter took note of his deprivations, as we shall see. But his most musical poem 'Calico Pie', though gently comical, has the true elegiac ring in its simplicities. It brings the wheel of poetry around and back to Sir Thomas Wyatt's Tudor lyric, 'They flee from me that sometime did me seek,/With naked foot stalking in my chamber/ . . . sometime they put themselves in danger, /To take bread at my hand.' Three centuries later another poet, Lear, in 'Calico Pie' is forsaken by birds, by fish, by mice, by insects. Creation recedes from him. The refrain

They never came back,
They never came back,
They never came back,
They never came back to me

pierces through to Lear's solitary suffering with a note more convincing than that of the 'idle tears' laments of his close friend Tennyson. Edward Lear knew himself to be a grotesque, like Hans Andersen, a kind of ineligible dunce. So Lear peopled the world of his imagination with figures even more stricken than he: sappy, goofy Simple Simons—aspects of himself, as of everyone else. That is the secret of their universality. Sometimes these ludicrous heroes are one-up on the complacent crowd that gawks at them. When defeated—smashed, baked, drowned, barbarously and amusingly demolished—they vanish, forever capering, to be forever unforgotten.

In the limericks Lear's creations make assets of their deformities and afflictions. Lear himself perambulated an outsized nose. And the very first figure in his *Book of Nonsense*

. . . was an Old Man with a nose,
Who said, 'If you choose to suppose
That my nose is too long, you are certainly wrong!'
That remarkable Man with a nose.

In the limericks Lear's drawings supplied the wit which his

slack, repetitive last lines never attempted. As pictured, the serpentining nose of his first old man, looped and knotted, is not at all too long: it serves some children as a jump-rope. (If a nose is said to be too long, the question is, 'Too long for what?') One of large-nosed Lear's old men used his proboscis to support a light when he fished at night. Another turned his into a trumpet. On the nose of a third 'Most birds of the air could repose.' And as for chins, when a chin is called too sharp, is it not ideal for playing the harp? (As in the instance of a 'Young Lady whose chin/Resembled the point of a pin.')

Lear's antic personages not only compensate for their deformitie and afflictions, but they also defy the world by goings-on that the etiquette books could never have thought to proscribe. One of them runs up and down in his Grandmother's gown. A second gets smashed for bumping at a gong all the day long. A curtseying old lady twirls round and round till she sinks into the ground. In bygone days England had its share of eccentrics. As the Beatles age, we may see their like again. Eccentrics have grown scarce. If, as Bergson said, humour rises from the mechanization of life, it may be that automation has pre-empted eccentricity and transferred it to the mixmasters and univacs. Still, Lear, thou shouldst have been living at that hour of recent history when a certain Old Person from Moscow on a table did thump with his shoe, at one of mankind's most august assemblages.

Such monkey business as that is the theme of Lear's limericks, which in the 1850s must have afforded a lurid commentary to Darwinism. In the limericks citizens comport themselves like apes and bears. Witness the

> *. . . Old Man of Peru*
> *Who never knew what he should do;*
> *So he tore off his hair, and behaved like a bear . . .*

or the

. . . Old Person of Chile
Whose conduct was painful and silly;

the

. . . Old Person of Anerley,
Whose conduct was strange and unmannerly;

the

. . . Old Person of Buda,
Whose conduct grew ruder and ruder.

the

. . . Old Man on the Border,
Who lived in the utmost disorder.

Most distrubing in all this senescence is the 'Old Person of Bromley',

Whose ways were not cheerful or comely;
He sat in the dust, eating spiders and crust.

The agitated individuals of Lear's limerick world move from despair to death. On adjacent pages one finds a Young Lady of Clare: 'When she found she was tired, she abruptly expired.' And opposite sits the 'Old Man of Cape Horn,'

Who wished he had never been born;
So he sat on a chair till he died of despair.

And we remember Edward Lear's brothers and sisters, cast out into the working world, whose lives were concluded before they had well begun.

Death is a leading topic of Lear's limericks. Death has long been seen as comical. The skull maintains its grin. Graveyards are for whistlers as well as sleepers. Gallows wit will long outlive the institution of capital punishment. And lovers of limericks must laugh until they weep. Like all wise mourners they must weep until they laugh—over the Old Man of Madras who was

There was an Old Man of the Hague, whose ideas were excessively vague:
He built a balloon, to examine the moon,
That deluded Old Man of the Hague

FROM EDWARD LEAR'S *A Book of Nonsense*

killed by the length of the ears of the creamcoloured ass he rode upon; or, more understandably, over the old man killed by the conduct of his children. Here, too, are the baked people, the choked people, the smashed people. The comic violence is that of our frenetic film cartoons. Lear's limericks must have brought into Victorian parlours welcome release of licensed rudeness. And the ultimate rudeness is violent death. Also, in his limericks Lear, like all of us, is trying to get used to death, to dull its sting. In a late limerick he became calm enough to write: 'Which concluded that Person of Cromer.'

I have looked into the limericks for Lear's inner world because, of all his poems, they are by far the most spontaneous. They must have emerged from his subconscious virtually unedited. Not nearly all of them are alarming or dire. Some convey the deep charm he must have had, according to children and others who flocked about him, and also according to the young Queen Victoria, who greatly enjoyed her art lessons with Mr Lear. Is there not the Edward Lear hypnotic charm working through an old man who hoped to smile a 'horrible Cow' into submission?

I will sit on this stile, and continue to smile,
Which may soften the heart of that Cow.

Elsewhere we see Lear with lap and beard full of nesting children. Characteristically he turns them into birds:

There was an old man with a beard
Who said, 'It is just as I feared.
Two Owls and a Hen, four Larks and a Wren,
Have all built their nests in my beard.'

So, with his beard full of birds, in a society whose bonnet was full of bees, we leave Lear among the limericks. I have explored these to the neglect of more subtle poems. One is the saga of the Jumblies, which, were it less delirious, could be a noble contribution to heroic literature. Edward Lear had genius. His creations have a strange dignity. It is perhaps only by the —for us—fortunate circumstance of the poet's despair and self-deprecation that his intense poetic phantasms should have emerged humbly as owls and pussycats, ducks and kangaroos. They form an indispensable part of English poetry; and because of them the days of Lear's pilgrimage are unlikely to vanish. Anyway, as he himself remarked:

Ere the days of his pilgrimage vanish,
How pleasant to know
Mr Lear.

[1966]

Meg, Jo, Beth, Amy, and Louisa

ELIZABETH JANEWAY

Meg, Jo, Beth, and Amy are a hundred years old on 3 October, and except for Natasha Rostova, who is almost exactly their contemporary (*War and Peace* appeared over the years 1865 to 1869), the Marches must be the most read about and cried over young women of their years. In my time we read *Little Women* of course, but we liked to think it was because our sentimental mothers had loved the book so and urged it on us. For all I know, this is still the cover story today, but just the same, the answer to 'Have you read *Little Women*?' is still 'Of course.' In the last week I've heard it from three Americans, an Italian, and an English girl, all in their twenties—the English girl quoted the whole opening: 'Christmas won't be Christmas without any presents', it begins, in case you've forgotten—and a mother of teenagers assured me that her daughters were even now devouring the works of Miss Alcott. Read *Little Women*? Of course.

Why? It is dated and sentimental and full of preaching and moralizing and some snobbery about the lower classes that is positively breathtaking in its horror: that moment, for instance, when old Mr Laurence is improbably discovered in a fishmarket, and bestows his charity on a starving Irish woman by hooking a large fish on the end of his cane and depositing it, to her gasping gratitude, in her arms. It is as often smug as it is snug, and its high-mindedness tends to be that peculiar sort that pays.

Brigid Brophy, writing in *The New York Times Book Review* a few years ago, called it a dreadful masterpiece, and the judgement stands (though not, I think, quite on Miss Brophy's grounds). And yet here it is in a new and handsome centennial edition, as compulsively readable as it was a century ago when publisher Thomas Niles's nieces overrode their uncle's doubts and urged him to bring it out.

Its faults we can see in a moment. They cry to heaven, and when Miss Brophy dwelt at length on the literary sin of sentimentality which falsifies emotion and manipulates the process of life, she hardly had to cite evidence. *Little Women* does harp on our nerves, does play on our feelings, does stack the cards to bring about undeserved happy outcomes here and undeserved come-uppance there. But that is not the whole story, and couldn't be, or there wouldn't be all those girls with their noses in the book right now and all those women who remember the supreme shock of the moment when Jo sold her hair; when Beth was discovered on the medicine chest in the closet with scarlet fever coming on; when Meg let the Moffats dress her up; when Amy was packed off, protesting and bargaining, to Aunt March's stiff house.

No, *Little Women* does manipulate life but it is also *about* life, and life that is recognizable in human terms today. Miss Alcott preached, and the conclusions she came to are frequently too good to be true; but the facts of emotion that she started with were real. She might end by softening the ways to deal with them, but she began by looking them in the eye. Her girls were jealous, mean, silly, and lazy; and for a hundred years jealous, mean, silly, and lazy girls have been ardently grateful for the chance to read about themselves. If Miss Alcott's prescriptions for curing their sins are too simple, it doesn't alter the fact that her diagnoses are clear, unequivocal, and humanly right. When her girls are good, they are apt to be painful; but when they are bad, they are bad just the way we all are, and over the same things. It must have been a heavenly relief a hundred years ago to learn that one's faults were not unique. Today I suspect that it is a relief to be told to take them seriously and struggle with them; that it is important to be good.

This general background of human interest makes *Little Women* still plausible, but it is hardly enough to keep it a perennial classic. The real attraction is not the book as a whole, but its heroine, Jo, and Jo is a unique creation: the one young woman in nineteenth-century fiction who maintains her individual independence, who gives up no part of her autonomy as payment for being born a woman—and who gets away with it. Jo is the tomboy dream come true, the dream of growing up into full humanity with all its potentialities instead of into limited femininity: of looking after oneself and paying one's way and doing effective work in the real world instead of learning how to please a man who will look after you, as Meg and Amy both do with pious pleasure. (So, by the way, does Natasha). It's no secret that Jo's story is the heart of *Little Women*, but just what that story represents has not, to my knowledge, been explored, and I think it is worth looking at.

We shall have to work back and forth from Louisa May Alcott's life to her book, but no one has ever denied that Jo is Louisa and that a great deal of her story is autobiographical. The very fact that *Little Women* was written so quickly makes that conclusion inescapable: two and a half months for the first part and two months for the second. More clearly in life, but clearly enough in her book, Louisa-Jo wanted to become the head of the family. In part, this was necessity. Bronson Alcott suffered from a kind of obsessional generosity that appears at times to have verged on *folie de grandeur*, and his wife and daughters learned early to shift for themselves, for Papa's plans not only went astray, they were apt to ignore the existence of his family completely.

Then there came a time—Louisa was eleven—when Bronson Alcott all but deserted his wife and daughters and went off to join a Shaker colony with his English friend, Charles Lane, who (as his wife put it) had almost hypnotic power over him. In the end he did not go, but suffered so powerfully from the crisis that he did in fact abdicate the father's role in the family. In that frequent nineteenth-century gesture of despair, he took to his bed and turned his face to the wall. None of this was hidden from Louisa. She and her older sister Anna made part of the family council which discussed Mr Alcott's decision to go off with his friend to the celibate Shakers or to stay.

This clumsy agony is glossed over in *Little Women*, where absent Mr March is away as a chaplain during the Civil War. But the pressure on Jo to hold her family together by working and earning is all there, and so is the emotion of the one who aspires to play the role of responsibility when it has become vacant. When Meg is falling in love, Jo blurts out in fury, 'I just wish I could marry Meg myself, and keep her safe in the family.' This is of course treated as a joke, though sociologist students of the incest taboo in the nuclear family would find it of interest. It is, at any rate, indicative of Jo's desire to become the responsible head of the household, and the last half of the book is devoted to her effort to achieve this end, which in her life she did achieve.

This aim explains her refusal to marry handsome Laurie, the next-door hero. Their relationship has always been that of two equals, which in nineteenth-century America (and in some places today) implies two equals of the same sex. Twice at least Laurie suggests that they run off together, not for love-making but for adventure, very much in the manner and mood in which Tom Sawyer and Huck Finn plan to run away from comfort and civilization. Again when Jo speaks to her mother about the possibility of marriage to Laurie, Mrs March is against it 'because you two are too much alike.' So they are, and so—with no explanations ever given—Jo refuses Laurie, and the reader knows she is right, for Jo and Laurie are dear friends, competitors and not in the least a couple. It is worth noting that the two other adored nineteenth-century heroines who say 'No' to the hero's proposal give way in the end, when circumstances and the hero have changed: Elizabeth Bennet and Jane Eyre. But Jo says 'No' and does not shift.

The subtlety of Miss Alcott's character drawing (or self-knowledge, if you will) comes through here, for Jo is a tomboy but never a masculinized or lesbian figure. She is, somehow, an idealized 'New Woman', capable of male virtues but not, as the Victorians would have said, 'unsexed'. Or perhaps she is really archaic woman, re-created out of some New-World-frontier necessity when patriarchy breaks down. For Jo marries (as we all know! Who can forget that last great self-indulgent burst of tears when Professor Bhaer stops, under the umbrella, and asks 'Heart's dearest, why do you cry?'). Yes, Jo marries and becomes, please note, not a sweet little wife but a matriarch: mistress of the professor's school, mother of healthy sons (while Amy and Laurie have only one sickly daughter), and cheerful active manager of events and people. For this Victorian moral tract, sentimental and preachy, was written by a secret rebel against the order of the world and woman's place in it, and all the girls who ever read it know it.

[1968]

Beatrix Potter

GRAHAM GREENE

'It is said that the effect of eating too much lettuce is soporific.' It is with some such precise informative sentence that one might have expected the great Potter saga to open, for the obvious characteristic of Beatrix Potter's style is a selective realism, which takes emotion for granted and puts aside love and death with a gentle detachment reminiscent of Mr E. M. Forster's. Her stories contain plenty of dramatic action, but it is described from the outside by an acute and unromantic observer who never sacrifices truth for an effective gesture. As an example of Miss Potter's empiricism, her rigid adherence to what can be seen and heard, consider the climax of her masterpiece *The Roly-Poly Pudding*, Tom Kitten's capture by the rats in the attic:

'Anna Maria,' said the old man rat (whose name was Samuel Whiskers), 'Anna Maria, make me a kitten dumpling roly-poly pudding for my dinner.'

'It requires dough and a pat of butter, and a rolling pin,' said Anna Maria, considering Tom Kitten with her head on one side.

'No,' said Samuel Whiskers. 'Make it properly, Anna Maria, with breadcrumbs.'

But in 1908, when *The Roly-Poly Pudding* was published, Miss Potter was at the height of her power. She was not a born realist, and her first story was not only romantic, it was historical. *The Tailor of Gloucester* opens:

In the time of swords and periwigs and full-skirted coats with

FROM *The Tale of Tom Kitten*

flowered lappets—when gentlemen wore ruffles, and gold-laced waistcoats of paduasoy and taffeta—there lived a tailor in Gloucester.

In the sharp details of this sentence, in the flowered lappets, there is a hint of the future Potter, but her first book is not only hampered by its period setting but by the presence of a human character. Miss Potter is seldom at her best with human beings (the only flaw in *The Roly-Poly Pudding* is the introduction in the final pages of the authoress in person), though with one human character she succeeded triumphantly. I refer of course to Mr MacGregor, who made an elusive appearance in 1904 in

The Tale of Benjamin Bunny, ran his crabbed earth-mould way through *Peter Rabbit,* and met his final ignominious defeat in *The Flopsy Bunnies* in 1909. But the tailor of Gloucester cannot be compared with Mr MacGregor. He is too ineffective and too virtuous, and the atmosphere of the story—snow, and Christmas bells and poverty—is too Dickensian. Incidentally in Simpkin Miss Potter drew her only unsympathetic portrait of a cat. The ancestors of Tom Thumb and Hunca Munca play a humanitarian part. Their kind hearts are a little oppressive.

In the same year Miss Potter published *Squirrel Nutkin.* It is an unsatisfactory book, less interesting than her first, which was a good example of a bad *genre.* But in 1904, with the publication of *Two Bad Mice,* Miss Potter opened the series of her great comedies. In this story of Tom Thumb and Hunca Munca and their wanton havoc of a doll's house, the unmistakable Potter style first appears.

It is an elusive style, difficult to analyse. It owes something to alliteration:

Hunca Munca stood up in her chair and chopped at the ham with another lead knife.

'It's as hard as the hams at the cheesemonger's,' said Hunca Munca.

Something too it owes to the short paragraphs, which are fashioned with a delicate irony, not to complete a movement, but mutely to criticize the action by arresting it. The imperceptive pause allows the mind to take in the picture: the mice are stilled in their enraged attitudes for a moment, before the action sweeps forward:

Then there was no end to the rage and disappointment of Tom Thumb and Hunca Munca. They broke up the pudding, the lobsters, the pears, and the oranges.

As the fish would not come off the plate, they put it into the red-hot crinkly paper fire in the kitchen; but it would not burn either.

It is curious that Beatrix Potter's method of paragraphing has never been imitated.

The last quotation shows another element of her later style, her love of a precise catalogue, her creation of atmosphere with still-life. One remembers Mr MacGregor's rubbish heap:

> *There were jam pots and paper bags and mountains of chopped grass from the mowing machine (which always tasted oily), and some rotten vegetable marrows and an old boot or two.*

The only indication in *Two Bad Mice* of a prentice hand is the sparsity of dialogue; her characters had not yet begun to utter those brief pregnant sentences, which have slipped, like proverbs, into common speech. Nothing in the early book equals Mr Jackson's, 'No teeth. No teeth. No teeth.'

* In 1904 too *The Tale of Peter Rabbit*, the second of the great comedies, was published, closely followed by its sequel, *Benjamin Bunny*. In Peter and his cousin Benjamin Miss Potter created two epic personalities. The great characters of fiction are often paired: Quixote and Sancho, Pantagruel and Panurge, Pickwick and Weller, Benjamin and Peter. Peter was a neurotic, Benjamin worldly and imperturbable. Peter was warned by his mother, 'Don't go into Mr MacGregor's garden; your father had an accident there; he was put in a pie by Mrs MacGregor.' But Peter went from stupidity rather than for adventure. He escaped from Mr MacGregor by leaving his clothes behind, and the sequel, the story of how his clothes were recovered, introduces Benjamin, whose coolness and practicality are a foil to the nerves and clumsiness of his cousin. It was Benjamin who knew the way to enter a garden: 'It spoils people's clothes to squeeze under a gate; the proper way to get in is to climb down a pear tree.' It was Peter who fell down head first.

From 1904 to 1908 were vintage years in comedy; to these years belong *The Pie and the Patty Pan*, *The Tale of Tom Kitten*, *The Tale of Mrs Tiggy Winkle*, and only one failure, *Mr Jeremy Fisher*. Miss Potter had found her right vein and her right scene. The novels were now set in Cumberland; the farms, the village shops, the stone walls, the green slope of Catbells became the background of her pictures and her prose. She was peopling a countryside. Her dialogue had become memorable because aphoristic:

'I disapprove of tin articles in puddings and pies. It is most undesirable—(especially when people swallow in lumps).'

She could draw a portrait in a sentence:

'My name is Mrs Tiggy Winkle; oh yes if you please'm, I'm an excellent clear-starcher.'

And with what beautiful economy she sketched the first smiling villain of her gallery! Tom Kitten had dropped his clothes off the garden wall as the Puddle-Duck family passed:

'Come! Mr Drake Puddle-Duck,' said Moppet. 'Come and help us to dress him! Come and button up Tom!'

Mr Drake Puddle-Duck advanced in a slow sideways manner, and picked up the various articles.

But he put them on himself. They fitted him even worse than Tom Kitten.

'It's a very fine morning,' said Mr Drake Puddle-Duck.

Looking backward over the thirty years of Miss Potter's literary career, we see that the creation of Mr Puddle-Duck marked the beginning of a new period. At some time between 1907 and 1909 Miss Potter must have passed through an emotional ordeal which changed the character of her genius. It would be impertinent to inquire into the nature of the ordeal. Her case is curiously similar to that of Henry James. Something happened which shook their faith in appearances. From *The Portrait of a Lady* onwards, innocence deceived, the treachery of friends, became the theme of James's greatest stories. Mme Merle, Kate Croy, Mme de Vionnet, Charlotte Stant, these tortuous treacherous women are paralleled through the dark period of Miss Potter's art. 'A man can smile and smile and be a villain'—that, a little altered, was her recurrent message, expressed by her gallery of scoundrels: Mr Drake Puddle-Duck, the first and slightest, Mr Jackson, the least harmful with his passion for honey and his reiterated, 'No teeth. No teeth. No teeth', Samuel Whiskers, gross and brutal, and the 'gentleman with sandy whiskers' who may be identified with Mr Tod. With the publication of *Mr Tod* in 1912, Miss Potter's pessimism reached its climax. But for the nature of her audience *Mr Tod* would certainly have ended tragically. In *Jemina Puddle-Duck* the gentleman with sandy whiskers had at least a debonair impudence when he addressed his victims:

'Before you commence your tedious sitting, I intend to give you a treat. Let us have a dinner party all to ourselves!

'May I ask you to bring up some herbs from the farm garden to make a savoury omelette? Sage and thyme, and mint and two onions, and some parsley. I will provide lard for the stuff—lard for the omelette,' said the hospitable gentleman with sandy whiskers.

But no charm softens the brutality of Mr. Tod and his enemy, the repulsive Tommy Brock. In her comedies Miss Potter had gracefully eliminated the emotions of love and death; it is the measure of her genius that when, in *The Tale of Mr Tod*, they broke the barrier, the form of her book, her ironic style, remained unshattered. When she could not keep death out she stretched her technique to include it. Benjamin and Peter had grown up and married, and Benjamin's babies were stolen by Brock; the immortal pair, one still neurotic, the other knowing and imperturbable, set off to the rescue, but the rescue, conducted in darkness, from a house, 'something between a cave, a prison, and a tumbledown pig-sty', compares grimly with an earlier rescue from Mr MacGregor's sunny vegetable garden:

The sun had set; an owl began to hoot in the wood. There were many unpleasant things lying about, that had much better have been buried; rabbit bones and skulls, and chicken's legs and other horrors. It was a shocking place and very dark.

But *Mr Tod*, for all the horror of its atmosphere, is indispensable. There are few fights in literature which can compare in excitement with the duel between Mr Tod and Tommy Brock (it was echoed by H. G. Wells in *Mr Polly*):

Everything was upset except the kitchen table.

And everything was broken, except the mantelpiece and the kitchen fender. The crockery was smashed to atoms.

The chairs were broken, and the window, and the clock fell with a crash, and there were handfuls of Mr Tod's sandy whiskers.

The vases fell off the mantelpiece, the canisters fell off the shelf; the kettle fell off the hob. Tommy Brock put his foot in a jar of raspberry jam.

Mr Tod marked the distance which Miss Potter had travelled since the ingenuous romanticism of *The Tailor of Gloucester*. The next year with *The Tale of Pigling Bland*, the period of the great near-tragedies came to an end. There was something of the same squalor, and the villain, Mr Thomas Piperson, was not less terrible than Mr Tod, but the book ended on a lyrical note, as Pigling Bland escaped with Pig-Wig:

They ran, and they ran, and they ran down the hill, and across a short cut on level green turf at the bottom, between pebble-beds and rushes. They came to the river, they came to the bridge —they crossed it hand in hand—

It was the nearest Miss Potter had approached to a conventional love story. The last sentence seemed a promise that the cloud had lifted, that there was to be a return to the style of the earlier comedies. But *Pigling Bland* was published in 1913. Through the years of war the author was silent, and for many years after it was over, only a few books of rhyme appeared. These showed that Miss Potter had lost none of her skill as an artist, but left the great question of whither her genius was tending unanswered. Then, after seventeen years, at the end of 1930, *Little Pig Robinson* was published.

The scene was no longer Cumberland but Devonshire and the sea. The story, more than twice as long as *Mr Tod,* was diffuse and undramatic. The smooth smiling villain had disappeared and taken with him the pungent dialogue, the sharp detail, the light of common day. Miss Potter had not returned to the great comedies. She had gone on beyond the great near-tragedies to her *Tempest.* No tortured Lear nor strutting Antony could live on Prospero's island, among the sounds and sweet airs and cloudcapt towers. Miss Potter too had reached her island, the escape from tragedy, the final surrender of imagination to safe serene fancy:

A steam of boiling water flowed down the silvery strand. The shore was covered with oysters. Acid-drops and sweets grew upon the trees. Yams, which are a sort of sweet potato, abounded ready cooked. The breadfruit tree grew iced cakes and muffins ready baked.

It was very satisfying for a pig Robinson, but in that rarefied air no bawdy Tommy Brock could creep to burrow, no Benjamin pursued his feud between the vegetable-frames, no Puddle-Duck could search in wide-eyed innocence for a 'convenient dry nesting-place'.

[1933]

NOTE. On the publication of this essay I received a somewhat acid letter from Miss Potter correcting certain details. *Little Pig Robinson,* although the last published of her books, was in fact the first written. She denied that there had been any emotional disturbance at the time she was writing *Mr Tod*: she was suffering however from the after-effects of flu. In conclusion she deprecated sharply 'the Freudian school' of criticism.

Huckleberry Finn: a critical essay

T. S. ELIOT

The Adventures of Huckleberry Finn is the only one of Mark Twain's various books which can be called a masterpiece. I do not suggest that it is his only book of permanent interest; but it is the only one in which his genius is completely realized, and the only one which creates its own category. There are pages in *Tom Sawyer* and in *Life on the Mississippi* which are, within their limits, as good as anything with which one can compare them in *Huckleberry Finn;* and in other books there are drolleries just as good of their kind. But when we find one book by a prolific author which is very much superior to all the rest, we look for the peculiar accident or concourse of accidents which made that book possible. In the writing of *Huckleberry Finn* Mark Twain had two elements which, when treated with his sensibility and his experience, formed a great book: these two are the Boy and the River.

Huckleberry Finn is, no doubt, a book which boys enjoy. I cannot speak from memory: I suspect that a fear on the part of my parents lest I should acquire a premature taste for tobacco, and perhaps other habits of the hero of the story, kept the book out of my way. But *Huckleberry Finn* does not fall into this category of juvenile fiction. The opinion of my parents that it was a book unsuitable for boys left me, for most of my life, under the impression that it was a book suitable only for boys. Therefore it was only a few years ago that I read for the first time, and in that order, *Tom Sawyer* and *Huckleberry Finn*.

Tom Sawyer did not prepare me for what I was to find its sequel to be. *Tom Sawyer* seems to me to be a boy's book, and a very good one. The River and the Boy make their appearance in it; the narrative is good; and there is also a very good picture of society in a small midwestern river town (for St Petersburg is more western than southern) a hundred years ago. But the point of view of the narrator is that of an adult observing a boy. And Tom is the ordinary boy, though of quicker wits and livelier imagination than most. Tom is, I suppose, very much the boy that Mark Twain had been: he is remembered and described as he seemed to his elders, rather than created. Huck Finn, on the other hand, is the boy that Mark Twain still was at the time of writing his adventures. We look at Tom as the smiling adult does: Huck we do not look at—we see the world through his eyes. The two boys are not merely different types; they were brought into existence by different processes. Hence in the second book their roles are altered. In the first book Huck is merely the humble friend—almost a variant of the traditional valet of comedy and we see him as he is seen by the conventional respectable society to which Tom belongs, and of which, we feel sure, Tom will one day become an eminently respectable and conventional member. In the second book their nominal relationship remains the same; but here it is Tom who has the secondary role. The author was probably not conscious of this when he wrote the first two chapters: *Huckleberry Finn* is not the kind of story in which the author knows, from the beginning, what is going to happen. Tom then disappears from our view; and when he returns, he has only two functions. The first is to provide a foil for Huck. Huck's persisting admiration for Tom only exhibits more clearly to our eyes the unique qualities of the former and the commonplacess of the latter. Tom has the imagination of a lively boy who has read a good deal of romantic fiction: he might, of course, become a writer—he might become Mark Twain. Or rather, he might become the more commonplace aspect of Mark Twain. Huck has not imagination, in the sense in which Tom has it: he has, instead, vision. He sees the real world; and he does not judge it—he allows it to judge itself.

Tom Sawyer is an orphan. But he has his aunt; he has, as we learn later, other relatives; and he has the environment into which he fits. He is wholly a social being. When there is a secret band to be formed, it is Tom who organizes it and prescribes the rules. Huck Finn is alone: there is no more solitary character in fiction. The fact that he has a father only emphasizes his loneliness; and he views his father with a terrifying detachment. So we come to see Huck himself in the end as one of the permanent symbolic figures of fiction, not unworthy to take a place with Ulysses, Faust, Don Quixote, Don Juan, Hamlet and other great discoveries that man has made about himself.

It would seem that Mark Twain was a man who—perhaps like most of us—never became in all respects mature. We might even say that the adult side of him was boyish, and that only the boy in him that was Huck Finn was adult. As Tom Sawyer grown up, he wanted success and applause (Tom himself always needed an audience). He wanted prosperity, a happy domestic life of a conventional kind, universal approval, and fame. All these things he obtained. As Huck Finn he was indifferent to all these things; and being composite of the two, Mark Twain both strove for them and resented their violation of his integrity. Hence he became the humorist and even clown: with his gifts, a certain way to success, for everyone could enjoy his writings without the slightest feeling of discomfort, self-consciousness, or self-criticism. And hence, on the other hand, his pessimism and misanthropy. To be a misanthrope is to be in some way divided; or it is sign of an uneasy conscience. The pessimism which Mark Twain discharged into *The Man That Corrupted Hadleyburg* and *What is Man?* springs less from observation of society, than from his hatred of himself for allowing society to tempt and corrupt him and give him what he wanted. There is no wisdom in it. But all this personal problem has been diligently examined by Mr Van Wyck Brooks; and it is not Mark Twain, but *Huckleberry Finn,* that is the subject of this essay.

You cannot say that Huck himself is either a humorist or a misanthrope. He is the impassive observer: he does not interfere, and, as I have said, he does not judge. Many of the episodes that occur on the voyage down the river, after he is joined by the Duke and the King (whose fancies about themselves are akin to the kind of fancy that Tom Sawyer enjoys), are in themselves farcical; and if it were not for the presence of Huck as the reporter of them, they would be no more than farce. But seen through the eyes of Huck, there is a deep human pathos in these scoundrels. On the other hand, the story of the feud between the Grangerfords and the Shepherdsons is a masterpiece in itself; yet Mark Twain could not have written it so, with that economy and restraint, with just the right details and no more, and leaving to the reader to make his own moral reflections, unless he had been writing in the person of Huck. And the *style* of the book, which is the style of Huck, is what makes it a far more convincing indictment of slavery than the sensationalist propaganda of *Uncle Tom's Cabin.* Huck is passive and impassive, apparently always the victim of events; and yet, in his acceptance of his world and of what it does to him and others, he is more powerful than his world because he is more *aware* than any other person in it.

Repeated readings of the book only confirm and deepen one's admiration of the consistency and perfect adaptation of the writing. This is a style which at the period, whether in America or in England, was an innovation, a new discovery in the English language. Other authors had achieved natural speech in relation to particular characters—Scott with characters talking Lowland

Scots, Dickens with cockneys—but no one else had kept it up through the whole of a book. Thackeray's Yellowplush, impressive as he is, is an obvious artifice in comparison. In *Huckleberry Finn* there is no exaggeration of grammar or spelling or speech, there is no sentence or phrase to destroy the illusion that these are Huck's own words. It is not only in the way in which he tells his story, but in the details he remembers, that Huck is true to himself. There is, for instance, the description of the Grangerford interior as Huck sees it on his arrival; there is the list of the objects which Huck and Jim salvaged from the derelict house:

We got an old tin lantern, and a butcher-knife without any handle, and a bran-new Barlow knife worth two bits in any store and a lot of tallow candles, and a tin candlestick, and a gourd, and a tin cup, and a ratty old bedquilt off the bed, and a reticule with needles and pins and beeswax and buttons and thread and all such truck in it, and a hatchet and some nails, and a fish-line as thick as my little finger, with some monstrous hooks on it, and a roll of buckskin, and a leather dog-collar, and a horseshoe, and some vials of medicine that didn't have no label on them; and just as we was leaving I found a tolerable good curry-comb, and Jim he found a ratty old fiddle-bow, and a wooden leg. The straps was broke off, but barring that, it was a good enough leg, though it was too long for men and not long enough for Jim, and we couldn't find the other one, though we hunted all round.

And so, take it all round, we made a good haul.

This is the sort of list that a boy reader should pore over with delight; but the paragraph performs other functions of which the reader would be unaware. It provides the right counterpoise to the horror of the wrecked house and the corpse; it has a grim precision which tells the reader all he needs to know about the way of life of the human derelicts who had used the house; it (especially the wooden leg and the fruitless search for its mate) reminds us at the right moment of the kinship of mind and the sympathy between the boy outcast from society and the Negro fugitive from the injustice of society.

Huck in fact would be incomplete without Jim, who is almost as notable a creation as Huck himself. Huck is the passive observer of men and events, Jim the submissive sufferer from them; and they are equal in dignity. There is no passage in which their relationship is brought out more clearly than the conclusion of the chapter in which, after the two have become separated in the fog, Huck in the canoe and Jim on the raft, Huck, in his impulse of boyish mischief, persuades Jim for a time that the latter had dreamt the whole episode.

'. . . my heart wuz mos' broke bekase you wuz los', en I didn' k'yer no mo' what become er me en de raf'. En when I wake up en fine you back agin', all safe en soun', de tears come en I could a got down on my knees en kiss' yo' foot, I's so thankful. En all you wuz thinkin' 'bout wuz how you could make a fool uv ole Jim wid a lie. Dat truck dah is trash; en trash is what people is dat puts dirt on de head en dey fren's en makes 'em ashamed.' . . .

It was fifteen minutes before I could work myself up to go and humble myself to a nigger—but I done it, and I warn't ever sorry for it afterwards, neither.

This passage has been quoted before; and if quote it again, it is because I wish to elicit from it one meaning that is, I think, usually overlooked. What is obvious in it is the pathos and dignity of Jim, and this is moving enough; but what I find still more disturbing, and still more unusual in literature, is the pathos and dignity of the boy, when reminded so humbly and humiliatingly that his position in the world is not that of other boys, entitled from time to time to a practical joke; but that he must bear, and bear alone, the responsibility of a man.

It is Huck who gives the book style. The River gives the book its form. But for the River, the book might be only a sequence of adventures with a happy ending. A river, a very big and powerful river, is the only natural force than can wholly determine the course of human peregrination. At sea, the wanderer may sail or be carried by winds and currents in one direction or another; a change of wind or tide may determine fortune. In the prairie, the direction of movement is more or less at the choice of the caravan; among mountains there will often be an alternative, a guess at the most likely pass. But the river with its strong, swift current is the dictator to the raft or to the steamboat. It is a treacherous and capricious dictator. At one season it may move sluggishly in a channel so narrow that, encountering it for the first time at that point, one can hardly believe that it has travelled already for hundreds of miles and has yet many hundreds of miles to go; at another season it may obliterate the low Illinois shore to a horizon of water, while in its bed it runs with a speed such that no man or beast can survive in it. At such times it carries down human bodies, cattle, and houses. At least twice, at St Louis, the western and the eastern shores have been separated by the fall of bridges, until the designer of the great Eads Bridge devised a structure which could resist the floods. In my own childhood, it was not unusual for the spring freshet to interrupt railway travel; and then the traveller to the east had to take steamboat from the levee up to Alton, at a higher level on the Illinois shore, before he could begin his rail journey. The river is never wholly chartable: it changes its pace, it shifts its channel, unaccountably; it may suddenly efface a sandbar and throw up another bar where before was navigable water.

It is the River that controls the voyage of Huck and Jim, that will not let them land at Cairo, where Jim could have reached freedom; it is the River that separates them and deposits Huck for a time in the Grangerford household; the River that reunites them and then compels upon them the unwelcome company of the King and the Duke. Recurrently we are reminded of its presence and its power.

When I woke up, I didn't know where I was for a minute. I set up and looked around, a little scared. Then I remembered. The river looked miles and miles across. The moon was so bright I could a counted the drift-logs that went a-slipping along, black and still, hundreds of yards out from shore. Everything was dead quiet, and it looked late, and smelt *late. You know what I mean—I don't know the words to put it in.*

. . . It was kind of solemn, drifting down the big still river, laying on our backs looking up at the stars, and we didn't ever feel like talking loud, and it warn't often that we laughed, only a little kind of a low chuckle. We had mighty good weather as a general thing, and nothing ever happened to us at all, that night, nor the next, nor the next.

Every night we passed towns, some of them away up on black hillsides, nothing but just a shiny bed of lights, not a house could you see. The fifth night we passed St Louis, and it was like the whole world lit up. In St Petersburg they used to say there was twenty or thirty thousand people in St Louis, but I never believed it till I see that wonderful spread of lights at two o'clock that still night. There warn't a sound there; everybody was asleep.

We come to understand the River by seeing it through the eyes of the Boy; but the Boy is also the spirit of the River. *Huckleberry Finn*, like other great works of imagination, can give to every reader whatever he is capable of taking from it. On the most superficial level of observation, Huck is convincing as a boy. On the same level, the picture of social life on the shores of the Mississippi a hundred years ago is, I feel sure, accurate. On any level, Mark Twain makes you see the River, as it is and was and always will be, more clearly than the author of any other description of a river known to me. But you do not merely see the River, you do not merely become acquainted with it through the senses: you experience the River. Mark Twain, in his later years of success and fame, referred to his early life as a steamboat pilot as the happiest he had known. With all allowance for the illusions of age, we can agree that those years were the years in which he was most fully alive. Certainly, but for his having practised that calling, earned his living by that profession, he would never have gained the understanding which his genius for expression communicates in this book. In the pilot's daily struggle with the River, in the satisfaction of activity, in the constant attention to the River's unpredictable vagaries, his consciousness was fully occupied, and he absorbed knowledge of which, as an artist, he later made use. There are perhaps only two ways in which a writer can acquire the understanding of environment which he can later turn to account: by having spent his childhood in that environment—that is, living in it at a period of life in which one experiences much more than one is aware of; and by having had to struggle for a livelihood in that environment—a livelihood bearing no direct relation to any intention of writing about it, of *using* it as literary material. Most of Joseph Conrad's understanding came to him in the latter way. Mark Twain knew the Mississippi in both ways: he had spent his childhood on its banks and he had earned his living matching his wits against its currents.

Thus the River makes the book a great book. As with Conrad, we are continually reminded of the power and terror of Nature, and the isolation and feebleness of Man. Conrad remains always the European observer of the tropics, the white man's eye contemplating the Congo and its black gods. But Mark Twain is a native, and the River God is his God. It is as a native that he accepts the River God, and it is the subjection of Man that gives to Man his dignity. For without some kind of God, Man is not even very interesting.

Readers sometimes deplore the fact that the story descends

to the level of *Tom Sawyer* from the moment that Tom himself reappears. Such readers protest that the escapades invented by Tom, in the attempted 'rescue' of Jim, are only a tedious development of themes with which we were already too familiar —even while admitting that the escapades themselves are very amusing and some of the incidental observations memorable.[1] But it is right that the mood of the end of the book should bring us back to that of the beginning. Or, if this was not the right ending for the book, what ending would have been right?

In *Huckleberry Finn* Mark Twain wrote a much greater book than he could have known he was writing. Perhaps all great works of art mean much more than the author could have been aware of meaning: Certainly *Huckleberry Finn* is the one book of Mark Twain's which, as a whole, has this unconsciousness. So what seems to be the rightness of reverting at the end of the book to the mood of *Tom Sawyer* was perhaps unconscious art. For Huckleberry Finn, neither a tragic nor a happy ending would be suitable. No wordly success or social satisfaction, no domestic consummation would be worthy of him; a tragic end also would reduce him to the level of those whom we pity. Huck Finn must come from nowhere and be bound for nowhere. His is not the independence of the typical or symbolic American Pioneer, but the independence of the vagabond. His existence questions the values of America as much as the values of Europe; he is as much an affront to the 'pioneer spirit' as he is to 'business enterprise'; he is in a state of nature as detached as the state of saint. In a busy world, he represents the loafer; in an acquisitive and competitive world, he insists on living from hand to mouth. He could not be exhibited in any amorous encounters or engagements, in any of the juvenile affections which are appropriate to Tom Sawyer. He belongs neither to the Sunday school nor to the reformatory. He has

---

[1] *e.g.* '*Jim* don't know anybody in China.'

no beginning and no end. Hence, he can only disappear; and his disappearance can only be accomplished by bringing forward another performer to obscure the disappearance in a cloud of whimsicalities.

Like Huckleberry Finn, the River itself has no beginning or end. In its beginning, it is not yet the River; in its end, it is no longer the River. What we call its headwaters is only a selection from among the innumerable sources which flow together to compose it. At what point in its course does the Mississippi become what the Mississippi *means*? It is both one and many; it is the Mississippi of this book only after its union with the Big Muddy—the Missouri; it derives some of its character from the Ohio, the Tennessee, and other confluents. And at the end it merely disappears among its deltas; it is no longer there, but it is still where it was, hundreds of miles to the North. The River cannot tolerate any design to a story, which is its story, that might interfere with its dominance. Things must merely happen, here and there, to the people who live along its shores or who commit themselves to its current. And it is as impossible for Huck as for the River to have a beginning or end—a *career*. So the book has the right, the only possible concluding sentence. I do not think that any book ever written ends more certainly with the right words:

But I reckon I got to light out for the Territory ahead of the rest, because Aunt Sally she's going to adopt me and sivilize me, and I can't stand it. I been there before.

[1950]

Arthur Ransome: charting the course

Today one author, who will be eighty years old next January, still stands head and shoulders above all living English authors of children's books. When diehards, believing that the only good children's books are the old books, join battle with moderns who maintain that today's child is not too badly served after all, the argument almost invariably begins or ends with the remark, 'But, of course, there is always Arthur Ransome.'

There is, of course, Arthur Ransome, and parents as well as children can be grateful for that fact. Dr Ransome is almost the only modern writer for children whose books grown-ups habitually read for their own pleasure. He has a small but enthusiastic following of adult admirers; like Miss Yonge, Miss Alcott, and, to a lesser extent, Mrs Molesworth, he is the object of a cult. This is the more strange in that Dr Ransome is essentially a writer *for*, and not about, children. He never gives a thought to the adult who may be reading the story aloud; his books are entirely free from those asides which grownups find so attractive and children so irritating because incomprehensible. Between childhood and the adult world there is a great gulf fixed—Dr Ransome has both his feet firmly planted on the children's side of that gulf.

What is his secret? First and foremost, he can always make us turn over to the next page. Will John succeed in reefing the mainsail in spite of the force of the North Sea gale? Can Dick and Dorothea, sailing a sledge over the frozen lake, ever reach the North Pole? Will Black Jake and the wicked crew of the Viper catch the Swallows and Amazons in Wildcat? Bedtime or not, even a grownup will agree to go on reading; none of us can wait to know the answer. Dr Ransome forces the reader to ask that basic and essential question, 'What happens next?' This is something which many of the real immortals too often fail to do; does anybody burn to know what actually *happens* to Richard Feverel, for instance, or to Lord Jim? A novel can be a great book, but if its pages are not turned over quickly it must in one vital respect be accounted a failure. Many authors possess the complex gift of character-drawing: few excel, as Dr Ransome excels, at the simple art of narration. Yet where children's books are concerned this is an essential gift, for the child does not ask 'Please talk to me about people', he simply says 'Tell me a story.'

Not, of course, that Dr Ransome's character-drawing is inadequate. His grown-up characters are one-dimensional, but that is the way grownups appear to the eyes of childhood. His children, however, we know as intimately as we know Miss Yonge's children or Miss Alcott's, far more intimately than we know those of E. Nesbit or Frances Hodgson Burnett. What is more—and this is surely an acid test—although no hint of the future is ever given, we know what is going to happen to them when they are grownup.

Some intellectuals stigmatize Dr Ransome's children as middle-class morons. Middle class they may be, but after all, like everyone else in life or literature they have to belong to some class or other, so why not the middle one? To clear Dr Ransome of the fashionable charge of snobbishness it is only necessary to point out that Joe, Bill, and Pete, of *Coot Club* and *The Big Six*, are all the children of working men, and that Pete at least is one of his author's favourite characters. And those critics who describe the Swallows and Amazons as morons can only be thinking of Nancy, who is indeed slightly moronic, like very many other girls of her age. They must have forgotten all about Titty and Dorothea. No two of Dr Ransome's children are alike, and it is worth noticing how well he has differentiated between the characters of these two clever little girls, dear Titty of the artistic, imaginative temperament, and Dorothea, the plodding intellectual.

Dorothea's brother Dick, bespectacled and scientific, would seem to be a character very much after Dr Ransome's own heart, for Dick thoroughly shares in his creator's passionate interest in technicalities, in the way in which things are made or done. When he invents a marvellous piece of mechanism by which an alarm is made to ring every time a carrier pigeon enters the loft, and the alarm actually goes off, it is difficult to tell which is the more elated, Dick or his creator. 'Dick, who had stopped short as the pigeon flew down, smiled a slow, happy smile. The thing had worked. Sophocles had rung the bell.' Perhaps Dr Ransome is also smiling a slow, happy smile. Yes, the thing has worked—and after all, it was he who actually thought up that clever contrivance.

So too when he describes exactly how John manages to raise the sunken Swallow or how Dick constructs a crucible in which to melt down ore, he is clearly enjoying every word he writes, just as Kipling is enjoying himself when he describes the workings of a railway engine or a steamship. And, again like Kipling, Dr Ransome manages to make these pages of technical description ring absolutely true. In all his stories there is only one passage at which the knowing grownup is tempted to cock an unbelieving eyebrow—the occasion in *Swallowdale* when John is given his very first lesson in the difficult art of fly-fishing. (How many *Swallows and Amazons* enthusiasts know or remember that Dr Ransome is the author of one of the best books on fishing ever written?) Immediately he rises a fish, and in another minute or two he catches one, whereupon the equally unskilled Susan has a try and gets a fish in her turn—and all this too in a Lake District tarn.

It may well be, however, that when Dr Ransome was John's age there were more fish in Lake District tarns than are to be found in them today, for as a rule he is not to be faulted on local detail. He is very sparing with descriptions of scenery, so sparing indeed that the imperceptive might begin to doubt whether he has in fact much feeling for places. But his strong sense of locality is proved by the fact that readers who know and love the Broads take a special pleasure in *Coot Club*, *The Big Six*, and *Secret Water*. Northerners, however, seldom appreciate these stories properly. They prefer to be at home with the Swallows and Amazons in that country where the good plain names, Beckfoot, Holly Howe, Crag Gill, even the sensible surname of Blackett, ring like bells to an exile from the north.

This power of setting stories fairly and squarely in a known countryside (and with maps to help too) certainly makes for reality, and reality is Dr Ransome's strength. His is not an impossible nor even a highly improbable world. Given a sensible parent like Mrs Walker, given above all a Mate Susan—'on questions of milk and drinking-water and getting able seamen to bed in proper time, Susan was the one the natives trusted'—it is not impossible that four children should go sailing and camping alone, it is not impossible that they should thwart a burglar or help to put out a forest fire, nor is it even entirely impossible that with a boy of John's calibre in charge—'You'll be a seaman yet, my son'— they should sail across the North Sea on a night of stormy weather and arrive safely in Holland. These are the things which most children want to do and imagine themselves as doing, the things too which many a grownup would choose, could they have their childhood over again.

But in another, more abstract sense, Dr Ransome's world is a world of reality. Above all things children hate a cheat. Nothing can be more disconcerting to a child-reader than to find that what appeared to be high drama is in fact a joke—the author is not serious, he does not believe in his own situations. Seen from this angle, *The Rose and the Ring*, for instance, is a book which should never be given to a child; it is impossible to forget the disillusioning shock of the discovery that Princess Angelica, Betsinda-Rosalba, Giglio, and poor Bulbo preparing to die with the rose between his teeth, are no more substantial than Alice's pack of cards, their thrilling adventures nothing but dreary farce. All the time that hearts have been beating faster and faster with excitement horrid Mr Thackeray has been sniggering up his sleeve.

For this reason, unless the author's touch is very sure, fantasy can be a dangerous element in a children's book. Fairy stories are, of course, excepted, because with a fairy story the child knows from the very beginning that he is in the world of make-believe. Trouble begins when the child, believing himself to be in one world, suddenly finds that he is in the other and that the grownups are smiling because he has mistaken fantasy for fact. Dr Ransome would never laugh at his readers in this manner, but nevertheless small children are often puzzled and a little disconcerted by his two fantasies, *Missee Lee* and *Peter Duck*. In the other stories the Swallows and Amazons are creatures of flesh and blood, yet here they are behaving almost in fairy-tale manner, enjoying adventures quite beyond the bounds of possibility. It is all very confusing, and a little destructive of belief. But for teenagers and grownups, who have learnt to recognize different levels of reality, these two stories are perhaps the most 'real' of all. If asked to name their favourite Ransome most grownups would vote for *Peter Duck*, with the wonderful last chapter singing its way up-Channel to the tune of 'Spanish Ladies'. The whole book is a masterly piece of writing, full of good straight excitement, but echoing too with overtones.

At the back of all Dr Ransome's stories there is always a hint of seriousness. They have their 'moments of truth' just as a good adult novel should, clearest of all perhaps in the two fantasy-tales, but to be recognized also in the more prosaic books, in *Pigeon Post*, for instance, when the scared child Titty throws

confessional; he is professional. He writes and draws his books, not as envelopes of covert or unconscious self-revelation, but to please and entertain himself and his young readers.

I believe that into one of these two classes—the confessional or the professional—any notable children's classic is apt to fall.

Kenneth Grahame, born a Scot in 1859 lived most of his life in England, dying in 1932. He was reared by his maternal grandmother. The older Grahame (the mother had died) coolly abandoned the four little Grahames, an action which was forever after to influence Kenneth's views on the character of grownups. The young Grahame, had he been properly educated, would have made an excellent backwater don, and we should probably be minus *The Wind in the Willows*. But his heavy-Victorian uncle would not pay the fees for Oxford and instead arranged for Kenneth to take a post in the Bank of England. His charm, natural intelligence, and physical attractiveness helped the dreamy young man to rise in the bank until in 1898 he became its secretary, and his financial future was assured.

Like many men he possessed no talent for that most exacting of professions, marriage; and like most men he married. (Someday, ten thousand years from now, the race will have advanced to the point where it will perhaps be one-tenth as exigent before granting a marriage licence as it is today before granting a plumber's licence.) Mrs Grahame was an impossible creature, affected, demanding, at bottom a fool. They had one child, Alastair, an unhappy, physically handicapped boy who, the evidence is now virtually all in, committed suicide at twenty by arranging to have a train run over him. There is no reason to suppose that the Grahames had any more ability at child-rearing than at making a harmonious marriage.

As was the case with so many eminent Victorians and Edwardians, Grahame led two lives. The first was imposed on him by his class: the Bank of England job, marriage, money-getting, paternity, respectability. The second was his dream life, the long, sad, halfhearted flight from what is called responsibility.

This dream life was his redress for many things: his father's cruelty; his dissatisfaction not so much with the Bank of England as with the England the bank stood for; his unhealthy relationship with his wife; his bohemian detestation of 'progress', industry, and trade; his aversion from the whole adult world, finding expression in a courteous misanthropy, an excessive love of nature, and an excessive idealization of animals.

Out of the conflict between the imposed life and the buried life came four slim books. One, *Pagan Papers,* is Stevenson-and-water: arty, wistful essays, perfectly in the *fin de siècle* mood of the nineties. *The Golden Age* and *Dream Days* are re-creations of the life of childhood, oddly mingling an affectionate sympathy for the young and a restrained bitterness toward grownups—the 'Olympians', as he ironically termed them.

The only one of Grahame's books that will last is *The Wind in the Willows.* This story of the riverside adventures of the Mole, the Water Rat, the Badger, and the Toad is generally received as a delightful animal fantasy. Indeed it can be so read, particularly by children. But many readers have often vaguely felt it to be more than that, just as they know *Gulliver* to be more than a story about little people and big people. Some of us perhaps find ourselves wondering about the conceited Mr Toad, in many ways an odd character for a child's book. By making Mr Toad a rich man was not Grahame quietly expressing his opinion of his money-making era, as Dickens did more explicitly? By making Mr Toad motor-mad was he not suggesting that the nineteenth century was to its own cost abandoning a life lived simply and naturally?

And then the book is not of one piece. Part of it seems simple and pleasant enough: the conversion of Mole to the delights of river life; the dangers Mole and Rat run in the Wild Wood and their rescue by Badger; Toad's transgressions and his final rehabilitation by the sorely tried but loyal friends. But other parts of the book are allegorical, even philosophical, and young readers will almost surely pass over them lightly. With the chapter called

'The Piper at the Gates of Dawn' and at several other points the tone alters. What was a humorous fancy about talking animals turns into a pagan hymn or a sly but not trivial commentary on the inferiority of humans to beasts.

All these matters are at last fully illuminated in the pages of Mr Green's biography. I found it admirable, if a mite solemn—for occasionally the author loses sight of the fact that after all Grahame is a one-book author, and a minor one at that. He is almost over-perceptive. Poring over Grahame with a magnifying lens he discovers more than a few things not open to the natural vision. What remains once these qualifications are registered is a fascinating exploration of a life that was a fiasco, in which all the major problems were side-stepped, the life of a charming, talented but essentially weak man. Yet out of his very failure, his hidden resentments, his reluctance to face up to the demands of his hard century, Grahame drew *The Wind in the Willows.* The sources of the little masterpiece are traced by Mr Green in his subject's conscious and unconscious life, much as John Livingston Lowes, that supreme literary sleuth, tracked down in *The Road to Xanadu* the operations of the mind that produced *The Ancient Mariner.*

Mr Green's conclusions are subtle and various, but one can sum them up by saying that in all his work, and particularly in *The Wind in the Willows,* Kenneth Grahame was revenging himself on the adult world which he had been forced to join and on the century whose materialism his sensibility could not accept. He said once that he was 'not a professional writer'. It is true; he was a confessional one. The book that he stoutly protested he wrote for children was a letter written in invisible ink to himself.

On the other hand there is Dr Seuss. I have known Ted Geisel for many years. (The 'Seuss' is his mother's maiden name, the 'Dr' represents the PH.D. he never quite managed to collect.) I do not care to infuriate him by suggesting that he has no unconscious and that those extraordinary animals he draws are not symbolic but merely the consequence of his liking to draw extraordinary animals. He may have a complete set of private despairs that he fondles lovingly in the dark—I would be the last man to deprive him of them. He may have a dandy buried life. I wish to state, however, that if he has one it is not reflected in any of the delightful children's books he has written and drawn during the last twenty-five years. While it may not be quite the decent thing these days to say of a friend, I believe Dr Seuss has not only added to the general store of happiness but that he is himself a happy man.

He is also—which such greater artists as Kenneth Grahame were not—a professional writer of juveniles. I do not mean that he writes with cold calculation for a shrewdly gauged market. On the contrary, he writes and draws as he does because he feels that way. But he knows exactly what he is doing. He aims to create nothing more than what meets the eye or ear. He is not *using* his books for any purpose beyond entertaining himself and his readers. *The Wind in the Willows* is a dream. But *On Beyond Zebra* (which deals with the letters of the alphabet after z, such as YUZZ, UM, and HUMPF) and *Horton Hears a Who!*, though far more extravagant, are not dreams. They are ingenious solutions, exploited with unique humour and slyness and absurdity, of the standing problem of the juvenile-fantasy writer: how to find, not another Alice, but another rabbit hole.

The Geisels have no children ('You make 'em—I amuse 'em,' says Dr Seuss), and while he likes youngsters well enough, he does not claim any transcendental understanding of the juvenile mind. (Grahame, it might be noted, did not particularly care for *real* children, only for his dream children, just as Lewis Carroll detested boys and didn't care much for girls once they got beyond Lolita's age.) The sordid fact is that to be a good writer of juveniles you don't have to love children, any more than you have to love criminals to write *Crime and Punishment*.

Ted Geisel turned into Dr Seuss more or less accidentally. Early in his career his absurd animals began to brighten the pages of the old *Judge*. But they did not pay dividends until they were transferred to the world of the Flit advertisements. He might have pursued his career of extermination indefinitely had it not been for his wife, who has all the qualities Elspeth Grahame lacked. Once, returning from Europe on the *Kungsholm*, Mr Geisel, like the man in Mark Twain's story (Punch in the presence of the passenjare!), found himself mumbling over and over to the beat of the ship's engines:

> *And that is a story that no one can beat,*
> *And to think that I saw it on Mulberry Street.*

In order to prevent their lives from being darkened by the continued repetition of this couplet, Mrs Geisel persuaded him to invent a story in which it might reasonably appear. The result was his first book, *And To Think That I Saw It on Mulberry Street*. It was rejected by twenty-seven publishers, on four grounds:

1. Fantasy doesn't sell.
2. Verse doesn't sell.
3. It had no 'pattern', whatever that meant.
4. It wasn't 'practical'—that is, it didn't teach the child how to become a better child, or grownup, or mortician.

The twenty-eighth publisher was densely ignorant of the juvenile market. He published the book for a fantastic reason—he liked it. Since then Dr Seuss's books (according to my calculations there are twenty of them) have sold something in the neighbourhood of four million copies. His *The Cat in the Hat* should be within sight of the million mark. It is probably the most influential first-grade reader since McGuffey. Using only 223 different words, it manages to tell a story that for the first time in the history of beginners'-grade education actually amuses the tot, and so persuades him that reading is a worthwhile experience.

Dr Seuss is a craftsman, not an allegorist, or a satirist in disguise. He modestly ascribes much of his success to the fact that he is his own illustrator, permitting him to make every page pull double weight. In his own way he is as mad about language as Flaubert was. Once he spent five hours in his publisher's office working over a single line of verse until he had removed an extra beat that bothered his ear. In the next room he overheard the editor trying to persuade a lady novelist, whose talents tend to the copious, to remove 75,000 words from her new book. (The editor lost.)

Dr Seuss also believes that children (and grownups too—there's quite a serious Seuss cult) like him because he *bucks* the trend in children's books, supplying oddity instead of wholesome instruction, wild humour instead of mere pleasantness, and the unbelievable instead of a duplication of the child's familiar environment. Whatever may be the good Doctor's secret, there is no doubt that he is the most successful writer in his field today, and a true professional. Whether his work will last, as *The Wind in the Willows* has lasted, is another matter. Possibly the absence of that very ambiguous element you find in Kenneth Grahame, that teasing sense of other meanings and under-meanings, destine it to a shorter life than children's classics saturated with the confessional element. At the moment Dr Seuss is single-handedly changing the reading habits of hundreds of thousands of American children. That's enough for any one man. Somebody ought to give him that PH.D. he's always hankered after.

[1962]

Among the wild things

NAT HENTOFF

My son Nicholas, three and a half, was jumping up and down on his bed.

'I want to wash your hands,' my wife said.

'I don't care,' Nicholas replied.

'Lunch is ready.'

'I don't care.'

'It will get cold.'

'I don't care.'

The leaping continued. Then my wife asked, 'Who *are* you?'

'Pierre!' Nicholas announced.

The next jump was the most ambitious yet, and Nicholas fell off the bed. As he rubbed his knee, my wife asked, 'Are you hurt?'

In a much softer voice, he replied, 'Yes, Mother Bear.'

Mother Bear is a large, comfortable source of reassurance in *Little Bear,* a series of four books written by Else Holmelund Minarik and illustrated by Maurice Sendak. The Pierre whom Nicholas had been emulating is the hero of a book called *Pierre,* which is part of the four-volume *Nutshell Library* written and illustrated by Maurice Sendak. Pierre, even after he is swallowed by a famished lion, will say only 'I don't care.' On top of a chest of drawers next to Nicholas's bed is a large picture of a dancing creature with horns, sharp teeth, yellow eyes, and a scaly body. He is a wild thing—an inhabitant of *Where the Wild Things Are,*

FROM MAURICE SENDAK'S *Higglety Pigglety Pop!*

a book written and illustrated by Maurice Sendak. Some reviewers of children's books have asserted that the wild things are frightening but Nicholas finds them quite funny.

My son's familiarity with Maurice Sendak's creations is shared by a sizable and constantly growing number of American children under eight. As a writer, as an illustrator, and as both, Sendak has been associated with a number of successful children's books of the past decade. In addition to the *Little Bear* series, the *Nutshell Library,* and *Where the Wild Things Are,* there have been *A Hole Is to Dig,* written by Ruth Krauss, *The Bat-Poet* and *The Animal Family,* both written by the late Randall Jarrell, *Lullabies and Night Songs,* with music by Alec Wilder, and *Hector Protector.* More than fifty other children's books contain illustrations by Sendak, and more than half a dozen have texts by him; many of them sell well enough to keep Sendak surprised by his affluence.

Sendak has trouble believing in his commercial success largely because his creations are so much at variance with the sort of thing that usually sells well in his field. Far too many contemporary picture books for the young are still populated by children who eat everything on their plates, go dutifully to bed at the proper hour, and learn all sorts of useful facts or moral lessons by the time the book comes to an end. The illustrations are usually decorative rather than imaginative, and any fantasy that may be encountered either corresponds to the fulfilment of adult wishes or is carefully curbed lest it frighten the child. Many of these books, homogenized and characterless, look and read as if they had been put together by a computer. Sendak's work, on the other hand, is unmistakably identifiable as his. He will not illustrate to order, increasingly depending on himself as the writer and, when he illustrates the texts of others, choosing only those that seem real to him. 'Maurice is not an artist who just does an occasional book for children because there's money in it or because he thinks it will give him an easy change of pace,' Sendak's editor, Ursula Nordstrom, who is director of the children's book department of Harper & Row, has said. 'Children's books are *all* he does and all he wants to do. His books are full of emotion, of vitality. When one of his lines for a drawing is blown up, you find that it's not a precise straight line. It's rough with ridges, because so much emotion has gone into it. Too many of us—and I mean editors along with illustrators and writers of children's books—are afraid of emotion. We keep forgetting that children are new and we are not. But somehow Maurice has retained a direct line to his own childhood.' Sendak, moreover, does not subscribe to the credo that childhood is a time of innocence—a point of view that, as it is usually interpreted, results in tales and pictures soothing to parents but unreal to the children. The young in Sendak's books—particularly the books he writes himself—are sometimes troubled and lonely, they slip easily into and out of fantasies, and occasionally they are unruly and stubborn. Nor are they the bright, handsome boys and softly pretty little girls who are so numerous in so many picture books for children. The Sendak boys and girls tend to appear truncated, having oversized heads, short arms, and quite short legs.

In the past few years, I have become increasingly interested in Sendak's work, reading his books for my own pleasure as well as for the amusement of my children. His drawings, I have found, are oddly compelling. Intensely, almost palpably alive, they seem to move on the page and, later, in memory. This quality is pervasive in *Where the Wild Things Are*, the story of a boy named Max who assumes a demonic face and puts on a wolf suit one night and makes mischief. His mother calls him a 'WILD THING!' and Max answers, 'I'LL EAT YOU UP!' He is sent to bed without his supper. Standing in his room, Max watches a forest grow until it becomes the world. An ocean tumbles by with a boat in it for Max, and he sails to where the wild things are. The wild things—a colony of monsters—try to frighten Max, but frowning fiercely, he commands them to be still. Cowed, they make Max King of the Wild Things. Then, at Max's order, a rumpus begins— six wordless pages of howling, dancing, tree-climbing, and parading by Max and the wild things. Max presently stops the revels, though, and sends the wild things to bed without *their* supper, and then, feeling lonely, gives up his crown. The wild things so hate to see Max leave that they try to scare him into staying, but he is not intimidated, and he sails back to his room, where he finds his supper waiting for him.

As I studied the pictures of Max and his companions, it seemed to me that I had never seen fantasy depicted in American children's books in illustrations that were so powerfully in motion. Brian O'Doherty, the former art critic of the *New York Times*, has written that Sendak is 'a fantasist in the great tradition of Sir John Tenniel and Edward Lear', and I agree. O'Doherty has also described Sendak as 'one of the most powerful men in the United States', in that he 'has given shape to the fantasies of millions of children—an awful responsibility.' I had known a few men who possessed power, but never this kind of power, so I made arrangements to meet the creator of the wild things.

Sendak, a bachelor, lives in a duplex on Ninth Street between Fifth and Sixth Avenues. On the street level he has a bedroom and a large living-room with a piano and a profusion of bookcases, one of them reserved for first editions (he has close to two hundred) of works by Henry James. On the floor below are a spacious kitchen, a dining-room with a brick fireplace, and a small studio, lit only by the lamp over Sendak's drawing-board, which is to the left of the room's entrance. On the walls of the studio are paintings, photographs, and posters advertising art exhibits. A bookcase near the studio door contains an extensive collection of children's books, formed largely around Sendak's favourite illustrators: Randolph Caldecott and George Cruikshank of nineteenth-century England; Ludwig Richter and Wilhelm Busch of the same period in Germany; A. B. Frost and Edward Windsor Kemble, Americans who between them spanned the last half of the nineteenth century and the first three decades of this one; Ernst Kreidolf, a Swiss artist of those years; and, among contemporaries, the late Hans Fischer of Switzerland and André François of France. To the right of Sendak's drawing-board is a worktable, and above this is a peg-board supporting a swarm of objects. Among them are talismans—a brontosaurus constructed for him by a nephew, for instance—and postcard reproductions of paintings by Watteau, Goya, William Blake, and Winslow Homer; there are also a number of toys that Sendak has brought back from Europe, where he goes about every other year. Across the room from the worktable an imposing high-fidelity unit stands on top of another bookcase, this one containing a large record collection in which works by Mahler, Mozart, Beethoven, Wolf, Wagner, and Verdi are heavily represented. What dominates the room, however, is a huge photograph. Taken at an orphanage in Sicily, it shows a ten-year-old girl standing sidewise in front of a whitewashed wall. She is wearing a ragged white dress, a fly has alighted on her back, and she looks out into the room with enormous black eyes. Her hand is on her hip—a pose that is frequently assumed by the children in Sendak's books.

The first day I visited his studio, Sendak, a short, shy man with dark-brown hair and green eyes, smiled after he saw me staring intently at the picture. 'It's hard to get away from her, isn't it?' he said. 'If you stay here long enough, you'll find that her eyes follow you around the room.' He moved in front of the photograph. 'Her face is unfinished—a round, beautiful child's face—but her eyes tell you she could be forty-five years old. Such knowledge and pain are already there. I couldn't do without her.'

A Sealyham terrier came in. This, I was told, was Jennie, who was twelve years old and had a tendency to brood. Jennie has appeared in most of Sendak's books, often looking more cheerful than she does in real life. Having sniffed at me briefly, Jennie left. Sendak lit a cigarette. As I looked at him, I found that he reminded me of the children in his books, and I told him so. 'Yes, they're all a kind of caricature of me,' he said. 'They look as if they'd been hit on the head, and hit so hard they weren't going to grow any more. When I first started showing my work to children's-book editors about seventeen years ago, they didn't encourage me, and a major reason was the kind of children I drew. One editor, I remember, told me they were too European. What she meant was that they seemed ugly to her. And even now I'll get a letter at least twice a year from a librarian who wants to know why my children are so drab. Well, they're not drab, but they're not innocent of experience either. Too many parents and too many writers of children's books don't respect the fact that kids know a great deal and suffer a great deal. My children also show a great deal of pleasure, but often they look defenceless too. Being defenceless is a primary element of childhood. It's not that I don't see the naturalistic beauty of a child. I'm very aware of that beauty, and I could draw it. I know the proportions of a child's body. But I am trying to draw the way children *feel*—or rather, the way I imagine they feel. It's the way *I know* I felt as a child.' Sendak leaned forward and continued, 'It may be that in projecting how I felt as a child onto the children I draw I'm being terribly biased and inaccurate. But all I have to go on is what I know—not only about my childhood then but about the child I was as he exists now.'

I looked puzzled, and Sendak smiled. 'You see, I don't believe, in a way, that the kid I was grew up into me,' he said. 'He still exists somewhere, in the most graphic, plastic, physical way. It's as if he had moved somewhere. I have a tremendous concern for him and interest in him. I communicate with him—or try to—all the time. One of my worst fears is losing contact with him.' Sendak frowned. 'I don't want this to sound coy or schizophrenic, but at least once a day I feel I have to make contact,' he went on. 'The pleasures I get as an adult are heightened by the fact that I experience them as a child at the same time. Like, when autumn comes, as an adult I welcome the departure of the heat, and simultaneously, as a child would, I start anticipating the snow and the first day it will be possible to use a sled. This dual apperception does break down occasionally. That usually happens when my work is going badly. I get a sour feeling about books in general and my own in particular. The next stage is annoyance at my dependence on this dual apperception, and I reject it. Then I become depressed. When excitement about what I'm working on returns, so does the child. We're on happy terms again. Being in that kind of contact with my childhood is vital to me, but it doesn't make me perfectly certain I know what I'm doing in my work. Especially in books for children under six. I don't think anyone really knows what kids that young like and what they don't like. They're formless, fluid creatures—like moving water. You can't stop one of them at any one point and know exactly what's going on. A child may react strongly to a book because it reaches him emotionally in some way the author intended. Then again, it may be that he once saw a duck from a train window and never saw one again until he looked at the book, and though the book is rotten, he loves it because there's a duck in it. Once in a while I encounter reactions to one of my books that make me think I may be getting some idea of what happened. From letters and from talking to parents and librarians I've found out that, of the four books in the *Nutshell Library*, *Pierre* is invariably the favourite with children. But here too, I don't know what level the child is reacting on. On one level *Pierre* is slapstick. Then, the text has a rhythmic quality—the repetition that kids like—and some children may be drawn mainly by that. On another level, Pierre is defiant—irrationally so when it comes to the lion that finally eats him—and the child may enjoy a surface identification with the fun of rebellion. And, on a deeper level, Pierre is saying 'I'm *me*. I'll be what I am and I'll do what I want to do.' The book that children have reacted to most strongly, though, is *Where the Wild Things Are*. They wear out copies at libraries and keep rereading it at home. Some have sent me drawings of their own wild things, and they make mine look like cuddly fuzzballs. My wild things have big teeth. Some of *their* wild things not only have big teeth but are chewing on children. I have yet to hear of a child who was frightened by the book. Adults who are troubled by it forget that Max is having a fine time. He's in control. And by getting his anger at his mother discharged against the wild things he's able to come back to the real world at peace with himself. I think Max is my truest creation. Like all kids, he believes in a world where a child can skip from fantasy to reality in the conviction that both exist. One seven-year-old boy wrote me a letter.' Sendak rose, rummaged through a file folder in the bookcase, found the letter, and handed it to me. The boy had written, 'How much does it cost to get to where the wild things are? If it is not too expensive my sister and I want to spend the summer there. Please answer soon.'

Fantasy, I learned in subsequent visits to the studio, has been familiar terrain to Sendak from his earliest years. He was born in Brooklyn on 10 June 1928, the youngest of three children of Philip and Sarah Sendak. (His sister, Natalie, was eight when he was born, and his brother, Jack, was five.) Both parents had come to America before the First World War from Jewish *shtetls*, or small towns, outside Warsaw. The father, who worked in the garment district, told his children long stories, based on tales he remembered from his childhood and alive with myth and fantasy. 'He was a marvellous improviser, and he'd often extend a story for many nights,' Sendak recalls. 'One short one I've always wanted to make into a book was about a child taking a walk with his father and mother. He becomes separated from them. Snow begins to fall, and the child shivers in the cold. He huddles under a tree, sobbing in terror. An enormous figure hovers over him and says, as he draws the boy up, "I'm Abraham, your father." His fear gone, the child looks up and also sees Sarah. He is no longer lost. When his parents find him, the child is dead. Those stories had something of the character of William Blake's poems. The myths in them didn't seem at all factitious. And they fused Jewish lore with my father's particular way of shaping memory and desire. That one, for instance, was based on the power of Abraham in Jewish tradition as the father who was always there —a reassuring father even when he was Death. But the story was also about how tremendously my father missed his parents. Not all his tales were sombre though. My father could be very witty, even if the humour was always on the darker side of irony.'

In addition to the tales his father told and occasional stories told by his mother, books, to which Sendak early formed a passionate attachment, also stimulated his imagination. His sister gave him his first books—*The Prince and the Pauper* and *The Three Musketeers*. Besides being fascinated by the contents of the books, he was drawn to them as physical entities. 'I can still remember the smell and feel of the bindings, of those first two books,' he says. 'I didn't read them for a long time. It felt so good just having them. They seemed alive to me, and so did many other inanimate objects I was fond of. All children have these intense feelings about certain dolls or other toys. In my case, this kind of relationship, if you can call it that, was heightened because up to the age of six I spent a lot of time in bed with a series of illnesses. Being alone much of the time, I developed friendships with objects. To this day, in my parents' home there are certain toys that I played with as a child, and when I visit my parents I'm also visiting those toys.'

In *Kenny's Window*, which was published in 1956 and was the first book that Sendak wrote as well as illustrated, he distilled much of his own childhood—the attachment to particular objects, the fantasy, the loneliness. Kenny wakes from a dream and remembers meeting in a garden a rooster who gave him seven questions to answer. In the course of searching for the answers, he has serious conversations with several of his toys. Kenny is angered by a favourite Teddy bear, who reproaches him for having been left under the bed all night, but soon Kenny writes the bear a poem assuring him of his love and that conflict is resolved. In fantasy, Kenny journeys to Switzerland and talks with a goat in order to find the answer to one of the rooster's questions: 'What is an only goat?' An only goat, Kenny finally learns, is a lonely goat who is not allowed by an overprotective master to do what he most enjoys doing. There is also a meeting, on the roof of Kenny's house, with a talking, flying horse. Kenny resolves not to tell his parents about the horse and its ability to talk and to fly. ('They'd say it was a dream. They don't know how to listen in the night.') Another crisis occurs when one of Kenny's two favourite lead soldiers reminds the other of a promise Kenny has broken—to take care of them always. The first soldier is chipped in four different places. He complains to Kenny. Enraged at being made to feel guilty, Kenny exiles the chipped soldier to the outside ledge of his window in the cold, but then he brings the soldier in again and tells him he has not broken his promise. When the rooster later asks Kenny one of the seven questions again—'Can you fix a broken promise?'—Kenny answers, 'Yes, if it only looks broken, but really isn't.'

In his adult life, Sendak's rapport with particular inanimate objects has not been limited to the toys in Brooklyn. One afternoon in his studio, he pointed out to me several pens on his drawing-board and said, 'Some of these pens are with me and some are against me. In a store, some look as if they want to be sold to me. Others will fight me to the end. I may antagonize some and not be able to win back their friendship, but others are less stubborn.' He picked up a small, smooth rock. 'This is a friend,' he said. 'I found him on a beach in Italy in 1953. He goes with me on all my trips.' Sendak looked at me somewhat warily, and added, 'I suppose that sounds strange.' Since I have similar feelings about an old lighter and three pipes, I was able to tell him it didn't.

Sendak did have other friends besides objects as he grew up. He had a close relationship with his brother Jack. Both boys enjoyed drawing, and one of their amusements was making books. These combined cut-out newspaper photographs and comic strips with sketches of the Sendak family. The books were bound with tape, had elaborately illustrated covers, and contained a good deal of painstaking hand lettering.

'I was always conscious of usable material for books,' Sendak recalls. 'I remember examining my grandmother all the time and placing her in various fantasies. And I was so conscious of the streets on which I lived that I can remember now in complete detail—how many houses there were, who lived in which house, what the people looked like. During my early teens, I spent a lot of time at the window sketching the kids at play, and those sketchbooks are, in a sense, the foundation of much of my later work. Maybe that's another reason the children in my books are called European-looking. Many of them resemble the kids I knew growing up in Brooklyn. They were Jewish kids, and they may well look like little greenhorns just off the boat. They had—some of them, anyway—a kind of bowed look, as if the burdens of the world were on their shoulders.'

The Sign on Rosie's Door, a Sendak book published in 1960, begins with the dedication:

Remembering *Pearl Karchawer*
all the Rosies
and Brooklyn.

Rosie is a girl with an unusually lively imagination, and she gets her friends—who do indeed look like Jewish children on the streets of Brooklyn—to take part in her fantasies. At one point Rosie, sitting on a cellar door and covered from head to foot in a red blanket, identifies herself as 'Alinda the lost girl'. 'Who lost you?' asks a neighbourhood literalist. 'I lost myself,' Rosie answers. Like the fantasies in *Kenny's Window* and a number of Sendak's other stories, Rosie's often involve highly active play. She announces that her 'Magic Man' is coming, and all the children close their eyes because he will not appear otherwise. They hear her speak to him, and when they are allowed to open their eyes again Rosie tells them that the Magic Man has informed her that they can all be firecrackers. Rosie and her friends proceed to leap and dance through several pages.

When the teenage Sendak wasn't making books, he was reading other people's. Though some were stories for children, his reading was indiscriminate. His sister subscribed to the Book-of-the-Month Club, and he read many of the volumes she received. 'Now I can't remember any children's books or artists that profoundly influenced me in those years except Walt Disney,' he says. 'I now say it to my shame, yet he did something tremendous for me. His pictures did move, and they often embodied lots of fantasy. With whatever money I had, I'd buy his colouring and cut-out books, and I made animated sequences of my own based on his characters. And when I saw Disney's *Snow White and the Seven Dwarfs* at the Radio City Music Hall, I had an inkling of what it was I especially wanted to do. It was only later that I could see how Disney had despoiled beautiful stories and had abused the idea of animation. Kids don't always know about the vulgar and tasteless, and to me Disney was a god. I remember a Mickey Mouse mask that came on a big box of cornflakes. What a fantastic mask! Such a big, bright, vivid, gorgeous hunk of face! My ambition was to work for Disney.'

Sendak graduated from Lafayette High School, in Brooklyn, in 1946. 'I was an art major in high school, but we had no real instruction—I just sat and did what I wanted to,' he says. After school and weekends he had worked for All American Comics, his job being to adapt 'Mutt and Jeff' strips for comic books, fitting them into the page, filling in backgrounds, and extending the story line when necessary. He enjoyed this work, but school, by contrast, was a place of acute discomfort. 'Nearly every morning, in order to get there, I had to talk myself out of a state of panic,' he says. 'I couldn't stand being cloistered with other children, and I was usually so embarrassed that I stammered.'

After graduation he went to work full time at Timely Service, a window-display house in lower Manhattan, beginning in a warehouse, where he helped construct store-window models of such figures as Snow White and the Seven Dwarfs out of chicken wire, papiermâché, spun glass, plaster, and paint. 'It was one of the best times of my life,' Sendak says. 'I was in Manhattan and, for the first time, I knew people who were artists, who considered their work for Timely Service just a job to enable them to do real painting at night in their cold-water flats. There were all kinds of people I'd never met in Brooklyn.' When he had been at Timely Service for nearly two years, he was promoted to the department that conceived the window-display designs to be built in the warehouse. There he was unhappy. 'The department consisted of another kind of artist—people in their fifties who had never got anywhere,' he recalls. Sendak left the display house in the summer of 1948, and during the next two months, at home in Brooklyn, he and his brother constructed six intricate animated wooden toys, performing scenes from *Little Red Riding Hood, Little Miss Muffet, Hansel and Gretel, Aladdin's Lamp, Old Mother Hubbard,* and *Pinocchio.* The pieces, five of which Sendak now has in his studio, are in the tradition of eighteenth-century German lever-operated toys. When a lever on Little Red Riding Hood's basket is pulled, for instance, a ferocious wolf leaps out of bed and Little Red Riding Hood collapses. The Sendak brothers took their toys to F. A. O. Schwarz. Their work was received with respect, but an official at the store pointed out that it would be too costly to reproduce the toys in large quantities. 'Nor were we ready to compromise, if a compromise had been suggested,' Sendak says. 'We wanted a workshop of the little old men creating the little wooden parts, and we would not have permitted any kind of plastic substitute.' Ultimately, though, Richard Nell, Schwarz's window-display director, was sufficiently impressed by the way in which Maurice Sendak had painted the toys to hire him as an assistant in the construction of window displays. (His brother, meanwhile, although he went on to work in the electronics field, has also written several children's books, two of which Maurice has illustrated.)

Sendak worked at the toy store for three years, and attended evening classes at the Art Students League during most of that time. 'It was the only kind of school I could endure, because it was freewheeling,' he says. 'What you learned depended on what you wanted to learn.' Sendak took classes in life drawing, oil painting, and composition, and feels that he benefited particularly from the instruction in composition he was given by the illustrator John Groth. 'He was important for me because he gave me a sense of the enormous potential for motion, for aliveness, in illustrations,' Sendak recalls. 'And he himself was so deeply committed to the field that he showed how much fun creating in it could be.'

At F. A. O. Schwarz, Frances Chrystie, the store's book buyer, who was a friend of Sendak's, knew that he was eager to try illustrating children's books, but when she suggested introducing him to Miss Nordstrom—partly because Harper's was the publisher whose children's books he most admired—he demurred, out of shyness. Miss Chrystie thereupon arranged for Miss Nordstrom to 'happen by' one day, in the spring of 1950, when Sendak had tacked up a broad variety of his pictures on the walls of the store's studio. The next day Miss Nordstrom called Sendak and offered him the opportunity to illustrate Marcel Aymé's *The Wonderful Farm.* He accepted, and the book was published in 1951. This was not the first time Sendak's work had been published; in 1947 he had done diagrams and spot drawings for *Atomics for the Millions,* written by Hyman Ruchlis, one of his high-school teachers, and three years later he had illustrated a book about the Sabbath, *Good Shabos, Everybody,* for the United Synagogue Commission on Jewish Education, but *The Wonderful Farm* was the first real children's book he had worked on. 'It made me an official person,' Sendak now says.

In 1952 Sendak became widely known in the children's-book field as the illustrator of Ruth Krauss's *A Hole Is to Dig.* The book was quite unconventional for its time. It had no story. Instead, Miss Krauss, by talking with and listening to children, had assembled a series of children's definitions, among them 'A face is so you can make faces', 'Buttons are to keep people warm', 'A whistle is to make people jump', and—a particular favourite with the book's readers—'A tablespoon is to eat a table with.' The general idea of *A Hole Is to Dig* has since been repeated many times, often coyly. But Sendak's small people, seen at play among themselves, sticking out their tongues, closing their eyes in anticipation of being kissed by their dogs' tongues, wiggling their toes, and sliding delightedly in the mud, never seem saccharine.

An established illustrator had originally been considered for the assignment, but when he was shown simply a collection of definitions, he felt that there was no book in them at all. From the start, however, Sendak was enthusiastic about the book's possibilities. 'It was like being part of a revolution,' he says. 'This was the first time in modern children's-book history that a book had come directly from kids. The notion was so startling to some academics, in fact, that the book was included in a course at Columbia on the uses of language. And, you know, some of those definitions *have* become part of the language. Working on that book, I learned something else too. When it seemed to me to be all done, Ruth Krauss pointed out that I was giving the kids who would read the book middle-class attitudes toward their roles. I had the boys doing what boys were expected to do and girls doing what *they* were expected to do. God forbid a boy should be jumping rope! Of course, that isn't the way it is, and at the last minute I made some quick changes.'

A Hole Is to Dig prepared the way for such later works by others as *A Friend Is Someone Who Likes You, Love Is a Special Way of Feeling,* and *Happiness Is a Warm Puppy,* and it was influential in other ways too. Its format was small, and its success brought back what Sendak identifies as 'the little book', adding 'and, God help us, it hasn't stopped.' The book was printed on brown-tinted paper, and for the illustrations Sendak had deliberately used his most 'oldfashioned' style, his pen-and-ink drawings including a considerable amount of cross-hatching, in the tradition of nineteenth-century German and British illustrators.

The success of *A Hole Is to Dig* was such that Sendak was able to leave F. A. O. Schwarz, move to Manhattan, and become a free-lance illustrator. Assignments poured in, from Miss Nordstrom and from editors at other publishing houses, and in the years that followed Sendak illustrated the work of various writers. There have been seven more books by Ruth Krauss, and seven books for older children by the Dutch-born writer Meindert DeJong; and Sendak has also had the privilege of collaborating posthumously with Tolstoy *(Nikolenka's Child-*

hood), the German Clemens Brentano *(The Tale of Gockel, Hinkel & Gackeliah* and *Schoolmaster Whackwell's Wonderful Sons)*, the German Wilhelm Hauff *(Dwarf Long-Nose)*, and the American Frank Stockton *(The Bee-Man of Orn* and *The Griffin and the Minor Canon)*. In a preface to *The Griffin and the Minor Canon*, Sendak describes his basic aim as an illustrator: 'I wanted at all costs to avoid the serious pitfall of illustrating with pictures what the author had already . . . illustrated with words. I hoped, rather, to let the story speak for itself, with my pictures as a kind of background music—music in the right style and always in tune with the words.'

Sendak elaborated on the degree to which he conceives his work musically in an article called 'The Shape of Music', which appeared in the Sunday *Herald Tribune* late in 1964. 'The spontaneous breaking into song and dance seems so natural and instinctive a part of childhood,' he wrote. 'It is perhaps the medium through which children best express the inexpressible; fantasy and feeling lie deeper than words—beyond the words yet available to a child—and both demand a more profound, more biological expression, the primitive expression of music.' Sendak is convinced that children will respond most spontaneously to illustrations that, in his words, 'have a sense of music and dance and are not something just glued onto the page.'

In the work of the illustrators that Sendak most admires, he invariably finds a musical quality that he terms 'authentic liveliness'. He points to the linear arabesques in the lamb's dance of death in Boutet de Monvel's drawings for La Fontaine's *Fables Choisies pour les Enfants*, and to the same artist's 'harmonic inventions' achieved by the subtle use of colour and line. In the work of Randolph Caldecott, Sendak is fascinated not only by the abundance of actual dancing, singing, and playing of instruments but also by the many ways in which Caldecott used the theme-and-variations technique, combining simple themes into what Sendak describes as 'a fantastically various interplay of images'.

When Sendak is at work, he not only thinks in musical terms but often has music playing. He begins by trying to find the composer and the piece of music that fit the mood and tone of the story on his drawing-board, and he may listen to many recordings before he hits on the right musical colours. 'Books, too, can be evocative for me when I'm working on a series of illustrations,' he says. 'I often turn to James, Stendhal, D. H. Lawrence, and Melville—especially James, with his acute sensitivity to what happens inside someone growing. But it is music that does most to open me up. That's why I have all these records—and I go to quite a lot of concerts too. The other night, for example, I was sitting here listening to *Die Meistersinger*, which I know by heart, and got excited about it all over again. What struck me this time was that Wagner, in some mysterious way, had made the atmosphere—the very night air—of Nuremberg into music. I could see the city and smell it. And that's the kind of thing I want to convey in my illustrations. The pictures should be so organically akin to the text, so reflective of its atmosphere, that they look as if they could have been done in no other way. They should help create the special world of the story. When this kind of drawing works I feel like a magician because I'm creating the air for a writer.'

In illustrating stories of his own, Sendak sometimes encounters an odd difficulty in performing this magic. 'I find myself writing things that I don't like to draw, as if I were two separate people,' he explains. 'As a writer I may, for instance, ask the illustrator part of me to draw too many specific details of a room or of clothes. As an illustrator, I most enjoy interpreting emotions. In *Where the Wild Things Are* those two selves fused, in that the illustrations were a complete imaginative backdrop to the feelings experienced in the course of fantasy. Being dreamlike and fluid, the scenes aren't hung up with the kind of particulars that are involved in aiming at literal verisimilitude.'

Where the Wild Things Are, which was published in 1963,

marked a key stage in Sendak's development. In 1964 the book received the Caldecott Medal, awarded annually by the American Library Association for the most distinguished American picture book for children. Sendak went to St Louis for the presentation, and in his acceptance speech he said, 'With *Where the Wild Things Are,* I feel I am at the end of a long apprenticeship. By that I mean all my previous work now seems to have been an elaborate preparation for it.' Miss Nordstrom says that *Where the Wild Things Are* is of singular historical importance because 'it is the first American picture book for children to recognize that children have *powerful* emotions—anger and fear as well as the need Max had, after his anger was spent, to be 'where someone loved him best of all".' She adds, 'A lot of good picture books have had fine stories and lovely pictures, and some have touched beautifully on basic elements in a child's life—physical growth, coming to terms with a new sister or brother, and the like. But it seems to me that *Where the Wild Things Are* goes deeper than previous picture books have gone.'

Miss Nordstrom was not surprised that the book met with some hostile reactions from critics and librarians. 'The furor reminded me of the New York Public Library's refusal to give shelf room to E. B. White's *Stuart Little* for some months back in 1945, when it came out,' she says. 'The statement that Mrs Little's second son was born looking very much like a mouse made one librarian there unable to sleep for three nights. Or so she told me. But the *children* who read and loved that book weren't thinking of any actual process of giving birth to a mouse—they thought it was nice to have a mouse in the family. There were even some negative reactions to *A Hole Is to Dig.* One librarian was appalled at the definition "A face is to make faces with." She said she didn't want *her* children making faces. And when *Where the Wild Things Are* came out, another librarian told me the book would frighten little children to death. "But Max *conquers* those monsters," I said. "He becomes king of the wild things." But she was obviously horrified, perhaps too horrified to imagine that children might react with pleasure to the book.' A reviewer for the *Journal of Nursery Education* mused, 'We should not like to have it left about where a sensitive child might find it to pore over in the twilight.' *Publisher's Weekly,* after saying that 'the plan and technique of the illustrations are superb,' cautioned, 'but they may well prove frightening, accompanied as they are by a pointless and confusing story.' Among the adults who were not traumatized by Max's journey was a critic for the *Library Journal,* who wrote, 'Each word has been carefully chosen to express Max's mood precisely,' and 'The wild things who acclaim him their king are at once both ugly and humorous.' The critic did, however, feel compelled to add, 'This is the kind of story that many adults will question and for many reasons, but the child will accept it wisely and without inhibition, as he knows it is written for him.' A reviewer for the Cleveland *Press* was also apprehensive about possible storms, noting, 'Boys and girls may have to shield their parents from this book. Parents are very easily scared.'

Sendak had expected a certain amount of angry reaction to *Where the Wild Things Are.* In his speech accepting the Caldecott Medal, he referred with some acerbity to those noncontroversial children's books that offer 'a gilded world unshadowed by the least suggestion of conflict or pain, a world manufactured by those who cannot—or don't care to—remember the truth of their own childhood.' Of these he said, 'Their expurgated vision has no relation to the way real children live. I suppose these books have some purpose—they don't frighten adults. . . . The popularity of such books is proof of endless pussyfooting about the grim aspects of child life, pussyfooting that attempts to justify itself by reminding us that we must not frighten our children. Of course, we must avoid frightening children, if by that we mean protecting them from experiences beyond their emotional capabilities; but I doubt that this is what most people mean when they say "We must not frighten our children." The need for half-truth books is the most obvious indication of the common wish to protect children from their everyday fears and anxieties, a hopeless wish that denies the child's endless battle with disturbing emotions.'

One afternoon, in his studio, Sendak told me more about his ideas on the proper use of fantasy in children's books. The light over his drawing-board was out, and we sat in near darkness. Characteristically, Sendak spoke softly and rapidly. Occasionally, as he grew more intense, his words bumped against each other in a slight stammer. 'There have to be elements of anxiety and mystery in truthful children's books, or at least there have to be in mine,' he said. 'What I don't like are formless, floating fantasies. Fantasy makes sense only if it's rooted ten feet deep in reality. In *Where the Wild Things Are* the reality is Max's misbehaviour, his punishment, and his anger at that punishment. That was why he didn't just have a cute little dream. He was trying to deal with imperative, basic emotions.'

Sendak leaned forward. 'Then, the fantasy has to be resolved,' he said. 'If Max had stayed on the island with the wild things, a child reading the book might well have been frightened. Max, however, comes home. Mind you, he doesn't say, "I'll never go there again." He *will* fantasize again, but the hope is that, like other children, he'll keep coming back to his mother. So the book doesn't say that life is constant anxiety. It simply says that life has anxiety in it. Here, let me show you one of the ways Caldecott conveyed this.'

From a bookshelf Sendak gently removed a first edition of *A Frog He Would A-Wooing Go* in the nineteenth-century British series *Randolph Caldecott's Picture Books* (which are, incidentally, still in print). He turned to a page showing the exterior of Mousey's Hall. Frog, accompanied by Mr Rat, is paying court to Miss Mouse. Two small girls and their parents are watching a cat and her kittens approach the house. 'Up to that point, Caldecott followed the usual plot,' Sendak said. 'He added this family to serve as an implied commentary on the action. The reader sees—but the family doesn't—the cat and her offspring devouring Miss Mouse and Mr Rat. Nor does the family see Frog, while escaping, being gobbled up by a duck as he crosses the pond. But here—in the last picture of the book—the girls and the parents are looking at Frog's hat, lying on a stone in the pond. The children are holding tightly onto their parents. The look on their faces is as if they are saying, "What a frightful thing must have happened! But we still have our parents to protect *us*." Caldecott went one step beyond the nursery rhyme by relating it to life. Except for Caldecott, illustrators of this story have generally pictured it as a rollicking farce—"Everybody gets eaten up. Ho-ho-ho!" But Caldecott, by bringing in that family, added an intimation of how grim reality can be. Even if the children didn't get the point explicitly from the drawings, the feeling was there. Caldecott did this sort of thing much better than I can. I don't have any evidence that he ever talked about what he was doing, but he often worked in this way. I grant that he himself may not have been all that conscious of expressing a touch of dread. Nor am I when I'm working.'

Sendak lit a cigarette. 'Recently I gave a lecture at Pratt Institute, and a student asked me if I ever sit down with the intention of doing a children's book dealing with anxiety,' he said. 'Of course I don't, I told him. If I did, I'd hardly be any kind of creative artist. When I write and draw I'm experiencing what the child in the book is going through. I was as relieved to get back from Max's journey as he was. Or rather, I like to think I got back. It's only after the act of writing the book that, as an adult, I can see what has happened and talk about fantasy as catharsis, about Max acting out his anger as he fights to grow.'

The room was now quite dark, and Sendak put on the light. 'For me, that book was a personal exorcism,' he went on. 'It went deeper into my own childhood than anything I've done before; and I must go even deeper in the ones to come.'

I asked him if he would continue to concentrate on books for younger children.

'Yes,' Sendak replied. 'There'll be exceptions, I suppose, but for the most part I like to work for children no older than seven or eight. With them, you can be freer in the use of fantasy and in various kinds of experimentation, because the picture itself still means a tremendous amount to them. There's no wall between them and the picture.'

A few weeks after this particular talk I moved my family to Fire Island for the summer. Sendak had taken a house there too, and we often met on the beach, where he sat for hours sketching. He and my son Nicholas came to know each other, but only slightly. Sendak does not extend himself to beguile children, but he is ready for conversation if they are. One afternoon Nicholas made a futile attempt to play with a group of older children who could run much faster than he could, and then trudged over to where Sendak and I were sitting. Seeing Nicholas sad, Sendak suggested that they dig a hole. When they had dug one, Nicholas jumped in and had himself covered with sand up to his shoulders. Then, observing that Sendak had been sketching, Nicholas asked, 'Can you make me a ferryboat?' Sendak did, and then drew other pictures at Nicholas's direction, including some of seagulls—creatures that my son is very fond of. The next day Sendak dropped in at our house with a watercolour scene that contained all the boats, birds, and fishes Nicholas had asked for the previous afternoon.

A few weeks later the three of us were on the beach again. In the interval, Nicholas had largely ignored Sendak and had not referred at all to the watercolour, which his mother had hung above his bed. I walked down the beach for a few minutes to talk to a friend, and when I returned Nicholas was chasing a sandpiper and Sendak was looking pleased.

'We've been in contact again,' Sendak said. 'These last few weeks I've been aware that he was conscious of me, but also that he had no desire to continue what we had going that day. Maybe I projected it, but I seemed to get the message: "Don't push it. Don't try to do it again just yet." But right after you left, he pointed to himself, pointed to the sky, and said, "Remember the seagull? Thank you for the picture." There was a huge smile on his face for maybe half a second, and then he ran after the sandpiper. I was very much moved, very grateful that he did remember—and that he told me so in that way. It was as if he were saying, "Don't be upset. I didn't forget. I still have the picture you brought me." ' Sendak laughed. 'I did feel we had reached each other again.'

On the way back from the beach, with Nicholas running down the road ahead of us, Sendak said, 'I get a kick whenever I see a child react to something I've drawn or written. I like getting the letters children write me, and I like having a chance to meet one who has enjoyed a book of mine. Not that I write basically for children. I really do these books for myself. It's something I have to do, and it's the only thing I want to do. Reaching the kids is important, but secondary. First, always, I have to reach and keep hold of the child in me.'

Nicholas and I stopped at our gate, and Sendak walked on down the road alone. At the crossing he turned around and waved. The wild thing trying to wrench the gate off its hinges paused to wave back.

[1966]

5 *Illustration*

Creation of a picture book

EDWARD ARDIZZONE

I am not an expert. I am a man with a family who has made up stories for his children. For the past thirty-four years I have been a practising artist, during which time I have painted many hundreds of pictures, illustrated over eighty books by various authors, written and illustrated ten of my own books, taught at the Royal College of Art in London, and done many other things. After so long a time, it is inevitable that one should have developed some ideas about one's craft.

The story of *Little Tim and the Brave Sea Captain*, the first of the Tim books, was invented twenty-four years ago. It did not spring ready-made to the mind, but started as a rather brief little tale made up on the spur of the moment to amuse my children. Luckily it did amuse them, so it was told again the next day and then the day after that and so on, and each time it was told again it grew somewhat in the telling until I finally found I had a story which I felt was worth illustrating and sending to the publisher.

Now this process of telling and retelling until it grows into something worthwhile has two major advantages. The first is that the script will inevitably be cast in a mould which is easily read aloud; and this is important, because the poor parents may well have to read the story over and over again. Secondly, and probably more important, the children will often make their own suggestions. They will add those wonderful inconsequential details which only children can think of and which, if incorporated in a tale, so greatly enrich the narrative.

When it comes to making the drawings for one's tale and writing down the tale to match the drawings, then a number of special problems arise, problems which are peculiar to the production of picture books. In picture books the drawings, of course, are as important as, or more important than, the text. The text has to be short, not more than two thousand words. In fact, the text can only give bones to the story. The pictures, on the other hand, must do more than just illustrate the story. They must elaborate it. Characters have to be created pictorially because there is no space to do so verbally in the text. Besides the settings and characters, the subtleties of mood and moment have to be suggested.

Now this is where the old convention of the balloon coming out of a character's mouth, with writing in the balloon, can be invaluable. Take a passage like this from *Tim to the Rescue*. The situation so far is that Ginger, who has anointed his hair with the Mate's hair restorer and whose hair is growing alarmingly, comes up before the ship's barber to have his hair cut for the umpteenth time. In the drawing, there is poor mop-headed Ginger with the tears streaming down his face, the barber with his scissors, and the Bosun. The text reads as follows: 'Seaman Bloggs, the ship's barber, said he was sick and tired of it, that his fingers were worn to the bone and that he ought to have extra pay.' But in the drawing, a balloon comes out of Bloggs's mouth in which is written, 'Blimey, Mr Bosun. I just can't, my thumb aches simply 'orrible.' While out of the Bosun's mouth comes another balloon in which is written, 'Mutiny, eh Bloggs!'

You will see at once that what is said in the balloon pinpoints the characters of Bloggs and the Bosun for us, as well as describing the tension in the ship due to the deplorable growth of

Ginger's hair. This would take a page or more of text to describe, and in picture books, with only sixty words to a page, there is not the room to spare. Balloons, however, must be used sparingly; otherwise one's book might take on the character of a strip cartoon, which would be sad indeed.

Now to make drawings which tell a story clearly and in which characters are portrayed convincingly and subtleties of mood conveyed is difficult. It demands some professional ability, more ability even than the writing of the text. There is an idea that the work of an amateur or inexperienced artist is suitable for books for little children, provided they have a certain spurious brightness of colour. Though there may be exceptions, I think this idea a bad one. Little children should have the best possible pictures to look at, and I think too that good or bright colour alone is not sufficient to make a good picture. Drawing is of paramount importance. The well-known picture-book classics by Kate Greenaway, Randolph Caldecott, Beatrix Potter, William Nicholson, and, nearer our own time, Jean de Brunhoff, are all impeccably drawn.

Writing the text for a picture book also has its particular difficulties, the main one being that the tale has to be told in so few words yet must read aloud easily and sound well when read. Another difficulty is that at the turn of each page, and one rarely has more than one hundred and twenty words between the turns, the text must end with a natural break, a note of interrogation or suspense. With rare exceptions, the professional writer who is no artist finds this extremely difficult, if not impossible, to do. Not being visually minded, he cannot leave out enough; he must elaborate; he cannot visualize how the picture will tell the story. And this, I think, is why the best picture books have been created by artists who have written their own text. It is a one-man job.

In what I have said I seem to have suggested that a good picture book should contain certain elements which can be defined and enumerated. Yet if somebody asked what made a good picture book, I would be hard put to say. Some genius might easily come along and break all the rules and produce a work of enduring delight. All the same, I feel sure that there is a basic quality or virtue common to all the finest work and, rather hesitatingly, I suggest it may be the quality of enjoyment. The author-artist must enjoy the act of creating his book. It must be fun for him and he must believe in it. Or rather, he must create a world in which, in spite of all sorts of improbabilities from an adult point of view, he can believe in one part of himself, the childish part.

Characters in the books must also have life. Tim, or Ginger who is not very clever and rather jealous, the disgruntled Bloggs, or the respectable Mrs Smawley must all act their parts and never act out of character. This is particularly so in the drawings. One must be able to believe in them.

To repeat what I have said, the author must enjoy creating this book and must believe in it. Put another way, one might say that, for the childish part of him, the story must be both possible and true, and of course in its childish framework it must have its own formal logic. You will notice in the splendid kingdom of Babar the Elephant how all the animals act quite logically in the given framework. Then, I think, the story might have that enduring appeal which makes it a classic. It will be a story that may well appeal to the childish element in the adults, as well as to the child.

However, let's take this question of the author's enjoyment of his work somewhat further and say the following, which sounds something of a paradox: the author-artist does not primarily create his books for children, but rather to amuse that childish part of himself. If this is so, and he may not always admit it, he will never be in danger of committing that cardinal error of writing and drawing down to children. Instead he will be writing up to himself. I am sure we are all agreed that this question of writing up or down for children is of the greatest importance. Little children love all books. They have no taste, and rightly so, and of course will read and look at anything with pleasure. All the more reason, therefore, that we should give them the best.

But what is the best, what sort of books should be given to children, what kinds of subject dealt with? I don't know, nor have I the courage or the knowledge to discuss the subject. This is surely the province of the educationalist and the child psychologist. All the same, I will be brave enough to say that I think we are possibly inclined, in a child's reading, to shelter him too much from the harder facts of life. Sorrow, failure, poverty, and possibly even death, if handled poetically, can surely all be introduced without hurt. After all, books for children are in a sense an introduction to the life that lies ahead of them. If no hint of the hard world comes into these books, then I am not sure that we are playing fair. In this respect, I think the old nursery rhymes are splendid. Their fine jingling rhymes, their words, sometimes cruel and sometimes gay and often meaningless to fit the jingle, are never sentimental. They seem to express a sort of racial experience which is the very stuff of life itself. Then again, take the beautiful stories of a writer like Hans Andersen. What a wonderful introduction they are to the poetry of the emotions, with the implication that children can enjoy sadness and the pleasure of tears at some sad tale as well as grownups.

Now in all this I may be wrong. But what I do find when I read to children, and what indeed I can be sure of, is that children, particularly little children, love the sounds of words for their own sake, which is why they so often love listening to verse. One should therefore be choosy as to the quality of the verse and prose one gives them. The prose in particular should not only be simple and lucid but should have a poetic cadence which will appeal to the ear. Long and difficult words can be used as long as they are explained as the text unfolds. Notice how cunningly Beatrix Potter does this. Children, in fact, love strange words, and I don't think it matters much if at first they don't understand them.

I am often asked why the Tim books are about the sea and

FROM EDWARD ARDIZZONE'S *Tim All Alone*

not about animals or fairies or other possibly more suitable themes. The answer, of course, is they are what they are because of the kind of artist I am. An artist's work is not really divisible into compartments. I like drawing people and creating characters visually and therefore the Tim books are primarily about people. They are about the sea because where else can one find a more splendid gallery of characters than on the little ships that sail around our coasts?

The scenes in the books are, to a great extent, drawn from old half-forgotten memories of past experiences. Not that I have suffered shipwreck or collision or fire at sea or any such adventures; but I made, as a child, the long sea voyage from China to England and have been at sea much since then and seen a gale or two. Now for me, these old half-forgotten memories are far the best to work from. Time has removed the inessentials, while nostalgia has given them a poignancy which no close or too well remembered thing can have. For instance, Tim's house by the sea was one we stayed in long ago. The beach that ran in front of it and stretched away as far as the eye could see we knew in all weathers. I dare say that the imperfections of memory and nostalgia have caused me to make this house with its odd balcony and the beach with its steep pebble bank and wooden greyness look more romantic in my drawings than they really are. But what of that! Surely for the purpose of illustration they are better for it.

The little ships that are pictured so often in the Tim books are based on very old memories indeed. I used to play on them as a child before the 1914 war. In those days we lived in Ipswich, a small seaport town on the east coast of England. It was a rough, tough, and lively little town and no bad place for boys to be in. Being a seaport town, there were the docks, and the docks were always full of a variety of craft—small coastal steamers carrying grain or china in their holds; Dutch boats, with their high bows and sterns, which sailed across the North Sea from Rotterdam and Antwerp; and barges with their great red sails. These barges carried cargo from port to port along the coast.

My cousin Arthur and I would play truant and spend many happy hours on these docks. The sailors were kindly men and we were given free run of their craft. The decks and the rigging were ours to play on, and we were allowed to explore both engine room and hold. The mates and bosuns and ordinary seaman—I knew them all. Changed they may be in my drawings. All the same, when I look over London Bridge and see the ships lying in the Pool of London below, they look little different from those of nearly fifty years ago and the men seem little different too from the men I used to know.

I have, in the course of years, illustrated many books by various authors, and many of these books have been for children. Illustrating other people's books is never quite as easy or so pleasant as illustrating one's own. If one has no feeling for a book, neither for its language nor imagery, then the task can be a difficult and weary one. As a professional, to get a book like this is all in the day's work and no excuse for making bad drawings, though I fear it sometimes leads to indifferent ones. On the other hand, when it comes to illustrating for a fine and poetic writer, then it is a different matter. To illustrate Walter de la Mare's *Peacock Pie* was sheer delight, and sheer delight it was, too, to illustrate the poems and prose of such writers as James Reeves and Eleanor Farjeon.

In all these books the very sound of the words is evocative of pretty pictures. It is as if the poems or stories take charge and illustrate themselves and one's pen is only a medium for their self-expression. In truth, I have found that all works by good authors, especially poetic ones, have this in common, whether they were written in prose or verse. That is, that the meaning of the words plus the sound of the words always produce a precise visual image. There is no ambiguity about them, and therefore the illustrator's task is made an easy one. For example, let's take the first verse of Walter de la Mare's 'Song of Enchantment':

A song of enchantment I sang me there
In a green wood by waters fair
Just as the words came up to me
I sang it under the wildwood tree.

Or take this poem of James Reeves's called 'The Street Musician':

With plaintive fluting, sad and slow
  The old man by the woodside stands.
Who would have thought such note could flow
  From such cracked lips and withered hands?

On shivering legs he stoops and sways,
  And not a passer stops to hark;
No penny cheers him as he plays;
  About his feet the mongrels bark.

But piping through the bitter weather,
He lets the world go on its way.
Old piper! Let us go together,
And I will sing and you shall play.

Now what more can an illustrator want than to have such verse to illustrate! The work of creation is done for him and all that remains is to make the drawings, and that is the easiest part of his task.

Before I finish, I would like to mention one book which is not strictly a children's book and which is by the author of some of the greatest prose ever written in the English language. The book is *The Pilgrim's Progress,* and I cannot resist including a short passage from the opening page: 'I dreamed, and behold I saw a man clothed in rags, standing in a certain place, with his face from his own house, a book in his hand, and a great burden upon his back. I looked, and saw him open the book, and read therein; and as he read, he wept and trembled; and not being able longer to contain, he brake out with a lamentable cry, saying, "What shall I do?" '

This is noble language, but to me the genius of Bunyan is shown in the phrase 'with his face from his own house'. This phrase instantly visualizes the scene for us. Christian has his back to his house. The house is obviously visible but must be some way off on the edge of a distant town, and the town itself must be surrounded by a flat, sad, and somewhat open landscape.

I illustrated the wonderful book about twelve years ago. But for twenty years before that it had been my ambition to do so. In fact, my first acquaintance with it came earlier still. I was a schoolboy when I was given a tiny pocket edition illustrated with many thumbnail engravings which delighted me. On looking back, I think it was this book, and particularly these little engravings, which started me off on my career. In a way, it crystallized in me the desire to become an illustrator and a painter.

It was many years before I could achieve this. I had to earn my living in various jobs in the city of London until I was twenty-six and it was only then that I could break away. Of course this long period of office work had its influence. It meant that I had little art school training. It also meant that I turned to the more exacting medium of watercolour, since oils took too long, and also, of course, to the graphic arts. If I had not had this long period as a clerk I might have been, for better or for worse, a very different sort of painter. Therefore I have no regrets.

To conclude, let me return for a moment to my own children's books. They were, of course, primarily written and illustrated to amuse the children, and I hope that the poor grownups who have read them over and over again do not find them too irksome. But all the same, they were still written largely to amuse that childish part of myself. I am afraid this is an awful confession to make, but alas I am not only incorrigible but also unrepentant, and so will go on concocting new works merely for the fun of it.

[1961]

Children's book illustration: the pleasures and problems

ROGER DUVOISIN

When I was offered the honour of speaking here for 'one full hour' about children's books, I worried a bit. The letter of invitation was clear: 'We want you to speak for one full hour.' This was flattering. To speak for one full hour without interruption is an opportunity never offered to most people. But it meant also, I took for granted, a formal *serious* talk. A formal serious talk, when 'amusing and fun' is probably more appropriate to describe the making of children's books. In the actual work of making a child's book, the artist had better keep his sense of humour and pleasure about him: if he forgets to do so, he may well end up with a book which will bore children. Therefore, I will mix fun and seriousness in trying to tell about my personal pleasures and problems in this delightful occupation of illustrating children's books.

First, I must say I have a suspicion that more than a few artists who write and illustrate children's books have not deliberately chosen the occupation: they discovered its pleasures accidentally while doing some sort of stories with drawings as a form of play with their own children. It does not take long when playing in this fashion to have the rough form of a lively story, and all done with the participation of the children themselves. In executing this little feat the artist may be astonished to discover a previously unknown talent in himself.

Everyone who has improvised stories and pictures in the presence of a few children knows the fun one can have in that game. When this act has life and humour, the children's eager eyes and laughter are pleasant rewards. Even the bored looks which come to the children's faces when the story and the pictures lack inventiveness are part of the amusement. Bored looks spur one to higher feats of imagination in order to bring back the laughs.

The making of children's picture books is indeed like playing with children. The game is on even when the author-illustrator sits alone at his drawing table. For he is really not as lonely as he seems to be. He has his abstract public with him, as have artists in every field. In his case it is a public made up of two kinds of children. First, there is the child *he* was, a child who is very much present and who inspires him and helps him understand the other children. Second, there are the abstract children who are watching over his shoulder.

From his own childhood, he remembers the things, impressions, attitudes which impressed him most. He remembers his childhood conceptions of people, of animals, of scenes, and of books which were part of his world.

From the abstract children watching over his shoulder, he will have the fresh, unexpected, imaginative conceptions which they have expressed during games or conversations. In this give and take with his abstract public of children the illustrator will learn to let his imagination flow more freely.

There is in the maker of children's books what is in most adults in their relations to children: that little sneaking desire to teach and to moralize, to pass on to children what we think of our world. A picture book is such a fine medium for this exercise that it is difficult to resist the temptation. Even if these sentiments are carefully hidden in the book they are generally there, and so much the better. The children's-book maker has the added pleasure of believing that he has done more than merely entertain. Personally, I like to think that while children read my books they do not waste their time on the hundreds of toy trucks, cars, tractors, and bulldozers which fill most children's rooms nowadays, or on some of those books of useless facts.

The modern picture book with its large pages, its wealth of colour made possible by modern processes of reproduction, is a tempting invitation to the artist to play with his brush and pen. The fine books which have been published in recent years prove that more and more artists of talent are eager to join in the fun.

This fun is apparent to anyone who walks into public or school libraries or into bookstores. And it is fun which is spreading far and wide, for the modern picture book has invaded the world. I have seen picture-book stores all over Europe, east and west. I have seen a few in Iran. In an Iranian bookstore, a clerk brought out a book which he said was the outstanding picture book in Iran. I told him that I had seen two better ones in the office of a Teheran publishing firm. 'I do not think that could be,' he answered, 'this one was chosen by the American Institute of Graphic Art for their book *The Children's Books of Asia*.' And indeed, he brought me the book which, until then, I had never seen. It was a most interesting book. This indicated that in Asia there were bookstores with children's-book departments such as the one I was visiting. There are very few of these stores in poor countries, however.

One might ask where all this is taking the children's-book creators. What standing have they won in our society? Who will take seriously artists who spend so much of their time playing with children and children's books? Not many people, in my own experience. Not even their own children. When I filled out an application for a passport last year, I wrote 'Children's book illustrator and writer' in the space for 'occupation'. When the clerk saw this he looked up with a wink and a smile

FROM ROGER DUVOISIN'S *Petunia*

and said, 'Hm, children's books, eh?' There was absolutely no doubt that he meant, 'Hm, harmless fellow.' Or at a party of serious business people, a lady friend is liable to introduce you to a grave-looking gentleman and say, 'This is Roger Duvoisin; he is the author of *Petunia the Silly Goose.*' This is sure to bring another wink and a smile. A third example is that of my granddaughter, who was asked when she was nine, 'Well, Anne, do you write stories for children as does your grandfather?' 'Oh yes,' she replied, 'I do write children's stories, but when I grow up I will write grownup stories.'

Anne can be forgiven for she did not know that generally speaking one has to be a grownup to write and illustrate stories which children will enjoy. But as for those grave, practical grownups, I know it is they who are foolish, they who should be smiled and winked at. Their attitude does not give me the slightest inferiority complex. I have no apologies to offer for being part of a zoo of imaginary animals, geese, hippopotamuses, rabbits, lions, raccoons, bugs, crocodiles, and others. These animals are my loyal friends and my wife's too. We have much affection for them. Together we do our best to make the imaginative stories and fantasies which children need to develop their imagination and to learn about reality.

Instead of living in a zoo I could just as well live among fairies, dragons, dwarfs, and giants. They are just as necessary to children. But I love my zoo and I prefer to draw animals. Besides, animals have been used as symbols of men and to represent the gods and the world of magic ever since men could talk.

But there is also a serious aspect to the making of children's books, an aspect which at times demands very much hard work. This other aspect of children's books concerns the illustrations from an artistic point of view. That is to say that while the artist desires to communicate his own pleasure to children, he wants to do so with illustrations that are original in their conceptions, that are well composed in their designs and colours. In this he is driven by his own need to experiment and to try to improve his art, and he is encouraged by the importance the art in children's books has acquired as an art form.

The two aspects of illustrating children's books—the fun aspect and the serious artistic aspect—should not be separated really, for they are part of one overall effort to make a book as good and as beautiful as possible. But I will separate them here for the purpose of making it easier to explain, if I can, what an illustration is and what makes it beautiful.

The modern picture book, then, must be considered as more than a vehicle to carry stories and pictures to children in order to amuse them and give food to their imagination—and to amuse their authors at the same time. It is also a most interesting medium for artists to experiment in with colours and design—to invent to their heart's content. This is why many talented artists have been attracted to the picture book, not only for the fun of it but also for the opportunities it offers for their art. The result is that the best children's books have become art creations without losing the particular qualities which give pleasure to children.

Imagine a layman listening to one artist as he explains to another artist what he is trying to do in working on a new book. What he may hear will make him wonder whether the poor child has not been completely overlooked in the problems the artist is trying to solve. These problems may pertain only to the proportions of margins to the interest of the white spaces and coloured shapes, to the inventiveness of the design, to the relationship of the various colours, and other such problems.

Where is the child in all these things? Has he been sent to bed to leave the grownups to discuss serious things without being disturbed? The answer is that the child is very much present indeed. One of the reasons for making a page which is well designed is to tell the story with more simplicity, more verve, clarity, and impact; to give importance to what is important; to eliminate what destroys the freshness, the originality of the page; in other words, to make a page which will be more easily read by the child. A well-designed page will also educate the child's taste and his visual sense. A beautiful book is a beautiful object which the child may learn to love.

The modern children's-book illustrator is not isolated from the turmoil of the art world around him. Instinctively or consciously, sometimes too consciously, he tries to swim in the current with varying degrees of success, depending on his talent. He wants to present to children books which reflect what he has learned from the new developments in art.

What these developments are everyone interested in painting and the graphic arts knows very well, but it seemed to me that it would be interesting to speak about them here and to tell how they are affecting the making of children's books.

Roughly, the extraordinary things which happened to painting during the nineteenth and twentieth century—its evolution away from representation and toward pure abstraction—have made the art of illustration what it is today. Illustration in some of its forms has long been confused with painting, and it is this evolution of painting toward abstraction which has helped clarify the difference between the two. However some confusion still exists. Illustration, in its narrow meaning, is an art whose purpose is to complement a text in a book or a magazine, to tell the story pictorially. But an illustration can tell a story without the help of a text. In this wider meaning, an illustration is a form of independent writing. It is pictorial literature.

It can even be said that illustration antedates the written word, for many of the prehistoric paintings or drawings were illustrations. For instance, those of the Tassili region in North Africa often describe scenes of the material or religious life of the people who made them: hunting, war, dance scenes, etc. The religious frescoes and paintings of the medieval period and the Renaissance were, for the people who could not read, what the illustrations in a picture book are for the child who has not yet learned to read. They told pictorially the stories and legends the people had heard.

A painting can be an illustration. A large painting which describes a battle scene can be merely a painted illustration and not a true painting. That is, its end may be strictly literary: to tell the story of a battle. Two well-known French painters of the nineteenth century—the historical painter Detaille and the great painter Delacroix—serve well as examples of this. When Detaille did a battle scene his purpose was simply to tell a highly sentimentalized, romanticized version of that battle. He painted the figures, the arms, and the uniforms down to the last button with a precise realism, like a storyteller who can't help putting in all the details. To Delacroix, however, the battle scenes he chose to paint were but subjects on which to work out abstract problems of painting. Even if, superficially, one will see only romantic pictures of battle scenes in the works of these two painters, the fact remains that Delacroix painted a painting while Detaille painted an illustration. This is how paintings can be confused with illustrations and illustrations with paintings.

Painting is the independent, abstract creation of an artist—abstract whether the subject which started it on its way remains or disappears in the process of creation, or whether there ever was any subject to begin with.

The arbitrary division between abstraction and representation in a painting has sometimes been explained by replacing a painting by a page of Chinese writing. To a person who cannot read Chinese, such a page is simply a beautiful abstract design. It means nothing, it only satisfies the visual senses. If, by some magic, the person admiring the abstract design of the page could suddenly understand the Chinese language and Chinese writing, the page would automatically cease to be a beautiful abstract design affecting the visual sense. It would become a poem about a lake, or a Chinese tale, or any other piece of writing. Only the trained artist may continue to admire the beauty of the abstract design.

Now, the point where a representational painting ceases to be a painting and becomes an illustration is not a well-defined one. The layman can take comfort in the fact that painters themselves do not always agree on the matter.

Up to the nineteenth century, no artist had left in writing his opinion of what makes a painting a true painting. We have only the opinions of writers who, for centuries, have considered that painting was an imitation of nature. In other words, a painting was a picture or illustration or literature.

The Greeks—for example, Aristotle—had expressed this opinion. The Greek paintings, the drawings on the Greek vases, all their art and sculpture were imitations of nature. They were representations of mythological figures or of everyday scenes. Unfortunately, we do not know what the artists thought of their art.

The paintings of the Romans reached an astonishing degree of realism. Many are pure illustrations painted on walls. They reveal to us the most intimate details of everyday life and the Roman's pictorial conceptions of their mythology.

The art of Byzantium was an interlude. Its almost abstract art ended realism and literature in art for several hundred years.

But toward the end of the thirteenth century the famous painter Giotto brought back realism and literature in painting. Whatever the value of his paintings as true paintings, their realism was the reason for his very success. People of his day flocked to see his paintings. Never before had the figures and scenes of the church seemed so alive to them. His realism and illustrative talent were highly praised by the writers of his day and of later periods. For them Giotto had liberated painting from the conventions of Byzantine art.

With the discovery of the laws of perspective in the fifteenth century, painting became more than ever illustration for most everyone, even for some painters. It is probable that most of the princes who ordered these paintings saw in them masterful illustrations of religious, mythological, or historical literature, and illustrations of their personal feats.

The problem went on during the next centuries and is well demonstrated in the art criticism which has been written all along. Paintings were almost continuously judged for qualities which were literary ones. A quotation from an eighteenth-century writer will give a good example. It was written about a painting by the French painter Greuze which was titled 'The Death of a Wicked Father':

The death of a wicked father, abandoned by his children, tears the soul of the spectator. It is hair raising. Everything expresses the despair of the dead, the disorder and horror of his condition. The strong, deep, revolting impression made by the painting repulsed many spectators. There is here a sublimity, as well as a beauty which few souls could bear.

In this case the painter was expressing human feelings which could be expressed in words. This made his painting a piece of literature. So we can forgive the writer for wanting to put it down in writing.

But the great painters of every period most certainly knew that the representation of a subject was not what mattered most in a painting even though they could not have discussed abstraction in the way it is discussed today.

It was in the nineteenth century that painters began to be articulate about the problem. Delacroix seems to have been the first to write on the subject. He was not only a great painter, he could also write well about painting. His diary and his letters make extremely interesting reading for artists. As far as we know, he was the first to express concern because people misunderstood paintings. When he painted he was not writing, he said. He had nothing to tell in mind. His paintings were only meant to reach the senses. In other words, what was of value in them was felt and could not be expressed in words. He also seems to have been the first to question the necessity of the subject. Its elimination was, of course, the most effective way to clear the misunderstanding. It is ironical that Delacroix ended up by being the victim of the subject. The subjects he chose for his paintings were so romantic that the paintings have not been popular in our century. But painters still see the true art in his paintings under their romantic dress.

More and more painters toward the end of the last century expressed the opinion that painting was a creation, an abstraction, not an imitation of nature, not literature. This led to twentieth-century painting, to pure non-representational art.

But painting also ceased to appeal to the layman. Spectators were so accustomed to considering painting as pictures or illustrations that their reactions were ones of revolt and anger when they first saw the paintings whose subjects were beginning to break up. They were frustrated at not recognizing their illustrations and accused the painters of mocking them. I remember the indignation that was created by a poster when I was a child. It represented a large horse done in stone lithography. The horse was not particularly distorted, but it was green. A green horse! Who had ever seen a green horse! That slight departure from realism was enough to bring a wave of protests.

While the painters were slowly effecting the divorce of illustration from painting, dismembering the subject, planning its final murder, the professional book illustrators had a good time.

Illustrated books were popular during the nineteenth century. There were many professional illustrators of talent who were often accomplished craftsmen in wood or copper engraving and in the new reproduction process of stone lithography. These illustrations were printed in black, but were sometimes coloured by hand. During the second half of the century the printing of colour overlays was perfected. But illustrators generally followed the tradition of realism and of closely following the text with exact literalness.

Children's-book illustrators were also busy during this time. What is remarkable is how some of these illustrators remained solidly wedded to the contemporary literature they illustrated. *Alice in Wonderland* and Tenniel comes to mind first as the classic example. When we think of Alice, we think of Tenniel's conception of her, and if we read the book without Tenniel's illustrations something is missing. At the turn of the century, *The Wind and the Willows* and Arthur Rackham is another example. We may not like now the mannered style of Rackham but his illustrations are well wedded to the story.

Even when an illustrator was not the contemporary of the author whose books he illustrated, his name could be closely associated with these books. Doré was such an illustrator. His drawings were not particularly distinguished, nor was he concerned with well-composed pages, but he had enormous verve and imagination. His name was for long identified with some of the classics he illustrated. Among these are masterpieces which are loved by children. They are Perrault's *Mother Goose Tales* and La Fontaine's *Fables*. In *Mother Goose Tales* Doré added to the fantasy of the tales; his forests were as dark, frightening, and mysterious as fairy-tale forests should be, and the romanticism of his castles lingered for a long time in the minds of readers.

But one of the most important things that happened to illustration during the nineteenth century was the interest that some major painters began to take in the work of illustrating books. It was a modest beginning at first, in the sense that few of these painters illustrated books. But it was the beginning of an interest which continued to grow and became extremely important during our century.

By a strange coincidence, the first of the major painters to express concern that his paintings were being mistaken for literary work was also the first to put his hand to the literary work of illustrating a book. He was Delacroix. Delacroix illustrated the *Faust* of Goethe on lithographic stones. It was, of course, the very personal creation of a great artist. Goethe himself was pleased with the vigour and power of these illustrations and was generous enough to say that they were superior to his text in the conception of some scenes. The book became a classic example of the combination in one book of a great writer and a great artist. Delacroix also illustrated *Hamlet* and other dramas.

A few more nineteenth-century artists, such as Turner, Manet, Rodin, did book illustrations. But it was in the twentieth century that their number really became important: Toulouse-Lautrec, Picasso, Matisse, Derain, Dufy, Miro, Redon, Juan Gris, Maillol, Klee, Chagall, even Calder and others. Recently, Rauschenberg did pages for Dante. Picasso himself illustrated a long list of books: poetry by his friends, novels, Greek classics, even Buffon's *Natural History.*

These painters who, little by little, led painting to nonfigurative art also brought new conceptions to book illustration. They were often in their own art the equals, if not the betters, of the writers whose works they illustrated. With their creative powers, they could not simply see their illustrations as the servants of a text and illustrate with literalness and realism. They did away with these conceptions. They illustrated on their own terms though they kept within the spirit of the particular piece of literature they chose to illustrate.

What interested them in this literature was that it offered their creative imaginations a base from which to invent graphic ideas.

There has been much criticism expressing disapproval of the liberties these artists took with the literature they illustrated, but it was these liberties as well as the greatness of their art which make their work in book illustration valuable and defensible.

Literature is an art which has its own conceptions and its own means of expressions. It does not need help from another art, unless the writer himself has planned it that way. Illustrations which impose the artist's conception of a novel with definitiveness and precise literalness come like a screen between the author and his readers. The illustrations interfere in a very unpleasant way with the readers' own dreams.

But illustrations as done by the superior artists are related to the text in a free, loose, subtle way; they leave the reader free to interpret the writing with complete freedom. And he has the added pleasure of doing the same with the illustrations.

One can see the difference between the two conceptions by comparing the illustrations done for the same literary work by two artists. Doré illustrated an edition of Rabelais's *Gargantua* which had much success in his time. His illustrations had verve and boisterousness, but they fixed the scenes and personages of the book with such realism and definitiveness that the reader had no choice but to see Gargantua as Doré saw him. Derain's illustrations, half a century later, had much success also, but they are only free suggestions of Renaissance art and styles and of Rabelais's figures. They make fine pages which leave the reader free to see his own Gargantua. Thus, just as painters were extricating painting from illustration, they gave illustration some of the abstract features of painting.

It is worth saying here, also, that the pure abstract painters, that is the painters who have completely eliminated the subject in conceiving their paintings, have never illustrated books. Illustrative art and abstract art are too opposed to each other.

Now, after this very simplified history of the confusion between illustration and painting, we are back where we started: our modern picture book.

It may seem irrelevant to spend so much time speaking of the relationship between illustration and painting and of the evolution of painting toward abstraction in a talk about the minor art of children's-book illustration; it may also seem preposterous to imply that children's picture books have such noble ancestry.

But all these things are what makes our picture books what they are now.

In eliminating the representational from painting, painters were better able to examine what painting was. All the graphic arts profited from the discoveries the painters made.

Illustrators were able to learn the importance of the design which holds the narrative elements together in a page and gives order and visual qualities to that page. They could reflect over the conception that what makes a painting beautiful is not what it represents, a conception which to some extent is applicable to illustration. What makes an illustration beautiful is not its descriptive qualities but its underlying graphic inventions. Even in children's-book illustrations it is worth while to think of the narrative elements as materials with which to build a beautiful page instead of concentrating on them for their own sake.

Then there was the realization that literalness and realism were to the illustrator what the cage is to the bird. Having gotten out of the cage, illustrators found the most pleasant freedom in relating illustrations to a text, in composing pages, and in using colours.

Illustration profited much from abstract painting in spite of the opposition between the two. The treatments of surfaces, the use of space, the colour relations, the free, dramatic forms and lines, etc., of abstract paintings teach much to the illustrator.

However, the children's-book artist must think about all this within the very special art of picture books. Because making a picture book is like playing with children, the particular way children react to the world around them cannot be forgotten. This need not be a limitation; on the contrary, limitations are a challenge and a source of inventions.

With their uninhibited vision, children do not see the world as we do. While we see only what interests us, they see everything. They have made no choice yet. We do not see what sort of buttons a man we pass in the street has on his coat or how many there are, unless we are a button maker. But a child cares and will count the buttons if he can. He will care just as much about the tiny ladybug which falls accidentally on the dining-room table as about the grownups who sit around it. More, in fact. The child's interests are infinite and he sees the tiniest details of his world as well as the biggest forms. And he does not say, 'I do not understand.' He looks and sees. He lives among wonders and the children's book artist only has to take him by the hand, so to speak, to lead him toward the most imaginative adventures.

The child also has the tendency to enjoy this detailed world of his in terms of happenings, of things being done, in other words, in terms of stories.

In their own art, the children are not aware of abstract considerations. They are not concerned with colour harmony or colour contrast, with composition and design. Their art is only a sort of writing, however beautiful it might be sometimes. With it they tell a story. If a child is asked to explain a painting he has made, he will most likely tell what is happening in it. 'This is a woman going to the market to buy fruit. This is a truck driver climbing on his truck. This is the sea, full of fish which the fisherman will catch.'

I still remember an experience I had with my elder son when he was four. It illustrates what I have just said. One day his mother took him up the Hudson River to Nyack. When they returned I asked him if he had liked the beautiful river with hills on both sides. He thought for a while and said, yes, he did. There was a boat on it which smoked and which had a little house in the middle. A door opened and a man came out of the house and went to look into the water. The only thing which struck him was an action, a little story. So let's give the child all the stories he wants.

Another quality children possess is their love and understanding of the humorous side of things. This also can be a rich source of ideas for the maker of children's books. Not only can he laugh with the child as he makes his books, but he can tell the most serious and important things while he laughs.

I have said enough, I think, to show that the artist and author cannot complain that the making of children's books has limitations. Those limitations rather resemble a jail whose windows and doors open wide into a beautiful paradise. The degree of talent of the children's-book maker may be the only limitation.

In the art itself, I think we will see artists taking more and more liberties. Even abstract art can have a place in a child's book under certain circumstancees. If the artist is inclined to search for his page designs and for his colours by using the elements of the story in rough, free, almost abstract forms, he will be tempted to leave his page almost in the rough abstract condition. The forms, the bright colour surfaces which are not cut or soiled by details, the white spaces which remain pure have a freshness, a force, and an interest which they may lose when details and precisions are brought in. The artist may then be searching for a simpler and more ingenuous way of telling the necessary story.

When the artist writes his own story, he can conceive both his text and illustrations simultaneously, thus making the text and pictures help each other as they develop the story. He even can make his illustrations first with great freedom and get ideas for the text from them. In this case, the text may be like the threads the dressmaker uses to hold the pieces of material which will form the dress.

This matter of abstraction and illustration recalls to my mind a fascinating experience I had with a friend of mine, a well-known abstract painter. He wanted to illustrate a charming story he had invented for his children, but never having illustrated before, he came to live with us for a few days to work out the problem. In spite of his talent for drawing, making illustrations was for him like speaking the language of an unknown country. He could no longer see the story in literary terms when he tried to imagine the various scenes with his brush on the paper. To see visually the sequence of these scenes as they were described in his own story and translate them pictorially proved impossible for him. After several days a pile of nice miniature abstract paintings had been made, none telling any story. Yet when I think of this now, it seems to me that a few well-placed details drawn with the pen might have transformed the abstractions into story-telling pages. This experience demonstrates, however, how difficult it is to join two art conceptions which are so opposed to each other. It demonstrates also that in picture books, as in every art form, everything is worth trying.

As I come to the end of the 'one full hour' I see that I could ramble on for another hour, but I think you can see now that the making of children's books can be as great a source of satisfaction for the artist as the finished book can be a source of pleasure for the child.

[1965]

Randolph Caldecott

FREDERICK LAWS

The kind of books we give to children are an indication of what we think and feel about childhood, and these beliefs and emotions lie close to the heart of our national culture. Mr F. J. Harvey Darton's history of *Children's Books in England* is a more serious history of England than most volumes which recite the names of battles and Acts of Parliament. It is no simple story of progress. Broadly speaking, in the eighteenth century parents and publishers fussed little about the young. They were presumed to be small adults and dressed as such. They could read such grownup books as interested them, but like the lower classes they found their pleasure in books mainly in the fairy tales, songs, and stories of adventure crudely printed in chap-books from the pedlar's pack. One publisher of genius, John Newbery, began catering especially for children, and by the end of the century he had a host of followers. Newbery called himself 'the friend of children', and his books were friendly and entertaining. But in the early nineteenth century children's books became both a flourishing business and a very serious matter. Their authors, though benevolent, edifying, and even understanding, were scarcely *friendly* to the child reader. The books had to save children's souls and to stuff their minds with suitable facts. According to the author of *The Fairchild Family*: 'All children are by nature evil, and while they have none but the natural evil principle to guide them, pious and prudent parents must check their naughty passions in any way that they have in their power, and force them into decent and proper behaviour and into what are called good habits.' Story books might help to frighten them into virtue. But fairy tales and nursery rhymes were irrational, uninformative and even immoral. Cinderella, for instance, 'paints some of the worst passions that can enter into the human breast, and of which little children should, if possible, be totally ignorant; such as envy, jealousy, a dislike to mothers-in-law and half-sisters, vanity, a love of dress, etc., etc.' Fortunately this dreary and barbarous attitude to the young was not universal, and great writers who *liked* children came along. Gaiety, poetry, nonsense, and the ancient heritage of folklore were brought to the nursery by Edward Lear, Lewis Carroll, Hans Andersen, and the translators of Grimm in the 1840s, 50s, and 60s. When Walter Crane, Kate Greenaway, and Randolph Caldecott began drawing for children they were under no public compulsion to be morally edifying or factually informative. Children were no longer supposed to be 'young persons' whose taste would be much the same whether they were five or fifteen. So long as they pleased children they were free; indeed Crane wrote that 'in a sober and matter-of-fact age Toybooks afford perhaps the only outlet for unrestricted flights of fancy open to the modern illustrator who likes to revolt against the despotism of facts.'

Since the eighties books for children have grown steadily in prestige and numbers and our attitude to children has altered immensely. The child is anything but downtrodden. His innocent eye is the final court of appeal for many aesthetic extremists. A pack of writers from Barrie downwards have envied his dream world. A contemporary illustrator might well seek to escape from the despotism of fantasy. Educational extremists say that 'the wisdom of the child' should decide what he ought to learn. The severest criticism of a children's book now is that it might frighten its readers.

In 1878 when Caldecott published his first picture book the

child had not become such a domineering father of the man. But the social and aesthetic importance of the baby's book was well established. Ruskin had denounced the pious ugliness of 'the literature which cheap printing enables the pious to make Christmas presents of for a penny . . . full of beautiful sentiments, woodcuts and music . . . Splendid woodcuts, too, in the best Kensington style, and rigidly on the principles of high, and commercially remunerative, art, taught by Messrs Redgrave, Cole, and Company.' He felt it would lead to: 'Ruin—inevitable and terrible, such as no nation has yet suffered . . . Yes—inevitable. England has to drink a cup which cannot pass from her—at the hands of the Lord, the cup of His fury;—surely the dregs of it, the wicked of the earth shall wring them and drink them out.'

The illustrations of the old chapbooks had been coarse in colour and vulgar in design. Even decently produced books as late as 1850 had the colour added to them in patches by children working in large groups. About 1868 the processes of colour printing took a leap forward in convenience and potential beauty. Walter Crane was inspired by Japanese colour prints: 'Their treatment in definite black outline and flat brilliant as well as delicate colours, vivid dramatic and decorative feeling struck me at once.' And as he worked with Edmund Evans, a printer of rare skill and taste, he was able to experiment successfully in adapting his ideas to mass colour printing. Evans printed the work of Caldecott and Kate Greenaway too, and played a considerable part in setting good standards of quality as the new mechanical processes developed.

Walter Crane's *The Baby's Opera* is a remaining classic of the nursery, and when he illustrated the same nursery rhymes as Caldecott he could excel him in beauty of design. But his vein of humour was not strong, and his elegant figures in Pre-Raphaelite attitudes were more decorative than illustrative. He tried to make his books train the taste of their readers, and made them a vehicle for his ideas about furniture and decoration.

Kate Greenaway was Caldecott's other chief rival. She drew beautiful children in costumes which she said were of the eighteenth century but which, in fact, came from her own imagination. Her gracefully sentimental work was so popular that the fashions she invented for children of the past became real. Kate Greenaway dresses and bonnets, made uglier of course, were worn by children here, in France, and in America. Ruskin alternated between grossly overpraising her work and cramping her style by trying to make her draw correctly.

Caldecott illustrated two or three books for Mrs Juliana Ewing —the best of them being *Jackanapes*—and was evidently sympathetic to her lively though elevating storytelling. His real reputation with infants, however, rests upon the picture books whose texts are either nursery rhymes or songs or ballads of the eighteenth century. The origins of the nursery rhyme are unquestionably ancient, but splendidly obscure. Theorists have claimed to find sources and parallels for them in anthropology; others hold that they are linked with popular political satire. It is all quite inconclusive, and the rhymes remain, magical fragments which add to nobody's store of knowledge, improve no infant characters, but persist in giving delight. Caldecott's affection for the late eighteenth century has been mentioned before. His idea of the period has nothing in common with the rational, elegant, witty, unregenerate *dix-huitième* in which Lytton Strachey discovered a spiritual home. It was almost as reliable as history, however. The poems which Caldecott raised almost to the true fame of anonymity included two by Oliver Goldsmith—the *Elegy on the Death of a Mad Dog* from *The Vicar of Wakefield* and his *Elegy On The Glory of Her Sex Mrs Mary Blaize*. It may be worth noting that the *Vicar of Wakefield* itself was nostalgic and pastoral—an escape from sophisticated London to old-fashioned country people. The 'good old days' seem to be progressively recessive. Neither of these poems were meant for children though Goldsmith, through his friendship with Newbery, wrote more for children than for adults. They are nonsense in a way, but the verbal nonsense of paradox and anti-climax rather than the image-nonsense of dream poetry. Caldecott made them live by ignoring their critical wit and exploiting every 'sympathetic' touch for all it was worth. The Mad Dog himself is a famous charmer:

The dog and man at first were friends
But when a pique began,
The dog, to gain some private ends,
Went mad, and bit the man.

In three drawings Caldecott makes it clear that the friendship was based on the gift of bones, that the pique was a matter of jealousy of a cat, and that the madness was an unfortunate private matter which 'the wondering neighbours' were impertinent to discuss.

Caldecott's choice of Robert Bloomfield's *Farmer's Boy* needs no explaining. It illustrates itself with a new animal on every page which those young persons who have learnt few words can nevertheless greet with appropriate noises. *John Gilpin* by William Cowper is more an older child's book. The riding and the misfortunes make active pictures, but babies may agree with Miss Greenaway that the accidents and sufferings of a nice old man are more distressing than funny.

Samuel Foote's *Great Panjandrum* is queerest of all. Foote wrote it to annoy the actor Macklin, famous for his Shylock. Macklin retired from the stage to keep a coffee-house and hoped to attract custom to it by giving lectures. Foote knew that sooner or later he would boast of his actor's skills in memorizing anything at a single hearing, and attended his lecture armed with *The Great Panjandrum*. This was a piece of nonsense from which each vestige of consecutive thought, every memory aid of association, and all sane meaning had been carefully excluded. Where Caldecott found it I cannot imagine. Foote's witty though scurrilous farces had been off the stage since his death in France after a prosecution as notorious in its time as that of Oscar Wilde. *The Life and Bonmots of Samuel Foote,* which contains the Panjandrum, was not a common book. The life was scandalous and the bonmots often regrettably coarse. But he *did* find it, and in no time dons and clergymen were sending translations of it into the Greek or Hebrew to *Notes and Queries,* and the young had adopted it is an excellent difficult thing to learn by heart.

His illustrations for this Dadaist masterpiece are an extreme example of the method of work and the peculiar fitness of his sort of imagination for the entertainment of small boys and girls. It is clear that he did his first drawings while telling a story to a child on his knee. The book of *Lightning Sketches For The House That Jack Built* proves that. So, obviously, did Edward Lear, and we are told the same of Lewis Carroll. It keeps your story moving at a proper pace. You find out when you are permitted to elaborate or digress and when you *must* have pictures to carry you over an unknown word or an ambiguous phrase.

Caldecott had kept the severely literal visual imagination which I believe to be characteristic of young children. The thing imagined for them is not of another order of reality from the thing seen. After all, you can see it in your head. They are willing to accept flexible conventions in imagining, will grant for the sake of fun that a cloud is very like a camel or Father like a bear. Yet their fancy has hard edges and is not at home off the solid earth. Until corrupted by whimsical elders, they prefer what they know or can see to fanciful inventions.

In picturing the Panjandrum, Caldecott leaves no point unsharpened and no bridgeable gap unbridged. 'So she went into the garden to cut a cabbage-leaf to make an apple-pie; and at the same time a great she-bear, coming down the street, pops its head into the shop. What, no soap? So he died, and she very imprudently married the Barber; and there were present the Picninnies, and the Joblillies, and the Garyulies, and the

FROM RANDOLPH CALDECOTT'S *Sing a Song for Sixpence*

great Panjandrum himself, with the little round button at top; and they all fell to playing the game of catch-as-catch-can, till the gunpowder ran out at the heels of their boots.' The she-bear goes down a real streeet—in Whitchurch. The regrettable shortage of soap directly causes death. The round button at top of the Panjandrum proves him a schoolmaster, and the gunpowder which ran out at the heels of the boots of the dancers, though unexplained, is clearly drawn in.

He brought the same thoroughgoing habits of realistic visualization and explanation to nursery rhymes, and the purist may object to such hard-and-fast interpretation. His most elaborate piece of exposition comes in *Sing a Song of Sixpence* which he changed to a Song *for* Sixpence without authority. The lines

Sing a song for sixpence
A pocketful of rye
Four-and-Twenty blackbirds
Baked in a pie.

are given eight pictures. An old lady gives a little girl sixpence, presumably for having sung. The girl gives it to a man chopping wood. The man buys or acquires a poacher's pocketful of rye which he takes home. His children set a blackbird trap in the snow, and evidently catch twenty-four birds which their mother bakes in a pie. This *looks* a likely story, but it is more probable that the first two lines of the song mean nothing at all. However, parents with children who ask Why? are fully covered. And the birdtrap picture is a very charming colour design. Humanitarians may disapprove of the whole blackbird incident. I can only report that at the age of three a kindly daughter of mine found the picture with the birds beginning to sing a sad one, on the grounds that the little girl with the spoon might get no dinner.

Another piece of rationalizing one might regret is the lowness of the moon jumped over by the cow. But no parent will regret the introduction of pigs to explain what fun the little dog laughed at. An insufficiency of pigs is one of the great faults of modern children's books.

The most famous of all Caldecott's drawings came in his first picture book—*The House That Jack Built.* The Dog that Worried the Cat sits there exhausted by his effort but happy in the consciousness that that effort has been virtuous, while behind him threatens the unsuspected, inevitable cow. Tragic irony and the madness of pride could not be more precisely expressed.

Story and picture have merged so closely in these books that to pick out a single page as a specimen of drawing is like removing a line from a sonnet. Each sketch depends on what went before and what comes after. The girls opening the gate here have been eavesdropping on the proposal scene just ended and will join the indignant heroine in chasing the kind gentleman. The dog slinking off on the right has been making up to the milkmaid's dog before and will be driven away by it afterwards. His set pieces in colour sometimes achieve dignity—the fine lady on a white horse is unquestionably handsome—and they have vigour and gaiety always. But his great achievement is the creation of a fluid style of pictorial storytelling which is as natural and as pleasant as friendly conversation.

[1956]

6 The modern scene

Science fiction

SHEILA EGOFF

You can, if you wish, class all science fiction together; but it is about as perceptive as classing the works of Ballantyne, Conrad and W. W. Jacobs as 'the sea-story' and then criticising that.

—C. S. Lewis: *An Experiment in Criticism* (1961)

C. S. Lewis was perfectly right, of course—science fiction defies simple definition. In its classic form, as represented by Arthur Clarke's *A Fall of Moondust* and Fred Hoyle's *Fifth Planet,* it extrapolates closely and logically from known scientific fact into conjecture. At the other extreme imagination runs wild and becomes science fiction 'space-opera', replete with bug-eyed monsters, space cows, humanoids, or telepathic FBI agents.

Under this broad umbrella of subject, style, and mood, science fiction may embrace past, present, and future; fantasy and harsh reality; horror and humour; the trite and the sublime. It is the literature of pure escapism and it may also be the vehicle for biting criticism of contemporary society, as in H. G. Wells's famous *The Time Machine* (1895). If you will, it is often children's literature for adults and it may equally well be the child's easiest entry into speculations that trouble the adult mind. Most important, science fiction, with its present immense popularity, is something of a literary phenomenon and for good or bad it has made an impact that cannot be ignored.

This complex, debatable, seemingly modern genre probably had its origins in the most obvious of motivations: simple curiosity. Science fiction began where its first tradition may well end—with man's yearning to land on the moon, now spectacularly fulfilled. The first moon stories were hardly scientific. In A.D. 200 Lucian of Samosata in his *True History* projected his travellers to the moon by means of a water spout and wind. Thirteen hundred years later the Italian poet Ariosto wrote *Orlanda Furioso* (1532) in which the hero, Astolpho, in search of Orlando's lost wits, goes in Elijah's chariot to the moon where things lost on earth—including wits—are to be found. In the last part of the fifteenth and the early part of the sixteenth century came the discoveries in astronomy of Copernicus and Galileo. However, writers such as Cyrano de Bergerac, Daniel Defoe, and Bishop Godwin still got their travellers to the moon by magic; even the German astronomer Kepler used a dream in his *Somnium*.

The scientific approach arrived with the late nineteenth century. In 1872 the Académie Française gave high praise to several science-fiction books by Jules Verne, the man who has been called the father of modern science fiction because he described so many things that were invented shortly afterwards—the aeroplane, the submarine, electric lights, the Atlantic cable. His *From the Earth to the Moon* (1870) describes a vehicle little different from Apollo 11 except in its method of propulsion. If written today it could be considered a light satire on our present manned flights to outer space. The Englishman, Frenchman, and American who make the flight have not even planned out how they are going to land on the moon, nor what they will do when they get there. They spend a great deal of their time having fabulous meals and imbibing French wine. Realizing that they will never reach the moon owing to an error in mathematics, they orbit it, plunge down into the Pacific Ocean, and when the projectile is opened to rescue them they are quietly playing dominoes.

Periodically science catches up with fiction by making real the fantasies of writers. The LM landing on the moon in July 1969 was one occasion (the atomic bomb on Hiroshima was another) that raised the question: has the advance of science caused the death-knell of science fiction? The question is purely academic. Apollo 8 and 9 and 10 and 11 are far more likely to destroy lovers' odes to the moon than science fiction, for there have been other traditions at work besides space flights, although many literary critics would disclaim them. Man's dissatisfaction with his present state produced the utopias—Sir Thomas More's *Utopia* (1516), Edward Bellamy's *Looking Backward* (1888), William Morris's *News From Nowhere* (1891). Fear of a sterile future produced Aldous Huxley's *Brave New World* (1932) and George Orwell's *Nineteen Eighty-Four* (1949). It is argued that these books are not science fiction at all but simply imaginative works of literature that make some statements about the destiny of mankind. Indeed, a science-fiction buff might reject them as lacking the usual conventions of the trade—space travel, telepathy, or ray guns. It is true they were not written as science fiction, but as they express some innovation in science and technology, some change in the natural order or the effects of such change, the label fits.

The term science fiction is fairly new. It is attributed to Hugo Gernsbeck, who founded the first radio magazine in 1908 and who later inserted what he liked to call *scientifiction* into his other publications, such as *Science and Invention.* It was soon simplified to science fiction. From the 1920s on most science-fiction writers of standing and virtually all without standing were first published in such magazines as *Amazing Stories* and *Astounding Stories.* But like Gresham's law of money, the bad drove out the good. What chiefly developed was the 'space opera'—plots that were lifted from cheap westerns and detective stories and transferred to outer space. All that was needed was a flying human or an attenuated Martian for a plot to be called science fiction. The paperback pulps soon added a mixture of horror and perversion to create what has been called the 'Mesozoic' period of science fiction—the Age of Monsters. Today reasonably respectable magazines such as *Galaxy* and *Analog* can be enjoyed by the average science-fiction fan. Many others, however, rate only a glance of incredulous horror. As well as the utmost crudity in format and illustration, they reflect their readership by advertisements of all forms of the occult. The writing and invention are unspeakable: 'Mr Frederic Troff looked down at himself and choked back a cry of dismay. His legs were on backwards and his toes pointed to the rear.' 'She dropped her gaze to the box . . . Inside was her own head.'

The major writers of the period between 1920 and 1950 wrote chiefly *science* fiction; that is, the emphasis was on science. With the exception of the works of Olaf Stapledon, Edwin Balmer and Richard Wylie, Robert Heinlein, Karel Capek, and a few others, little remains except the short stories that now turn up in anthologies. But there is no doubt that writers such as these prepared a small but enthusiastic body of readers for great and continuing technological change. From the 1950s on this writing became more and more science *fiction* and fiction of a speculative kind. Yes, we could travel to the moon, *but* did we have a right to take our wars and our divisions and our diseases to another planet? Yes, we could release atomic energy, *but* what would be the effect upon our culture? Yes, we could drop a hydrogen bomb, *but* what would be the effects of radiation?

The writers of science fiction in the fifties and early sixties appeared to agree with Walter de la Mare that 'The future is easier to cope with than the past, but it may also be more important than the present.' In book after book the writers appear to be acting as the conscience of the human race. The future is not a great unknown; it will be exactly based on what man does in the present. E. B. White in 'The Morning of the Day They Did It', in his *Second Tree from the Corner* (1954), describes the devasting results of trying to prevent war by establishing the SPCA—Space Platform for Checking Aggression. In John Wyndham's *Consider Her Ways* (1961) a woman of the twenty-first century, living in what most of us would consider a sterile world, argues convincingly about the effects of the twentieth-century concept of romance (woman's place is in the home using consumer goods) upon twentieth-century woman. When the world's food supply is destroyed in John Christopher's *The Death of Grass* (1957), the question is asked: Do we kill to protect and provide for our families? What price civilized behaviour in the face of disaster? In *The Martian Chronicles* (1950), Ray Bradbury effectively uses almost every gimmick of pulp science fiction to state, in a weird and fantastic way, that until we conquer ourselves we are not ready to conquer another planet.

Science fiction for children cannot be separated from its parent body any more than children's books in general can be separated from the mainstream of literature. The same rules hold. However, the young of today are more sophisticated than the young of the past and are often more knowledgeable about science than adults. Thus their 'willing suspension of disbelief' has to be based on more realism. Much science fiction for children seems to have stemmed from the sensational magazines for boys that were published in the late nineteenth and early twentieth century. Stories of fantastic inventions and interplanetary wars were the general fare in such periodicals as *Boys' Magazine*, *Union Jack*, *Boys' Friend*, and *Boys' Herald*. If they lacked scientific plausibility, they made up for this in pace and action. All too many stories written for children today are not only poorly conceived and badly written but downright dull. As a youthful reader once pointed out, they are poor fiction and bad science. In 1947 Robert Heinlein churned out *Rocket Ship Galileo* in which a scientist and three high-school students go to the moon in a 'do-it-yourself' rocket constructed in the backyard. Only one parent questions the project. In his *Farmer in the Sky* (1950) a space ship is hit by a meteor and the young hero plugs the hole with his jacket until the great ship can be repaired. Gary Turner in *Stranger from the Depth* (1967) envisions a lizard man who has been preserved for a hundred million years and then comes to life, a dubious idea that has been used about fifty times.

The volume of publishing in this field for children is still fairly slight and both the best and the worst of it edge more towards fantasy than realism. William Pène Du Bois's *The Twenty-One Balloons* (1947) tells of a professor's balloon trip to a fabulous island built on a diamond mine, and his *Peter Graves* (1950) describes the hilarious efforts of an eccentric inventor and a young boy to find some practical uses for a peculiar new metal called 'furloy' (mission impossible). Donald Suddaby's *Lost Men in the Grass* (1940) relates the chilling adventures of a shrunken man in the insect world. These books are marvellous fabrications, but like all good fantasy they are firmly based on authentic detail and concrete description. They are science fiction because they are based on some form of motivational machinery other than the supernatural—so much so that the reader can say 'half of this story is true and the other half might very well have happened' (which cannot be said of fantasy). Undisciplined science-fiction fantasies for children are numerous. A little worse than typical are the books by André Norton (*Star Man's Son, Star Rangers, Star Gate*), which concern atomic devastation and are dependent for atmosphere on the creation of indefinite primitive worlds, on weird, ugly, and distorted creatures and the casual use of odd words and unpronounceable names—Tolkien on a 'trip'.

A plausible use of science can be found in the books by the French writer Paul Berna—translated into English as *Threshold of the Stars* (1958) and *Continent in the Sky* (1959). The former describes the life of a group of school children who live on a French space station where they learn lunar geography and think they have discovered a group of saboteurs. They do not get to the moon, but the impression is conveyed that some day they will. Children are able to absorb a good deal about modern science and know, for example, that man cannot live on the other planets without oxygen. The best realistic science fiction for children respects such knowledge. Paul Berna in *Continent in the Sky* overcomes the problem by establishing a plant on the moon that generates an artificial atmosphere capable of supporting human life. Donald Suddaby in *Prisoners of Saturn* (1957) invents an even more ingenious device. Here the Saturnians have created an energy screen that allows human life to exist as well as their own race.

The most ambitious and successful science-fiction project for children has been John Christopher's trilogy—*The White Mountains* (1967), *The City of Gold and Lead* (1967), and *The Pool of Fire* (1968)—about three boys of the future who help to save earth from the domination of the alien Masters. In spite of some anachronisms and careless writing, the cities of the Tripods and defeated earth struggling back to scientific knowledge are carefully enough described to make an absorbing if conventional futuristic science-fiction tale. There are also books for the young that use the conventional science-fiction techniques casually and concentrate on the conflicts that arise because of changing or differing values in various societies: Poul Anderson's *The High Crusade* (1960), Alan Nourse's *Raiders from the Rings* (1962), Robert Heinlein's *Starship Troopers* (1959) and *Podkayne of Mars* (1963).

Science fiction for children is not literature; there is as yet no novel in the field that welds scientific fact and/or sociological speculation with strong literary qualities to give it universal appeal. Nothing yet matches the best in other genres, such as fantasy and the realistic or historical novel for children. This may be because writers of science fiction are more concerned with themes than with their presentation. But if science-fiction writing for children is facile, it is readable (i.e. clear and straightforward) and it seems to cast a hallucinogenic spell on many young readers. Indeed, science fiction may have found its most appreciative audience among the young.

The reasons for this are as diverse as the literature itself and the interests of young people, and several are applicable to the varied reading interests of adults. The sensational aspect of science fiction appeals as undisciplined, lurid fantasy has always appealed. Its simplicity is also attractive—science fiction makes small demands intellectually and stylistically. Then there is its 'scientificness'. Science not only pervades our lives but it is also an 'in' thing: it is used to sell everything from bread to hair spray to soap flakes and in a quantitative sense it is matched in mass-media advertising only by sexual symbolism. It also satisfies a desire for quick and easy access to information. Much of the information it imparts is no more than the popular understanding of the week-end magazines, but in the *scientific* science-fiction novel, one that has an imaginative view of scientific possibilities, a good deal of information can be picked up—an explanation of the Moebius strip or an introduction to the principles of William of Ockham—in the way that a certain amount of history can be gleaned from an authentic historical novel.

All of these reasons pale beside the one that has made modern science fiction somewhat of a cult among the young. It is the only literature being written today that is making large statements about our transitional society, and it often does this either by issuing dire Savonarola-like warnings or by dressing up polemics with hilarious or deliberately shocking divertissements. When it does this it speaks clearly, although in allegory, of the psychic structure of our time.

It seems fairly clear that the youth of today suffer a disillusionment with the present order that in many cases is understandable. They look around them and see war, intolerance, racism, poverty, injustice, and also that very little is being done about these things. There is a two-fold reaction to this disillusionment. The first is a desire for a radically different world and it finds satisfaction in the uncluttered statement, the instant solution, the black or white decision. Adults turn to realism or pragmatism when faced with complexities—the slow, solid way of working out difficulties. A generation enamoured of the sensational and the simplistic sees only that rationality betokens failure. In *A Canticle for Leibowitz*

(1959) man does it again—brings about an atomic holocaust not once, but twice. The solution? Flight (for a few) to another planet where presumably things will be better. *Flowers for Algernon* (1958), made into a movie called *Charly*, represents another aspect of disillusionment—the 'put on' about the adult world. Charly quite happily goes back to his moronic state when he finds that his artificially stimulated high I.Q. causes dissent and suspicion among people who treated him kindly or jokingly in his former state.

The second reaction of young people to the disillusionment they feel is that if the situation cannot change, human nature should. Science fiction also suggests this possibility; however, it does not do so in the humanistic tradition of the gradual development of character. Like the old Greek nature myths, science fiction is little concerned with the complexities of human character. As Edmund Crispin, a leading British commentator on science fiction, has pointed out:

The characters in a science fiction story are usually treated rather as representatives of their species than as individuals in their own right. They are matchstick men and matchstick women for the reason that if they were not, the anthropocentric habit of our culture would cause us, in reading, to give too much attention to them and too little to the non-human forces which constitute the important remainder of the dramatis personae...

Whether it is Orpheus lost in the underworld or Pierre Boulle's astronaut doomed to die on the moon, we are sad for mankind rather than for an individual. Instead of showing human beings in relationship with another human being, science fiction tends to show human beings in relation to a thing—an alien, a monster, a machine, a new form of society. The *deus ex machina* of science fiction—a black cloud, a monolith, a robot or an alien—represents a higher controlling force to which man should aspire. While the western humanist clings to the fear of the dehumanizing effect of the machine, the young are rebelling against the old-line human machines while taking the mechanical machine for granted and even admiring its 'cool' precision.

The American novelist and critic Leslie Fiedler, in an article in *Partisan Review* (Fall, 1965), borrows a popular S/F term in describing the young of today as the 'new mutants' who are living at the beginning of the post-human era and to whom machines are an extension of themselves. Science fiction often appears to be saying that earthlings are unequal to the problems of human life. Back in 1950 Isaac Asimov in *I, Robot* had a leading robot psychologist say to a reporter from the Interplanetary Press:

To you, a robot is a robot. Gears and metal; electricity and positrons. Mind and iron. Human-made. If necessary, human-destroyed. But you haven't worked with them, so you don't know. They're a cleaner, better breed than we are.

Science fiction's presentation of man's need to change his own nature is also evident in two books by Robert Heinlein, written a decade apart, that are quite characteristic. It is perhaps significant that the earlier of these, *Red Planet* (1949), was written specifically for the teenage reader while the later adult novel, *Stranger in a Strange Land* (1961), has such a following among young people that it has almost produced a cult—perhaps because it is a futuristic myth whose theme is the emergence of the 'new mutants'. But Heinlein develops this theme out of the earlier book.

In *Red Planet* the central human character is a boy, Jim Marlowe, one of the early colonists of Mars. He has befriended a Martian—or, as it seems, a rather primitive species of Martian—called a 'bouncer'. This creature, which Jim has named Willis, is quite endearing but it also possesses some amazing talents, among them an ability to mimic to perfection any conversation, music, or other sound it has heard.

Besides the form of Martian life represented by Willis, there is another kind: creatures twelve feet or more in height with three legs and eyes on stalks. But the reader is never conscious of any grotesquerie in the appearance or manner of these creatures; or if their appearance seems grotesque, their manner does not. They are always dignified and calm, in contrast to the humans of the story who are perpetually quarrelling among themselves. The most meaningful form of relationship on Mars is the 'sharing of water', and the Martians spend a great deal of their time sitting around passively 'growing together'. Only Jim Marlowe and Doctor Macrae, representing respectively youthful idealism and crusty wisdom, are capable of any kind of rapport with the Martians, who exist, we discover, on a higher evolutionary level than human beings. In *Red Planet* the degrees of good and evil in the various human characters, and of their success, are related to their ability or inability to appreciate the special powers of the non-humans and to identify with them. In this book, written some two decades ago, we have the first appearance of the myth of Fiedler's 'post-human' world.

In *Stranger in a Strange Land* Heinlein carries the fascination with the human relating to the non-human a step further, to the point where its relevance to contemporary youth can be seen more clearly. In this later book the Martians are off stage, as it were, but their influence is even more inescapable than in the *Red Planet* (where they resemble a *deus ex machina*): the power of Martian life operates through a human 'mutant'. The central character of *Stranger in a Strange Land* is Valentine Michael Smith who, soon after his birth, survived the crash of an early expedition from Earth to Mars and was raised by Martians after the death of his parents. Smith returns to Earth speaking only the Martian language and with some of those typical Martian faculties we were introduced to in the earlier novel. Like Willis, Smith has an astonishingly retentive memory; he also has the ability to make objects or people vanish. Like the Martians, Smith spends a great deal of time in a seemingly comatose state in which complex mental issues are resolved. These elements of Martian life, and also the water ceremony and the 'growing together', are all transported without alteration from *Red Planet* to *Stranger in a Strange Land.* But in the later book Heinlein introduces us to a new and significant Martian trait, the ability to 'grok'. This is supposed to be inexplicable in any human language, but from the context of the story it seems to be a kind of total comprehension, an understanding that encompasses and consumes its object. This is literally as well as figuratively true: the final stage in 'grokking' someone is to consume his body after his physical death.

The largest part of *Stranger in a Strange Land* is concerned with a struggle between high government officials and Smith's mentor, the writer Juval Harshaw, over Smith's supposed rights to ownership of Mars. But rather abruptly (although there are hints of the change early in the story), the direction of the narrative is altered midway. Smith undertakes to set up a kind of religion in which humans learn the powers of Martian life and how to evolve onto the higher planes of existence that Martians are capable of. But it is not a religion in any usual sense, as Jill, Smith's wife and his first convert, explains:

'It is a church, in every legal and moral sense. But we're not trying to bring people to God; that's a contradiction, you can't say it in Martian. We're not trying to save souls, souls can't be lost. We're not trying to get people to have faith, what we offer is not faith but truth—truth they can check. Truth for here-and-now, truth as matter of fact as an ironing board and as useful as bread, so practical that it can make war and hunger and violence and hate as unnecessary as . . . well, as clothes in the Nest. But they have to learn Martian. That's the hitch—finding people honest enough to believe what they see, willing to work hard—it is hard—to learn the language it must be taught in. This truth can't be stated in English any more than Beethoven's Fifth can be.'

Stranger in a Strange Land effectively approximates a society to which the young aspire—the new irrational spirit, the ideal of passive withdrawal into a Nirvana-like state. It ends with a vision of a new society or non-society founded by the neo-Martians. There is even a suggestion that the emulation by humans of Martian ways will reach such a degree that the 'new mutants' will be able to beat the Martians at their own game. Those humans who are incapable of grasping the qualities of the superior Martian culture will be eradicated; a new paradise, based on Martian perfection, will emerge.

Frank Herbert's *Dune* (1965) is another recent science-fiction novel in which science takes second place to mythology: the heroes live in caves, battle dragons, kill with swords and poisoned rings. It has a strong link with *Stranger in a Strange Land.* The new society here is based on the rise of a saviour who has mental powers beyond the normal. On a dry planet the sharing of water becomes not only a necessity of life but a religious ritual and so a form of communication that keeps a desperate band of people together.

In both *Stranger in a Strange Land* and *Dune,* the sects that develop are alien to the mores of Western culture. In other books, ranging in time from Olaf Stapledon's *Odd John* (1936) to John Wyndham's *The Midwich Cuckoos* (1957), the development of super-humans is emphasized, and in still others, such as Naomi Mitchison's *Memoirs of a Space Woman* (1946), all alien societies, even a butterfly world, are deemed worthy of study by advanced humans. All seem to prophesy the extension of the human into the non-human—or at least into a mutant.

But both *Stranger in a Strange Land* and *Dune* have characteristics that set them apart from other science fiction. They are extremely long books—over 400 pages—and they are ambitiously conceived: their mythology is worked out in almost fanatical detail. Compared with these novels, most other science fiction can be described as 'hit and run'—making a point with as little detail as possible.

If science fiction cannot be defined, it perhaps can be characterized. It is a transferred fairy tale with Mars as a never-never land; with the formidable scientist replacing the powerful 'old man' of the woods and scientific ingenuity replacing the supernatural. It allows an adult to reread about, and so to re-create, the monsters and strange events that he imagined as a child in dealing with the unknown oppression and the wonders he was surrounded by. It allows the young reader to find the large concepts of the fairy tale (good versus evil, life versus death, love versus hate) applied more directly to the world he sees around him. If this were not so, why would both children and adults read *Gulliver's Travels* and watch *Star Trek?*

Frequently condemned for its lack of style and characterization, and its simplistic approach to the great problems of existence, science fiction can nevertheless reveal a great moral if one reads it as allegory or myth. Mary Shelley's *Frankenstein,* written in 1817, is indeed a lesson in terror, but not in the Hollywood monster sense: it unveils the terror of man's failure to understand with his heart what he has created with his mind.

Science fiction has already provided young people with the prototypes of the dress they so avidly adopt today. The miniskirt, the boots, the belts, the talismans, the earrings for men are straight out of illustrated science-fiction magazines from the twenties through the forties. For those who are of an age between childhood and adulthood, science fiction also projects an irresistible vision. It can be receptive, as are the young, to a view that sees the earth itself as a new kind of planet. With its gadgetry and prophecy, its travel to past or future by spaceship, space warp, dreams, drugs, and the fourth dimension, science fiction often succeeds in looking at the old universe with new eyes.

If science fiction were to be divided and discussed under such headings as Early Space Voyages, Inventions, Discoveries and Predictions, Space the Conquerable, and Man and Machine, one theme would connect them all—man and himself. Science fiction does not provide answers; it offers a weapon rather than a philosophy. Ray Bradbury in his preface to *The Martian*

Chronicles gives this explanation: 'Science fiction is a wonderful hammer; I intend to use it when and if necessary, to break a few shins or knock a few heads, in order to make people leave people alone.'

[1969]

Fiction for teenagers

NAT HENTOFF

While I was working on my first novel for teenagers, *Jazz Country*, several writer friends tried to dissuade me from the project. Writing for small children, I was instructed, can be an art. Consider Maurice Sendak. But to try deliberately to reach an audience from twelve to sixteen is at best a craft, and a craft of a distinctly low order. No *serious* writer would expend creative energy on such a self-limiting assignment. Any teenager really involved with literature as pleasure has reached into the adult shelves. What were *you* reading when you were in your teens? Thinking back to that far distant country, I remembered enthusiasms for Arthur Koestler, Dostoevsky, Thomas Wolfe, and *A Portrait of the Artist As a Young Man*. See? Go write a novel, period, and if it's worth their time, young readers will get to it too.

I was persuaded they were right, but I went ahead anyway. I had not tried fiction before, and I thought this might be a trial run for a novel for grownups to follow. One such, *Call the Keeper*, did follow, and another will be published next year. But I am also involved in a second novel for teenagers, and now my serious writer friends are even more scornful than before. OK, now you know you can write adult fiction, or at least you know you can get it published. So why waste more time on child craft?

I had admitted to them that *Jazz Country* had indeed been diluted because of my preconceptions of what ought to be left out of books for 12+ (as the dust jackets identify their putative range). In the book I'd explored some of the fierce ambiguities in current relations—or rather, widening distances—between blacks and whites; but the language of the novel would not have offended the most zealous inheritors of Anthony Comstock's mission. Nor did the book deal with sex or drugs or anything else, except black nationalism, that might have alarmed the more insulated librarians.

Yet, diluted as it was, the book did reach what seemed to me a surprisingly large number of the young. Some wrote to me, and I met more in schools—ghetto and white 'advantaged'. My visits to those schools were hardly unqualified triumphs. Criticisms were sharp and frequent, both of me and of other writers of books for 12+. There were many more hang-ups in being young, I was told repeatedly, than were even intimated in most of the books they'd seen.

I began to read what other writers in the field were doing and agreed with the young critics that little of relevance is being written about what it is to be young now. There are occasional works of fiction about the past, about other countries, about the riddling truths in fantasy which do attract and hold some young readers; but the challenge is to make contact with the sizeable number of the young who seldom read anything for pleasure because they are not in it.

For the past two years, in addition to these school visits I have been asking others of the young what they read and what they would like to see in books. I start at home, where there are two teenagers who know, it sometimes seems, hundreds more. And during the research for various articles I do on education, I also bring up in conversations with adolescents the subject of reading. I have no statistics to bear out what has become an increasingly strong impression, but it seems to me that this generation of the young reads much less often outside school than mine did.

Granted that Marshall McLuhan is given to stating his 'probes', as he calls his theories, in hyperbolic terms, but my casual research does bear out his contention that 'television has created a huge gap between generations, between those who learned to read and write before TV, and those who came to TV first.' The TV generation, he asserts, wants 'depth and involvement' because it is attuned to an outer environment 'charged with messages'. Substantial sections of it are therefore in rebellion against the print-oriented ways of acquiring knowledge and pleasure. Or, if you like, pleasure through knowledge.

Of course there are exceptions, but most of the young I meet are more stimulated by television and by the pounding gestalt of tribal lyrics and electronics in the rock groups whose records they buy than they are by books. In ghetto classrooms, children who have been turned off reading—by teachers who have turned themselves off from the children—are bottomless repositories of radio commercials and song lyrics. The middle-class youngsters I see do their homework more or less, but once *those* books are shut they generally prefer the record player and television set as ways of involvement.

Is it possible, then, to reach these children of McLuhan in that old-time medium, the novel? I believe it is, because their primary concerns are only partially explored in the messages they get from their music and are diverted rather than probed on television. If a book is relevant to those concerns, not didactically but in creating textures of experience which teenagers can recognize as germane to their own, it can merit their attention.

One such book, written by a seventeen-year-old girl from Tulsa, is Susan Hinton's *The Outsiders*. Any teenager, no matter what some of his textbooks say, knows that this is decidedly not a classless society, and *The Outsiders* examines the social and physical warfare between a group of slum youngsters, 'the greasers', and the progeny of the upper middle class in Tulsa, 'the Socs'. Miss Hinton, with an astute ear and a lively sense of the restless rhythms of the young, also explores the tenacious loyalties on both sides of the class divide. Her plot is factitious at times, but the book has been widely read among heterogeneous sections of the young because it stimulates their own feelings and questionings about class and differing life-styles.

Another book which will, I think, have a long active life in libraries in diverse neighborhoods is Paula Fox's *How Many Miles to Babylon?* This one is marked 10+, but it transcends any such confines. Miss Fox is an authentic novelist who can project herself into mind of a ten-year-old black boy in Brooklyn with an unsentimental but deeply affecting understanding of what it is to be alone though loved, frightened though reasonably brave. Unlike most fiction for the young which is set in the ghetto, the book is not in the least homiletic. The boy James is himself, not a précis of sociological studies. And the ghetto is seen through him:

He walked quickly. He was afraid of this street—the old brown houses were all shut up, boards nailed across the doors, windows all broken and nothing to see behind the windows except the dark rooms that always looked like night. There were piles of things on the street in front of the houses but each day there was a little less. The baby carriage he had seen last Friday was gone. The old stove was still there. Too big to carry, he guessed. Where had the people gone? One day he had seen a man up on one of the stoops kicking at the boarded-up door. 'My things, my things . . .' he had cried.

I mention only two books because this is not intended as a survey of actuality writing for children. So much is not being written about that I prefer to focus on what is missing. To many children, for one example, school is a place of fear. In a sophomore class in a New York high school which is not known to be rigidly academic, a boy bites his lip to keep from crying because he has received a 67 in a math test. Will he be able to get into a 'good' college if this keeps up? And if he doesn't, what will become of him? Is he already a failure?

A high school girl writes to the New York *Times* Sunday magazine:

I'm wasting these years of preparation. I'm not learning what I want to learn. . . . I don't care about the feudal system. I want to know about life. I want to think and read. . . .

My life is a whirlpool. I'm caught up in it, but I'm not conscious of it. I'm what you *call living, but somehow I can't find life. Days go by in an instant. I feel nothing accomplished in that instant. So maybe I got an A on that composition I worked on for three hours, but when I get it back I find it means nothing. It's a letter* you *use to keep me going.*

Every day I come in well prepared. Yet I dread every class; my stomach tightens and I sit tense. I drink coffee morning, noon and night. At night, after my homework, I lie in bed and wonder if I've really done it all. Is there something I've forgotten? . . . I wonder what I'm doing here. I feel phony. . . . You wonder about juvenile delinquents. If I ever become one, I'll tell you why it will be. I feel cramped. I feel like I'm locked in a coffin and can't move or breathe. There's no air or light. All I see is blackness and I've got to burst. Sometimes I feel maybe something will come along. Something has to or I'm not worth anything. My life is worth nothing. It's enclosed in a few buildings. . . . It goes no further.

And yet this far from uncommon sense of suffocation throughout the long years in which the young are 'prepared' is muted, if it is present at all, in fiction about school life.

Outside school, there are anxieties and moral conundrums endemic to today's youth which are only glancingly acknowledged in books about them. For a young man near draft age, what is courage in America in 1967? Does the state have the right to make him kill, and be killed, in a distant war which many in this country, including perhaps his parents, oppose? Is it cowardly of him to stay in college as long as he can? Is it cowardly or courageous to resist the draft or to apply for exemption as a conscientious objector? Is it the war he's against or the possibility of his death in it? These are central, agonizing questions and should quicken and complicate the imaginations of those who write fiction for the young. But so far as I know, no novel about this dilemma exists.

There are the complex temptations and fears about sex in a time of an alleged sexual revolution. Increasingly virginity has to be justified, but stubbornly it is by far more girls than the rhetoric of the young would indicate. Where is the line between love and sex being used? If sex is so natural an act, why do so many doubts and guilts persist? What of the small but growing number of parents who are advising adolescent daughters of the most effective ways of avoiding pregnancy? Do I wish my parents were like that, and if I don't, what *is* it I'm afraid of? Them or me? And for young males, 'making out' in sex is becoming as insistent a pressure as keeping grades high. And if you don't 'make out', what's wrong with you? Are you already a failure in *that* too?

What of the failures of adults? Remarkably absent from most fiction for the young is any real density of perception of the ways in which they look at and react to the adults with whom they live. The corroded marriages; the chronic, dreary lies; the business 'deals' and income-tax inventions; the squabbles about money; the smallness of 'grownup' satisfactions. I know of no fiction for the young that convincingly digs into the effects of the high incidence of divorce on shifting families: that perpetual stranger in the house, the stepfather; the varieties of ambivalent obligations to the real but outside father; the half-brothers and half-sisters who have to be coped with. Contemporary American family life is full of broken and loose ends, but where are the books about it in which teenagers can recognize mazes similar to their own?

The list of missed opportunities to involve the young in fiction about them also includes the microcosm of the hippie. Hippies not only are increasing in numbers, but their methods of encapsulation fascinate more and more of those who do not make the leap into inner space. At least not yet. What are those islands like? There are perils as well as arcane adventures in these enclaves as traffic in pot and drugs becomes big business not to be left entirely to amateur free-enterprisers. What happens to some of the ingenuous runaways to these Casbahs of the flower people? What is there to *do* between inner trips? How organic are the extended communities? What are the frictions inside them? The Haight-Ashbury hippies held a 'funeral of the Hippies', heralding the 'birth of the Free People'. But what does that mean? Are they now, as they say, really free of concern about the future? How free can you be? And what are their relations with the smouldering unfree blacks and Puerto Ricans in the neighbourhoods in which they camp?

And as for books for and about young blacks and Puerto Ricans themselves, so far non-fiction has been far more resonant of where they're at than most novels concerning the underclass. *Go Tell It on the Mountain* and *Invisible Man* will last as literature; but the ghettos have changed, and there is nothing yet in fiction, for teenagers or adults, that gets to the molten core of the rising pride in blackness among ghetto youth, the new directions of *machismo,* the thrust to build new nations within this nation, and the splintering frustrations which are baleful corollaries of that thrust.

Having projected some of the possibilities in fiction for the young, I am left with the question of whether writing for teenagers need be self-limiting. There is no reason it has to be if the writer can free himself of his own strictures concerning what books for 12+ ought to leave out in terms of language and subject matter. That means—and my serious-writer friends were correct—writing a novel, period. The conflict then will not be inside the writer but between him and certain librarians and certain editors in the juvenile departments of publishing houses—at this stage, probably most librarians and most editors of books for the young. If they resist language and themes which the writer knows are essential if his book is to be real to the young, then he will find out if he has indeed written a novel, period. For if he has, it will interest adult readers too and can be published as part of the adult trade list. Adolescents will find the book if it speaks to them.

In one junior high school I visited, a librarian took me into her office and cautioned me not to be 'too free and outspoken' with the youngsters I was about to meet. 'They can absorb only so much,' she said. 'They have to grow into what life is all about. And I should tell you, they're not very sophisticated. They don't read much, or well.' For the next two hours I was hit with a barrage of questions, opinions, and counter-arguments about sex, pot, race, capitalism, Vietnam, religion, violence, non-violence, revolution, black power. I've rarely been involved in so sustainedly intense an exchange of views, and at the end I was exhausted because they had forced me to look much harder at the consistency of some of my own convictions than I had for some time.

The librarian was unhappy at a number of turns the conversation had taken, and after a peremptory good-bye she stalked off. 'Hey,' one of the younger children said as I started to leave, 'have you dug this?' He pulled from his pocket a beat-up paperback copy of *The Autobiography of Malcolm X*.

[1967]

The present state of English children's literature

JOHN ROWE TOWNSEND

To write about the state of children's books in England is a daunting task for any one person. The trouble is not so much the size and complexity of the subject; one can deal with that by admitting frankly that a single article cannot cover everything and by concentrating on what seems at present to be the essentials. It is rather that there are widely differing viewpoints, and a picture that is true from one of them may look quite false from another.

The division, generally unacknowledged, is between what I call the 'book' people and the 'child' people. Authors, publishers, and critics are professionally involved with books and are bound to look first at the book, because that is their job. Teachers and parents are concerned with the total development of the child, in which the book is only one element. For them, naturally, the child is in the middle of the picture; they ask what the book is doing for *him*, not for the author or the publisher or the map of children's literature. Somewhere in the middle ground are the librarians. In Britain, at least, I would say that public librarians tend by their professional training to be book people; school librarians tend by their professional training to be child people. At present some of the child people are disagreeing loudly with the book people.

It is just possible to imagine a person who could reconcile the viewpoints and make a single, balanced, all-round assessment. He would be an author who was also a publisher, a critic, and a bookseller. He would study children's literature on an international scale; he would have at least a dozen children of his own, of assorted tastes and intelligence; he would spend part of his year working in public and school libraries, part teaching children, part sitting beside them in school and playing beside them in the playground. He would need a fifty-hour day, a ten-day week, a hundred-week year. He does not, of course, exist.

Put in the shoes of this paragon, I can only declare my own interest and viewpoint and do my best. I am a writer and reviewer and review-editor of books for children. I am, willy-nilly, in the bookmen's camp. True, I have three children, and this might seem—as it certainly seems to me—to make me in some degree a child person. But my children are nonstop book-gobblers; I am always told that they are not typical and don't really count. I shall try, writing as a bookman, to give a brief account of some of the best contemporary British authors and their books; to say something about the economics of writing and publishing 'quality' books for children; to consider (with an eye on the child people) whether we are really producing the books that British children want and need, rather than those we think fit for them, and how far we are equipped for actually getting the book to the child.

To begin, then, with the books we have. My firm belief is that we are doing well; that British children's books are better today than ever before, and that, adding to them the growing number of first-class foreign books now being brought into the country, we are offering our children unprecedented wealth.

I am concerned here with British rather than foreign books, and especially with fiction. The improvement has been spectacular, and has mainly been since the mid-century. Between the wars our children's books were in an indifferent state. There were, it is true, some highlights—the Winnie-the-Pooh books, *Mary Poppins*, John Masefield's *Midnight Folk*, the Arthur Ransome *Swallows and Amazons* series, Tolkien's *Hobbit*, a few others—but the general level was low, and the most characteristic productions were anaemic pseudo-fairy tales and talking-animal books for young children, and weary formula-type school and adventure stories for older ones. The Second World War and the years just after it were, inevitably, rather barren periods. Though a few able prewar veterans like Geoffrey Trease and Noel Streatfeild were and still are writing, the renaissance came in the early fifties with the emergence of a new wave of writers headed by Rosemary Sutcliff, William Mayne, and Philippa Pearce.

The historical novel for children had been rid of a good deal of its old gadzookery in the 1930s by Geoffrey Trease (whose radical anti-romantic Robin Hood novel *Bows Against the Barons*, first published in 1934, has lately been successfully reissued). In Rosemary Sutcliff's hands it has reached a new level of seriousness and of what I can only call contemporaneity: that is, the sense that history is here and now; that people in the past were real people coping with universal problems rather than picturesque figures in fancy-dress charades. I do not think Miss Sutcliff has yet surpassed her sequence set in Roman Britain: *The Eagle of the Ninth* (1954), *The Silver Branch* (1957), and *The Lantern Bearers* (1959), with *Dawn Wind* (1961) in the position of a sequel and *The Mark of the Horse Lord* (1965) standing strongly apart.

William Mayne is a remarkable writer in whom quantity and quality have gone happily together. In fifteen years he has written something like forty books. He is still quite a young man and shows every sign of eventually reaching the hundred mark. In the mid-1950s he revived the school story—in Britain a literary form of respectable antiquity and past achievement—with four stories set in a cathedral choir school, of which the first and best was *A Swarm in May* (1955). He wrote too a series of spectacular treasure hunts, in which strange treasures were sought and found in mysterious, complicated ways. In the present decade his best book among those I know (and I will admit that I have not read all forty) is *Earthfasts* (1966), in which, uncharacteristically, he makes use of the supernatural: too often a cheap and easy device in children's books, but here rehabilitated by the highly individual Mayne treatment.

Philippa Pearce is a contrast to Mayne in productivity, for in a writing career of similar length to his she has written only a handful of books. But in quality she is his equal. Some good judges indeed claim her as Britain's best living children's-book writer, and personally I rank *Tom's Midnight Garden* (1958) as the outstanding British children's book of the last quarter-century. *Minnow on the Say* (1955) is, by coincidence, a somewhat Mayne-like treasure hunt; *A Dog So Small* (1962) explores a child's longing for a pet and the difficulty of reconciling his obsession with outside reality; and in *The Children of the House* (1968) Miss Pearce has developed from a manuscript by Brian Fairfax-Lucy a strange, sad, and obviously true story of the underprivileged rich.

These were, to my mind, the new leaders of the 1950s, and I would bracket with them C. S. Lewis, whose seven 'Narnia' books appeared between 1950 and 1956, and also Mary Norton; for although Miss Norton's first book was some years earlier her most memorable work, *The Borrowers*, and its three successors came out between 1952 and 1961.

In the 1960s a further wave of writers has emerged. The most notable names are those of Alan Garner, Leon Garfield, and K. M. Peyton. Garner began, with *The Weirdstone of Brisingamen* (1960) and *The Moon of Gomrath* (1963), as a writer of wild and whirling fantasies in which people claimed to detect strong resemblances to J. R. R. Tolkien. His work developed strongly with *Elidor* (1965), a many-layered book which could be read as a straight adventure story by quite young children, but differently and symbolically by older readers in the light of the

Grail legend and *The Golden Bough.* Then in 1967 came *The Owl Service.* This story, in which the power of ancient myth breaks violently through into a modern situation, has been discussed by all, hated by a few, and universally acknowledged as brilliant; and it scored a unique double by winning this year's Carnegie Medal and also the *Guardian* award for children's fiction.

Leon Garfield's three books, *Jack Holborn* (1964), *Devil-in-the-Fog* (1966), and *Smith* (1967), are vivid, violent, and exuberantly masculine. They are no-holds-barred adventure stories, but are also something more, for they are constantly at grips with problems of identity and of good and evil. All three are set in the eighteenth century and written in a style that vaguely suggests that period but is really pure Garfield.

K. M. Peyton, like Garfield, whom she resembles in no other way, is a writer whose books are set in the past but who is not an historical novelist. Though she has a strong feeling for time and place her true concern is always for people, their individual complexities and their relationships. Her two latest books, *Thunder in the Sky* (1966), and *Flambards* (1967), are undoubtedly her best.

But in picking out these few names I risk obscuring what I think is probably the most encouraging feature at present, and that is the high *general* level of books being put out by the leading publishers. Rosemary Sutcliff, although in my view she is in a class of her own, is not by any means our only historical novelist of quality. Among many others are Ronald Welch, Philip Rush, Cynthia Harnett, Hester Burton, C. Walter Hodges, and the late Henry Treece (whose last book, *The Dream-time,* set in the Stone Age, was a close runner-up for the latest Carnegie Medal and would surely have won it against any competition other than that of *The Owl Service*). And on the sidelines is the uproarious unhistory of Joan Aiken who writes about an England-that-never-was, with King James III on the throne and the Hanoverians plotting his downfall.

A few years ago I was lamenting that so much talent was devoted to battles long ago and so little, relatively, to the novel of contemporary life. This complaint could still be made, but not now so forcibly. The writers of modern-life novels—a phrase by which I do not mean to imply only heavy social realism—are not so obviously in the front rank, but they are coming on. Barbara Willard, John Verney, Anne Barrett, Catherine Cookson, and Roy Brown are among the writers with good work to their credit, and I suppose I can claim to have made some contribution myself in this field. A welcome transfusion has come from Australian writers, possibly outside my strict terms of reference but too good to omit in this context; they include Ivan Southall, Nan Chauncy, H. F. Brinsmead, Joan Phipson, and Patricia Wrightson.

In fantasy, where traditionally British writers have excelled, the 1960s have not quite matched the work of C. S. Lewis and Mary Norton in the fifties. Borderlines are, as always, hard to draw, and the best work of the sixties has been rather on the frontiers of this category. There is not much in common, except quality of imagination, between the alarming worlds of Alan Garner and the nostalgic ones of Helen Cresswell's *The Piemakers* (1967) and *The Signposters* (1968). Lucy Boston's *The Sea Egg* (1967) is, however, in the mainstream of the best English fantasy and fully maintains the standard of her 'Green Knowe' stories. In science fiction we have not done well; the best children's writers, it seems, have not been attracted to science fiction and the best science fiction writers have not felt impelled to write for children; but John Christopher has brightened the picture immensely with his three splendidly conceived and written novels, *The White Mountains* (1966), *The City of Gold and Lead* (1967), and *The Pool of Fire* (1968).

Picture books for young children are a thoroughly international field. In the early postwar years only Edward Ardizzone seemed in the first rank as a writer-artist, but today we also have Charles Keeping and John Burningham in this class. Brian Wildsmith is, so far as I know, an artist only, but a superb one.

Victor Ambrus and Antony Maitland have done their best work as artists on behalf of other people, but have also written and illustrated books of their own.

On the whole this is a creditable array of talent, and there is much more that I have not been able to mention. The outlook for the future, too, seems reasonably encouraging. Publishers always hold their cards close to their chests and do not disclose the financial results of their children's departments. But it is generally agreed that bringing out 'quality' books for children is profitable as well as satisfying. The reasons are roughly the same as in the United States. For one thing, children's books keep on selling 'forever', or at any rate for a few years, rather than the few months of the average adult novel. For another, the insitutional market, now believed to account for seventy-five to eighty per cent of home hardback sales, provides steadily growing support. A representative sampling of thirty-two local authorities recently made by the Library Association shows that in spite of the present severe financial problems in Britain, expenditure on children's books rose from an average of 6.145 pence per head of population in 1965-6 to 6.936 pence in 1966-7 and 7.848 pence in 1967-8. These are increases of more than ten per cent a year, and the rising trend seems likely to continue. The survey also shows spectacular variations in spending between different authorities, and my guess is that the laggards are more likely to catch up than the vanguard to slow down. Many publishers are able to sell a good proportion of their children's-book output in overseas, especially Commonwealth, markets; in addition, American and foreign-language rights in books of any merit are readily sold. Finally, a growing amount of co-operative publishing across frontiers, especially of picture books, gives increased sales and lower costs.

Financial prospects for authors are hard to assess. Antony Kamm and Boswell Taylor, in *Books for the Teacher* (1966), presented an analysis of actual production costs for a book by 'quite a well-known professional author' of the kind that 'provides the basis of the fiction section of the school library', and this analysis showed the author's total receipts, from the first and only edition of five thousand copies, to be £225. As remuneration this is derisory; it would be necessary for a man to write a book a month to maintain even a modest standard of living. But observation suggests that a great many writers of children's books do far better. The keys to financial viability for an author are a backlist of established titles and the sale of foreign, especially American, rights. The British are too reticent to quiz each other about their finances, and statistics are scanty, but two 'quality' writers, who are both professionals and both fairly prolific, are reputed to earn £5,000 and £3,000 a year respectively. If this seems unimpressive it should be remembered that British authors in general are poorly paid; an inquiry by the Society of Authors in 1965 showed that only one-sixth of them made as much as £1,050 a year. My guess is that on the average the writer of children's fiction does no worse, and perhaps better, than the adult novelist.

The question, from the point of view of the prospects for British children's literature, is not whether authors are adequately paid but whether they will continue to come forward; and there is every sign that they will. One assumes either that they can subsist on their earnings or that they have other jobs or private incomes. One assumes above all that they are not really commercially motivated. In terms of creative satisfaction there is certainly much to be said for writing for children.

Here I had better speak for myself. It seems to me that children are the most stimulating audience a writer could wish for. You are no longer much confined by the bounds of what is 'suitable'; for it is, thank goodness, well accepted by now that children will pass unharmed over material they are not yet ready to understand. You can take up your themes afresh as if the world were new, rather than return to them wearily for audiences that have heard everything already. You cannot expect children to put up with formlessness, turgidity, pomposity, emperor's clothes—but that is a discipline, not a restriction. You can expect from the reading child as much intelligence and imagination as from any adult, and far more willingness to live the story.

But . . . 'the reading child'. There goes a phrase that trips the switch; that turns me over to another viewpoint on the same situation; that cuts short my contemplation of the splendid new books, the happy publishers, the growing expenditure of libraries, the authors so well-rewarded psychologically if not financially. The reading child, yes, for him it is a wonderful world; but what about the *un*reading children, the majority?

Aidan Chambers, himself a writer, pointed out in a letter to the *Times Literary Supplement* (28 April 1966)) that 'sixty per cent of our children are unwilling readers; *can* read but don't much; have little useful access to school libraries and never go into the public ones. . . . Where writers and literature are concerned there is little for them or concern about them.'

That this gap exists is undeniable, and no one can be happy about it. Which side do we bridge it from? Mr Chambers claimed that ordinary children needed honest books about their own personal relationships and everyday lives; he blamed authors and publishers for not supplying them. Since then he has acted on his beliefs, being deeply involved in one hardback and one paperback series intended for older and reluctant readers. So far the books do not appear to have made a great impression, and it is not in fact self-evident that the 'ordinary' child wants or needs to read about ordinary lives. It could well be that books about wizards and pirates and tigers would open more windows for him. But whether or not Mr Chambers is on the right lines there are many people, especially practising teachers, who support him passionately and articulately. They care, and they have something to care about.

In the last resort one can only, in all humility, take a view and stick to it until convinced that it is wrong. There is no logical compromise. Mr Chambers and many who think like him believe that it is up to authors and publishers to cater to the unliterary majority. Authors and publishers feel, I think, sometimes guilty but nearly always helpless. They are doing their best, they say; they cannot change their ways without betraying their calling.

Mine is the view, admittedly, of a bookman. It seems to me that writers and publishers and critics, if they take their work seriously, have no real option. The writer's job is to write the best book he can, whatever it may be. The publisher's job is to publish the best book he can, whatever it may be. The critic's job is to acknowledge excellence, to see through the bad or mediocre; and if his judgements are to mean anything he must judge children's books by much the same standards as any others. The fallacy in the case put forward by the school of why-don't-you-write-for-the-ordinary-and-not-the-elite-child is, I think, this: that they start, unconsciously, from the premise that 'books are special', but then propose to rob books of the quality that makes them special. Without excellence, recreational books have no particular claim on the time and attention of children or anyone else. Cultural crusaders could more usefully turn their attention to the mass media, especially television. A book is not a form of mass communication, it is an individual thing. It speaks to one child here, to another there; it can do no more and should not try. To push or popularize books is self-defeating because it is contrary to their very nature. A book does not jostle for attention among the throng of competing attractions. A book is there, waiting, and you can get to know it if you wish.

No; I am sure the self-respecting author and publisher should not risk devaluing their work by doctoring it to suit those who would otherwise reject it (and will probably still reject it). In any case, if a good author is not doing what he sees as his best work he is not good any more, and the bad author will deservedly play him off the field. I have a feeling we would do better in England to set about reducing the numbers of nonreading children. There will always be children to whom books have little or nothing to offer, and where necessary individual defeat must be accepted. But there are, I am sure, vast numbers of children who could perfectly well enjoy the pleasures of reading if only they could be made aware of them. The machinery in this country for producing children's books is excellent, efficient, and in good working order. The machinery for introducing children to books is much inferior, and only works for those who don't need it.

Britain in fact is far behind the United States (which itself could do better than it does). Part of our trouble is that the education system has not yet taken account of children's literature. It has no status; it is not seen as being important. No university English department will look at it. Hardly any school of education runs organized courses. Teachers, while in college, are understandably concerned to pass their examinations; and when they start teaching they have a hundred and one other things to do and to know about. They can hardly be blamed for not devoting time to the professionally unrewarding study of children's books. Even teachers of English, in my experience, most often know little or nothing about modern children's literature. And it was only last week that I heard of a primary school teacher who was totally baffled by a reference to *The Borrowers*. When teachers know so little, what can be expected of parents, and what help are children likely to get?

I have no doubt that there will be improvement over the next few years, party through belated following of American trends and partly through stirrings at our own grassroots. This year an international summer school in children's literature, the first of its kind, has been held at Loughborough Library School. There are moves afoot to set up a centre for children's literature, though nobody so far seems to know exactly what it should do. People here and there in the educational world are sitting up and taking notice. So far it is doubtful whether organized effort has done as much to get good books to children as the Puffin branch of Penguin Books has done by the simple means of making quality paperbacks available by the hundred thousand at prices children can afford. But on balance I am optimistic. There are better days ahead. Maybe we shall not actually reach that golden age when English children will read as naturally as they breathe. But I believe that more and more good books will be there, and more and more children will get pleasure from reading them. And after a generation or two we may even become a nation that cares as much about what its children read as about what they eat and wear.

[1968]

Precepts and pleasures: changing emphases in the writing and criticism of children's literature

SHEILA EGOFF

When Caxton began printing in England in 1476, the child was still looked upon as a miniature adult and was merged into the adult world. With the gradual realization that the child's natural carefree ways were a barrier between adult and child, adults hastened to teach the child 'manners', and the first books for children were books of manners and 'courtesie'. What more palatable candy coating for the traditional morals of mankind than Aesop's *Fables*? Here was an ideal way to present acceptable actions to the child—by means of talking animals. Caxton printed the first English edition in 1484 and the work rapidly became part of the schoolroom tradition.

The Puritan concept of sin that took hold in the seventeenth century led to a slight change in the accepted view of children: they were still thought of as miniature adults but they now had to be specially trained. And so a separate stream of children's books began. 'Children are not too young to die,' said the Puritans, 'they are not too little to go to hell,' and a great spate of writing and publishing supported this view. What was described by later generations as the 'brand of hell' school of writing reached its peak in 1671 with James Janeway's *A Token For Children: Being an Exact Account of the Conversion, Holy and Exemplary Lives and Joyful Deaths of several Young Children.* The Puritans contended that books of this kind gave the highest pleasure to children, 'that of studying and enjoying the Will of God'. What emerges from an overall look at the children's books of this period is a picture of a society that was narrow and intolerant, that saw children as separate from adults even while it brought the full force of adult values to bear upon them. It also reveals a remarkably consistent viewpoint. This society knew exactly what it wanted for its children: happiness in the next world.

Although the tone of religious ferocity was to abate in children's books until they became only mildly moralistic, the spirit of fear engendered by the Puritan era lingered in them for about a hundred and fifty years. Few books were free of religious overtones. The title of a spelling book of 1705 reads: *A Help to True Spelling and Reading . . . Here are also the Chief Principles of Religion laid down in a plain and easie Metre.* In Dr Aikin's and Mrs Barbauld's *Evenings at Home* (1792), a kind of junior encyclopaedia, with suggestions for keeping children out of mischief, a section on geography reads:

Asia lies east of Europe; it is about 4,800 miles long, and 4,300 broad; bounded on the North by the Frozen Ocean, by the Pacific on the East, by the Red Sea on the West, and the Indian Sea on the South. This, though the second, is the principal quarter of the globe; for here our first parents were created, and placed in the garden of Eden . . .

A somewhat less grim view of pleasure in the Puritan sense was offered by a seventeenth-century philosopher. In *Some Thoughts Concerning Education* (1690) John Locke urged that children should be brought to pleasure in reading, but through animal stories accompanied by pictures. Although his choice of books was very narrow—Aesop's *Fables* and *Reynard the Fox* were his strongest recommendations—he enunciated the first great principle about children and reading. 'Children do not like to be constrained to read,' he warned, 'any more than adults.'

John Locke was not listened to in his day and it would appear that he had only one disciple, in the person of John Newbery who, in 1744, set up his bookshop for children in St Paul's churchyard. Newbery intended to please children, but his break with tradition came in the way he approached them rather than in the contents of the books he published for them: he provided stories with the obvious morals of the time but in a gayer, more childlike way than his contemporaries. He covered his books with flowery and gilt' Dutch paper; he added woodcuts that illustrated the text, though they were crude in execution; with his bookshop he provided a place children could call their own and he supplemented his stock of books with baubles to delight a child—tops, pincushions, and games. Newbery has been called the 'commercial dynamo' of his time in the field of publishing. As a publisher his activities included much of what is good and bad in publishing for children today. He commissioned writers (it is supposed that Oliver Goldsmith was the author of Newbery's *Goody Two Shoes*); he saw the market for children's books as well as the need; and he had other ventures associated with his publishing (in *Goody Two Shoes* it is noted that little Marjory's father died from a want of Dr James's fever powder—a patent medicine sold by Newbery).

The overall influence of John Newbery was slight and fleeting—although the marketing lesson remained. The deliberate motives of both writers and critics throughout the eighteenth century and well into the nineteenth were the constraint and edification of children through books written for them. The emphasis continued to be on children and what was thought to be their needs rather than on literature, and children's books became tools for the educational process. The chief influence on English children's books came from France with the publication of Rousseau's *Emile* (1762) and its translation into English in 1762.

Rousseau's idea of bringing up a child in a natural state, far from the corrupting influences of civilization but with an adult always at hand to teach and explain, was seized upon by writers for children. A flood of books was unleashed that portrayed children as constantly and of necessity under the surveillance of adults, who turned even a glance at a butterfly into a lesson on entomology or a sermon on the brevity of life. Hence Thomas Day in *Sandford and Merton* (1795-8) shows a minister, Mr Barlow, undertaking the complete education of two boys (obviously at the expense of his clerical duties) and turning the rich, bad child into a duplicate of the good farmer's son. Mrs Sherwood in *The History of the Fairchild Family* (1818-47) shows a father and mother devoting all their time to their children, who get into trouble whenever they are freed from parental supervision. Who in the 1960s would not expect such children to get into trouble the moment parental supervision was relaxed? For Rousseau's disciples the solution to this problem was not to encourage children to develop moral responsibility of their own from an early age; it was to make the external application of a moral code yet more stringent. The naughty Fairchild children are taken to visit a gibbet to see the body of a criminal who 'had hung there some years'.

Time brought modifications. The grip on children's books shifted from the French master (much misinterpreted by his English followers) to a group of English women and clergymen of Established, Unitarian, Evangelical, and Quaker persuasion. This included Dr Aikin, Mrs Barbauld, Mrs Trimmer, Mrs Sherwood, Maria Edgeworth, Mary Belson, Mary Elliott, Dorothy Kilner, and many others. Their motives were best expressed by Mrs Trimmer in her magazine *The Guardian of Education* (1802): 'to contribute to the preservation of the young and innocent from the dangers which threaten them in the form of infantine literature.' Their vehicles were the Moral Tale and the Matter-of-Fact Tale, which were devoted to telling children how to behave, extolling missionary work among the heathen and cramming the children with elementary information that was little more than religious didacticism. A geography book of 1818 contains this passage:

Q. *What do the I-tal-i-ans wor-ship?*
A. *They wor-ship i-dols and a piece of bread.*
Q. *Would not God be ang-ry that I-tal-ians wor-ship i-dols and a piece of bread?*
A. *God is ang-ry.*

The literature of the 'moral' school mixed a liberal dose of menace in with its precepts. If children do not obey adults they will be punished and the punishment will be carried out. The heroine of Maria Edgeworth's *Rosamond* is told not to buy a purple jar. She does so and has to go shoeless and misses out on a treat. In much of the writing, death, the ultimate threat, is introduced. Moreover, God will see to it that death is the outcome of wrongdoing. In a little book of 1801 called *Pleasant Tales, to improve the mind and correct the morals of youth* (no irony is intended in the word 'pleasant'), we meet Patty's cousin who was haughty and arrogant and who, having the misjudgement to marry her father's valet, was thrust out into the snow in true *East Lynne* style. The book ends thus:

Patty put her poor Cousin to bed, where she lingered a few hours, and then expired, saying—'had I been GOOD, I should have been HAPPY; the GUILTY and the UNFEELING can never taste of PEACE.' Patty lived long and happily, a striking example to the world, that HONESTY, FILIAL DUTY, and RELIGION, are well-pleasing in the sight of the Almighty who is the punisher of VICE, and the liberal rewarder of VIRTUE.

Charles Lamb in a famous letter to Coleridge commented on the effects of this type of book rather than on its spirit: 'Mrs Barbauld's stuff has banished all the old classics of the nursery. . . Think what you would have been now, if instead of being fed with tales and old wives' fables in childhood, you had been fed with geography and natural history.' The old classics of the nursery were not specifically designed for children but were literature they had taken for themselves—myth, faerie and folklore, romances, nonsense rhymes, and such adult books as *Pilgrim's Progress* (1678), *Robinson Crusoe* (1719), and *Gulliver's Travels* (1726). These classics existed in a kind of underground movement, however—they were not dead.

Each era has produced what can be described as a public literature for its children; that is, a model of what society desired for them. Leonard de Vries's *Flowers of Delight* (1965), which gives a sampling of what was available for children from 1765-1830, shows how prominent this public literature was. Here is the round of *Easy Lessons, The Parental Instructor*, and stories containing 'caution and instruction for children'. Mr de Vries has included a few folktales and nonsense rhymes that tend only to heighten the dreariness of the writing considered 'good' for children. This literature came in horizontal waves from 1700 to 1900, but always cutting across it vertically was the literature of delight, the literature of mankind. As Paul Hazard has put it, children have simply refused to be oppressed and have taken what they wanted, be it Malory's *Le Morte d'Arthur* or Blake's *Songs of Innocence*. They had in addition the hundreds of little chapbooks that flooded England in the eighteenth century through the chapmen who sold them for a penny along with ribbons and needles and pins and thread. In these crude little books was stuff to make the sky turn round —*The Babes in the Wood, Valentine and Orson*, and *The Death and Burial of Cock Robin*.

Since 'Up with didacticism!' was the battle cry of the guardians of public morality, the fairies were in retreat. Denigrations of imagination, pleasure, and faerie were not new of course. Plato in *The Republic* condemned the Homeric epics for portraying the passions of men in the form of gods. In 1554 Hugh Rhodes, a gentleman of the king's chapel, urged parents in his *Book of Nurture to* keep their children from 'reading of feigned fables, vain fantasies, and wanton stories, and songs of love, which bring much mischief to youth.' About the same time, Roger Ascham, the otherwise enlightened tutor of Queen Elizabeth I, was exclaiming against *King Arthur* for the young. The Puritans almost succeeded in driving out imagination and pleasure by the sheer numbers of their own kind of book, but nothing exceeded the attempts of the writers of the moral tale in the late eighteenth and early nineteenth century for either ferocity or length of attack on imaginative literature. And when George Cruikshank in his *Fairy Library* rewrote the old tales such as 'Puss in Boots' and 'Cinderella' as temperance tracts, it seemed as if fear and didacticism in children's books were to last forever. Even Charles Dickens's now-famous article, 'Frauds on the Fairies'—a spirited attack on Cruikshank's emasculated moralizing versions of the old tales—was seemingly an insufficient counterthrust. Time, however, was on the side of the underground movement.

Yet the authors of the moral tale meant so well. Their concern for the good of children is obvious: they were the first to pay attention to the children of the poor through the Sunday School movement. As writers they often used the English language with power and precision; they wrote with a passionate conviction that most modern writers for children should envy; and their plots were skilfully contrived to give concrete support for abstract ideas. In *Simple Susan* (1796) Maria Edgeworth uses a disagreement between a farmer and a lawyer to make her point:

'Then why so stiff about it, Price? All I want of you is to say—'

'To say that black is white, which I won't do, Mr Case; the ground is a thing not worth talking of, but it's neither yours nor mine; in my memory, since the new *lane was made, it has always been open to the parish, and no man shall enclose it with my good will.—Truth is truth, and must be spoken; justice is justice, and should be done, Mr Attorney.'*

'And law is law, Mr Farmer, and shall have its course, to your cost,' cried the attorney, exasperated by the dauntless spirit of this village Hampden.

In retrospect it can be seen that until about 1850 the books deliberately intended for children were judged on their extra-literary qualities. They were used to preach, teach, exhort, and reprimand. However, their captive audience, children, resisted literature that was didactic and explicitly moral in favour of literature that was pleasurable—and *implicitly* moral. They were helped by the indestructible qualities of literature itself and by a few defenders such as Charles Lamb and Charles Dickens. As a result the underground movement held its own sufficiently to provide the inspiration for the flowering of children's literature that was to come.

Linked to this flowering was a change in attitude towards children. If the seventeenth century discovered the child, the Victorians may be credited with discovering childhood—that is, a state distinct from that of adulthood. While the writers of the past had said, in effect, 'Give me a child and through books we will see to it that his manners, religion, and outlook on life are exactly what we adults want', the writers of the late Victorian period idealized and sentimentalized the child. They saw childhood as the time of innocence untrammelled, as epitomized in Wordsworth's famous lines, 'Heaven lies about us in our infancy!/Shades of the prison-house begin to close/Upon the growing boy.' Influenced also by Coleridge and William Morris, who had released fantasy and mythology for adults, they expressed this new spirit of childhood through the play of their original and inventive minds. Their audience was ready-made in the offspring of the wealthy middle class that emerged in the second half of the nineteenth century. These children were kept in the nursery, guarded and cherished by nannies who, while excellent disciplinarians, seemed to have had their heads stuffed with 'old wives' tales'. For these children, and sometimes for individual children or groups of children, there appeared works of original genius (some by writers who were strongly entrenched in the world of adult literature): Ruskin's *The King of the Golden River* (1851), Thackeray's *The Rose and the Ring* (1855), Kingsley's *The Water-Babies* (1863), Carroll's *Alice's Adventures in Wonderland* (1865), Mrs Ewing's *The Brownies* (1870), MacDonald's *At the Back of the North Wind* (1871) and *The Princess and the Goblin* (1872), Mrs Molesworth's *The Tapestry Room* (1879), and many, many more. There is no evidence to show that these books were attacked as being unsuitable fare for children. This may be because they in no way broke the moral tradition of children's literature. While telling fascinating tales, their authors simply raised morality to a higher degree, indeed to a universal order. Children's literature in the best moral and humanistic tradition had been born.

But no one type of literature ever has its way completely. Another brand of fantasy, helped by a revolution in the method of printing, was reaching out to another group of readers. Rotary presses disgorged masses of boys' sensational magazines, perhaps as a reaction to the moral constraints of previous ages or even as a revolt against the Victorian social conscience that was expressed in the works of Dickens and Thackeray. In literary lineage the serial stories in magazines such as *The Boys of England* (1866), *The Boy's Standard* (1875), and *Jack Harkaway's Journal* (1893) were related to gothic novels like Horace Walpole's *The Castle of Otranto* (1764) and Mrs Radcliffe's *The Mysteries of Udolpho* (1794) and were reinforced by the rise of the 'penny dreadfuls' and the 'penny parts' of the 1830s. In format, illustration, content, and popularity, these magazines were matched only by the rise and influence of the comic book in the mid-twentieth century. This was the beginning of mass-media publishing for the young and of the syndicated writer.

One of the chief publishers of these magazines was Edward Lloyd, who boasted that they were given to the office boy to read to test their suitability for the general public. At first they were not aimed at the juvenile market, but the scalp-tingling subject matter easily enticed boys who had little else to read in the adventure line after they had read *Robinson Crusoe* and *Quentin Durward*. One good book creates a desire for another and in those days there was virtually little else that was in the class of these two novels.

It is hard to believe that the 'bloods', as these stories came to be called, formed a part of the stream of children's literature, and it is harder to be objectively critical of them. Highly noticeable is the monotonous style, which was lavish in description and overloaded with detail. Pages are spent in building up an atmosphere of dread and mystery by utilizing mouldy dungeons, clanking chains, rusty daggers, and ethereal music. Then at the end comes a refusal to admit the existence of the supernatural: a laboured explanation of the mysterious events reduces the tale to nothing more than an illusion or a prank. Like the series books of today, anyone who understood the formula—even the office boy—could take over the writing. And the most cavalier approach was allowable. It is said that on one occasion the writer of a boy's serial became ill and left his hero bound and gagged on the edge of a cliff with the villain ready to do him in. The substitute writers could not think of a way to rescue the hero. The more practised writer, returning a few days later, picked up his pen and wrote: 'With one bound the hero broke his bonds.' (Syndicated writing is still with us today, both in its sensational magazine form and in the Bobbsey Twins and Nancy Drew series, in which the ten-year-old twins can out-detect the Japanese police force and Nancy can drive a golf ball two hundred and twenty-five yards straight down the fairway.) The boys' 'bloods', like their modern counterparts, were often regarded as quite legitimate escapism. In a seeming reinforcement of this attitude a noted critic of the time observed that 'the British boy cares as much about style as a pig about asparagus'. It is ironic that the remark was made about *Treasure Island:* Stevenson was considered to be wasting his talent on books for boys. However, when children had an opportunity to escape to genuine romance in *Treasure Island* they did so in great numbers, and succeeding generations of all nations have kept it very much alive. According to the pattern set by the boys' magazines, this novel was first serialized in the magazine *Young Folks* in 1881. It was called *The Sea Cook* and the author used a pseudonym, Captain George North.

Along with the literature of fantasy and sensationalism, in which *Treasure Island* showed that high adventure was not incompatible with good writing, didactic novels were still being produced—survivors from the earlier trend. The *Peter Parley* annuals (from the 1820s to the 1870s) were a long series chiefly composed of mini-essays of encyclopaedic variety compiled or written by numerous writers, both English and American. In the annual for 1871 appears a typical fictional effort entitled 'Found Wanting; or He Would Be a Traveller'. In this story a boy who has the sea in his blood agrees to stifle his own natural desires and enter his grandfather's counting-house. Eventually the grandfather sees the boy's unhappiness and allows him a trip on a luxury liner. On the voyage the boy falls down the stairs (the captain's, no less) and is crippled for life. Both he and the grandfather 'comprehend the hand of Providence in the matter'.

All this time English children's books travelled across the Atlantic and were published in the United States, many in pirated editions. Original American children's books paralleled the English ones, as can be seen from such titles as *Spiritual Milk for Boston Babes* (1684), *The School of Good Manners* (1796), *Little Nancy; or, The Punishment of Greediness* (1824). Richard Darling's excellent book, *The Rise of Children's Book Reviewing in the United States, 1865-1881* (1968), shows that it was in the United States rather than in England where some soul-searching was first done about the nature and mission of children's books and the nature of the child. The Reverend Samuel Osgood, a Unitarian clergyman, stated a philosophy close to that of the early twentieth century. Boys and girls are adults in 'nature', he said, but not in 'development'. Children have intelligence and wills that should be respected. 'Children not only want the true thing said to them, but want to have it said in a true and fitting way.' By thus emphasizing literary execution as early as 1865, Osgood helped to provide the climate of taste and talent in which the great American children's books of the nineteenth century were to flourish: Louisa May Alcott's *Little Women* (1868), Frank Stockton's *The Bee-man of Orn and Other Fanciful Tales* (1887), Mark Twain's *The Prince and the Pauper* (1881), Howard Pyle's *Otto of the Silver Hand* (1888) and *Men of Iron* (1891).

According to evidence supplied by Mr Darling, American reviews of children's books were of a higher order than those appearing in England at the time. Few books, however, were judged on their intrinsic merit as literature; the effect of the book on the child still took priority. Nevertheless the whole ferment of the time regarding children's books, the rise of children's libraries, the influx of talented writers and illustrators from Europe, and the development of criticism pointed to what in fact turned out to be the case: that in all the activities surrounding the production and use of picture books and the many categories of non-fiction for children, the twentieth century would belong to the United States.

The major writers of children's books from about 1900 to the late 1950s exhibited a tremendous unanimity of purpose in their view of childhood. For in spite of the changes in books for adults caused by two world wars, a depression, advances in medicine, transportation, and communication, and a freer expression about morality as well as changes in literary style, children's literature remained stable. It seemed as though twentieth-century writers for children had learned a lesson from the Golden Age of Victorian children's books: literature was for pleasure rather than for admonition. Fantasy, with its revelation of great truths and its strong appeal to the imagination, was still the highest form of writing engaging the talents of acknowledged serious writers. Kenneth Grahame, J. R. R. Tolkien, E. B. White, C. S. Lewis, and Rumer Godden did not shy away from difficult themes. *The Wind in the Willows* celebrates human relationships as well as the joys of the countryside; *The Hobbit* offers a quest that never ends as well as a search for gold; *Charlotte's Web* makes death acceptable by dealing with it in terms of the life-and-death cycle of an insect; the Narnia books speak gently of the beliefs and ethics of Christianity; and *The Dolls' House* exposes jealousy and hatred in the miniature world of dolls. Such themes were not used didactically or obtrusively, however. These writers stripped away the last vestiges of sentimentality and preaching from the classics of childhood. With consummate artistry they welded their own moral philosophy to a dramatic form, and it is probably this accomplishment as much as any other that makes a great book great.

Adult attitudes to children in the first half of the twentieth century can be directly seen in the realistic stories of child and family life. On the whole they are set in a world of delight and innocence, which is described lovingly and nostalgically, almost with Maurice Sendak's 'near-obsession' with childhood. The world of childhood is still separate from that of adults: the children are busy and happy about their own affairs while the adults hover on the periphery of their lives, ready to step in at times of danger or need. But the children are generally equal to most situations. There is little introspection and less ugliness or downright hardship than in real life. There were war stories, stories of poor children, stories of children with problems, but they were few in number, and such subjects were not emphasized. Most books were primarily adventure stories that, in the hands of writers of talent, gave a clear, steady, conservative view of life for children. Childhood, it seems, was the best of all possible states. This is the literary world of Edith Nesbit, Arthur Ransome, Eleanor Estes, Lois Lenski, Noel Streatfeild, Lucy Boston, William Mayne, and many others.

The survival rate of books written between 1900 and 1960 has been remarkably high. Only a few books deliberately written for children before 1900 have survived to be read today. The most notable examples are: Edward Lear's *The Book of Nonsense* (1846), Lewis Carroll's *Alice's Adventures in Wonderland* (1865), Louisa May Alcott's *Little Women* (1868), George MacDonald's *The Princess and the Goblin* (1872), Robert Louis Stevenson's *Treasure Island* (1882). An extremely large group from the turn of the century on, however, now forms much of the basic reading of children of today: *Mary Poppins, The Borrowers, Island of the Blue Dolphins, Call It Courage, Johnny Tremain, Doctor Dolittle, The Eagle of the Ninth, The Children of Green Knowe, The Moffats,* and *The Wolves of Willoughby Chase* are only a few lasting books out of hundreds. This difference cannot be accounted for solely by an increase in the number of books published. In the nineteenth century the book business for children was also remarkably big, widespread, and affluent. The difference is in the writers. The major writers of the twentieth century have seen children as a challenging audience demanding their highest efforts and children have responded to their integrity.

'Only the more rugged mortals should attempt to keep up with current literature,' said George Ade many years ago. What would he have said if he had been faced with just one year's publications in the 1960s? With some 6,000 titles in the English language published annually for children (including some few hundred reissues and new editions), it would be futile to attempt a survey and misguided to try to offer genuine criticism. Generalizations are always tempting, however, and the subject invites some.

It appears that current children's books reflect the society they were written in to a degree not known since the seventeenth century and that they are overwhelmingly carrying on the traditional mission of children's books: to inform and instruct the young. There have been changes in style and theme in the books published in the last few years, and it is not surprising that the greatest changes appear in American fiction. Even a superficial study of North American society in the sixties reveals confusion, uneasiness, a shifting of values, a preoccupation with the psychology of individual and group problems, and a strong desire, particularly on the part of young people, to be told the truth, no matter how it distresses adults to tell it to them. Technical and electronic advances admit us to McLuhan's global village and force immediate decisions of conscience on us all, but we have very sketchy background information about the problems brought to our attention. Almost every hitherto accepted idea and principle about the conduct of life is being challenged. Pressure on the individual is intense and the feeling of being threatened is very real. The age of faith has passed and what is to fill the void? For many of the young the solution is to withdraw from bigness, from the multiversity and corporate business, from government and the mass media, and to become engaged in a rediscovery of humanity on a more personal level.

Where American books are concerned the condition of North American society is being translated into children's books quite clearly, but with one notable difference from the past. As society in general does not seem to know what to say to its children and cannot express itself with one voice, we have both a literature of 'personal decision', which suggests that each young person has to come to terms with life on an individual basis, and a literature of conformity. Many writers move uneasily between the two, exhibiting their own cloudy view of life and of contemporary problems. The form most writers use is realistic fiction or contemporary-scene fiction and they try to 'tell it like it is' in areas such as the 'personal' problems of young people, race relationships, alcoholism, drug addiction, violence, and war. These books are chiefly aimed at the senior elementary-school child or the junior high-school student.

Many books deal with family problems or problems of growing up, such as Lee Kingman's *The Year of the Raccoon* (1966),

Christie Harris's *Confessions of a Toe-Hanger* (1967), and Maia Wojciechowska's *The Hollywood Kid* (1966). In most cases the young people are at odds with their parents and/or their siblings. Such books tend to be facile exploitations of tensions that are quickly and remarkably resolved by conformity.

In other books tensions are built up because of such social problems as divorce—Vera and Bill Cleaver's *Ellen Grae* (1967) and *Lady Ellen Grae* (1968); alcoholism—Regina Woody's *One Day At a Time* (1968); poverty—Frank Bonham's *The Nitty Gritty* (1967); and war—John R. Tunis's *His Enemy His Friend* (1968). All of these books have a brittle style that could be considered 'mod' by the younger generation, but unfortunately they have soft and flabby answers to the questions they deliberately raise. It is perhaps too simple to say that children's books are bringing children faster into the adult world than ever before. Television has a prior influence in this regard; and in many cases these books are merely a reflection of what the child has already encountered on TV. (Indeed they share their most notable characteristic with the mass media: superficiality.) Due to the mass media and the pressures of modern society, children have now rejoined the adult world from which they were separated in the previous century. However, we adults of the 1960s only half accept them and in our half acceptance we provide them with books that are only half honest. The alcoholic mother in Regina Woody's book makes a remarkable recovery when her young daughter solves the family's financial crisis and John Tunis would have us believe that his German officer made a decision when he did not.

The flood of books on Negroes deserves some attention. Their intent is beyond reproach: to provoke sympathy and gain understanding for an oppressed group. Beginning in the 1950s there were some rather cautious books of this kind. One example is Hope Newell's *A Cap for Mary Ellis* (1952), in which two educationally advanced and well-adjusted Negro girls are selected to enter a hitherto all-white nursing school. The books of the 1960s have attempted to come to grips with more fundamental issues. Frank Bonham's *Durango Street* (1965) deals with 'inner-city' poverty and gang warfare and Natalie Carlson's *The Empty Schoolhouse* (1965) and Bella Rodman's *Lions in the Way* (1966) are about school integration. As high as their moral purpose is, these are still rather one-sided books that encourage white children to be kind to Negroes, to see their problems, and to accept the civil-rights legislation. The Negroes are portrayed as good, kind, religious, indeed 'square'—the middle class with black skins. Or, as in *The Empty Schoolhouse* and *Lions in the Way*, the white community comes to an understanding of Negroes only when violence is seen as a threat to themselves. The writers of these books may feel that they are doing their bit for social protest, but the results are too often false. Such books are merely another form of condescension that is very far removed from the outraged protests of Negro writers of adult literature; they bear almost no relation to how Negroes see themselves and the society they live in. It is interesting that two books have been praised as much for the fact that they indicate chiefly by illustration that the young protagonists are Negro as for their intrinsic merit: Paula Fox's *How Many Miles to Babylon?* (1967) and E. L. Konigsberg's *Jennifer, Hecate, Macbeth, William McKinley and Me, Elizabeth* (1967).

The authors of all these books show quite clearly society's ambivalent attitude toward children: wanting them to be informed and yet to conform; wanting problems to be presented realistically while taking such a hesitant step towards realism that only half-truths result, which can be more dangerous than ignorance. Most of the children's books on Negro life and problems lack, besides literary qualities, honesty, integrity, and genuine knowledge. The best books about Negroes will be written by black writers; hopefully these writers will have the power and insight of the many black writers who have distinguished themselves in the adult field.

The personal decision-making stream of writing can be represented by such books as Martha Stiles's *Darkness Over the Land* (1966), about the inner conflict of a boy growing up in Nazi Germany in the Second World War; Nat Hentoff's *I'm Really Dragged But Nothing Gets Me Down* (1968), on the problems of American boys facing the Vietnam draft; and Barbara Wersba's *The Dream Watcher* (1968), about a boy who worries because he is 'different':

I'm the only person in America who doesn't belong to a group. I'm not square and I'm not hip. I'm not a hood. I'm not an intellectual. I'm not an athlete. And what else is there?

Darkness Over the Land, with all its commonplace writing, has a clearly defined theme that makes the whole greater than the sum of its parts. In most other books of this type the major issues are either complicated or simplistic; in both cases they are undramatic. They also frequently imply that the young protagonist's decision—to engage in draft counselling, for example, or to become 'somebody'—is *the* big decision and that he need never make another one.

It is a fact that the desires of young people—to know what adults are all about, to understand themselves in the most complicated and diversified era man has yet experienced, to fulfil themselves in a world where the socially acceptable nine-to-five jobs and suburbia are holding less and less appeal, to see reflected in books written for them the view of the world that they really hold—do *not* preclude satisfying their requirements in genuine works of literature. That problems should provide themes for children's literature is not being questioned, for they should if literature is to reflect life, but it is clear that in most cases the demand for problem books is being filled by highly superficial and mediocre writing.

One view of the problem books, which says that if a problem exists it should be presented to the young reader in as realistic a way as possible, often implies that such literary values as style, characterization, plot, and the welding of a philosophy of life to a literary form must take second place. The opposite view is based on a literary standard and all that it demands. Generally speaking the modern American realistic school of writing is almost aggressively unliterary. Most authors appear to be amateur writers dragged into active existence by the great demand for the problem book, not because they have something to say to the young and can say it well. Their efforts are almost without plot and read like socio-psychological case-studies that are entirely devoid of interpretation and significance. Is bibliotherapy really an excuse for poor literature even though the problems—racial inequality, drug addiction, unmarried mothers, alcoholic fathers—are important ones? What answers do these books give to the problems they set up? Whatever they are, they tend to be one-dimensional answers to multi-dimensional problems. The vision in most current writing is very, very narrow—in the setting up of the problem, in the resolution of it, and in the intended readership. In most instances several problems are settled for a lifetime in the last chapter. One can only wonder if the generation gap is so great that adults have to suspend their reasoned judgement in order to 'keep with it' so far as young people and their cares are concerned. It can be argued that in the hands of a real writer the problems of a fifteen-year-old with a famous movie-star mother could be made absorbing and significant. So they could, but only if the writer can make pain and sorrow and joy universal, so that every reader can say of the protaganist 'That's me!' and of the theme 'I know it's true.'

We now know a great deal about children clinically and psychologically, but what do we know of their literary needs? It would appear that in purporting to be realistic, present-day writers forget that realism is a distillation, not a simple ingredient or a fixed attitude. Realism as it is presented in most books for children is an encumbrance rather than a release. As Sir Laurence Olivier once pointed out, 'If you cut out the nose of a portrait by Rembrandt and pushed your own nose through, the nose would be real enough, but as a painting it would be disastrous.' Much of modern realistic writing for children is just this: adults ludicrously playing at deception. The artificial quality of these books is never more evident than in their endings. All too often they conclude on a note of moralizing or of sweetened uplift. At the end of Barbara Wersba's *The Dream Watcher* (1968) the young hero 'finds' himself, as do most other young American heroes and heroines.

Of course not all current writers contribute to the slice-of-life genre; there are a few who do not slavishly pursue verisimilitude but prefer to write on a more symbolic level. Significantly it is such authors—notably Louise Fitzhugh in *Harriet the Spy* (1964) and *The Long Secret* (1965) and Julia Cunningham in *Dorp Dead* (1965)—who are the most controversial. The objectives and successes of these two writers can be seen in contrast to a more obviously realistic book, such as Marilyn Sachs's *Veronica Ganz* (1968).

In *Harriet the Spy* we gather first of all that Harriet's parents have not found the time to take a large part in her upbringing and have entrusted most of it to her nurse, Ole Golly. We are given a fairly detailed portrait of Ole Golly, though not of the other adults in the book. She comes from an impoverished and uninspiring background (the book begins with a visit to her grotesque, simple-minded mother), but she compensates for the dreariness of her youth with enormous intellectual pretensions. She has a fondness for inserting into a conversation dimly understood quotations from famous writers, no matter how irrelevant they may be. Undoubtedly it is Ole Golly who influenced Harriet to keep a diary as a prelude to her future writing career. Harriet's character is really quite consistent with the description we are given of Ole Golly's part in her upbringing. In a permissive atmosphere in which her ideas are taken seriously by her nurse, she has come to believe that all experience must be explored; at the same time she has been taught that she can and indeed must be objective in her observation of this experience:

Miss Whitehead's feet look larger this year. Miss Whitehead has buck teeth, thin hair, feet like skis, and a very long hanging stomach. Ole Golly says description is good for the soul, and clears the brain like a laxative.

Harriet gets carried away and deliberately spies upon people to get the material she so accurately records in her diary. She comes to realize that 'some people are one way and some people are another and that's that.' In the book's denouement, which has horrified many adults, Harriet learns about human relations that 'Ole Golly was right. Sometimes you have to lie.'

The people she spies upon are her neighbours, her teachers, her parents, and her friends. None of them is 'real' in the sense that we could imagine such people existing in our own world. They are all exaggerations, even caricatures, yet they are real as symbols of the follies of contemporary society. Harriet's parents are presented far more realistically than most parents in modern children's books. At the beginning they ignore their parental responsibilities, but they do come to Harriet's aid when she is in trouble and so do her teachers. This runs counter to the current American trend of making adults ineffectual, which implies that children are in opposition to adults. (American children seem to be hurried into adulthood; yet in books, adulthood is not presented as an entirely felicitous state. But this is a topic for another paper.)

Opinions of *Harriet the Spy* have been sharply divided. It has been lauded for its 'realism' and condemned as being 'warped and unpleasant'. Both views misinterpret Miss Fitzhugh's approach to life, which, if it is to be pigeon-holed, should be described as 'naturalistic' rather than 'realistic'. She introduces into children's literature a mode of fictional writing that adults have learned how to deal with adequately in their own literature but that they do not quite know what to make of in a children's book. For example, an adult would not read Evelyn Waugh's *The Loved One* and think it was an accurate representation of

American funerary practices, yet through its distortions the book tells us a great deal about life in southern California and indeed about contemporary life in general. But when Louise Fitzhugh in somewhat the same way brings a child to terms with adult life and in the process reveals its unpleasantness and dishonesty, she is criticized for her lack of fidelity. What is hampering judgement here is simply an old tradition of children's literature that life is fundamentally good and beautiful and that all the virtues will have their own reward.

Marilyn Sachs's *Veronica Ganz* might be described as a more realistic and generally 'acceptable' book than *Harriet the Spy*. But it is precisely Mrs Sachs's faithfulness to a limited reality that ultimately makes this book a lesser accomplishment than either of Miss Fitzhugh's novels. The turning-point comes when Veronica, realizing the power and privileges of being a female, loses all the aggressive instincts that have dominated her mind and actions up to that moment. Certainly Veronica has suffered from the break-up of her parent's marriage, from having lived in grinding poverty, and from having to fight all her fellow pupils into submission in order to gain a sense of position among them. Is it consistent with the realistic background that Mrs Sachs has so faithfully described that Veronica could undergo such an instantaneous and presumably permanent transformation? Because Mrs Sachs is not faithful to the inner reality of her book, it is marred by a certain dishonesty. Her message of the power of womanhood goes against the laws of both her created universe and the universe of the reader. In *Harriet the Spy* the reader only has to look at its inner reality to see the relevance of that reality to the one he knows. In *Dorp Dead* Julia Cunningham also portrays life as she sees it, believing that, in the total experience, the unhealthy lip-licking kind of brutality that she has been accused of exploiting is actually inseparable from the realization of love and personal fulfilment of the young protagonist, Gilly: had he not been the victim of a sadistic adult, he would have become entrapped in a cage of self-alienation.

The disapproving critical reception of these unusual novels by Louise Fitzhugh and Julia Cunningham suggests that while mediocrity is acceptable or at least tolerated, distortion for artistic reasons and anything pathological are not, even when they are used to widen the reader's vision of life and society. It is sadly apparent that the majority of adult critics of children's books prefer a message imposed from without rather than one that grows out of the novel itself.[1]

Realistic novels in the established tradition of children's literature, while not neglected by American writers, are being produced in greater numbers in England and Australia. Echoes of Louisa May Alcott, Arthur Ransome, and Eleanor Estes continue to reverberate in stories that have real plots, self-reliant children, and timeless themes and settings. These books have fewer instant problems and solutions. In John Rowe Townsend's *Gumble's Yard* (1961) a group of poor children, deserted by an uncle and his common-law wife, solve a mystery and help capture some criminals. At the end of the story Kevin quite naturally feels that after all the exciting events some dramatic change should come into his life, but circumstances do not allow a change. The children have a choice between an unsatisfactory life and public welfare. Yet the book ends on a note of practical cheer:

We walked three abreast, with Sandra in the middle. And as we turned the corner into our own street I felt happy and burst out singing.

'Hark at him!' said Sandra. 'Not a care in the world.'

'Where does it hurt, Kevin?' asked Dick with mock sympathy.

'I'll hurt you in a minute!' I said.

And we started a friendly scuffle, the kind that happens a dozen times a day.

On the whole, British children's fiction tends to carry on the tradition of children's literature that was set in the late-Victorian

---

[1] See Anthony Metie, 'Notes on Some Recent Fiction for Children', Canadian Association of Children's Librarians *Bulletin* (Fall 1968), pp. 37-43.

age and was carried on into the 1950s; a large proportion of these novels reflect literary discipline and a flair for language, and (more frequently than in American novels) the resolution of theme usually stems from characterization and from the inevitability of events. Not all British books are praiseworthy, of course, nor do they all avoid current issues: British publishers are not above offering books like Gertrude Kamm's *Young Mother* (almost a 'how-to-do-it' book on illegitimacy). But the mainstream of writing tends toward the realistic adventure story rather than the problem book. Gerald Durrell's *The Donkey Rustlers* (1968) is a zany 'cops-and-robbers' story and the fact that two wealthy children help a poor friend is an integral part of the plot rather than a lesson in generosity. Helen Cresswell's *The Piemakers* (1968) is a charming and original 'tall tale'. Patricia Wrightson's *I Own the Racecourse* (Australian, 1968), in which a group of boys disagree over how to help a mentally retarded friend who takes their game of owning things seriously, manages to convey a world of concerned childhood rather than the American concept of 'growing up' or 'coming to terms with life'. None of these writers, and indeed fewer British writers than American, inhibit their style because they are writing for children.

While current American writing is notable for a group of new writers who are busy with immediate social and personal problems, a goodly number of established and new British writers prefer to write about the past, an area in which American writing has been weak. The British historical novel for children has had a long tradition and its modern practitioners are among the best: Rosemary Sutcliff, Geoffrey Trease, Hilda Lewis, Naomi Mitchison, Ronald Welch, and Hester Burton. The rising star in this field is Leon Garfield, who has called forth comparisons with Fielding, Hogarth, and Dickens. Not merely concerned with creating a strict historical setting, he conveys the very atmosphere of time past. Using the ingredients of melodrama—pickpockets, highwaymen, smiling villains, cut-throat sailors, stolen documents and diamonds, escapes and hurried journeys—he welds them into tales of high adventure that have their own inner purpose. The only direct problem Mr Garfield poses to readers is how to put a book of his down.

The difference between the past and the present in children's literature can be as clearly seen through its critics as through its practitioners. Although the first 350 years of its history produced no coherent objective body of criticism, there were many expressive voices. With the exception of John Locke, they all spoke as one in emphasizing that children's books could be deliberately and legitimately used as propaganda and that their effectiveness was to be judged by their powers of persuasion upon the young. Modern critical writing on children's literature either states or intimates varying (almost contradictory) views on its nature and purpose. Critics of adult literature, say from Coleridge to T. S. Eliot, had different approaches to criticism, but they had no doubt at all about the *nature* of the beast they were discussing. Literature was simply the best that had been thought and written and it was the critic's business to understand it, to interpret it, and to promote it. Contemporary critics of books for children tend to bring widely differing conceptions of what children's literature is to their evaluation and interpretation of it. 'One of the mistaken assumptions about the nature of children's literature is that it involves the same elements and hence the same criteria as adult literature,' writes one critic, while another asks, 'Should children's books be rated in any lesser way [than adult literature]?' A third asks for judgements of modern children's books based on the classics of children's literature. Walter de la Mare has said that 'only the rarest kind of best in anything can be good enough for the young'; C. S. Lewis believed that no book was really worth reading at the age of ten that was not equally (and often far more) worth reading at the age of fifty; and a popular, pragmatic view is that since children's books are chiefly intended for reading practice, it does not matter what children read as long as they do read. Some true believers, of course, manage to hold all opinions at once.

Criticism, as opposed to book reviewing, first emerged in the writings of Anne Carroll Moore, who headed the children's department in the New York Public Library. Her 'views and reviews' of children's books were brought together in such volumes as *Roads to Childhood* (1920), *New Roads to Childhood* (1923), *Crossroads to Childhood* (1926), and *The Three Owls Notebooks* (1925-7). The first three were reprinted in 1961 as *My Roads to Childhood.* In the introduction to this book Frances Clarke Sayers pays tribute to Miss Moore's critical judgement.

How adept she was at discovery. She was first to discern, upon their initial appearance, what was unique and enduring in such giants on the scene as Hendrik van Loon, Carl Sandburg, Dr Seuss . . . and hundreds of others. She was a discoverer and proclaimer, a celebrant of originality. No book was judged in a vacuum. She drew upon her knowledge of life, as well as of books, and she saw childhood as something more than progressive stages of physical and psychological growth.

The most startling and innovative idea of the 1920s was the founding in 1921 of *The Horn Book Magazine* as a review devoted exclusively to children's books and planned to interest children as well as teachers, parents, and librarians. Its title recalls Randolph Caldecott's *Three Jovial Huntsmen,* and its aim was 'to blow the horn for fine books for boys and girls—their authors, their illustrators, and their publishers'. At least two of the outstanding qualities of the early issues of *The Horn Book* deserve comment here. One was its recognition of writing for children as an international field. It was far from being parochially American, and through articles as well as book-notes it introduced American readers to Juliana Horatia Ewing, Leslie Brooke, Walter de la Mare, and to continental European writers. Its second great strength, which is the strength of all great critical writing, was the enduring value of much of its criticism. It is remarkable that as early as 1924, Alice Jordan (then Supervisor, Work With Children, Boston Public Library) deplored the 'series books', which continued unabated through the 1960s. 'We believe that long series are stultifying,' she wrote, 'that mediocrity in books for children is more universal and more baffling to combat than sensationalism.' *The Horn Book* was also responsible for the translation and publication in 1944 of the most perceptive book ever written about children and their reading—the wise, witty, and humane *Books, Children and Men* by Paul Hazard.

Critical acumen and a spiritual outlook are combined in the most important book we have on the criticism of children's literature: *The Unreluctant Years: A Critical Approach to Children's Literature* (1953) by Lillian H. Smith, for many years Head of Boys and Girls Division, Toronto Public Library. While a good many publications discuss children's literature and even more survey it, only *The Unreluctant Years* gives shape and judgement to the literature itself in rational, coherent terms backed up by evidence. The sub-title of the book indicates that the emphasis is on works of literature. Although children, their tastes, and their individual differences are not ignored, Miss Smith urges that only 'recognition of an underlying soundness or unsoundness in writing, theme and content will serve to keep in the field of children's books those that will bring a deeper and more lasting pleasure to children.'

As well as being a declaration of Miss Smith's personal philosophy, *The Unreluctant Years* brought into prominence an approach to children's books that had been crystallizing since the 1860s in England and the United States. Children may not always be able to judge and appreciate excellence in writing, but this fact, far from permitting inferior work, places on writers the obligation to meet the highest standards of integrity and artistry. *Caveat emptor* may be a sufficient guide for the marketplace, but only the unthinking or the unscrupulous will regard children as fair game for tasteless, spurious, or talentless writing.

The evidence from the past supports this viewpoint. Literature that is 'outer-directed' rather than 'inner-directed' will simply fade away or join historical collections to amuse future generations by its quaintness or idiocy. Only the 'literature of power', as De Quincey put it, 'the literature that speaks ultimately to the higher understanding of reason', will last.

But is this philosophy in tune with the tempo of the schizophrenic sixties? The reading tastes of children are changing. Books of fantasy appear to be declining in numbers, quality, and readership. Books about 'real life' are on the increase. Children's literature in North America is dominated by books that are 'outer-directed'—works of fiction that offer thinly disguised instruction on psychological and sociological themes, as the didactic books of an earlier period dealt with religion and morality. Such books—hastily written, speedily published, whose only interest derives from the topicality of their subjects—are no more realistic than soap operas. They are false sociology and bad literature.

Painfully and ironically enough, this vogue for non-literature comes at a time when we have produced young people who are better informed, more sophisticated, and more troubled by adult values than any other generation in history. They sit with their parents around the same television set and watch the same programs, they read the same newspapers, and in many cases they own the same paperbacks, for they are reaching out for adult books just as they have done in the past whenever their own literature did not satisfy them. They present a challenge to children's literature that with few exceptions modern writers and publishers have not yet met or fully comprehended.

[1969]

Contributors

EDWARD ARDIZZONE Born in Haiphong, Vietnam, Ardizzone attended school in England. He was always interested in drawing, but it was not until he was in his mid-twenties that he was able to take up art professionally. He has illustrated over a hundred books, both for adults and children, and his name is particularly associated with the *Tim* books, the first and perhaps most popular of which, *Little Tim and the Brave Sea Captain*, was published in 1936. He has won several awards for his children's books, including the Kate Greenaway Medal for *Tim All Alone* in 1956.

JORDAN BROTMAN Born in Calgary, Alberta, Brotman grew up in Vancouver and San Franciso. He got his doctorate at the Berkeley campus of the University of California and now teaches English at Sacramento State College. He is a journalist and novelist. His novel *Doctor Vago* won a prize and is available in paperback.

ROGER DUVOISIN After spending his childhood in Switzerland, Duvoisin studied design as a young man in Lyons and Paris and later settled in the United States, where he has become well known as an author and illustrator of children's books. *Petunia* and *Lovely Veronica* brought him recognition as an artist capable of combining imagination and humour. In 1948 he was awarded the Caldecott Medal for *White Snow, Bright Snow*.

SHEILA EGOFF Born in Maine, Sheila Egoff was educated in Ontario. She graduated from the University of Toronto and went to the University of London for graduate studies. Returning to Canada, she became actively engaged in library work, first in the east and since 1962 in Vancouver where she is an Associate Professor in the School of Librarianship at the University of British Columbia. Her special interest for many years has been in library services to boys and girls. She has written articles on this subject and a study of Canadian children's books, *The Republic of Childhood: A Critical Guide to Canadian Children's Books in English* (1967).

T. S. ELIOT American-born, but resident in England from 1914 until his death in 1965, Eliot is recognized as one of the most influential writers of the twentieth century. His poetry, though generally serious and complex, includes a few diversions such as *The Hippopotamus* and *Old Possum's Book of Practical Cats.* His best-known essays deal with poetic theory, doctrines of criticism, the classics, and the place of religion in society.

JASON EPSTEIN Vice-president of Random House, he is also president of Epstein and Carroll, publishers of the Looking Glass Library, which specializes in reprinting children's classics.

CLIFTON FADIMAN Known to the general public through his appearances on radio and television programs, Clifton Fadiman has also been a frequent contributor of articles, essays, and reviews to periodicals in the United States. Some of these writings were collected in *Party of One* (1955), *Any Number Can Play* (1957), and *Enter, Conversing* (1962). He is a member of the Editorial Board of the Book-of-the-Month Club.

MARTIN GARDNER American journalist and freelance writer. Many of his articles have been published in philosophical journals, and his column on recreational mathematics appears regularly in *Scientific American.* He is the author of *Fads and Fallacies in the Name of Science* and *Relativity for the Millions* and editor of *The Annotated Alice.*

RUMER GODDEN The well-known English novelist was born in Sussex in 1907 and was brought up chiefly in India. She has spent lengthy periods of her life in India, which forms the setting for *Black Narcissus, The River,* and several other novels. *The Doll's House,* published in 1946, was the first of her successful children's stories.

DIANA GOLDSBOROUGH A Canadian writer known for her witty reviews and travel articles and for her wide knowledge of children's books, Diana Goldsborough is on the editorial staff of *The Canadian,* published in Toronto.

ROGER LANCELYN GREEN Author of *Andrew Lang, A. E. W. Mason, The Lewis Carroll Handbook,* and other biographical works, Green has made a particular study of children's books and authors. His publications include retellings of the great myths and legends.

GRAHAM GREENE Noted writer of fiction. Some of his novels *(The Power and the Glory, The Heart of the Matter, A Burnt-out Case)* reveal the author's concern with moral and theological dilemmas; in others *(The Third Man, Our Man in Havana)* the element of entertainment predominates. Graham Greene has also written short stories, travel books, and critical essays and articles on many different subjects. His *Collected Essays* was published in 1969.

NAT HENTOFF Author, publisher, one-time radio announcer, Hentoff has been a staff writer for the *New Yorker* since 1960. One of his main interests is jazz, and the subject has formed the theme for two of his books, *The Jazz Life* and *Jazz Country*. Also apparent in Hentoff's writing is his concern for young people and the problems they face in society today.

MICHAEL HORNYANSKY Chairman of the English Department at Brock University in St Catharines, Ontario. His popular children's book, *The Golden Phoenix and Other French-Canadian Folk Tales*, is a retelling of French-Canadian stories collected by Marius Barbeau.

ELIZABETH JANEWAY Born in Brooklyn, New York, she attended Barnard College. She is a frequent book reviewer and the author of several novels, including *The Walsh Girls* and *Daisy Kenyon*. Mrs Janeway's two sons supplied ideas for some of her children's books. Her most recent publication is a children's story, *Ivanov Seven* (1967).

EDMUND LEACH University Reader in Social Anthropology and Provost of King's College, Cambridge, Leach has conducted research in anthropology in Formosa, Borneo, Ceylon, and many other places. He has reported on his work in professional journals and in such studies as *A Village in Ceylon*. In 1967 Dr Leach gave the Reith Lectures for the BBC, taking as his subject 'A Runaway World?'

C. S. LEWIS After holding other academic appointments, Lewis was Professor of Medieval and Renaissance English at Cambridge University from 1954 until his death in 1963. He was a man of varied literary gifts: a novelist, literary critic, and the author of essays on Christian theological and moral problems. Three of his novels, including the well-known *Out of the Silent Planet*, are philosophical fantasies of life on other planets. His *Narnia* stories for children, written between 1950 and 1956, are allegorical in character.

MARION LOCHHEAD Born in Lanarkshire, Scotland, Marion Lochhead was educated at Wishaw High School and Glasgow University. She is the author of numerous biographical and historical works. Of the latter, *Their First Ten Years* examines the place of children in Victorian society. *St Mungo's Bairns* and *On Tintock Tap* are children's stories.

HELEN LOURIE Psychiatrist and author, wife of Anthony Storr (see below). Since 1962 she has devoted her full time to writing. *Stories for Jane* (1952) was the first of several books for children. Her other writings have included *Freud for Jung* (1963), written under the pseudonym Irene Adler, and frequent contributions to the *Times Literary Supplement* and *New Society*.

DONNARAE MACCANN Studied music at Santa Monica City College and international relations at the University of California. Since 1957 she has been librarian of the University Elementary School on the Los Angeles campus of the University of California. She has lectured on library subjects and written a study of book illustration, *The Child, the Artist and the Book* (1962).

WILLIAM H. MAGEE For four years Dean of the College of Arts and Letters at the University of Alaska, Dr Magee is at present Associate Professor of English at the University of Calgary. He has contributed papers to the *University of Toronto Quarterly*, *Culture*, the *Dalhousie Review*, and other Canadian periodicals. The subjects in which he has a special interest are Canadian literature and the eighteenth-century British novel.

PENELOPE MORTIMER The wife of John Mortimer, the English playwright and novelist, Penelope Mortimer has raised a large family and in addition has established a reputation as a writer of fiction; her best-known novel is *The Pumpkin-Eater*. Many of her short stories have been published in the *New Yorker*. A selection of these appeared in 1960 under the title *Saturday Lunch with the Brownings*.

EDWARD W. ROSENHEIM, JR. Professor of English at the University of Chicago. His books include *What Happens in Literature* (1960) and *Swift and the Satirist's Art* (1963).

LILLIAN H. SMITH A Canadian librarian, now retired, Miss Smith is remembered for her long and distinguished service at the Toronto Public Library. Starting with limited resources, she built up in over forty years a children's collection that has become recognized as one of the best in North America. Her approach to the evaluation of children's books has had enormous influence. In 1962 the American Library Association presented her with the Clarence Day Award for her work in Toronto and for her book on children's literature, *The Unreluctant Years: A Critical Approach to Children's Literature*.

ANTHONY STORR Educated at Winchester and Cambridge, Anthony Storr qualified as a physician in 1944 and has since specialized in psychiatric work. In addition to his practice as an analyst, he finds time for appearances on British television and radio and writes articles and book reviews. He has also written three books, including *Human Aggression.*

ROSEMARY SUTCLIFF Born in Sussex, the daughter of an English naval officer, Rosemary Sutcliff first embarked on a career as an artist and was elected a member of the Royal Society of Miniature Painters. After the Second World War she gave up painting for writing historical fiction for children and adults. Her many outstanding children's novels include *The Eagle of the Ninth, The Shield Ring, Simon* and *The Mark of the Horse Lord.* In 1959 she was awarded the Carnegie Medal for *The Lantern Bearers.*

J. R. R. TOLKIEN First reaching a wide public as author of the three-fold saga *The Lord of the Rings,* Tolkien is also an authority on medieval English literature and philology and was Merton professor of English language and literature at Oxford University from 1945 to 1959. The mythical creatures who inhabit *The Lord of the Rings* originally made their appearance in a children's book, *The Hobbit,* written in 1937 when Tolkien was professor of Anglo-Saxon at Oxford.

JOHN ROWE TOWNSEND Born and brought up in Leeds, Townsend attended Cambridge University where he edited the university newspaper. Subsequently he embarked on a career in journalism, gaining much of his experience on the staff of the *Guardian,* first as sub-editor then later as editor of the international edition. An active interest in the social conditions of poor children prompted him to write his first novel, *Gumble's Yard.* Its success led to other books for children. In the last few years he has conducted courses in children's literature at Manchester and Sheffield Universities.

PAMELA TRAVERS A native of Australia, Pamela Travers has spent most of her life in England. Her literary career began with the writing of poetry; then for a number of years she contributed articles to the *Irish Statesman* and to English magazines. For her own entertainment while recovering from an illness she began to write the *Mary Poppins* stories, which have brought her international fame.

ALISON WHITE Dr Alison White teaches courses in Children's Literature and Practical Criticism at the University of Alberta. Born in the United States, she studied at institutions there and in Great Britain. Before settling in Alberta and becoming a Canadian citizen, Dr White held academic appointments in Illinois, Wisconsin, and Indiana. Her critical writings have received wide circulation in magazines and professional journals.

ALAN MORAY WILLIAMS A graduate of King's College, Cambridge, Williams entered the field of journalism and was appointed special correspondent of the *Sunday Times* in Norway in 1950. His newspaper work has taken him to all parts of Scandinavia, and since 1956 he has been managing editor of Scandinavian Features Service, with offices in Copenhagen. Apart from contributions to newspapers and periodicals, he has written *Children of the Century, The Road to the West,* and *Russian Made Easy.*

Selected bibliography

ARBUTHNOT, MAY HILL. *Children and Books.* 3rd ed. Glenview, Ill., Scott, Foresman, 1964.

A general approach, designed as a source book for teachers and students of children's literature. The persuasive style, the emphasis on the reading needs and interests of children, and thorough bibliographical data, are among the features that make this an important though not a definitive study.

Children's Literature: A Guide to Reference Sources. Prepared under the direction of Virgina Haviland. Washington, D. C., Library of Congress, 1966.

This annotated bibliography describes books, articles and pamphlets selected on the basis of their estimated usefulness to adults concerned with the creation, reading or study of children's books. It is arranged under broad headings such as 'History and Criticism', 'Authorship', 'Illustration', and then under more specific headings, thus bringing like subjects together. A useful guide both in building a collection on children's literature and as an aid to research for an individual, it is attractively printed, bound, and illustrated.

CROUCH, MARCUS. *Treasure Seekers and Borrowers: Children's Books in Britain 1900-1960.* London, Library Association, 1962.

A survey of writing and illustration based on the trends in living and thought that have affected children's books. In a sense it up-dates Harvey Darton's *Children's Books in England: Five Centuries of Social Life,* but it does so without the scholarship and objectivity that is more easily applied to the distant past. It is, however, valuable for what it does attempt: a chronological look at modern British trends in writing for children.

DARLING, RICHARD. *The Rise of Children's Book Reviewing in America, 1865-1881.* New York & London, R. R. Bowker, 1968.

A valuable piece of research that will have to be taken into account in any future histories of children's literature and in the development of criticism about it. The activity that surrounded children and their books during this period, particularly as it was reflected in the major literary periodicals, is well described and documented. The author occasionally mistakenly considers book reviewing—excellent though many of the examples are—to represent a genuine, objective body of critical writing on children's literature.

DARTON, F. J. HARVEY. *Children's Books in England: Five Centuries of Social Life.* 2nd ed. Cambridge University Press, 1958.
The first major work to relate children's books to evolving social and moral attitudes towards young people, *Children's Books in England* is a book that no serious student should be unacquainted with. It gives an authoritative and scholarly review of the historical conflict between instruction and entertainment in children's literature.

EGOFF, SHEILA. *The Republic of Childhood: A Critical Guide to Canadian Children's Literature in English.* Toronto, Oxford University Press, 1967.
Sheila Egoff's provocative survey of Canadian children's books since 1950 frankly compares the relative weaknesses and strengths of a burgeoning literature with significant British and American publications. The annotated booklists provide honest and objective judgements.

EYRE, FRANK. *Twentieth Century Children's Books, 1900-1950.* London, Longmans, 1952.
An introduction to modern developments in British children's books for readers outside the United Kingdom. This brief but intensive study gives information on main publishing trends, picture books, fiction, and contemporary authors. A revision is being prepared for publication in 1970.

FENWICK, SARA I., ed. *A Critical Approach to Children's Literature.* University of Chicago Press, 1967.
Twelve papers originally presented at the 31st Annual Conference of the University of Chicago Graduate Library School. They deal with important current issues and stress the need for informed, perceptive criticism.

FISHER, MARGERY. *Intent Upon Reading: A Critical Appraisal of Modern Fiction for Children.* Revised Edition. Brockhampton Press, 1964. (First published in 1961.)
Influenced by her own childhood reading and that of her children and backed by years of experience as a reviewer of children's books, Mrs Fisher provides a thoughtful and at times sparkling commentary on fiction (mostly British) from 1930 to 1963. Books and writers are discussed under

broad groupings, with major writers receiving extra attention. In 1962 Mrs Fisher began publishing her highly valuable book-reviewing journal, *Growing Point.*

GREEN, ROGER LANCELYN. *Teller of Tales: Children's Books and Their Authors from 1800 to 1964.* Revised edition, London, Edmund Ward, 1965.
With its emphasis on bibliographical material and chronological arrangement, this discussion of British authors and children's books is a useful reference guide to individual authors and to the classic books.

HAZARD, PAUL. *Books, Children and Men.* Translated by Marguerite Mitchell. Boston, Horn Book, 1944.
A wide-ranging philosophical discourse about children and their books. Some think the 'Give us wings' approach limits its usefulness, but for its richness of allusion and its profound interpretation of childhood, it continues to occupy an important place in the literature on children's books.

A Horn Book Sampler: On Children's Books and Reading. Selected from Twenty-five Years of The Horn Book Magazine, *1924-1948.* Edited by Norma R. Fryatt. Boston, Horn Book, 1959.
The main characteristic of *The Horn Book* has always been its personal and intimate view of children's books and their authors and illustrators and the *Sampler* reveals this quality very strongly, as well as the close link between the magazine's editors and contributors. In the ferment of 1969 these articles have a nostalgic ring, but they deserve all the more to be read and re-read to remind us of enduring values.

HURLIMANN, BETTINA. *Three Centuries of Children's Books in Europe.* Translated and edited by B. W. Alderson. London, Oxford University Press, 1967.
Bettina Hürlimann gives a highly informative and warm appraisal of children's literature. She discusses major European authors and books against a background of British and American developments. Her lively style is admirably complemented by the translator's comments and book-lists.

HURLIMANN, BETTINA. *Picture-Book World.* Translated and edited by B. W. Alderson. London, Oxford University Press, 1968.
Generously illustrated in full colour and black and white, this is a valuable survey of picture-books from around the world and an impressive revelation of the artistry that is being applied to the modern picture-book. There are suggestions for further reading and information and a bio-bibliographical appendix.

MAHONY, BERTHA E. and others, eds. *Illustrators of Children's Books, 1744-1945.* Boston, Horn Book, 1947.

A handsome production with very full treatment of artists and developments in illustration and techniques. Part I consists of descriptive articles on the history and growth of illustrated books. Parts II, III and IV provide extensive biographical and bibliographical data.

MEIGS, CORNELIA and others. *A Critical History of Children's Literature.* New York, Macmillan, 1953.

This survey of children's books is one of the most comprehensive works of its kind and is widely used as a text in children's literature courses. Most of the book is concerned with American writing, though there is some discussion of parallel developments in Great Britain. A veritable mine of information, it is, however, a book to use with caution since some of the information is misleading or inaccurate. A new edition would be welcome to correct errors and to provide a chapter on the writers of the last two decades.

MORRIS, CHARLES H. *The Illustration of Children's Books.* London, Library Association, 1957.

Reviewing briefly the main developments in British children's illustrated books, Newbery to 1950, this pamphlet provides an introduction to the subject and offers useful guidelines for further study.

PELLOWSKI, ANNE. *The World of Children's Literature.* New York & London, R. R. Bowker, 1968.

This world bibliography of works about children's literature is a model of research and organization. It offers spirited (if brief) interpretations of various national literary scenes and, besides the merely enumerative bibliography, adds the continuing excitement of a creative approach in the essays preceding the bibliographies and in the annotations. Its scope is wide, covering all aspects of the subject: public and school library work with children and books, national book clubs, programs, bibliographies, anthologies, indexes, etc. The arrangement is by large geographical areas, which makes good sense since it brings related literatures—for example those of Denmark, Norway, and Sweden—together. Under each separate country, entries give complete bibliographical details and in most cases the library location (the method of entering is well explained). The major sources are the Library of Congress, the International Youth Library, and the New York Public Library. The annotations are in English, while the majority of entries are in the language of the country.

PITZ, HENRY C. *Illustrating Children's Books: History, Techniques, Production.* New York, Watson-Guptill, 1963.

Though largely technical in emphasis, this work is also a valuable source of general information on the art of illustrating children's books.

SMITH, JAMES STEEL. *A Critical Approach to Children's Literature.* New York, McGraw-Hill, 1967.

One of the most recent textbooks on children's literature. The first chapter suggests that the author is bringing an original point of view and a fresh outlook to his subject. What follows, however, contributes very little that is new, and some of the critical theories presented are open to question.

SMITH, LILLIAN H. *The Unreluctant Years: A Critical Approach to Children's Literature.* Chicago, American Library Association, 1953.

Miss Smith brings sound literary taste, a wide background of reading in both adult and children's literatures, and a fine writing style to her discussion of traditional and modern children's books, which is also given distinction by her high standards and a penetrating insight into children's reading interests. Her analyses of outstanding children's books offer criteria for evaluation that cannot fail to benefit anyone working in the field. The book is now available in paperback as a Viking Compass Book.

THWAITE, M. F. *From Primer to Pleasure: An Introduction to the History of Children's Books in England from the Invention of Printing to 1900.* London, Library Association, 1963.

Intended as an introduction to more detailed studies, *From Primer to Pleasure* possesses considerable merit in its own right. It is both well researched and eminently readable. Of particular interest to teachers and librarians is the coverage of nineteenth-century developments.

TOWNSEND, JOHN ROWE. *Written for Children: An Outline of English Children's Literature.* London, Garnet Miller, 1965.

A survey of quality, this very informed study suffers from compression but offers the kind of enlightened views to be expected from a distinguished critic and author.

VIGUERS, RUTH H. and others (eds.). *Illustrators of Children's Books, 1946-1956.* Boston, Horn Book, 1958.

One of the standard works on illustration. Patterned upon and supplementing Mahony (above), it brings the record of illustration in children's books nearer to date. (A further volume edited by Lee Kingman and others covers the period 1957-1966.)

Index

ONLY CONNECT

Readings on children's literatur

Edited by Sheila Egoff, G. T. Stubbs, and L. F. Ashl

This collection of forty essays on children's literature in English, m
of which were first published in the 1960s, encompasses literary histo
and criticism, standards, changing tastes, the child's response to boo
writers and their writing, illustration, and recent books. In making th
selection, the editors looked for insight and informed contempora
thinking, and the essays they have chosen from diverse and in so
cases inaccessible periodicals combine strong content and lively writi
Among the contributors are Edward Ardizzone, Roger Duvoisin, T.
Eliot, Jason Epstein, Clifton Fadiman, Rumer Godden, Roger Lancel
Green, Graham Greene, Nat Hentoff, Michael Hornyansky, Elizabe
Janeway, C. S. Lewis, Penelope Mortimer, Edward W. Rosenheim J
Lillian H. Smith, Rosemary Sutcliff, J. R. R. Tolkien, John Ro
Townsend, and P. L. Travers. One of the editors, Sheila Egoff, has co
tributed a discussion of science fiction and a long and valuable ess
on historical changes in children's literature and modern trends, wi
comments on some recent novels.

Librarians, parents, teachers, and students will find that *Only Conn*
is an informed and useful commentary on an important field of writi
and publishing, superseding all other such compilations.

SHEILA EGOFF, the author of *The Republic of Childhood: A Critical Gu*
to Canadian Children's Literature in English, is Associate Professor in t
School of Librarianship, University of British Columbia. G. T. STUB
and L. F. ASHLEY teach in the College of Education of that universi

OXFORD UNIVERSITY PRES